INFORMATION MODELLING AND KNOWLEDGE BASES XXXV

Frontiers in Artificial Intelligence and Applications

The book series Frontiers in Artificial Intelligence and Applications (FAIA) covers all aspects of theoretical and applied Artificial Intelligence research in the form of monographs, selected doctoral dissertations, handbooks and proceedings volumes. The FAIA series contains several sub-series, including 'Information Modelling and Knowledge Bases' and 'Knowledge-Based Intelligent Engineering Systems'. It also includes the biennial European Conference on Artificial Intelligence (ECAI) proceedings volumes, and other EurAI (European Association for Artificial Intelligence, formerly ECCAI) sponsored publications. The series has become a highly visible platform for the publication and dissemination of original research in this field. Volumes are selected for inclusion by an international editorial board of well-known scholars in the field of AI. All contributions to the volumes in the series have been peer reviewed.

The FAIA series is indexed in ACM Digital Library; DBLP; EI Compendex; Google Scholar; Scopus; Web of Science: Conference Proceedings Citation Index – Science (CPCI-S) and Book Citation Index – Science (BKCI-S); Zentralblatt MATH.

Series Editors:
Nicola Guarino, Pascal Hitzler, Joost N. Kok, Jiming Liu, Ramon López de Mántaras,
Riichiro Mizoguchi, Mark Musen, Sankar K. Pal, Ning Zhong

Volume 380

Recently published in this series

ISSN 0922-6389 (print)
ISSN 1879-8314 (online)

Information Modelling and Knowledge Bases XXXV

Edited by

Marina Tropmann-Frick
University of Applied Sciences Hamburg, Germany

Hannu Jaakkola
Tampere University, Finland

Bernhard Thalheim
Christian Albrechts University Kiel, Germany

Yasushi Kiyoki
Keio University, Japan

and

Naofumi Yoshida
Komazawa University, Japan

IOS Press

Amsterdam • Berlin • Washington, DC

ISBN 978-1-64368-476-5 (print)
ISBN 978-1-64368-477-2 (online)
doi: 10.3233/FAIA380

Publisher
IOS Press BV
Nieuwe Hemweg 6B
1013 BG Amsterdam
Netherlands
e-mail: order@iospress.nl

For book sales in the USA and Canada:
IOS Press, Inc.
6751 Tepper Drive
Clifton, VA 20124
USA
Tel.: +1 703 830 6300
Fax: +1 703 830 2300
sales@iospress.com

LEGAL NOTICE

The publisher is not responsible for the use which might be made of the following information.

PRINTED IN THE NETHERLANDS

Preface

Information Modeling and Knowledge Bases has become an important technology contributor for the 21st century's academic and industry research. It addresses the complexities of modeling in digital transformation and digital innovation, reaching beyond the traditional boarders of information systems and computer science academic research.

The amount and complexity of information itself, the number of abstraction levels of information, and the size of databases and knowledge bases are continuously growing. The diversity of data sources combines data from traditional legacy sources to stream based unstructured data having need for backwards modelling. Conceptual modelling is one of the sub-areas of information modelling. The aim of this conference is to bring together experts from different areas of computer science and other disciplines, who have a common interest in understanding and solving problems on information modelling and knowledge bases, as well as applying the results of research to practice. We also aim to recognize and study new areas of modelling and knowledge bases to which more attention should be paid. Therefore, philosophy and logic, cognitive science, knowledge management, linguistics, and management science as well as machine learning and AI are relevant areas, too.

In the conference, there will be three categories of presentations, i.e., full papers, short papers, and invited papers. The international conference on information modelling and knowledge bases originated from the co-operation between Japan and Finland in 1982 as the European Japanese conference (EJC). Then professor Ohsuga in Japan and Professors Hannu Kangassalo and Hannu Jaakkola from Finland (Nordic countries) did the pioneering work for this long tradition of academic collaboration. Over the years, the conference gradually expanded to include European and Asian countries, and gradually spread through networks of previous participants to other countries. In 2014, with this expanded geographical scope, the European Japanese part in the title was replaced by International. The conference characteristics include opening with a keynote session followed by presentation sessions with enough time for discussions. The limited number of participants is typical for this conference.

The 33rd International Conference on Information Modeling and Knowledge Bases (EJC 2023) held at Maribor, Slovenia constitutes a research forum for the exchange of scientific results and experiences of academics and practitioners dealing with information and knowledge. The main topics of EJC 2023 cover a wide range of themes extending the knowledge discovery through Conceptual Modelling, Knowledge and Information Modelling and Discovery, Linguistic Modelling, Cross-Cultural Communication and Social Computing, Environmental Modeling and Engineering, and Multimedia Data Modelling and Systems. The conference has also been open to new topics, related to its main themes. In this way, the content emphases of the conferences have been able to adapt to the changes taking place in the research field.

The EJC 2023 was hosted by the Faculty of Electrical Engineering and Computer Science of the University of Maribor, Slovenia on June 5 – June 9, 2023. The contributions of this proceeding feature eighteen reviewed, selected, and upgraded publications as well as one keynote and three invited contributions that are the result of presentations, comments, and discussions during the conference. We thank all colleagues for their support in making this conference successful, especially the program committee, organization committee, and the program coordination team, especially Professor Naofumi Yoshida, who maintains the paper submission and reviewing systems and compiles the files for this book.

Editors
Marina Tropmann-Frick
Hannu Jaakkola
Bernhard Thalheim
Yasushi Kiyoki
Naofumi Yoshida

About the Conference

Program Committee Co-Chairs
Yasushi Kiyoki, Keio University, Japan
Marina Tropmann-Frick, Hamburg University of Applied Sciences, Germany

Program Committee Members
Bostjan Brumen, University of Maribor, Slovenia
Petchporn Chawakitchareon, Chulalongkorn University, Thailand
Pierre-Jean Charrel, University of Toulouse and IRIT, France
Xing Chen, Kanagawa Institute of Technology, Japan
Ajantha Dahanayake, LUT University, Lappeenranta, Finland
Marie Duzi, VSB-Technical University of Ostrava, Czech Republic
Anneli Heimburger, University of Jyväskylä, Finland
Jaak Henno, Tallinn University of Technology, Estonia
Sami Hyrynsalmi, LUT University, Lahti, Finland
Hannu Jaakkola, Tampere University, Finland
Tommi Mikkonen, University of Helsinki, Finland
Jorgen Fischer Nilsson, Technical University of Denmark, Denmark
Tomoya Noro, Fujitsu Laboratories Ltd., Japan
Jari Palomaki, Tampere University, Finland
Bernhard Rumpe, RWTH Aachen, Germany
Shiori Sasaki, Musashino University and Keio University, Japan
Jari Soini, Tampere University, Finland
Virach Sornlertlamvanich, SIIT, Thammasat University, Thailand
Tetsuya Suzuki, Shibaura Institute of Technology, Japan
Naofumi Yoshida, Komazawa University, Japan

General Organizing Chair
Hannu Jaakkola, Tampere University, Finland.

Organizing Committee Chairs
Xing Chen, Kanagawa Institute of Technology, Japan
Tatjana Welzer Družovec, University of Maribor, Slovenia

Local Organizing Committee
Tatjana Welzer Družovec, University of Maribor, Slovenia
Marko Hölbl, University of Maribor, Slovenia

Program Coordination Team
Naofumi Yoshida, Komazawa University, Japan
Tatjana Welzer Družovec, University of Maribor, Slovenia
Tatiana Endrjukaite, Transport and Telecommunication Institute, Latvia

Contents

x

Information Modelling and Knowledge Bases XXXV
M. Tropmann-Frick et al. (Eds.)

doi:10.3233/FAIA231144

Modelology — The New Science, Life and Practice Discipline

Bernhard THALHEIM [1]

Christian-Albrechts-University Kiel, Christian-Albrechts-Platz 4, 24118 Kiel, Germany

Abstract. Every object and every idea can be used as a model *in an application scenario*, if it becomes useful in the scenario as an instrument in a function. Through this use and function, an object or idea becomes a model, at least for a certain or long time for the respective model user in its context and environment.

Models are **works of art of thinking**. They come in the most diverse forms: small ingenious, ever-present, medium-sized or even elaborate ones of imposing size and full of hidden secrets. Quiet ones, animated by a flash of inspiration. Groundbreaking and revolutionary. Methodically overwhelmingly sophisticated ones that stand on the shoulders of giants. Simple ones that are so well put together that everyone likes them and understands them and cannot refuse them.

Modelology is a novel discipline that handles model development and usage in a systematic and well-founded way. We introduce the central kernels of this new science, art, and culture.

Keywords. model-based reasoning, plausible reasoning, approximative reasoning, abduction, induction, explanation, hypotheses, empiric

1. Models — Almost Everywhere, At Any Time and For Many Things

Models are a universal instrument of human thought, human presentation, human activity, and socialising interaction. They reduce complexity, are less complicated, allow concentration on the essential and often work many times better than the complicated world surrounding us thus is difficult to understand and to comprehend. They are simply universal and allow us, on the one hand, to react quickly and, on the other hand, to process in depth. Models accompany the design of solutions, constructions and projects.

It is claimed that logic is the most essential part of the culture of thought. Logic includes not only the rigid canonical mathematical logic in Bauhaus style, the syllogistic spinning in Aristotle style, various logics of discourses, human logics for daily life, and the logic inherent in applications. In thinking, models are the accompanying and sufficiently simple instruments – even more so profound ones – of thought also for the step-by-step development of thinking.

Models use, as a result of modeling, a vivid and dependable presentation in a well-formed design to open up what is being considered in a way that the recipient can understand and process. They, thus, enable a differentiation, evaluation and meaning assignment of what is to be explored. They provide a sufficiently lasting meaning with a reference to what is presented and allow a recipient to appropriate it.

---

[1] bernhard.thalheim@email.uni-kiel.de

The instrument lore of the ingenious instrument makers seems to be outdated with the modern times. Neither an experimentalist nor a technologist who faces difficult problems will agree with this. Activities must be premeditated, tracked with understanding, and evaluated. Again, models are the companion in all activities and also in the systematic and well thought-out action.

Models accompany social life in particular. They enable people to cope in the simplest and at the same time sufficient way, as well as to act with each other in the context of the environment and the community. The challenging world, the biasing community, the systems in all varieties, and the wide range of tasks are often far too complicated and complex, so a wise reduction and orientation to the essentials while borrowing from what is already understood and proven as successful both in a quick way and with model-based thorough thinking with a wise use of models.

Models are also products of *human critical realism* [2]. They are constantly modified with new experiences, insights, failures and successes. They allow a skeptical distance and at the same time a successful processing paired with a hope for success. They allow us a cosmopolitan open-mindedness and an internalization of usable knowledge in all spheres of existence. They support all forms of thinking and are not just focused on rational thinking for problem solving as arguably one of the seven forms of human thinking. It is therefore inconceivable that once calculating machines can replace our model thinking. Machines – of whatever kind – will at best be partners or instruments. They need to be pre-conceived in all aspects both as an actual machine and second order machine that could incorporate pre-conceived changes. Encoding true human cognitive abilities is not only time-consuming and highly laborious, but is still in its reductionist infancy.

Since models do not follow an absolute concept of truth, they are always to be regarded with a reservation. They are often revised for new situations and in new contexts. They can make a claim to truth, but this is rather an exception. In contrast to the potential of science and technology, modeling always focuses on human limitations. Humans cannot consider arbitrarily complex things. It needs a concentration on the essential, an abstraction from the specific and a focusing.

Models are based on human capabilities and limitations. They are geared to efficiency and, in particular, to fast yet reliable solutions. It uses not only the intelligible processing, but also unconscious or preconscious abilities as well as to a large extent the intuition. Model science is as important a foundation as mathematics, where the art of calculating, measuring, analyzing, and comprehensible reasoning teaches a foundation of science and technology. We thus envision that a new model science in a similar form becomes a daily use science with a complex of techniques and methods, as variation, for exploration, design, representation and interaction. So far, a disciplinary foundation of model science is lacking. We now want to present such a foundation.

With this breadth of application, importance, and universality, it is surprising that a systematic model science is not a component of all disciplines or, in particular, a separate discipline apart from the sciences, technology, and life. A disciplinary model science or model lore exists in rudiments as [20] shows. However, a cross-disciplinary model science is missing so far, which is why we try to fill this gap. We will now introduce this new discipline, modelology, and outline its potential.

---

[2]Models are actually results of social interaction and activity as well as of conscious, subconscious and preconscious thinking as the "sixth" sense.

2. The Birth of a New Discipline

Human thought and action is universally accompanied by models in a variety of scenarios such as the following ones: (1) communication and negotiation, (2) conceptualisation, (3) description and representation, (4) system construction and optimisation, (5) system maintenance and control, (5) prescription and governing solution realisation, (6) steering and guiding, (7) reflection and discussion, (8) documentation and demonstration, (9) perception, (10) orientation and social life, (11) cogitation and cognition, (12) learning and explanation, (13) investigation and exploration, (14) socialisation and interaction, (15) substitution and agency, (16) interaction, and threescore more. They are the little helpers and brownies in all activities, all thinking, all recognizing and all living together. It is therefore astonishing why these universal helpers are not also systematically and scientifically widely researched and why not everybody has to learn and master the discipline of modeling like a school and university subject. Perhaps the diversity of model use is to blame. We want to introduce a new discipline here and explain the basics of modelology.

2.1. Models – Another Dimension Between Situations and Theories

Models mirror and then reflect observations and can also be used to explain and understand theories. Therefore, models are classically often regarded as material or ideal objects that can be located between the two dimensions of practical and scientific life as an intermediate between situations met in the state-of-affairs and the theories as depicted in Figure 1. However, this only addresses a few of the roles that models play. In addition, there are also models from engineering or even instructional models that cannot be located in this way. Nor can models simply be understood linguistically as special language constructs and therefore be reduced to a component of the semiotic triangle. Models can be expressed linguistically, but they do not have to be. People develop models even before they can speak. They also use models throughout their lives that they do not even represent linguistically.

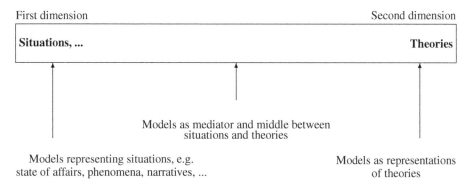

Figure 1. Classical view: Models as the middle and mediator between dimensions

If you look at the classical view in Figure 1 a little more closely, you quickly realize that models are not just something between the two dimensions – situations and theories –, but that they form an independent dimension. They are completely different in their variety, in their structure, in their use and in their theoretical foundation. Therefore, one must consider models as an independent dimension as shown in Figure 2.

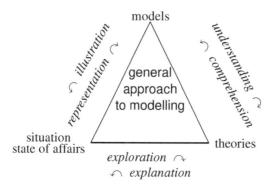

Figure 2. Modern view: Models – the third dimension between situations and science

Models are one of the main instruments in scientific research. They are considered to be the *third dimension of science* [20] [3]. Modelling is one of the four central paradigms of Computer Science [17] beside structures (in the small and large), evolution or transformation (in the small and large), and collaboration (based on communication, cooperation, and coordination). An independent sub-discipline is also to be developed for Computer Science, so that the huge body of knowledge can be widely used in a systematic and learnable form. Typical deficiencies of modelling in Computer Science are: ad-hoc modelling, modelling in the small, limited reuse of models, models are not understood as some kind of programs, and rigid separation into sub-disciplines without development of a common understanding and culture.

When considering the dimensions, we have left out engineering and also social life. Otherwise, models would be the fifth or sixth dimension.

2.2. The Conception of Model

Let us briefly remember notions to modelling in [14] (see also [15,16,17,18,19]) [4]:

"A **model** *is a well-formed, adequate, and dependable instrument that represents origins and that functions in utilisation scenarios."* [5,14]

"Its criteria of well-formedness, adequacy, and dependability must be commonly accepted by its community of practice (CoP) within some context and correspond to the functions that a model fulfills in utilisation scenarios.

The model should be well-formed according to some well-formedness criterion. As an instrument or more specifically an artifact a model comes with its *background*, e.g. paradigms, assumptions, postulates, language, thought community, etc. The background its often given only in an implicit form. The background is often implicit and hidden.

A well-formed instrument is *adequate* for a collection of origins if it is *analogous* to the origins to be represented according to some analogy criterion, it is more *focused* (e.g. simpler, truncated, more abstract or reduced) than the origins being modelled, and it sufficiently satisfies its *purpose*.

---

[3]The title of the book [3] has inspired this claim.

[4]We omit here a detailed bibliography of the more than 4000 works on models and further on the history of modeling already considered by us and refer especially to [4,9,10,11,13,20].

Well-formedness enables an instrument to be *justified* by an empirical corroboration according to its objectives, by rational coherence and conformity explicitly stated through conformity formulas or statements, by falsifiability or validation, and by stability and plasticity within a collection of origins.

The instrument is *sufficient* by its *quality* characterisation for internal quality, external quality and quality in use or through quality characteristics [14] such as correctness, generality, usefulness, comprehensibility, parsimony, robustness, novelty etc. Sufficiency is typically combined with some assurance evaluation (tolerance, modality, confidence, and restrictions).

A well-formed instrument is called *dependable"* [and thus reliable and trustable] "if it is sufficient and is justified for some of the justification properties and some of the sufficiency characteristics." [14]

2.3. Modelology: From Art to Theory and Culture

Art of modelling is the current handicraft and skills in planning, making, executing and as capacity to model well. It is going to become a practice-oriented apprenticeship due to systematic generalisation of modelling experience.

Current development of modelology can be understood as a *theory offer*. It is a scientific, explicit and systematic discussion of foundations and methods, with critical reflection, and a system of assured conceptions providing a holistic understanding. A theory offer is understood as the underpinning of technology and science similar to architecture theory. Theory offers do not constitute a theory on their own, rather are some kind of collection consisting of pieces from different and partially incompatible theories, e.g. sociology theories such as the reference group theory, network theories, economic theories such as the agent, Darwinian evolution theories, subjective rationality theories, and ideology theories.

In contrast to a theory offer, a *(scientific) theory* is a "systematic ideational structure of broad scope, conceived by the human imagination that encompasses a family of empirical (experiential) laws regarding regularities existing in objects and events, both observed and posited. A scientific theory is a structure suggested by these laws and is devised to explain them in a scientifically rational manner. In attempting to explain things and events, the scientist employs (1) careful observation or experiments, (2) reports of regularities, and (3) systematic explanatory schemes (theories)." [2].

Modelology will be a constructive theory (applicative, explicate, exploitative, explorative, prognosticative, predictive). It is based on principles, technology of modelling, reasoning, theory in the sense of Vitruvius, Semper, Alberti, and Gregor [1,7,12,21]. It provides practical (technical) and quality (esthetic) norms according to the goals of construction and guided by some background. It is, thus, a discipline or area of systematic theory founding with justified and established knowledge. Modelology is becoming a collective or particular discipline of study and learning acquired through the scientific method.

We envision that is going to become a culture as practised and well-accepted theory-backed technology and engineering and thus 'collective programming of the modelling mind'.

Modelology should provide answers to questions such as:

- What is a model? What are its essential elements? Which kinds of models reflect which task and support a solution of which problems? Which methods must be provided for a proper use of the model? Which methods support development and modernisation of models?

- In which cases is the model adequate? What are the limits and and where should this model not be used? In which case we can rely on a model? What means dependability of models?
- What are good models? Which models are effective? Which properties can be proven for models?
- How can models be integrated and composed?
- What are the correct activities for modelling?
- What is the added value of a model?
- Who can use the model how?
- What are the background theories of modelling?
- Why should a given model be where used? In what way? And by what means?

2.4. Modelology: Integrating Science of Modelling with Engineering of Models

Modelology is a new scientific discipline. This new discipline will be based on a well-ordered and comprehensible arrangement of findings and a well-founded system for a delimited subject area. It will be traced back to principles which are value-free, presuppositionless and objective. Terms, categories, inner connections, dependencies will be considered as well as general laws, theories and hypothetical proposals.

As in any such discipline, general disciplinary laws apply. For modellogy, e.g., the theorem of internal coherence applies as a generalization of the theorem of excluded contradiction, which requires that elements are not mutually exclusive but have a coherent context of meaning. The justification claim for models is derived from the utility and use of models depending on the requirements of the particular situation and the needs of a user community. Justification is therefore de- or inter-subjectified relative to the community. The quality requirements are also derived from this.

At the same time modelology is also the lore of the technique of thinking and acting consciously with appropriate methods. This lore also includes methods of design, development and utilization. It is accompanied, by formal procedures for designing models for the given community in appropriate situations, for mastering, skillfully using, and wisely advancing models in a web of models. This use also follows regularities for effective and efficient use. The appropriate means are provided with the methods and techniques for this.

In addition to the scientific claim to know something, there is therefore also the claim to do something in an integrated form. This engineering claim also includes thinking ahead and acting to achieve the goals, requirements, and concerns. Thus also action schemes and rule canons are a component of modelology.

In this context, models and modeling are not ends in themselves, but are seen as means and helpers to cope with all situations. Modelology is a theory of construction as well as an art of creating the artificial. This results in new research content, research methods, insights, proven approaches and also theories, which are also used in other disciplines, but have not been elaborated or have not been worked out.

This establishes a doctrine and lore that, starting from problems and research claims based on relevant tasks, leads to a modeling professionalism that also stands up to evaluation and scrutiny. This professionalism is based on a good number of principles such as systematic construction, credibility, dependability, usability, comparability, cost-effectiveness, relevance, and additionally multiple representation and coherence in model suites. In addition, there is the transfer and diffusion of the findings and methods into other disciplines and from these disciplines. This is an iterative and never ending co-evolution.

3. Theses of Modelology as a Summary of Findings and Experiences

We already discovered that the art and lore of models and modelling is far broader than often considered while trapped in the confines of a sub-discipline. 'Something' must not be named instrument or model while being an instrument or being a model. Modelling is a common practice in all branches of computer science and engineering.

Research and practice has produced a good series of results in studies of models and modelling which, although not generally compiled in full in this way, can be summarised in the form of theses based on the body of evidence. We first present theses on models, then on properties of models and at the end on the glory of using models.

3.1. General Theses of Modelology

Model science can be based on statements that already have a certain acceptance in the practice of modelling. We orient ourselves on ten central achievements of model studies.

1. Models are a universal instrument of thought, work, mediation and socialisation. They accompany being human also in the philosophies of nature and not only with the late dominance of technology and science.
2. Everything (from mind games to artefacts) can – but need not – serve as a model. Usually for a certain time, in a limited community or only for itself, in a context and thus a landscape.
3. Models should be suitable and appropriate, but not perfect. They should not be completely valid or free of contradictions. There are also pre-models, non-models, and un-models.
4. Models need their community of 'fans' who also need to have the possibilities and skills to use a model appropriately.
5. Mind games and artefacts are born, live, survive, pass away completely or temporarily, are taken up again and are also only understandable with the context and the disciplinary matrix. They can also take on completely different functions and roles in a different scenario.
6. Models and model-being change dynamically depending on the situation, context, recipient, school and collective of thought, model usage success, evolving concerns, and workshop as well as with use.
7. Models have their peculiarities and obstinacies, not only because of the form of expression used, but also because of their inner peculiarities, which do not even have to be explicitly inventible. These peculiarities and obstinacies partially overwrite or cover the properties of the origins. They can push themselves into the foreground.
8. Things, instruments and models can be modernised (evolutionary, revolutionary), integrated into other models, and prepared for other uses, disassembled or cannibalised.
9. Models do not have to be, not yet or not completely language-bound, as e.g. in biosemiotics.

10. Models integrate the existing world view of individuals or of a group of individuals without explicitly expressing this. They bring their own (disciplinary) matrix and implicitly integrate deep models.

Models accompany humans just like other tools and are therefore the "little helpers".

3.2. Theses on Specific and Important Properties of Models

Not everything is suitable as an instrument or even a model. There are commonalities that can be observed, like the case study in [20], in model studies. Everything can become a model if it is justified by the circumstances, properties, and the characteristics. Therefore, models also follow specifications for their properties.

11. There is not one model for a given task in a scenario, but many different options, so evaluation and assessment theory is also required.
12. Models are meant to simplify and focus. Therefore, a model cannot be universal.
13. Models are instruments and should above all be useful, i.e. a model-being presupposes being an instrument. They have a power of effect and of interpretation, a validity claim, need for recognition, and a specific impact.
14. Models are often and also deliberately misused, so that there is a need for an alert and trained mind and especially for model lore and modelology. Especially since models are also dedicatedly used as "secret doctrines"..
15. Models and instruments can also be perfected to allow automatic use. Usually this is associated with a special quality request.
16. Models were mostly developed by other members of the community, who shape the artifacts or world of thought with their own culture, view, experience and lifeworld without making this explicit.
17. Models have a life history together with the instrument-being and the (model) object/thing. The history can be permanent, broken, resumed, with new assignments for being, spiralling, etc.
18. Model elements can be freely or cared for associated with a meaning depending on use, user and community. Meanings can be injected e.g. terms or concepts.
19. There is not THE model, but many models are used at the same time in a loose or close association, whereby added value also arises precisely through this maintained coexistence.
20. Models can also consist of a model suite, i.e. a well-associated ensemble of models. The impact power usually increases in a suite.

As "little helpers", models are not arbitrary, but possess specific properties that can be postulated equally for all kinds of models (see first paragraph in Section 2).

3.3. Theses on the Usefulness of Models

The usefulness of models arises from the desire to master something. That is why models have to useful. The application game, thus, determines whether 'something' is a model, a pre-model, a non-model, or an un-model. The model-being is determined by the necessities, desires, opportunities, expectations, and hopes of an individual or of the community of practice. It is an agreement within this user community, in the current situation, current moment of time, and current (disciplinary) background. The model-being thus is determined through activities and context which are supported by a model. Models are tools that support thinking, imaging, signifying, minding, fantasising, processing, constructing, acting, undertaking, planning, organising, understanding, comprehending, considering, learning, agreeing, communicating, orienting, socialising, etc. These human intentions and the desire for support of any human endeavour determine the usefulness of 'something' as a model.

21. Models are useful, however 'useful' is understood. Use and added value dominate the nature of models. They are far more convenient than elaborated and fully developed theories or technologies. They correspond much more closely to human limitations.
22. Models have potential performance. Beyond this capability, models are not reasonably usable.
23. The usefulness of models in an application scenario is justified by a role in a function that the model plays in that scenario.
24. Roles, functions, nature, brand, and mission may be consistently changed, resumed, temporarily discontinued, or increasingly played out during the lifetime of models.
25. Model use can be intentional (planned, designed, knowing, intended) and unconscious (unintentional, preconscious, subconscious, involuntary, knowing, undesigned, unformed, oblivious, inattentive).
26. Models can also be possessed or owned as an instrument or model and are therefore for a general public to acquire first.
27. Mental (perceptual, intuitional, experiential, thinking, cognitive, orientational) models serve a user first. No awareness of mental models is necessary or assumed in a user.
28. Models often perform only in a (model) ensemble connected by multiple networks of relationships (alternatively meta-hypergraphs).
29. Model-based acting, representing, reasoning and interacting does not generally follow the laws of classical mathematical logic or mathematics.
30. Model-based reasoning is also based on other reasoning mechanisms than those of the exact sciences or the technical sciences. Essential components are plausible and approximate reasoning.

The everyday understanding of models and their use is – compared to the understanding in theory-oriented sciences – always diffuse, vague, fuzzy and fluid. The application in the sciences first follows the accepted patterns of these sciences and can be grasped more precisely. Engineering sciences are oriented towards the achievable result with multiple justifications.

We restricted ourselves to thirty theses while confessing that there are far more such theses that are commonly acceptable for model studies and especially for modelology.

4. Practical Modelology: Design with the Model House

Two central components of modelology are the doctrine of construction and the doctrine of use. Although everything can become a model, models do not fall from the sky. They have to be suitable for the intended use within the user community and also adequate for the subject matter as well as dependable so that the use does justice to the concern. This raises the question of whether the construction of models cannot be systematically and at the same time effectively accompanied by one or the other design procedure. There will not be just one system, but rather many different ones.

In the following, we will present a systematics that follows the generic conception of the model and that allows a targeted refinement to specific and thus also special models based on it. This systematics can be understood as *design pragmatics*. In this way, an optimal design can be found from a wealth of requirements placed on the model, some of which are contradictory.

4.1. The Conceptual Model of Model

The model definition does not yet allow to derive the structure and functionality of models directly. Therefore, a construction doctrine is also needed for models. Such a doctrine is based on the means of design and principles of order. It follows the paradigms, principles and assumptions of modelology as well as the postulates of application. This doctrine is based on a description of components. This is simplest by a development of a conceptual model of the model.

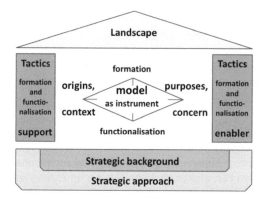

Figure 3. The conceptual model of model: General architecture of the "model house"

The conceptual world in Figure 3 includes the nature of the model in the application landscape (range of portfolio tasks of the model in scenarios of the community of practice (CoP)), the fundamentals (especially the strategic ones for the inner model behind the model as a matrix), and the instrumentation (i.e. the formation and functionalization) of the model based on tactical support and enablers. We use the *complementarity* inherent in the model on the one hand through the constructive formation and on the other hand through the range of functions provided. In models, origins (answer to the "whereof") are presented in a context based on a purpose and thus concern (answer to the "why" and "wherefore"). The rhombus in Figure 3 represents the worksheet for model construction and design. A paradigm analogous to design theory is the paradigm: *design follows purpose and concern.*

4.2. A Systematic and Stereotypical Approach to Design of Models

For the design of models, we use a detailing of the individual concepts of the conceptual model of the model using a step-by-step refinement of the given generic definition of models. Thus, step by step, first, the suitability as an instrument, second, the adequacy of the model, and third, the dependability of the model are constructed towards a specific model.

4.2.1. Landscaping

Models are not simply developed as universal instruments. They are intended to work in a specific application situation and in an application scenario for specific tasks based on the CoP's horizon of expectations. The model is embedded in a landscape with its situations, scenarios, the mission's goal and purpose, a CoP and also a usage situation. This also determines the nature of the model, the mission in this application and the brand of model.

Example 1 *For the articulation of the model as a special model example we use as a special descriptive model one that serves analysis, specification, clarification of a common understanding, and paraphasing for a development of an information system in a banking application with special orientation to the support of the bankers' work (different than for the bank employees).*

Therefore, in the roof of our model house, the concrete application, the functions of the model and thus the nature of the model, the mission and the corresponding brand are filled. The appropriate playground for representing the landscape within a design process is outlined in Table 1.

modelling playground	for landscape setting (scenario, nature, mission, brand)
issue	narrowing down and focusing the model on its tasks and functions
prerequisite	previous detailed analysis of the application (mostly future optimized); elaboration of the vocabulary of the application; delimitation of the stakeholders with their profiles;
activity	restriction to the essential in application on the basis of the real task and concern; detection of invariants beside declaration of origins of interest
subject	nature (whereof–as–what_for–in), mission (tasks in model portfolio), brand (demands and possibilities of the CoP) of model and its obligations; role in an application 'game' (and model journey)
supportive	"model business" conditions; potential infrastructure; model profile (goal, purpose, function)

Table 1. Further filling the model house: landscape specification

A *landscape* represents the general appearance with all interacting factors according to the characteristic rules as well as the containment in which the model integrated in it should function. The model (as instrument) inherits the essential core of the considered origins ('whereof') as invariants from them in its own way and transports this core to the result in appropriate (adequate, dependable) form to the result for the users respectively according to the different scenarios (model journey: wherein,where).

With the instrument-being of ideas and artifacts also the four-formed *nature* of the model is generally explainable on the basis of the concern or the central question. The *nature of being a model* is characterized by a *whereof (origins) – as (instrument) – what for (concerns) – in (scenarios of use)* pattern.

The *mission* describes the intended and hopefully successful use of "something" as a model in a context and situation and thus the application scenario.

The *brand* describes the possible acceptance of the model-being within the community of intended principal stakeholders.

4.2.2. The Design Worksheet

The worksheet presents an intentional model (model-what-is, model-as-should-be, what-how-why-when-where, model-used). It defines the development tasks and the composition of the model within the context of the landscape.

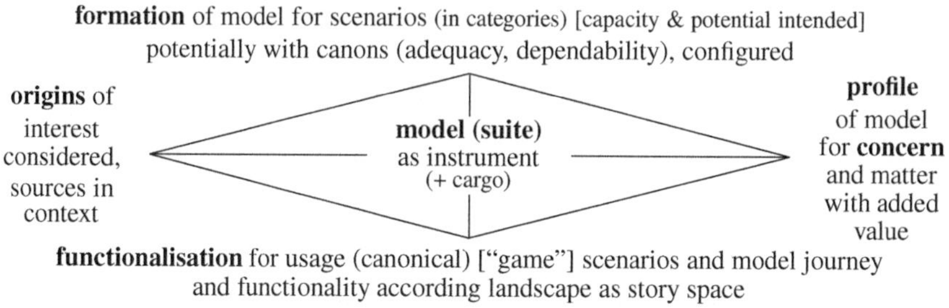

formation of model for scenarios (in categories) [capacity & potential intended]
potentially with canons (adequacy, dependability), configured

origins of interest considered, sources in context

model (suite) as instrument (+ cargo)

profile of model for **concern** and matter with added value

functionalisation for usage (canonical) ["game"] scenarios and model journey and functionality according landscape as story space

Figure 4. The worksheet for model (suite) design and configuration

The situation and scenario in which "something" is considered a model in the CoP, are clarified by the worksheet in a focussed and logical way as well as in a clear way by answering questions in the worksheet such as the following:

· *What models and model categories allow these model concern and matter to be addressed?*
· *What factors are going to characterise the model?*
· *What are the limitations of such a model category?*
· *Which functions are supported by the model in the given scenarios?*
· *What reliability can be expected with it?*
· *How can the game of sufficiently precise analogy and parsimonious focus be resolved?*
· *Which CoP acts in which role, endeavor, and execution?*
· *What support and equipment should the model have as an instrument?*
· *What contribution can "something" have as a model in the given situation?*
· *To what extent can the model continue to be used as the situation changes?*
· *What potential and capacity does such a model have and lack?*
· *What shape and form should the model have as a well-formed and usable tool?*
· *Is the chosen orientation to the given approach and implicit model sufficient?*

The worksheet in Figure 4 and Table 2 serves as an orientation of the further construction of the model.

modelling worksheet   for the task field of model design and construction according its usage

issue	clear outline of the task field for design
prerequisite	concern is precisely conceived and understood
activity	clarification of formation and functionalisation requirements; acceptable strategic direction; proposed framework for canonical features of the model
subject	set the frame for model configuration that is properly usable
supportive	adapted as far as possible to the current application

Table 2. Further filling the house: design worksheet according usage

Example 2 (continuing Example 1) *The model is canonically formed based on well-known business data structures common in the application as a data structure description model suite for various data usages and equipped with the usual functionality for object-relational analysis, development and design for a coordinated and appropriate specification of the banker's work.*

4.2.3. The Strategic Matrix

The strategic matrix underpins the model-being and thus also the instrument by an intrinsic, deep, and hidden model fundament in two foundational directives, first, by an approach or methodology, and second, by adopting model experiences that have already been tested. The *disciplinary matrix* generalizes the approaches of T. Kuhn and L. Fleck [6,8]: (1) strategic components and paradigms, (2) beliefs and values within the CoP, (3) experiences based on experienced examples, (4) a guiding question as the main concern, and (5) methodologies or approaches. Methodologies also include pattern, templates, directives, guidelines, and methods.

A model community shares a "philosophy" and also techniques of model development and of model use. We can think of the matrix as a strategic background behind the model that is often only implicit. The matrix directs model-based acting and thinking from one side and contributes to the control of the model design from the other side. Both directives also fill in the justifications for being a specific or specialised model.

Example 3 (continuing Example 2) *The model incorporates the application background (e.g., the way models are thought about, represented, handled), the approach to development (e.g., the database life cycle), the way they are implemented (e.g., concrete system environments), and the world of banking (e.g., organizational theory, specific banking doctrines, bankers' thinking).*

Most of the time, the underlying strategy is more of an "as-usual" practice that has become naturalized and doesn't need to be thought about. However, only a deliberate choice of disciplinary matrix leads to truly reliable and thus dependable models. Table 3 demonstrates the breadth of strategic choices that should be explicitly known. Often, the strategy matrix is simply taken from older and well-known analog applications without critically questioning this and also having it available.

modelling playground	for matrix configuration
issue	selection of intrinsic background, model basis, and foundation
prerequisite	well-defined and understood theories and practices
activity	paradigms and culture elaboration; describing essentials of thought school, commonsense, conventions, conceptions, classification system; proper approach and methodology selection, method canon specialisation; explication of restrictions, practices, guidance; incorporation and refinement of existing experience; pattern and canon injection; opportunity space reification; donor model investigation; regulatory frameworks and rules; meta-models for formation and functionalisation; strategems and stereotypes
subject	characterising disciplinary matrix in all of its facets
supportive	injectable shepherding fundaments for intrinsic (deep, inner) model

Table 3. Further filling the house: explicit and sophisticated treatment of disciplinary matrix

The strategy, like the tactics, is implicitly assumed without presenting it. Thus, a model can only be understood by extracting these components. The model does not speak for itself, but speaks only when this background is collected in a dedicated way.

4.2.4. The Tactical Workshop

Often goal, purpose and function of models are simply treated as synonyms. A *goal* is a triform relation (is-state, goal-state, usage CoP). A *purpose* extends the goal by the means to achieve the goal. A *function of model* relates the purpose to actual and intended scenarios. Therefore, *tactical equipment* based on existing *workshops* serves to realize the purpose. We can consider separately the support and the enabling equipment for the formation and functionalization.

Example 4 (continuing Examples 1, 2 and 3) *A banker's information system thrives on the naturalized understanding of how a bank (such as the bank of Japan) works, what processes are performed and in what form (e.g., specific balance sheets), concepts and terms, accepted theories, and also common practices. For a realization as an information system we need as functionality also linguistic forms (e.g. of the banker's everyday life), means of representation (e.g. languages for conceptual modeling), and also the language of the systems (e.g. database systems within a selected DBMS paradigm).*

modelling playground   for supporting and enabling the formation and functionalisation

issue	incorporation of tactical capability and equipment for proper design and usage
prerequisite	available world knowledge (encyclopedia, abstract notion spaces, semantics, pragmatics, reference models, conceptualisation) and prowess (techniques, routines, terms, common-sense, practices, helpers) for formation and functionalisation
activity	importing and injecting world experience while considering CoP agreements, generic and other models, common understanding, formation steering; exploiting and applying methods and techniques while considering common design guidelines, experience, functionalisation steering
subject	extrinsic tactical incubation and reuse of workshops
supportive	right pedigree for CoP

Table 4. Further filling the house: supported and enabled by workshops and toolboxes

Table 4 explains the workshop and toolboxes used as ways of supporting and enabling the composition of a usable model. In detail, this then provides for the following, with the specifics of the toolboxes also entering implicitly:

(1) The support of "something" as a model is done by an import or modified adoption of donors, carriers, bases, world knowledge, general personal views and ideas in the CoP, bases used, the accepted and practiced ordering system, etc. It is therefore the usable and used *support world knowledge*. Models have an environment for support and enablement, similar to a workshop. They need a carrier, an underpinning or support, and a foundation. They integrate donor models as well as knowledge from the application domain such as conceptual worlds. The thinking, conceptual, and possibility space is presupposed for models as a tactical environment in a focus for indexing, constituting, and representing.

(2) The equipment and arrangement of a "something", which is used as a model, includes all used aids, which can be described with the image of an instrumentarium of a workshop. Models have an environment to support, equip, and enable. Being a model is made possible by tools for their design and use, esp. methods provided. They are equipped with techniques as well as a design and use methodology from the field of application. A frequently used tool are languages adapted to the application domain, e.g. for communication and dialogs within a CoP. Other tools support actions with models directly or methodically. In addition, there is also a meta-equipment based on the chosen strategy

and landscape. The workshops provide the model means on the basis of *enabling world prowess*.

4.2.5. Final Design

With the background and possible tools accurately captured, one can also proceed to a canonical design of models based on a configuration. The configuration of model-being summarizes the nature, landscape, strategy, and tactics as an adaptation of model-being to the model situation. It is often taken as a given. For example, in teams or exercise tasks for conceptual descriptive database design, such a raw version is already assumed in order to focus on the specific origins based on the given function in an application scenario, i.e., to configure a model both on the one hand for the transmitter and on the other hand for the receiver. This configuration with a "blank" as a work piece is used to systematically perform a model composition and develop a setup for both formation and functionalisation. In many cases, such a "blank" version is conveniently used as a starting point based on existing experience. The configuration leads directly to a derived *disciplinary model conception* on the basis of the deep intrinsic model [17]:

"Given a configuration for modeling. A disciplinary model *is a model with preconfig-ured canonical adequacy and dependability that functions according to the requirements of the configuration in intended scenarios"* within the discipline.

The disciplinary model concept is aligned with the *core* (for models on the na-ture and landscape), the *common approaches* and *methodologies*, and the implicit *expert knowledge* (i.e. implicit models for a disciplinary model) and the *available means* (for models on the supporting and enabling) within the setting of the given discipline.

Example 5 *In addition to the widely studied conceptual description model (e.g. paper 44 in collection 4 [14]), the prescription model is of particular value. A* conceptual pre-scription database structure model in the global-as-design approach *consists of*
(1) a database schema expressed by means of a conceptual modelling language with di-rectives for interpretation of used constructs within the DBMS,
(2) a conceptualisation that reflects the meaning of used constructs within the applica-tion,
(3) a collection of views for both support of business users and system operating (i.e. including realisation functionalisation),
(4) realisation templates with pragmas for realisation of the database within a given platform setting, and
(5) a declaration of model's canonical adequacy and dependability.

In Table 5 we follow the usual approach to the operational execution of the model de-sign. For this purpose the canonical additions, the situation facts and the well-formedness are executed step by step like in a thinking space on the basis of the rules in a *"way of designing and thinking"*.

Example 6 (finalising Examples 1–4) *For the example, we assemble the individual components, push implicit but intrinsic components into the background, and design the model within the accepted postulates of the application and paradigms using the matrix, as well as chosen tactical principles. Figure 5 briefly visualizes the conceptual model of a descriptive database structure model of our bank information system application for bankers. The scheme in the picture is just one of many for the application.*

modelling playground	for finalising design of a useful model
issue	operational development of model
prerequisite	accepted configuration (or canon); known world/application knowledge and prowess; concentrated, focused version of the world of Origins; completed and coordinated worksheet
activity	cutting away all details that are not necessary for the specific scenario; choice of the best abstraction, analogies, and foci; gradual and coherent step-by-step development based on the matrix with tactical tools
subject	design of the final model with concern orientation
supportive	sophisticated composition is beneficial

Table 5. Final filling the house: operational and final design, construction and composition

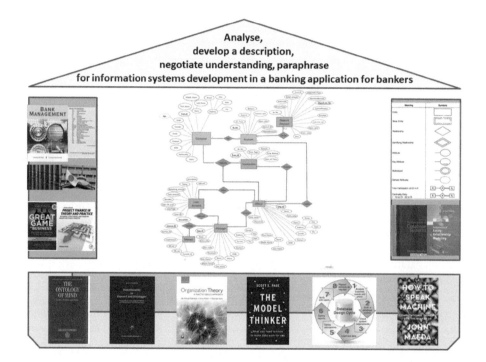

Figure 5. The conceptual model of the Banker's information system model

Most often, the conceptual model of a model is hidden after composition and only the final product of the design process is given as in Figure 5 as the inner part of the conceptual model of the model. Cutting away landscape, worksheet, strategic, and tactical decisions is not without problems and can also lead to misinterpretation such as the apparent universality of object orientation. We note that often instead of looking holistically at the complete model with its background and workshop, one only looks at the ocularly "normal" model as a representative result, cutting away the entire context.

In Table 6, we now sketch the operational evolution of the many individual models for the different roles of bankers. This sketch follows the general operational design steps.

modelling playground	for finalising design of a useful model
issue	operational development of a banker's model suite
prerequisite	accepted matrix, esp. bank pedigree, banker's knowledge; perfectly understood
activity	stepwise and systematic formation of a number of coherent and integrated banker's models (in a model suite) and provision of best available functionality for information system
subject	design of banker's model suite within the role setting of bankers
supportive	negotiated and tested structuring with sample data

Table 6. Final filling the house: design frame for Example 5

5. Practical Modelology: Utility, Usage, and Usefulnes

For model use, we are so far only aware of case studies for specific models. Therefore, this section will be kept short. A general theory of model use is still an outstanding research and development task. We will only sketch an approach to such a theory of use in the following. The usage side of modelology also needs a pragmatism underpinning.

Model usage can be examined with the 3U rule (utility + usability + usefulness)). Special attention is paid to the form of usage (way of acting & working). An approach of the form "accept it and use it" has often been advocated and leads to rapid modification or even rejection of models, especially when the specifics of an application must be considered.

Example 7 *(the disciplinary model in Example 5 for our running Example 6) A use of models for an – accompanied by automatisms – development of systems seems to be reserved for the later realisation. In the M2P (model_to_program) approach this can be realized at least in a template form. We can illustrate this for prescription models in our application. Database programming includes besides the automatic transformation or compilation of the actual structures also maintenance of the integrity and consistency of the database. The directives specify the way in which the individual constructs are to be translated. The pragmas set the generated structures into the context of the DBMS, as in the C++ compilation, so that with a three-step compilation (structure, conversion of the directives, optimization with the pragmas) to a large extent automatically also the entire realisation can be generated including the trigger networks and the macro state-based treatment (e.g. initial, running, archived) (see papers 33, 36, 46 – 48 in collections [14]).*

We can essentially distinguish three uses of models.

Apply and employ the model: The model or the model suite is put into service and is used directly on the basis of its tasks, e.g. for practical problem solving, and then validated to see whether the solution also corresponds to the concern. The model remains so even after its use. Typical model types of this form are description, construction, prescription, documentation, explanation, mastery, and (re)presentation models.

Operate with the model: The model or the model suite sufficiently fully substitutes for the origins, produces an appropriate effect, performs as expected when applied, and is used instead of origins functionally in the context of the concern in its current form and environment. Typical model types of this form are communication, replacement, substitution, reasoning, negotiation, theoretical, cogitation, optimisation, steering and intuition models.

Utilise the model: The model or the model suite coexists with the application, is constantly reused and modified with the applications based on the concerns as well as specialized if necessary. Typical model types of this form are learning, discovery, reflection, investigation, orientation, and socialisation models. agent, circumstance, degree, duration, explanation, group, instrument, manner, means, place, purpose, role, time

We already introduced in detail the rational and intuitive methods in the EJC 2021 keynote paper in paper 41 in [14]. Figure 6 illustrates the other types of model use.

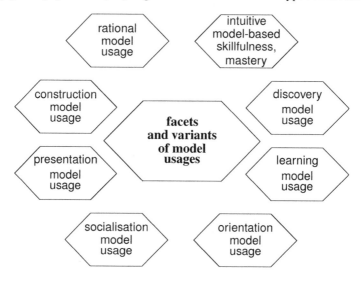

Figure 6. Facets of model usage

6. Finally

In this paper we have focused on model design, although model usage deserves an even more extensive presentation. The basics of modeling are also missing, which have only been elaborated in fragments so far. A methodology also used here is stereotyping for both model development and use. Models are universal instruments of thought and action. Therefore a modelology is not conceivable without a theory of application. So far, we have tested this doctrine on applications in Computer Science, Business Informatics, Medicine, and historical sciences such as Egyptology and Archeology. However, the spectrum of applications is much broader.

References

[1]   L.B. Alberti. *On the art of building in ten books.* MIT Press, Cambridge. Promulgated in 1475, published in 1485, 1988.

[2]   S. Bosco, L. Braucher, and M. Wiechec. *Encyclopedia Britannica, Ultimate Reference Suite.* Merriam-Webster, 2015.

[3]   S. Chadarevian and N. Hopwood, editors. *Models - The third dimension of science.* Stanford University Press, Stanford, California, 2004.

[4]   C. Eck, H. Garcke, and P. Knabner. *Mathematische Modellierung.* Springer, 2008.

[5]   D. Embley and B. Thalheim, editors. *The Handbook of Conceptual Modeling: Its Usage and Its Challenges.* Springer, 2011.

[6]   L. Fleck. *Denkstile und Tatsachen, edited by S. Werner and C. Zittel.* Surkamp, 2011.

[7]   S. Gregor and D. Jones. The anatomy of a design theory. *Journal of Association for Information Systems,* 8(5):312–335, 2007.

[8]   T. Kuhn. *The Structure of Scientific Revolutions.* University of Chicago Press, Chicago, Illinois, 2nd, enlarged, with postscript edition, 1970.

[9]   R. Müller.   Model history is culture history. From early man to cyberspace. http://www.muellerscience.com/ENGLISH/model.htm, 2016. Assessed Oct. 29, 2017.

[10] C. P. Ortlieb, C. von Dresky, I. Gasser, and S Günzel. *Mathematische Modellierung: Eine Einführung in zwölf Fallstudien.* Vieweg, 2009.

[11] A. A. Samarskii and A. P. Mikhailov. *Principles of mathematical modelling: Ideas, methods, examples (Translated from Russian, 1997).* CRC Press, 2001.

[12] G. Semper. *Die vier Elemente der Baukunst.* Braunschweig, 1851.

[13] B. Thalheim. *Entity-relationship modeling – Foundations of database technology.* Springer, Berlin, 2000.

[14] B. Thalheim. Models, to model, and modelling. *collections of papers.* https://www.researchgate.net (search keyphrase "Towards a theory of models, especially conceptual models and modelling"), also academia.edu, 2009-2021.

[15] B. Thalheim. Artificial intelligence enhanced by modelling. *Intellectual Systems – Theory and Application,* 26(1):359–365, 2022.

[16] B. Thalheim. Model-based reasoning for investigating the heart capability. In B. Lohff and J. Schaefer, editors, *Cardio-Physiology Challenging Empirical Philosophy,* volume II, pages 162–199, Norderstedt, 2022. BoD.

[17] B. Thalheim. Models: The fourth dimension of computer science – towards studies of models and modelling. *Software & Systems Modeling,* 21:9–18, 2022.

[18] B. Thalheim. Auf dem Wege zur Modellkunde. In *Modellierung 2022,* volume P-324 of *LNI,* pages 11–32, Bonn, 2023. Gesellschaft für Informatik e.V.

[19] B. Thalheim. Modellkunde: kurz & knapp. In C.L. Loeben, editor, *Modellkunde und Ägyptologie im Dialog. Essays,* Berlin, 2023. Kulturverlag Kadmos.

[20] B. Thalheim and I. Nissen, editors. *Wissenschaft und Kunst der Modellierung: Modelle, Modellieren, Modellierung.* De Gruyter, Boston, 2015.

[21] Vitruvius. *The ten books on architecture (De re aedificatoria).* Oxford University Press, London, 1914.

Remark: We have also refrained from an extensive bibliography due to the brevity of this paper on the new discipline modelology. A small bibliography would quickly come up with a few hundred necessary entries.

More detailed information on our research papers can be found on research gate in collections *[14]*
     at   https://www.researchgate.net/profile/Bernhard_Thalheim .

We have omitted many of the references to these works in this paper and assume some knowledge of them.

See also the youtube channel "Bernhard Thalheim" (alternatively: search "modelology", "Modellkunde"), videos at https://vk.com/id349869409 or at https://vk.com/id463894395 (in German).

Information Modelling and Knowledge Bases XXXV
M. Tropmann-Frick et al. (Eds.)
© 2024 The Authors.
This article is published online with Open Access by IOS Press and distributed under the terms
of the Creative Commons Attribution Non-Commercial License 4.0 (CC BY-NC 4.0).
doi:10.3233/FAIA231145

A Context-Based Time Series Analysis and Prediction Method for Public Health Data

Asako URAKI[a,1], Yasushi KIYOKI[a], Koji MURAKAMI[a], Akira KANO[b]

[a] *Keio Research Institute at SFC, Keio University, Japan*
[b] *Fujimino Emergency Hospital*

Abstract. The important process of time series analysis for public health data is to determine target data as a semantic discrete value, according to a context from continuous phenomenon around our circumstance. Typically, each field of experts has their own fields' specific and practical knowledge to specify an appropriate target part of data which contains the key features of their intended context in each analysis. Those are often implicit, thus not defined as systematically and quantitatively. In this paper, we present a context-based time series analysis and prediction method for public health data. The most essential point of our approach is to express a basis of time series context as the combination of the following 5 elements (1: granularity setting on time axis, 2: feature extraction method, 3: time-window setting, 4: differential computing function, and 5: pivot setting) to determine target data as semantic discrete values, according to the time series context of analysis for public health data. One of the main features of our method is to create different results by switching time series contexts. The method realizes 1) introducing a new normalization (context expression) method to fix a target reference data for time series analysis and prediction according to a context, and 2) presenting a process to generate semantic discrete values reflecting the 5 elements. And the significant features of the proposing method are 1) our context definition realizes the closed world of the semantic differential computing on time axis from the viewpoint of database system, and 2) the 5 elements enable to explicit and quantify experts' semantic viewpoint of specifying a certain reference data according to a context for each analysis and prediction. As our experiment, we have realized analysis and prediction by applying actual public health data. The results of the experiments show the prediction feasibility of our method in the field of public health data, effectiveness to generate results for discussion regarding switching context, and applicability to express time series context of an expert knowledge for analysis and prediction as combination of the 5 elements to make the knowledge explicit and quantitative expression.

Keywords. Context-based System, Differential Computing, Time-series Analysis, Time-series Prediction, Public Health Data, Big Data, AI, Cyber-Physical System

1. Introduction

Analysis and Prevention for future situation from the past and current data are important activities to realize preemptive medicine for human health and early detection of spreading infection disease in nature and societies. As our background researches, our

---

[1] Corresponding Author, Asako Uraki, Keio University, Endo 5322, Fujisawa, Kanagawa, Japan; E-mail: aco@sfc.keio.ac.jp.

semantic computing method [9,10,12] and 5D World Map system [1,2,3,4,5,6,7,8,11] are applied to analysis from the viewpoint of personal health-situation and spreading of infection disease. The important process of time series analysis for public health data is to determine target data as a semantic discrete value, according to a context from continuous phenomenon around our circumstance. The phenomenon is expressed as continuous values or as just a raw discrete data along the time, independent of context. Difference of situations in the phenomenon on time axis expresses one of the key features of time series data, and differences are reflected with adjacent discrete values.

Typically, each field of experts has their own field's specific and practical knowledge to specify an appropriate target part of data which contains the key features of their intended time series context for each analysis. However, those are often implicit therefore not defined systematically and quantitatively.

In this paper, we present a context-based time series analysis and prediction method for public health data. The most essential point of our approach is to express a basis of time series context as the combination of the following 5 elements (1: granularity setting on time axis, 2: feature extraction method, 3: time-window setting, 4: differential computing function, and 5: pivot setting) to determine target data as the semantic discrete value according to the time series context of analysis and prediction for public health data. As our experiment, we realized analysis and prediction by applying actual public health data.

In General, to predict future situation, we need something previous things for reference, and results are different according to a context to confirm referential data for prediction. Figure 1 shows our main motivation of time series context to fix reference data for prediction with examples. By applying the blue part as most recent situation, the same kind of period, actual number, and rough movement, we can predict it as the blue dash line, by applying green part as previous lockdown period and precise movement with min-max ratio to predict how it goes the upcoming lock down period, we can predict it as the green dash line, by applying red part as historical other data period from max to 0 with the trend line to predict the overall pandemic forecasting, we can predict it as the red dash line. Those three examples express all-time series context to fix target reference data for prediction. We could find from those examples, the essential point of time series analysis and prediction is "to normalize a target reference data according to a context" as semantic discrete values, not only time range on time axis, but also size of sampling rate on time axis, quantification method for value, quantification method for difference along with time, and starting point of prediction.

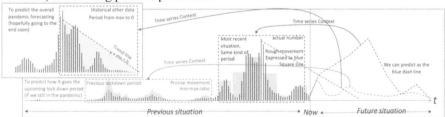

Figure 1. Motivation of time series context to determine reference data for prediction. This example shows prediction results should be different according to a reference data for prediction which reflects each context for analysis. The essential point of time series analysis and prediction is "to normalize a target reference data according to a context" as semantic discrete values, not only time range on time axis, but also size of sampling rate on time axis, quantification method for value, quantification method for difference along with time, and starting point of prediction.

Ordinally in time-series data analysis and prediction, we determine the target part of data along with time axis with an implicit expert knowledge as each context. Our main objective is to make it possible to explicitly express each context for determination of the target part of data. Then we are able to express certain context quantitatively, to make compatibility, to share the context quantitatively among the different analysis and prediction environment. By changing the context, we can get the different results for discussion and comparison between the different point of view, and to be able to review analytical results of phenomena among users and analyst. Our system enables to express expert knowledge of analysis and prediction on each specific field, and this makes it possible to analyze and discuss interdisciplinary between different fields. The meaning of our new context definition is to fix the closed world of the semantic differential computing on time axis from viewpoint of database system. So, we can normalize the targe part of data according to a context, and it means we can compare the feature extracted from the target data.

One of the main features of our method is to obtain different results by switching the time series context. Our concept to express time series context by 5 elements is shown in Figure 2. If we apply our new context definition to prediction, we are able to realize comparison and discussion between several prediction results for the same data by switching the time series context. Therefore, we are not focusing to evaluate the output results with the real data. Our method realizes quantitative comparison between different time series contexts. The main features of our method are summarized as follows; 1) introducing a new normalization (context expression) method to fix a target reference data for time series analysis and prediction according to a context, and 2) presenting a process to generate semantic discrete values reflecting the 5 elements. And the significant points of the proposing method are 1) our new context definition corresponds to fix the closed world of the semantic differential computing on time axis from the viewpoint of database system, and 2) the 5 elements enable to explicit and quantify experts' semantic viewpoint of specifying a certain reference data according to a context for each analysis and prediction.

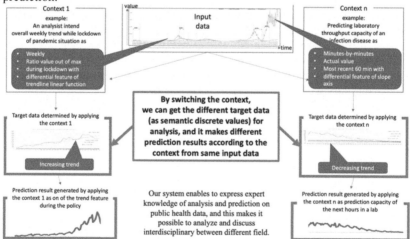

Figure 2. Concept of the context-based time series analysis and prediction method for public health data. The left side shows context 1 (ex: for overall weekly trend while lockdown of pandemic situation), and the right side another context n (ex: prediction laboratory throughput capacity of an infection disease). By switching those contexts, we can obtain the different target data (as semantic discrete values) for analysis, and it makes different prediction results according to the context from same input data.

The context definition is quite important to deal with interdisciplinary phenomenon between human and providence of nature, such as the field of health, medication, environment, and culture which are having time axis. As our experiment, we realized our system and context definition in the field of public health to analyze and prediction of infection disease. The experiments show the prediction feasibility of our method in the field of public health data, effectiveness to generate results for discussion regarding switching context, and applicability to express time series context of an expert knowledge for analysis and prediction as combination of the 5 elements to make the knowledge explicit and quantitative expression.

In the next section, we present our method by explaining overview and definitions of data and functions. In section 3, we show two experiments by applying actual public health data, and we conclude this paper in section 4.

2. A Context-based Time Series Analysis and Prediction Method for Public Health Data

In this section, we define a context-based time series analysis and prediction method for public health data. First, we explain overview of our method to process the 5 elements of context to analysis and prediction for public health data. Then we define 5 elements to express basis of a time series context to generate reference data as semantic discrete values of analysis and prediction according to the time series context, and we also define input data, confirmed reference data, and output data of our method.

2.1. Overview of the Context-based Time Series Analysis and Prediction Method

We realize our method by the following 4 steps to obtain analysis and prediction result. Overview of the proposing method is shown in Figure 3.

Step 1: Input data (continuous data/raw discrete data) along with time (before considering time series context)
   1. Input time series data for reference (IRD)
   2. Input time series data for prediction (ITD)

Step2: Define a time series context for analysis and prediction by combination of the 5 elements
   1. Granularity setting on time axis (GS)
   2. Feature extraction method (FEM)
   3. Time-window setting (TWS)
   4. Differential computing function (DCF)
   5. Pivot setting on time axis for prediction (PV)

Step3: Extract reference data and pivot according to the 5 elements defined in Step2
   1. Confirmed reference data (CRD)
   2. Time point of Pivot on ITD (PV)

Step4: Output prediction result according to the context
   1. Output prediction data (OPD)

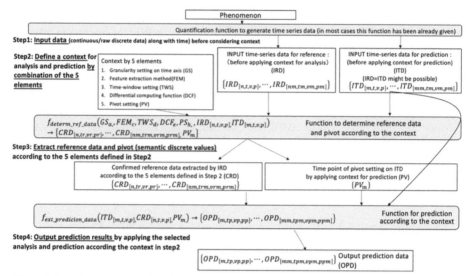

Figure 3. Overview of a context-based time series analysis and prediction method for public health data. We realize our model by the 4 steps to output prediction result.

2.2. Data Structure and Definition of 5 elements to express a time series context to determine semantic discrete values as target of analysis and prediction

Our approach is to express the basis of time series context for analysis and prediction as combination of the following 5 elements, Granularity setting on time axis (GS), Feature extraction method (FEM), Time-window setting (TWS), Differential computing function (DCF), and Pivot setting on time axis for prediction (PV) to determine the appropriate reference data as semantic discrete values on time axis.

In the field of analysis of time series data, we have many viewpoints for expressing time series context to determine reference data not only those elements but also for the specific criteria on each field. In this paper, we only focused on the analysis and prediction of public health data, and we designed it by applying the 5 elements with the expert knowledge which are previously implicit in the brain of each analyst. Therefore, by applying the 5 elements, we are able to express a time series context to determine reference data and pivot on time axis for analysis and prediction in the field of public health data. Each element has each role to determine reference data as explaining in the following subsections.

Granularity setting on time axis (GS): Setting granularity on time axis corresponds to fix a semantic sampling rate of reference data as semantic discrete values. For example, this setting is corresponding to normalize horizontal unit size when we make a chart. We have many conceptual numeral systems on time axis and its sampling size according to a context. The granularity setting in time (GS) includes two variables, original granularity in time (OG), and target granularity in time (TG). We define data structure of GS as the following.

$$GS_a \supset \{OG_b, TG_b\} \tag{1}$$

$(a = 1, am)(a = granularity\ control\ method\ id, am = maximum\ number\ of\ granularity\ control\ method)$
$(b = 1, bm)(b = granulairty\ id, bm = maximum\ number\ of\ granulairty)$

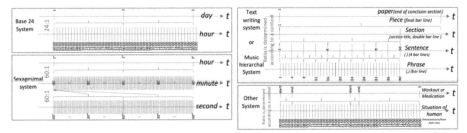

Figure 4. Examples of major granularity settings on time axis (GS), one of the most important elements which we can fix as one of the time series contexts. The left side shows base 24 system (24 ticks of conceptual and hierarchal structures between day and hour), and sexagesimal system (60 ticks of conceptual and hierarchal structures for second, minute, and hour), the right side shows conceptual systems on time axis, such as hierarchal text writing system of paper (hierarchal system between phrase, sentence, section, and paper), music hierarchal system (hierarchal system between note, phrase, section, movement, and a piece of music)

As shown in Figure 4, in general, as we can feel in daily life, we have many kinds of numeral systems on time axis, such as base 24 system (24 ticks of conceptual and hierarchal structures between day and hour), sexagesimal system (60 ticks of conceptual and hierarchal structures for second, minute, and hour). We also have several conceptual systems on time axis, such as hierarchal text writing system of paper (hierarchal system between phrase, sentence, section, and paper), music hierarchal system (hierarchal system between note, phrase, section, movement, and a piece of music) Moreover, we use specific segmentation to fix an important part of data by applying additional information other than data itself, such as heart beat rate during workout or not, blood pressure value in duration of medication or not. We have introduced the conceptual tick and the hierarchal system of music data as "grain and tree-structured granularity" for music analysis in our previous research [14]. By switching the system and selecting the level of granularity, we can specify an appropriate grain of data according to a context. Ordinally in the field of data analysis, the granularity of input data will be used as is the granularity of the targe data. Our model makes it possible to explicit desired granularity of context to generate reference data for each analysis and prediction. If we have an attention on larger granularity, the difference between data expresses comprehensive feature. Other cases, if we have another attention on smaller granularity, the difference between data expresses detailed differential feature of the data. For example, if the OG is hourly data, and TG is weekly data, we can control by applying the time system hierarchy to generate the size of TG.

Feature extraction method (FEM): Setting of the feature extraction method means normalization of values of reference data in a closed world of context for analysis and prediction. The feature extraction method is the quantification method to generate value of the reference data on time axis, such as ratio out of maximum number, specific quantity, semantic feature value on specific viewpoint, and so on. This setting corresponds to normalize vertical unit setting and value when we make a chart, to fix unit and values of feature of reference data as semantic discrete values. This process makes it possible to explicit desired viewpoint of feature extraction according to a context. For example, those are completely different between if we have an attention on actual value, ratio of certain data, or semantic other features. We define data structure of FEM as the following.

$$FEM_c \qquad\qquad\qquad\qquad (2)$$

$(c = 1, cm)(c = feature\ extraction\ method\ id, cm = maximum\ number\ of\ feature\ extraction\ method)$

Time-window setting (TWS): Setting the time-window means selection of intended range of time axis for each context. This process corresponds to normalize of range of horizontal axis when we make a chart, to fix intended range of time axis for each context. This process makes it possible to explicit desired focusing point of reference data according to a context for each analysis and prediction. In general, we have specific focusing point when we analyze data. By switching the time-window, we can only focus on an appropriate range of time axis according to a context. Those are completely different between if we have an attention on most recent time range, time range having similar situation (period during lockdown etc.), or semantically fixed other range (medication term etc.). Time-window setting (TWS) contains two variables, starting time point (TS) and ending time point (TE). We define data structure of TWS as the following.

$$TWS_d \supset \{TS_{tp}, TE_{tp}\} \tag{3}$$
$(d = 1, dm)$
$(d = time\_window\ setting\ id, dm = maximum\ number\ of\ time\_window\ setting\ method)$
$(tp = time\ point\ on\ IRD)$

Differential computing function (DCF): Setting of the differential computing method means switching type of ruler to calculate differential feature between adjacent data on time axis for each context. The differential computing method is a quantification method to calculate value of the difference of reference data on time axis, such as regressive curve, tilt/angle, slope, trend line linear, substruction, ratio between each substruction, a color system to calculate distance between colors, and so on. The determination of the differential computing method is often considered with the feature extraction method since in many cases, as both two are developed together in specific research field such as metadata generation method and the specific calculation system for the metadata. The determination of the differential computing method is often considered with the feature extraction method, since the both two are developed together in specific research field such as metadata generation method and the specific calculation system for the metadata in many cases. We define data structure of the DCF as the following.

$$DCF_e \tag{4}$$
$(e = 1, em)$
$(e = differential\ computing\ \text{function}\ id, em = maximum\ number\ of\ differential\ computing\ \text{function})$

Pivot setting (PV): Setting pivot means to fix an effective timing of starting prediction by applying reference data of each context. The pivot is a starting time point of prediction that matched the conceptual meaning of the starting time of prediction data, such as the same day of week, same month in a year, having a similarity in supportive data, having a similarity in reference data and prediction data, and so on. The pivot has also a role to adjust difference of meaning between starting point of reference data and the PV point of the prediction data by comparing those values. We define data structure of PV as the following.

$$PV_h \tag{5}$$
$(h = 1, hm)$
$(h = pivot\ setting\ id, hm = maximum\ number\ of\ pivot\ setting)$
$(tp = time\ point\ on\ ITD)$

2.3. Data Structure and Definition of Input Data, Reference data, and Output Data of the Context-based Time Series Analysis and Prediction Method

Our input data consists of the following two data, 1) Input time series data for reference (IRD) and 2) Input time series data for prediction (ITD). IRD is a base data for picking up reference data according to a context. ITD is previous part of desired prediction data. We define the data structure of the two inputs data as the following formula. ITD=IRD might be possible when if the IRD is also desired prediction data, and ITD=null might be also possible when if only for analysis. We define IRD and ITD as the followings.

Input time series data for reference (IRD):

$$\left\{IRD_{[n,t,v,p]}, \cdots, IRD_{[nm,tm,vm,pm]}\right\} \tag{6}$$
$(n = 1, nm)(nm = maximum\ number\ of\ IRD)$
$(t = 1, tm)(tm = maximum\ number\ of\ time\ point)$
$(v = 1, vm)(vm = maximum\ value)$
$(p = 1, pm)(pm = maximum\ number\ of\ parameter)$

Input time series data for prediction (ITD):

$$\left\{ITD_{[m,t,v,p]}, \cdots, ITD_{[mm,tm,vm,pm]}\right\} \tag{7}$$
$(m = 1, mm)(mm = maximum\ number\ of\ ITD)$

Confirmed reference data (CRD):

The data structure of the reference data is formalized as the following.

$$\left\{CRD_{[n,tr,vr,pr]}, \cdots, CRD_{[nm,trm,vrm,prm]}\right\} \tag{8}$$
$(rt = 1, trm)(trm = maximum\ number\ of\ time\ point)$
$(vr = 1, vrm)(vrm = maximum\ value)$
$(pr = 1, prm)(prm = maximum\ number\ of\ parameter)$

Output prediction data (OPD):

Data structure of the output data structure is formalized as the following.

$$\left\{OPD_{[m,tp,vp,pp]}, \cdots, OPD_{[mm,\ tpm,vpm,ppm]}\right\} \tag{9}$$
$(tp = 1, tpm)(tpm = maximum\ number\ of\ time\ point)$
$(vp = 1, vpm)(vpm = maximum\ value)$
$(pp = 1, ppm)(ppm = maximum\ number\ of\ parameter)$

2.4. Functions of the Context-based Time Series Analysis and Prediction Method

Function to determine reference data and pivot:

We define the function to determine reference data and pivot as the following.

$$f_{determine\_ref\_data}\left(GS_a, FEM_b, FW_{[ts,te]}, DCM_c, PV_h, IRD_{[n,t,v,p]}, ITD_{[nm,t,v,p]}\right) \rightarrow$$
$$\left\{CRD_{[n,tr,vr,pr]}, \cdots, CRD_{[nm,trm,vrm,prm]}, PV_m\right\} \tag{10}$$

Function for prediction according to the context:

We define the function for prediction as the following.

$$f_{extract\_predicion\_data}\left(ITD_{[m,t,v,p]}, CRD_{[n,t,v,p]}, PV_m\right) \rightarrow$$
$$\left\{OPD_{[m,tp,vp,pp]}, \cdots, OPD_{[mm,tpm,vpm,ppm]}\right\} \tag{11}$$

3. Experiment Study

We realized our experimental studies by applying COVID-19 number of confirmed cases data as the actual phenomenon of one of the public health issues.

Experiment 1:
    This experiment is to predict Covid-19 number of cases to expect tightness of testing throughput capacity of the Covid-19 (infection disease) in a laboratory during the coming week in Austria with single parameterized input data. The point of this experiment is to know what day of the week we need to expect maximum number of processing. A testing laboratory has implicit statistics that the number of confirmed cases is mostly synchronized with tightness day of the testing throughput capacity. The experiment 1 is one of the examples to realize prediction by applying own previous data of prediction target, single parameter value, and two kind of contexts comparison. To determine reference data for prediction, we set the following two contexts by an expert of analysis in the field of public health data. The time series context 1 is to reflect the most recent situation for prediction. The context 2 is to reflect the most similar situation in for prediction. By applying the two contexts to determine reference data to the prediction, we expect to get different prediction result according to each context. After the context setting process, context 1 selected the week starting from July 31st 2022, and the context 2 selected the week starting from April 24th 2022, and the pivot time point of prediction is at Aug 14th 2022, as shown in Figure 5.

Figure 5. Process to determine the confirmed reference data (CRD) for the context 1 and 2 of experiment1. The figure shows number of confirmed cases on every Sundays (as weekly data), and the red squares show two candidate weeks that matched condition of time-window setting (TWS) of the context 2. The most recent week from the candidates (the right red square) has been determined as the reference data (CRD). The green square shows time point of the pivot (PV) for prediction.

The important knowledge in the context setting of experiment 1 is to focus on the number of confirmed cases on Sundays, since most of the testing sites are closed on Sundays in Austria by business restrictions same as other DACH countries, and the confirmed cases on Sundays are expressing only the results from the regional core hospitals to care relatively severe conditioned patients. The expert of analysis in the field of public health data who set those contexts assumes that ratio comparing by the Sunday's number expresses one of the key features of situation of the following days on the week. Therefore, starting time point of the TWS and the PV is on Sunday in this experiment.

Input data and time series context 1 for experiment 1: to predict tightness of testing throughput capacity of the Covid-19 (infection disease) in a laboratory during the coming week in Austria **by reflecting the most recent situation for prediction.**

- Input time series data for reference (IRD) = Covid-19 number of confirmed cases in Austria which is published by ECDC [16]
- Input time series data for prediction (ITD) = prediction data is same as IRD, Covid-19 number of confirmed cases in Austria

- Granularity setting (GS)
  * Original granularity (OG) = daily
  * Target granularity (TG) = daily
- Feature extraction method (FEM) = actual number of confirmed cases
- Time-window setting (TWS) = most recent 1 week starting from Sunday on IRD
- Differential computing function (DCF) = ratio between starting point number of cases
- Pivot setting on ITD (PV) = the most recent Sunday on ITD

The confirmed reference data (CRD) for context 1 of experiment1 and the prediction output (OPD) are shown in Figure 6.

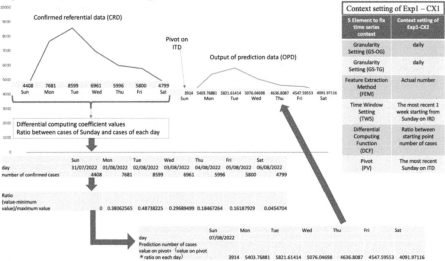

Figure 6. The confirmed reference data (CRD) and the prediction output (OPD) for context 1 of experiment1. The context setting is shown in top right table. The top left data (blue line) shows the most recent one-week data starting from Sunday which reflect the context 1, and the number of confirmed cases on each day calculated as the ratio between cases of Sunday and cases of each day as shown in the table. The ratio applied to predict the next one-week number of cases as the right bottom table. The output prediction data (OPD) is shown in top right (orange line).

Input data and time series context 2 for experiment 1: to predict tightness of testing throughput capacity of the Covid-19 (infection disease) in a laboratory during the coming week in Austria **by reflecting the most similar past situation (amount of change and absolute value) for prediction**
- Input time series data for reference (IRD) = Covid-19 number of confirmed cases in Austria which is published by ECDC [16]
- Input time series data for prediction (ITD) = prediction data is same as IRD, Covid-19 number of confirmed cases in Austria

- Granularity setting on time axis (GS)
    * Original granularity (OG) = daily (for reference data), weekly (for determination of reference data)
    * Target granularity (TG) = daily for prediction
- Feature extraction method (FEM) = actual number of confirmed cases
- Time-window setting (TWS) = most recent 1 week starting from Sunday that matched condition (condition: combination of slope trend (over two weeks of decreasing trend) and absolute value (the time point right after under 5000 cases))
- Differential computing function (DCF) = ratio between starting point number of cases
- Pivot setting on ITD (PV) = the most recent Sunday on ITD

The Process to determine the confirmed reference data (CRD) for the context 2 of experiment1 is shown in Figure 4, and the confirmed reference data (CRD) for context 1 of experiment1 and the prediction output (OPD) are shown in Figure 7.

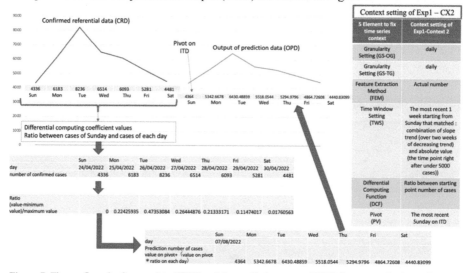

Figure 7. The confirmed reference data (CRD) and the prediction output (OPD) for context 2 of experiment1. The context setting is shown in top right table. The top left data (blue line) shows the one-week data that matched condition starting from Sunday which reflect the context 2, and the number of confirmed cases on each day calculated as the ratio between cases of Sunday and cases of each day as shown in the table. The ratio applied to predict the next one-week number of cases as the right bottom table. The output prediction data (OPD) is shown in top right (orange line).

Comparison between CRD (confirmed referential data), OPD (output prediction data), and the actual number of confirmed cases are shown in Figure 8. The left-side chart is result of context 1 of experiment1, and the right-side chart is result of context 2 of experiment. Dash line shows prediction data, double line shows CRD (confirmed referential data), and the solid line shows actual number of cases which later published from ECDC. By comparing OPD and the actual number of cases, the context 2 is closer than context 1.

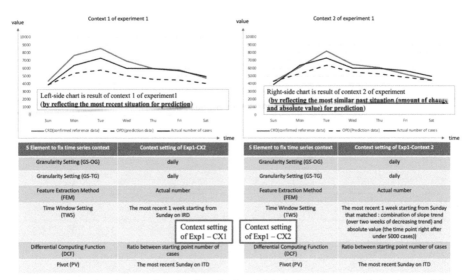

Figure 8. Comparison between CRD (confirmed referential data), OPD (output prediction data), and the actual number of confirmed cases. The context setting for each analysis are also shown in the bottom table. Left-side chart is result of context 1 of experiment1 (**by reflecting the most recent situation for prediction**), and the right-side chart is result of context 2 of experiment (**by reflecting the most similar past situation (amount of change and absolute value) for prediction**). Dash line shows prediction data, double line shows CRD (confirmed referential data), and the solid line shows actual number of cases which later published from ECDC. By comparing OPD and the actual number of cases, the context 2 is closer than context 1.

To confirm more applicability of our method, we reflect other several countries data. Figure 9 shows prediction results of Germany, Italy, and Slovenia. And the left-side chart is result of context 1 of experiment1, the right-side chart is result of context 2 of experiment 1, same as the experiment of the Austria's cases.

Results of the experiment 1 show following discussions.
- Prediction feasibility of our method in the field of public health data
- Realized quantitative comparison between different time series context
- Effectiveness to generate results for discussion regarding switching the setting of 5 elements to reflect better settings of time series context to the other prediction quantitatively
- Applicability to express time series context of an expert knowledge for analysis and prediction as the combination of 5 elements, to make the knowledge explicit and quantitative expression
- Realized quantitative comparison between different situation in several countries and time series context
- Especially the results of this experiment show that the setting of this context is more effective for DACH countries (Germany) where the test facilities are closed on every Sundays. Those results show discussion about setting the appropriate pivot is the important expert knowledge to reflect situations of public health.

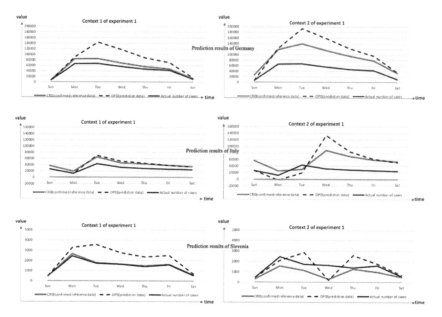

Figure 9. Comparison between CRD (confirmed referential data), OPD (output prediction data), and the actual number of confirmed cases of Germany (the top two results), Italy (the middle two results), and Slovenia (the bottom two results). Left-side chart is result of context 1 of experiment1 (**by reflecting the most recent situation for prediction**), and the right-side chart is result of context 2 of experiment (**by reflecting the most similar past situation (amount of change and absolute value) for prediction**). Dash line shows prediction data, double line shows CRD (confirmed referential data), and the solid line shows actual number of cases which later published from ECDC.

Experiment 2:

The experiment 2 is one of the examples to realize prediction by applying, other previous data of prediction target, multiple parameter value, and two kind of contexts comparison. Experiment 2 is focusing on switching two major variant, Alpha and Delta, during pandemic situation of Covid-19 in 2022 with multiparametric input data. This experiment is to predict the timing to reach over 90% ratio of a spreading (increasing) variant while switching with another variant. To determine reference data for prediction, we set the following two contexts to select input time series data for reference (IRD), by an expert of analysis in the field of public health data. The time series context 1 is to reflect the closer population, and the time series context 2 is to reflect the closer population density. By applying those contexts, we selected Covid-19 confirmed number of variant cases of nationwide data of United Kingdom and city level data of London as the input time series data for reference (IRD) which is published by government of United Kingdom [15]. Those areas have already switched majority from Alpha variant to Delta variant completely, and the Delta variant reached over 90% ratio. And we also selected Covid-19 confirmed number of variant cases of Saitama as input time series data for prediction (ITD) which are still in the half time point of switching majority from Alpha variant to Delta variant.

The important knowledge in the context setting of experiment 2 is to focus on closer population and closer population density. The expert of analysis in the field of public health data who set those contexts assumes that rapidness of switching two major variant is corresponding population density, and rapidness is slower in higher density area and rapidness is quicker in lower density area. We obtain different prediction result according to each context, and we also obtain basis to compare it for discussion of the expert's assumption.

In this experiment, we extract rapidness of switching two major variants by applying the rapidness calculation function which we already introduced in [13] as the differential computing function (DCF), and we reflect it to predict rapidness of Saitama (ITD) for the second half situation. The concept of the experiment 2 is shown in the Figure 10. For the other time series context were also set by the expert from an epidemiological laboratory in Japan for public health data analysis to express their desired context for this comparison.

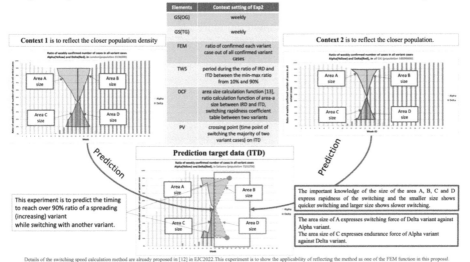

Figure 10. Concept of the experiment2 to predict the timing to reach over 90% ratio of a spreading (increasing) variant while switching with another variant. The context setting is shown in the top center table. The top left shows context 1 by applying London data (IRD) and confirmed reference data (CRD), and the top right shows context 2 by applying United Kingdom data (IRD) and confirmed reference data (CRD). The bottom shows time series prediction data of Saitama (ITD).

Input data and time series context 1 for experiment 2: to predict the timing to reach over 90% ratio of a spreading (increasing) variant while switching with another variant in Saitama <u>**by reflecting London (closer feature is population density) for prediction**</u>

- Input time series data for reference (IRD) = Covid-19 number of confirmed Alpha and Delta variant cases out of all confirmed variant cases in London (already switched the majority of the two variants) which is published by government of United Kingdom [15]. Population density of London is 4761 people/square kilometers.
- Input time series data for prediction (ITD) = Covid-19 number of confirmed Alpha and Delta variant cases out of all confirmed variant cases in Saitama (still in the half time point of switching majority from Alpha variant to Delta variant) which is collected by hospital and testing facility in Saitama. Population density of Saitama is 6127 people/square kilometers.

- Granularity setting on time axis (GS)
  * Original granularity (OG) = weekly for London, daily for Saitama

* Target granularity (TG) = weekly for both London and Saitama
- Feature extraction method (FEM) = ratio of confirmed each variant case out of all confirmed variant cases
- Time-window setting (TWS) = period during the ratio of IRD and ITD between the min-max ratio from 10% and 90%
- Differential computing function (DCF) = area size calculation function [13], ratio calculation function of area-a size between IRD and ITD, switching rapidness coefficient table between two variants
- Pivot setting on ITD (PV) = crossing point (time point of switching the majority of two variant cases) on ITD

The input time series data for reference (IRD) of London and the time series input data for prediction (ITD) of Saitama is shown in Figure 11.

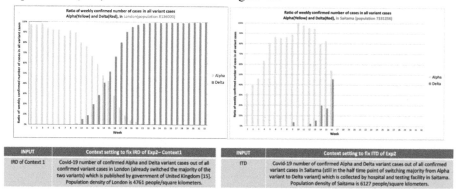

Figure 11. The left chart shows time series input data for reference (IRD) of London. The context setting to select IRD of Context 1 and ITD are shown in the bottom tables. The right chart shows time series input data for prediction (ITD) of Saitama. This data is time-series ratio of confirmed patient of each variant of Covid-19 which expresses situation of majority of variant of each area. London data shows situation is that this area is already switched the majority of the two variants. Saitama data shows situation that this area is still in the half time point of switching majority from Alpha variant to Delta variant.

Confirmed reference data for analysis (CRD) for context 1 of the experiment 2 is shown in Figure 12. The size of the area A, B, C and D express rapidness of the switching and the smaller size shows quicker switching and larger size shows slower switching.

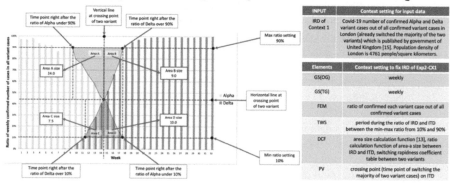

Figure 12. Confirmed reference data for analysis (CRD) of London for experiment 2 by applying 5 elements of context which expressing rapidness of switching two major variants. The context setting and IRD of Context 1 are shown in the right tables. The size of the area A, B, C and D express rapidness of the switching and the smaller size shows quicker switching and larger size shows slower switching.

Input data and time series context 2 for experiment 2: to predict the timing to reach over 90% ratio of a spreading (increasing) variant while switching with another variant in Sweden <u>by reflecting United Kingdom (population density is not closer) for prediction</u>

- Input time series data for reference (IRD) = Covid-19 number of confirmed Alpha and Delta variant cases out of all confirmed variant cases in United Kingdom (already switched the majority of the two variants) which is published by government of United Kingdom [15]. Population density of United Kingdom is 257 people/square kilometers (not closer).
- Input time series data for prediction (ITD) = Covid-19 number of confirmed Alpha and Delta variant cases out of all confirmed variant cases in Saitama (still in the half time point of switching majority from Alpha variant to Delta variant) which is collected by hospital and testing facility in Saitama. Population density of Saitama is 6127 people/square kilometers (not closer).

- Granularity setting on time axis (GS)
  * Original granularity (OG) = weekly for United Kingdom, daily for Saitama
  * Target granularity (TG) = weekly for both United Kingdom and Saitama
- Feature extraction method (FEM) = ratio of confirmed each variant case out of all confirmed variant cases
- Time-window setting (TWS) = period during the ratio of IRD and ITD between the min-max ratio from 10% and 90%
- Differential computing function (DCF) = area size calculation function [13], ratio calculation function of area-a size between IRD and ITD, switching rapidness coefficient table between two variants
- Pivot setting on ITD (PV) = crossing point (time point of switching the majority of two variant cases) on ITD

The input time series data for reference (IRD) of United Kingdom and the time series input data for prediction (ITD) of Saitama is shown in Figure 13.

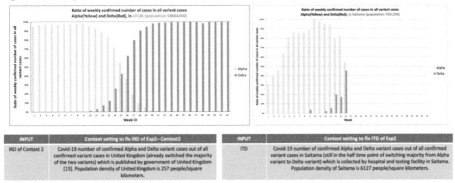

Figure 13. The left chart shows time series input data for reference (IRD) of United Kingdom. The context setting to select IRD of Context 2 and ITD are shown in the bottom tables. The right chart shows time series input data for prediction (ITD) of Saitama. This data is time-series ratio of confirmed patient of each variant of Covid-19 which expresses situation of majority of variant of each area. United Kingdom data shows situation is that this area is already switched the majority of the two variants. Saitama data shows situation that this area is still in the half time point of switching majority from Alpha variant to Delta variant.

Confirmed reference data for analysis (CRD) for context 1 of the experiment 2 is shown in Figure 14. The size of the area A, B, C and D express rapidness of the switching and the smaller size shows quicker switching and larger size shows slower switching. The area size analysis of the input time series data for prediction (ITD) of Saitama is shown in Figure 15.

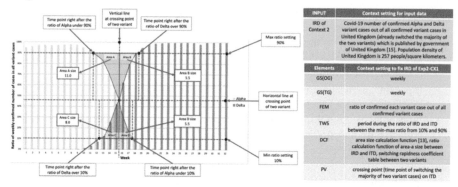

Figure 14. Confirmed reference data for analysis (CRD) of All UK for experiment 2 by applying 5 elements of context which expressing rapidness of switching two major variants. The context setting and IRD of Context 2 are shown in the right tables. The size of the area A, B, C and D express rapidness of the switching and the smaller size shows quicker switching and larger size shows slower switching.

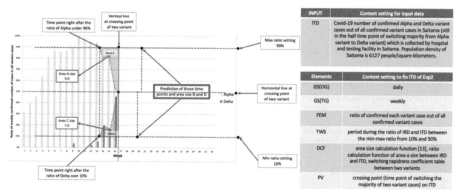

Figure 15. Area size analysis of the input time series data for prediction (ITD) of Saitama. The context setting and ITD are shown in the right tables. The area size of A expresses switching force of Delta variant against Alpha variant. The area size of C expresses endurance force of Alpha variant against Delta variant. This area size is differential computing result and it reflects feature of the Saitama data for the prediction in the next step processing.

Output data and comparison between context 1 and 2 of experiment 2:

By applying the London data and United Kingdom data of rapidness ratio between area A, B, C and D, we can get the prediction result of the Saitama after the crossing point as area size and the timing of the data over 90% ratio. The output prediction data (OPD) of the experiment 2 is shown in Figure 16 for both context 1 and 2.

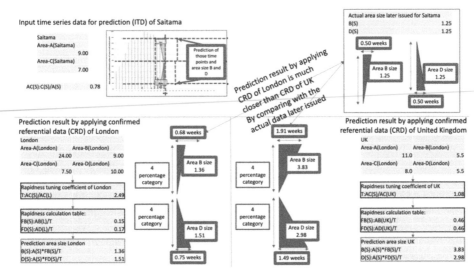

Figure 16. Result of Experiment-2 as the output prediction value (OPD) of Saitama. The bottom left values show prediction result by applying London data, and the bottom right values show prediction result by applying UK data. The top right values show the actual area size and week which later issued for Saitama. By comparing those results, the prediction results by applying CRD of London is much closer than CRD of UK to the actual data.

To confirm applicability of our method, we reflect other several countries data to our method. The results are shown in the figures below. Figure 17 shows prediction results of Austria, Germany, and Italy.

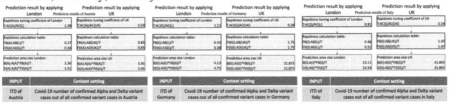

Figure 17. Result of Experiment-2 as the output prediction value (OPD). The left two columns for Austria, the middle two columns for Germany, and the right two columns for Italy. The left-side boxes of each country show prediction result by applying London data, and the right-side boxes show prediction result by applying UK data. The bottom tables show context setting to select ITD of each country.

Results of the experiment 2 shows following discussions.

- Prediction feasibility of our method in the field of public health data with the multiparametric input data
- Realized quantitative comparison between different time series context on different places which have different environmental feature
- Effectiveness for discussion regarding
  * switching the setting of 5 elements with field specific condition
  * processing different kind of granularity on time axis
    to reflect better settings of time series context to the other prediction quantitatively
  * Applicability of field specific function of public health data analysis to our presenting method

* Applicability of our method to various countries data which have different human environmental situation from the viewpoint of public health

4. Conclusion

We have presented a context-based time series analysis and prediction method for public health data. The most essential point of our approach is to express a basis of context as the combination of the 5 elements (1: granularity setting on time axis, 2: feature extraction method, 3: time-window setting, 4: differential computing function, and 5: pivot setting) to determine reference data as the semantic discrete value according to the context of analysis for public health data. As our experiment, we realized analysis and prediction by applying public health data. As our future work, we will design appropriate evaluation in this field to express the essence of our method, we will apply our method not only for prediction but also for datamining/analysis/search, and we will extend our method and the system to realize mutual understanding and knowledge sharing on global human-health issues in the world-wide scope.

Acknowledgement

We are grateful to Dr. Shiori Sasaki for essential and helpful discussion of this study.

References

[1] Yasushi Kiyoki, Xing Chen, "A Semantic Associative Computation Method for Automatic Decorative-Multimedia Creation with "Kansei" Information" (Invited Paper), The Sixth Asia-Pacific Conferences on Conceptual Modelling (APCCM 2009), 9 pages, January 20-23, 2009.

[2] Yasushi Kiyoki, Xing Chen, Shiori Sasaki, Chawan Koopipat, "A Globally-Integrated Environmental Analysis and Visualization System with Multi-Spectral & Semantic Computing in "Multi-Dimensional World Map"", Information Modelling and Knowledge Bases XXVIII, pp.106-122,2017

[3] Yasushi Kiyoki and Saeko Ishihara: "A Semantic Search Space Integration Method for Meta-level Knowledge Acquisition from Heterogeneous Databases," Information Modeling and Knowledge Bases (IOS Press), Vol. 14, pp.86-103, May 2002.

[4] Yasushi Kiyoki, Shiori Sasaki, Nhung Nguyen Trang, Nguyen Thi Ngoc Diep, "Cross-cultural Multimedia Computing with Impression-based Semantic Spaces," Conceptual Modelling and Its Theoretical Foundations, Lecture Notes in Computer Science, Springer, pp.316-328, March 2012.

[5] Yasushi Kiyoki: "A "Kansei: Multimedia Computing System for Environmental Analysis and Cross-Cultural Communication," 7th IEEE International Conference on Semantic Computing, keynote speech, Sept. 2013.

[6] Shiori Sasaki, Yusuke Takahashi, Yasushi Kiyoki: "The 4D World Map System with Semantic and Spatiotemporal Analyzers," Information Modelling and Knowledge Bases, Vol.XXI, IOS Press, 18 pages, 2010.

[7] Totok Suhardijanto, Yasushi Kiyoki, Ali Ridho Barakbah: "A Term-based Cross-Cultural Computing System for Cultural Semantics Analysis with Phonological-Semantic Vector Spaces," Information Modelling and Knowledge Bases XXIII, pp.20-38, IOS Press, 2012.

[8] Chalisa Veesommai, Yasushi Kiyoki, Shiori Sasaki and Petchporn Chawakitchareon, "Wide-Area River-Water Quality Analysis and Visualization with 5D World Map System", Information Modelling and Knowledge Bases, Vol. XXVII, pp.31-41, 2016.

[9] Chalisa Veesommai, Yasushi Kiyoki, "Spatial Dynamics of The Global Water Quality Analysis System with Semantic-Ordering Functions". Information Modelling and Knowledge Bases, Vol. XXIX, 2018.

[10] Yasushi Kiyoki, Asako Uraki, Chalisa Veesommai, "A Seawater-Quality Analysis Semantic- Space in Hawaii-Islands with Multi-Dimensional World Map System", 18th International Electronics Symposium (IES2016), Bali, Indonesia, September 29-30, 2016.

[11] Shiori Sasaki and Yasushi Kiyoki, "Real-time Sensing, Processing and Actuation Functions of 5D World Map System: A Collaborative Knowledge Sharing System for Environmental Analysis", Information Modelling and Knowledge Bases, Vol. XXVIII, IOS Press, pp. 220-239, May 2016.

[12] Shiori Sasaki, Koji Murakami, Yasushi Kiyoki, Asako Uraki: "Global & Geographical Mapping and Visualization Method for Personal/Collective Health Data with 5D World Map System," Information Modelling and Knowledge Bases (IOS Press), Vol. XXXII, pp. 134 – 149, 2020.

[13] Yasushi Kiyoki, Koji Murakami, Shiori Sasaki, Asako Uraki, "Human-Health-Analysis Semantic Computing & 5D World Map System" Information Modelling and Knowledge Bases (IOS Press), Vol. XXXIII, pp. 141 – 151, 2022.

[14] A. Ijichi and Y. Kiyoki: "A Kansei Metadata Generation Method for Music Data Dealing with Dramatic Interpretation "Information Modeling and Knowledge Bases, IOS Press, Vol.XVI, pp.170-182,(2004).

[15] UK Health Security Agency. Variant of Concern Technical Briefing 23. Available at: https://www.gov.uk/government/publications/investigation-of-sars-cov-2-variants-technical-briefings

[16] ECDC European Centre for Disease Prevention and Control, Data on the daily number of new reported COVID-19 cases and deaths by EU/EEA country, Available at : https://www.ecdc.europa.eu/en/publications-data/data-daily-new-cases-covid-19-eueea-country

40

Information Modelling and Knowledge Bases XXXV
M. Tropmann-Frick et al. (Eds.)
© 2024 The Authors.
This article is published online with Open Access by IOS Press and distributed under the terms
of the Creative Commons Attribution Non-Commercial License 4.0 (CC BY-NC 4.0).
doi:10.3233/FAIA231146

Towards a Definition of a Responsible Artificial Intelligence

Sabrina GÖLLNER [a], Marina TROPMANN-FRICK [a] and Boštjan BRUMEN [b]

[a] *Department of Computer Science, Hamburg University of Applied Sciences, Germany.*
sabrina.goellner@haw-hamburg.de, marina.tropmann-frick@haw-hamburg.de
[b] *Faculty of Electrical Engineering and Computer Science, University of Maribor,*
Slovenia.
bostjan.brumen@um.si
ORCiD ID: Sabrina Göllner https://orcid.org/0000-0002-1817-7440, Marina
Tropmann-Frick https://orcid.org/0000-0003-1623-5309, Boštjan Brumen
https://orcid.org/0000-0002-0560-1230

Abstract. Our investigation seeks to enhance the understanding of responsible artificial intelligence. The EU is deeply engaged in discussions concerning AI trustworthiness and has released several relevant documents. It's crucial to remember that while AI offers immense benefits, it also poses risks, necessitating global oversight. Moreover, there's a need for a framework that helps enterprises align their AI development with these international standards. This research will aid both policymakers and AI developers in anticipating future challenges and prioritizing their efforts. In our study, we delve into the essence of responsible AI and, to our understanding, introduce a comprehensive definition of the term. Through a thorough literature review, we pinpoint the prevailing trends surrounding responsible AI. Using insights from our analysis, we've also deliberated on a prospective framework for responsible AI. Our findings emphasize that human-centeredness should prioritized. This entails adopting AI techniques that prioritize ethical considerations, explainability of models, and aspects like privacy, security, and trustworthiness.

Keywords. Structured Literature Review, Artificial Intelligence, Responsible AI, Privacy-preserving AI, Explainable AI, Ethical AI, Trustworthy AI.

1. Introduction

Over the past few years, intensified research has been directed towards advancing Artificial Intelligence (AI), reflecting its increasing integration into various sectors. The European Commission, in 2020 and 2021, unveiled several documents, notably [1,2,3], outlining their strategic vision for AI. Their 2020 white paper "A European Approach to Excellence and Trust" proposes political strategies to amplify AI's potential benefits and mitigate its inherent risks. Their objective is to create a legal infrastructure in Europe, promoting trustworthy AI, anchored firmly in the core values and rights of EU citizens. Emphasizing a human-centric AI approach, the paramount importance of European values is highlighted. These documents tackle intricate challenges like ethics, privacy, and sustainability, underscoring the security's pivotal role within AI domains and introducing a stratified risk framework for AI systems.

An observation from the documents is the current absence of a unified European AI framework, shedding light on its political significance. Another crucial document, the "Communication on Fostering a European Approach to AI," sets out the EU Commission's roadmap. It underscores a *"human-centric, sustainable, secure, inclusive and trustworthy artificial intelligence (AI) [which] depends on the ability of the European Union"*.

The Commission's ambition revolves around fostering AI excellence, emphasizing collaboration, research augmentation, and funding prospects. The discourse on trust spirals towards innovation, with the EU's approach characterized as *"human-centered, risk-based, proportionate, and dynamic"*. The vision encapsulated is for an innovative, ethical, and human-focused AI. The document wraps up by highlighting the opportunity to support the EU's innovative prowess, competitiveness, and responsible AI deployment.

Moreover, the European Commission's "Proposal for a Regulation" details potential prohibitions in AI practices and stipulations for high-risk AI systems, with an emphasis on transparency. Notably, there's a discernible inconsistency in the terminologies used across political texts related to trustworthy AI, often leading to ambiguity. While the documents accentuate both the promise and perils of AI, they avoid a clear definition of trustworthy AI. The discourse touches upon aspects like ethical considerations, transparency, and safety, but without offering an unequivocal definition.

Our contention is that merely targeting trust, as vaguely outlined in these documents, doesn't suffice for AI integration. A broader "responsible AI" approach, resonating with European values, is imperative, where trust forms just an element of its broader responsibility. Consequently, in this paper, our quest is to discern the current academic consensus on *"trustworthy AI"* and probe if there's a definition for *"responsible AI"*. This understanding is crucial for steering towards *"excellence"* in AI.

In our endeavor to decipher responsible AI, we embark on a structured literature review, aiming to unveil its true essence. Our initial probe reveals a plethora of inconsistencies in terminologies not just in political texts but across various sources. Definitional overlaps for responsible AI, coupled with semantically similar terms, further complicate the landscape. Although paradigms exist in arenas like ethics and security, myriad challenges loom ahead. Best to our knowledge this is the first detailed and structured review about responsible AI. The structure of our paper is as follows: Initially, our research methodology, encompassing aims, objectives, as well as specifying the databases and research queries we used for searching, is detailed. We then go through extant literature to cull out definitions of responsible AI, compare them against analogous terms. From this analysis, we derive a definitive understanding of responsible AI. The ensuing sections encapsulate our core findings, underpinned by a meticulous analysis of every single paper regarding the terms "Trustworthy, Ethics, Explainability, Privacy, and Security" in a structured table and quantitative analysis of the study features. Culminating the paper, our discussion highlights the foundational pillars for nurturing responsible AI, and we conclude with our research constraints, inferences, and avenues for future research.

2. Research Methodology

In addressing our research queries, we conducted a systematic literature review (SLR) adhering to the guidelines delineated in [4]. The methodology and steps involved in our comprehensive literature review are expounded upon in the ensuing subsections, with a concise outline presented in the Systematic Review Protocol.

2.1. Research Aims and Objectives

In our current study, our objective is to delve into the multifaceted role of "Responsible AI" encompassing diverse facets like privacy, explainability, trust, and ethics. Our primary goal is to decipher the composite components that make up "responsible AI". Subsequently, we intend to survey the prevailing advancements in this domain. Concludingly, our focus will shift to pinpointing unresolved issues, potential challenges, and arenas that demand deeper investigative efforts.

In summary, we provide the following contributions:

1. Specify a concise Definition of "Responsible AI"
2. Analyze the state of the art in the field of "Responsible AI"

2.2. Research Questions Formulation

Based on the aims of the research, we state the following research questions:

- RQ1: What is a general or agreed on definition of "Responsible AI" and what are the associated terms defining it?
- RQ2: What does "Responsible AI" encompass?

2.3. Databases

In order to get the best results when searching for the relevant studies, we used the indexing data sources. These sources enabled us a wide search of publications that would otherwise be overlooked. The following databases were searched:

- ACM Digital Library (ACM)
- IEEE Explore (IEEE)
- SpringerLink (SL)
- Elsevier ScienceDirect (SD)

The reason for selecting these databases was to limit our search to peer-reviewed research papers only.

2.4. Studies Selection

To scour the various databases for relevant literature, we utilized the following search string:("Artificial Intelligence" OR "Machine Learning" OR "Deep Learning" OR "Neural Network" OR "AI" OR "ML") AND (Ethic* OR Explain* OR Trust*) AND (Privacy*).
Acknowledging the varied terminology often associated with "Artificial Intelligence",

we incorporated terms like "Machine Learning", "Deep Learning", and "Neural Network", viewing them as synonymous. Given the prevalent use of the acronyms AI and ML in many existing papers, these too were integrated into our synonym set. We used the wildcard asterisk (*) with terms like "Ethic", "Trust", "Explain", and "Privacy" to ensure all potential variations stemming from these root words were captured (for instance, explain would match "explainability"). Boolean operators, namely OR and AND, facilitated our search strategy. The OR operator allowed for inclusiveness of any terms, while the AND operator ensured all our specified categories intersected. Parentheses were used to demarcate these sets.

We focused our search on literature from 2020 and 2021, offering a snapshot of the most recent advancements. This search was executed in December 2021. Upon retrieval, results were ranked by relevance. This prioritization was essential, especially since certain databases, lacking refined search capabilities, yielded a multitude of unrelated documents. To exclude irrelevant papers, the authors followed a set of guidelines during the screening stage. Papers did not pass the screening if:

1. They mention AI in the context of cyber-security, embedded systems, robotics, autonomous driving or internet of things, or alike.
2. They are not related to the defined terms of responsible AI.
3. They belong to general AI studies.
4. They only consist of an abstract.
5. They are published as posters.

These defined guidelines were used to greatly decrease the number of full-text papers to be evaluated in subsequent stages, allowing the examiners to focus only on potentially relevant papers.

The initial search produced 10.313 papers of which 4.121 were retrieved from ACM, 1064 from IEEE, 1.487 from Elsevier Science Direct, and 3.641 from Springer Link. The screening using the title, abstract, and keywords removed 6.507 papers. During the check of the remaining papers for eligibility, we excluded 77 irrelevant studies and 9 inaccessible papers. We ended up with 254 papers that we included for the qualitative and quantitative analysis (see Figure 1).

3. Analysis

This section includes the analysis part in which we first find out which definitions for 'responsible AI' existed in the literature so far. Afterward, we explore content-wise similar expressions and look for their definitions in the literature. These definitions are then compared with each other and searched for overlaps. As a result, we extract the essence of the analysis to formulate our definition of responsible AI.

3.1. Responsible AI

In this subsection, we answer the first research question: What is a general or agreed on definition of 'Responsible AI', and what are the associated terms defining it?

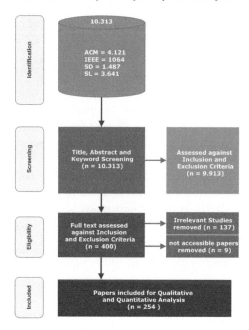

Figure 1. Structured review flow chart: the Preferred Reporting Items for Systematic Reviews and Meta–Analyses (PRISMA) flow chart detailing the records identified and screened, the number of full-text articles retrieved and assessed for eligibility, and the number of studies included in the review.

3.1.1. Terms defining Responsible AI

Out of all 254 analyzed papers, we only found 5 papers that explicitly introduce aspects for defining "responsible" AI. The papers use the following terms in connection with 'responsible AI':

- Fairness, Privacy, Accountability, Transparency and Soundness [5]
- Fairness, Privacy, Accountability, Transparency, Ethics, Security & Safety [6]
- Fairness, Privacy, Accountability, Transparency, Explainability [7]
- Fairness, Accountability, Transparency, and Explainability [8]
- Fairness, Privacy, Sustainability, Inclusiveness, Safety, Social Good, Dignity, Performance, Accountability, Transparency, Human Autonomy, Solidarity [9]

However, after reading all 254 analyzed papers we strongly believe, that the terms that are included in those definitions can be mostly treated as subterms or ambiguous terms.

- 'Fairness'[5] and 'Accountability' [5,6,7], as well as the terms 'Inclusiveness, Sustainability, Social Good, Dignity, Human Autonomy, Solidarity' [9] according to our definition, are subterms of Ethics.
- 'Soundness'[5], interpreted as 'Reliability' or 'Stability', is included within Security and Safety.
- Transparency [5,6,7] is often used as a synonym for explainability in the whole literature.

Therefore we summarize these terms of the above definitions to: "Ethics, Trustworthiness, Security, Privacy, and Explainability". However, only the terms alone are not enough to get a picture of responsible AI. Therefore, we will analyze and discuss what the *meaning* of the five terms "Ethics, Trustworthiness, Security, Privacy, and Explainability" in the context of AI is, and how they *depend* on each other. During the analysis, we found also content-wise similar expressions to the concept of "responsible AI" which we want to include in the findings. This topic will be dealt with in the next section.

3.1.2. Content-wise similar expressions for Responsible AI

During the analysis, we found that the term "Responsible AI" is often used interchangeably with the terms "Ethical AI" or "Trustworthy" AI, and "Human-Centered AI" is a content-wise similar expression.

Therefore, we treat the terms:

- "Trustworthy AI", found in [10,11,12,13,14,15,16], and [17] as cited in [18]
- "Ethical AI", found in [19,20,21,22,23], and [24] as cited in [25]
- "Human-Centered AI", found in [26] as cited in [23]

as the *content-wise similar expressions* for "Responsible AI" hereinafter.

3.2. Collection of definitions

The resulting collection of definitions from 'responsible AI' and 'content-wise similar expressions for responsible AI' from the papers results in the following Venn diagram:

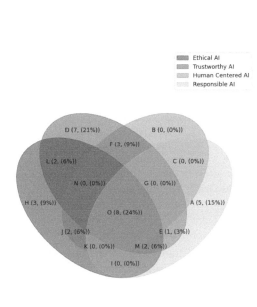

Set	Terms
A	Solidarity, Performance, Sustainability, Soundness, Inclusiveness
B	-
C	-
D	Equality, Usability, Accuracy under Uncertainty, Assessment, Reliability, Data Control, Data Minimization Reproducibility, Generalization User Acceptance
E	Social Good
F	Human-Centered, Human Control, Human Agency
G	-
H	Autonomy, Non-Maleficience, Trust
I	-
J	Human Values, Non-Discrimination
K	-
L	Compliant with Rules and Laws, Social Robustness
M	Human Autonomy, Dignity
N	-
O	Explainability, Safety, Fairness, Accountability, Ethics, Security Privacy, Transparency

Figure 2. Venn diagram

Analysis: We compared the definitions in the Venn diagram and determine the following findings:

- From all four sets there is an overlap of 24% of the terms: Explainability, Safety, Fairness, Accountability, Ethics, Security Privacy, Transparency.
- The terms occurring in the set of the definition for 'trust' only occurred in these, which is why this makes up the second largest set in the diagram. This is due to the fact that most of the terms actually come from definitions for trustworthy AI.
- There are also 6 null sets.

To tie in with the summary from the previous section, it should be pointed out once again that the terms 'Explainability, Safety, Fairness, Accountability, Ethics, Security Privacy, Transparency' can be grouped into generic terms as follows: Ethics, Security, Privacy, and Explainability.

We also strongly claim that 'trust/trustworthiness' should be seen as an outcome of a responsible AI system, and therefore we determine, that it belongs to the set of requirements. And each responsible AI should be built in a 'human-centered' manner, which makes it therefore another important subterm.

On top of these findings we specify our definition of Responsible AI in order to answer the first research question:

DEFINITION OF RESPONSIBLE AI

Responsible AI is **human-centered** and ensures users' **trust** through **ethical** ways of decision making. The decision-making must be fair, accountable, not biased, with good intentions, non-discriminating, and consistent with societal laws and norms. Responsible AI ensures, that automated decisions are **explainable** to users while always preserving users **privacy** through a **secure** implementation.

As mentioned in the sections before, the terms defining "responsible AI" result from the analysis of the terms in sections 3.1.1 and 3.1.2. We presented a figure depicting the overlapping of the terms of content-wise similar expressions of Responsible AI, namely "Ethical AI, Trustworthy AI, and Human-Centered AI", and extracted the main terms of it. Also by summarizing the terms Fairness and Accountability into Ethics, and clarifying the synonyms (e.g., explainability instead of transparency), we finally redefined the terms defining "responsible AI" as **"Human-centered, Trustworthy, Ethical, Explainable, Privacy(-preserving) and Secure AI"**.

3.3. Aspects of Responsible AI

According to our analysis of the literature, we have identified several categories in section 3 in connection to responsible AI, namely "Human-centered, Trustworthy, Ethical, Explainable, Privacy-preserving and Secure AI" which should ensure the development and use of it.

To answer the second research question (RQ2), we analyze the state-of-the-art of topics "Trustworthy, Ethical, Explainable, Privacy-preserving and Secure AI" in the following subsections. We have decided to deal with the topic of 'Human-Centered AI' in a separate paper so as not to go beyond the scope of this work. To find out the state of the art of the mentioned topics in AI, all 254 papers were assigned to one of the categories "Trustworthy AI, Ethical AI, Explainable AI, Privacy-preserving AI, and Secure AI", based on the prevailing content of the paper compared to each of the topic. The detailed analysis of these papers is beyond the scope of the present work and will be presented in our future work. Nevertheless, we highlight their most important features in the following subsections.

3.3.1. Trustworthy AI

A concise statement for trust in AI is as follows:

> *"Trust is an attitude that an agent will behave as expected and can be relied upon to reach its goal. Trust breaks down after an error or a misunderstanding between the agent and the trusting individual. The psychological state of trust in AI is an emergent property of a complex system, usually involving many cycles of design, training, deployment, measurement of performance, regulation, redesign, and retraining."*[27]

Trustworthy AI is about delivering the promise of AI's benefits while addressing the scenarios that have vital consequences for people and society.

In this subsection, we summarize which are the aspects covered by the papers in the category "Trustworthy AI" and what are the issues to engender users' trust in AI.

Trust must be an essential goal of an AI application in order to be accepted in society and that every effort must be made to maintain and measure it at all times and in every stage of development. However, trustworthy AI still remains as a big challenge as it is not addressed (yet) holistically.

3.3.2. Ethical AI

In this subsection, we list the findings in the field of ethical AI. In our opinion, the definition found in [28] best describes ethics in conjunction with AI:

> *"AI ethics is the attempt to guide human conduct in the design and use of artificial automata or artificial machines, aka computers, in particular, by rationally formulating and following principles or rules that reflect our basic individual and social commitments and our leading ideals and values [28]."*

During our analysis we noticed that Ethical AI deals often with fairness. Fair AI can be understood as *"AI systems [which] should not lead to any kind of discrimination against individuals or collectives in relation to race, religion, gender, sexual orientation, disability, ethnicity, origin or any other personal condition. Thus, fundamental criteria to consider while optimizing the results of an AI system is not only their outputs in terms of error optimization but also how the system deals with those groups."*[6]

In any case, the development of ethical artificial intelligence should be also subject to proper oversight within the framework of robust laws and regulations.

It is also stated, that transparency is widely considered also as one of the central AI ethical principles [29].

In the state-of-the-art overview of [30] the authors deal with the relations between explanation and AI fairness and examine, that fair decision-making requires extensive contextual understanding, and AI explanations help identify potential variables that are driving the unfair outcomes.

Mostly, transparency and explainability are achieved using so-called explainability (XAI) methods. Therefore, it is discussed separately in the following subsection.

3.3.3. Explainable AI

Decisions made by AI systems or by humans using AI can have a direct impact on the well-being, rights, and opportunities of those affected by the decisions. This is what makes the problem of the explainability of AI such a significant ethical problem. This subsection deals with the analysis of the literature in the field explainable AI (XAI).

We found an interesting definition in [6] which is quite suitable for defining explainable AI:

> *Given a certain audience, explainability refers to the details and reasons a model gives to make its functioning clear or easy to understand.[6]*

There are many different XAI techniques discussed in the literature. [6] as well as [31] give a detailed overview of the known techniques and their strengths and weaknesses, therefore we will only cover this topic in short.

First, the models can be distinguished into two different approaches to XAI, the intrinsically transparent models and the Post-hoc explainability target models that are not readily interpretable by design. These so-called "black-box models" are the more problematic ones, because they are way more difficult to understand. The post-hoc explainability methods can then be distinguished further into model-specific and model-agnostic techniques.

We can also distinguish generally between data-dependent and data-independent mechanisms for gaining interpretability as well as global and local interpretability methods.

The general public needs more transparency about how ML/AI systems can fail and what is at stake if they fail. Ideally, they should clearly communicate the outcomes and focus on the downsides to help people think about the trade-offs and risks of different choices (for example, the costs associated with different outcomes). But in addition to the general public also Data Scientists and ML Practitioners represent another key stakeholder group. In the study by [32] the effectiveness and interpretability of two existing tools were investigated; the results indicate that data scientists over-trust and misuse interpretability tools.

There is a "right to explanation" in the context of AI systems that directly affect individuals through their decisions, especially in legal and financial terms, which is one of the themes of the General Data Protection Regulation (GDPR) [33,34]. Therefore we need to protect data through secure and privacy-preserving AI-methods.

We will analyze this in the next section.

3.3.4. Privacy-preserving and Secure AI

As it was noted before, privacy and security are seen as central aspects of building trust in AI. However, the fuel for the good performance of ML models is data, especially sensitive data. This has led to growing privacy concerns, such as unlawful use of private data and disclosure of sensitive data[35,36]. We, therefore, need comprehensive privacy protection through holistic approaches to privacy protection that can also take into account the specific use of data and the transactions and activities of users [37] .

Privacy-preserving and Secure AI methods can help mitigate those risks. We define "Secure AI" as protecting data from malicious threats, which means protecting personal data from any unauthorized third-party access or malicious attacks and exploitation of data. It is set up to protect personal data using different methods and techniques to ensure data privacy. Data privacy is about using data responsibly. This means proper handling, processing, storage, and usage of personal information. It is all about the rights of individuals with respect to their personal information. Therefore data security is a prerequisite for data privacy.

There is a lot of research related to privacy and security in the field of AI and there is no approach yet to achieve perfectly privacy-preserving and secure AI and many challenges are left open.

3.4. Quantitative analysis

The final set of 254 high-quality studies was selected for an in-depth analysis to aid in answering the presented research questions.

Our choice of features is based on their content in each of the following categories, "Trustworthy AI, Ethical AI, Explainable AI, Privacy-preserving AI, and Secure AI", as derived from section 3.2. We analyzed the papers quantitatively. Table 1 presents study features along with their absolute and percentile representations in the reviewed literature as well as their sources.

The distribution of the paper is as follows: most papers covered the topic "Privacy-Preserving and Secure AI", followed by "Ethical AI" and then "Explainable AI" and Trustworthy AI.

Within the topic "Privacy-Preserving and Secure AI", most papers belong to "Federated learning", obviously being a very emerging research field in the time frame.

There were also many different papers that were not assigned to any specific category (see "Miscellaneous)" since the topic is very multifaceted.

In the topic area of "Ethical AI", the most common category was 'Miscellaneous', since the authors of the ethical AI field handle very different topics. In addition, second most of them could be assigned to the category 'ethical issues' since ths is a hot topic in the field of ethics. The rest of the papers dealt with ethical frameworks that try to to integrate ethical AI in context of a development process.

Most studies in the field oxf XAI deal with coming up with new XAI approaches to solve different explainability problems with new AI models. There were also a few that presented stakeholder analyses specifically in the context of explainability of AI models. Few of them presented miscellaneous topics that could not be assigned to any specific category or frameworks to integrate explainable AI.

In Trustworthy AI, we saw that most presented a review or survey on the current state of Trustworthy AI in research. There were also papers presented frameworks specially for trustwothiness or papers that reported on how Trust is perceived and described by different users.

Feature of a study	Representation	Percentage	Sources
Trustworthy AI (28/254, 11%) *			
Reviews and Surveys	9/28	32%	[11,17,38,13,39,14,40,41,42]
Perceptions of trust	4/28	14%	[43,44,45,27]
Frameworks	9/28	32%	[26,46,47,48,49,15,50,51,52]
Miscellaneous	6/28	28%	[53,54,55,56,16,57]
Ethical AI (85/254,34%) *			
Frameworks	19/85	22%	[35,58,59,7,20,60,29,24,61,62]
			[63,64,65,66,67,68,69,70,71]
Ethical issues	22/85	26%	[72,20,73,74,75,76,77,78]
			[79,80,81,28,82,36,83,84]
			[85,86,87,88,89,90]
Miscellaneous	33/85	39%	[91,19,92,93,94,95,96,22,21,97,98]
			[99,100,101,102,9,103,104]
			[105,106,107,108,109,110,111]
			[112,113,114,115,116,117,118,8]
Reviews and Surveys	10/85	12%	[119,120,121,122,123,124,125,126,127,30]
Tools	1/85	1%	[128]
Explainable AI (46/254 , 18%) *			
Reviews and Surveys	10/46	22%	[6,31,33,12,129,34]
			[130,131,132,133]
Stakeholders	7/46	15%	[134,135,136,137]
			[32,138,139]
XAI Approaches	14/46	30%	[140,5,141,142,143,144]
			[145,146,147,148,149,150,151,152]
Frameworks	4/46	9%	[153,154,155,156]
Miscellaneous	11/46	24%	[157,158,159,160,161]
			[162,163,164,165,166,167]
Privacy-preserving and Secure AI (95/254 , 38%) *			
Reviews and Surveys	10/95	10%	[168,169,170,171,172,37]
			[173,174,175,176]
Differential Privacy	12/95	13%	[177,178,179,180,181,182]
			[183,184,185,186,187,188]
Secure Multi-Party Computation	2/95	2%	[189,190]
Homomorphic Encryption	4/95	4%	[142,191,192,193]
Federated learning	35/95	37%	[194,195,196,197,198,199,200,201]
			[202,203,204,205,206]
			[207,208,209,210,211,212,213,214,215]
			[216,217,218,219,220,221,222]
			[223,224,225,226,227,228,229]
Hybrid Approaches	8/95	xx%	[230,231,232,233,234,235,236,237]
Security Threats	7/95	8%	[238,239,240,241,242,243,244]
Miscellaneous	16/95	17%	[245,246,247,248,249,250,251,252,253,254]
			[255,256,257,258,259,260]

Table 1. Quantitative Analysis

*percentage does not add up to 100 due to rounding.

4. Discussion

Several key points have emerged from the analysis. It has become clear that AI will have an ever-increasing impact on our daily lives, from delivery robots to e-health, smart nutrition and digital assistants, and the list is growing every day. AI should be viewed as a tool, not a system that has infinite control over everything. It should therefore not replace humans or make them useless, nor should it lead to humans no longer using their own intelligence and only letting AI decide. We need a system that we can truly call "responsible" AI. The analysis has clearly shown that the elements of ethics, privacy, security and explainability are the true pillars of responsible AI, which should lead to a basis of trust.

4.1. Pillars of Responsible AI

Here we highlight the most important criteria that a responsible AI should fulfill. These are also the points that a developer should consider if she wants to develop responsible AI. Therefore, they also form the pillars for the future framework.

Key-requirements for the Ethical AI are as follows:

- fair: non-biased and non-discriminating in every way,
- accountability: justifying the decisions and actions,
- sustainable: built with long-term consequences in mind, satisfying the Sustainable Development Goals,
- compliant: with robust laws and regulations.

Key-requirements for the privacy and security techniques are identified as follows:

- need to comply with regulations: HIPAA, COPPA, and more recently the GDPR (like, for example, the Federated Learning),
- need to be complemented by proper organizational processes,
- must be used depending on tasks to be executed on the data and on specific transactions a user is executing,
- use hybrid PPML-approaches because they can take advantage of each component, providing an optimal trade-off between ML task performance and privacy overhead,
- use techniques that reduce communication and computational cost (especially in distributed approaches).

Key-requirements for Explainable AI are the following:

- Human-Centered: the user interaction plays a important role and how he understands and interacts with the system,
- Explanations must be tailored to the user needs and target group
- Intuitive User interface/experience: the results need to be presented in a understandable visual language,
- Explainable is also feature to say how well the system does its work (non functional requirement),
- Impact of explanations on decision making process,

Key-Perceptions of trustworthy AI are as follows:

- ensure user data is protected,
- probabilistic accuracy under uncertainty,
- provides an understandable, transparent, explainable reasoning process to the user,
- usability,
- act "as intended" when facing a given problem,
- perception as fair and useful,
- reliability.

We define Responsible AI as an interdisciplinary and dynamic process: it goes beyond technology and includes laws (compliance and regulations) and society standards such as ethics guidelines and the Sustainable Development Goals.

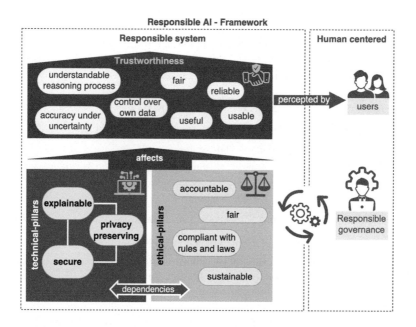

Figure 3. Pillars of the Responsible AI framework

Figure 4 shows that on the one hand there are social/ethical requirements/pillars and on the other hand the technical requirements/pillars. All of them are dependent on each other. If the technical and ethical side is satisfied the user trust is maintained. Trust can be seen as the perception of the users of AI.
There are also "sub-modules" present in each of the pillars, like accountability, fairness, sustainability and compliance in the field of ethics. They are crucial that we can say the AI meets ethical requirements.
Furthermore, the explainability methods must value privacy, meaning they must not have that much access to a model so that it results in a privacy breach. Privacy is dependent on security, because security is a prerequisite for it.
With each "responsible system" there are the humans that care for the system. The people who take care of the system must also handle it responsibly and constantly carry out

maintenance work and check by metrics whether the responsibility is fulfilled. This can be ensured by special metrics which are considered as a kind of continuous check as standard. This means responsible AI encompasses the system-side and the developer-side.

Human-Centered AI (mentioned in 3.3) needs to be considered as a very important part of responsible AI and it is closely connected to the approach "Human-in-the-loop". The human in the loop here is very important because this is the person who checks and improves the system during the life cycle. so the whole responsible AI system needs to be Human-Centered, too. This topic will not be dealt with in detail in this study, but is a part of the future work.

Therefore, responsible AI is interdisciplinary, and it is not a static but it is a dynamic process that needs to be taken care of in the whole system lifecycle.

4.2. Trade-offs

To fulfill all aspects comes with tradeoffs as discussed for example in [16] and comes for example at cost of data privacy. For example the methods that make model more robust against attacks or methots that try to explain a models behaviour and could leak some information. But we have fo find a way to manage that AI Systems that are accurate, fair, private, robust and explainable at the same time, which will be a very challenging task. We think that one approach to start with would be to create a benchmark for the different requirements that can determine to which proportion a certain requirement is fulfilled, or not.

5. Research Limitations

In the current study, we have included the literature available through various journals and provided a comprehensive and detailed survey on the literature in the field of responsible AI. In conducting the study, we unfortunately had the limitation that some journals were not freely accessible despite a comprehensive access provided by our institutions. Although we made a good effort to obtain the information needed for the study on responsible AI from various international journals, accessibility was still a problem. It is also possible that some of the relevant research publications are not listed in the databases we used for searching. Additional limitation is the time frame of searched articles; this was carefully addressed to include only the state-of-the-art in the field. However, some older yet still current developement might have been missed out.

Another limitation of the presented work is the missing in-depth analysis of the papers reviewed. Due to paper length constraints, we have omitted a detailed overview of each of the reviewed papers' contribution in each of the subsections of the section 3.3.

6. Conclusion

The field of AI is such a fast changing area and a legal framework for responsible AI is strongly necessary. From the series of EU-Papers on Artificial Intelligence of the last 2 years we noticed that "trustworthy AI" and "responsible AI" are not clearly defined, and as such a legal framework could not be efficiently established. Hence, the trust as a goal to define a framework/regulation for AI is not sufficient. Regulations for 'responsible AI' need to be defined instead. As the EU is a leading authority when it comes to setting standards (like the GDPR) we find it is absolutely necessary to help the politicians to really know what they are talking about. On the other hand, helping practitioners to prepare for what is coming next in both research and legal regulations is also of great importance.

The present research made important contributions to the concept of responsible AI. It is the first contribution to wholly address the "responsible AI" by conducting a structured literature research, and an overarching definition is presented as a result. The structured literature review covered 254 most recent high quality works on the topic. We have included a qualitative analysis of the papers covered.

By defining "responsible AI" and further analyzing the state of the art of its components (i.e., Human-centered, Trustworthy, Ethical, Explainable, Privacy(-preserving) and Secure AI), we have shown which are the most important parts to consider when developing AI products and setting up legal frameworks to regulate their development and use.

In the discussion section we have outlined an idea for developing a future framework in the context of Responsible AI based on the knowledge and insights gained in the analysis part.

In future work and research we will include a detailed analysis of the contribution of each of the analyzed papers to the defined aspects of responsible AI. Furthermore, the topic of Human-Centered AI and "Human-in-the-loop" should be developed in the context responsible AI. Other important topics to be worked upon are the benchmarking approaches for responsible AI and a holistic framework for Responsible AI as the overarching goal.

7. References

A complete list of 260 references is available at https://drive.google.com/file/d/1Fm-9hKkrY_YAzSO2TWec2L3lIqgPSmqm/view?usp=sharing, or by scanning the QR code below.

Figure 4. QR Code with the list of references

References

[1] European Commission. White Paper on Artificial Intelligence A European approach to excellence and trust. European Commission,.; 2020. Available from: `https://digital-strategy.ec.europa.eu/en/library/communication-fostering-european-approach-artificial-intelligence`.

[2] European Commission. Coordinated Plan on Artificial Intelligence 2021 Review. European Commission.; 2021. Available from: `https://digital-strategy.ec.europa.eu/en/library/coordinated-plan-artificial-intelligence-2021-review`.

[3] Commission E. Proposal for a REGULATION OF THE EUROPEAN PARLIAMENT AND OF THE COUNCIL LAYING DOWN HARMONISED RULES ON ARTIFICIAL INTELLIGENCE (ARTIFICIAL INTELLIGENCE ACT) AND AMENDING CERTAIN UNION LEGISLATIVE ACTS. European Commission.; 2021. Available from: `https://eur-lex.europa.eu/legal-content/EN/TXT/?qid=1623335154975&uri=CELEX%3A52021PC0206`.

[4] Kitchenham B, Brereton OP, Budgen D, Turne M, Bailey J, Linkman S. Systematic literature reviews in software engineering – A systematic literature review. Information and Software Technology. 2009;51:7-15.

[5] Maree C, Modal JE, Omlin CW. Towards Responsible AI for Financial Transactions. In: 2020 IEEE Symposium Series on Computational Intelligence (SSCI); 2020. p. 16-21.

[6] Alejandro Barredo Arrieta, Natalia Díaz-Rodríguez, Javier Del Ser, Adrien Bennetot, Siham Tabik, Alberto Barbado, et al. Explainable Artificial Intelligence (XAI): Concepts, taxonomies, opportunities and challenges toward responsible AI. Information Fusion. 2020;58:82-115. Available from: `https://www.sciencedirect.com/science/article/pii/S1566253519308103`.

[7] Eitel-Porter R. Beyond the promise: implementing ethical AI. AI and Ethics. 2021;1(1):73-80.

[8] Werder K, Ramesh B, Zhang RS. Establishing Data Provenance for Responsible Artificial Intelligence Systems. ACM Transactions on Management Information Systems. 2022 Jun;13(2):1-23. Available from: `https://dl.acm.org/doi/10.1145/3503488`.

[9] Jakesch M, Buçinca Z, Amershi S, Olteanu A. How Different Groups Prioritize Ethical Values for Responsible AI. In: 2022 ACM Conference on Fairness, Accountability, and Transparency. Seoul Republic of Korea: ACM; 2022. p. 310-23. Available from: `https://dl.acm.org/doi/10.1145/3531146.3533097`.

[10] level expert group on artificial intelligence H. Ethics guidelines for trustworthy AI e. European Commission.; 2019. Available from: `https://digital-strategy.ec.europa.eu/en/policies/expert-group-ai`.

[11] Jain S, Luthra M, Sharma S, Fatima M. Trustworthiness of Artificial Intelligence. In: 2020 6th International Conference on Advanced Computing and Communication Systems (ICACCS); 2020. p. 907-12.

[12] Sheth A, Gaur M, Roy K, Faldu K. Knowledge-Intensive Language Understanding for Explainable AI. IEEE Internet Computing. 2021;25(5):19-24.

[13] Wing JM. Trustworthy AI. Commun ACM. 2021;64(10):64-71.

[14] Zhang T, Qin Y, Li Q. Trusted Artificial Intelligence: Technique Requirements and Best Practices. In: 2021 International Conference on Cyberworlds (CW); 2021. p. 303-6. ISSN: 2642-3596.

[15] Li B, Qi P, Liu B, Di S, Liu J, Pei J, et al. Trustworthy AI: From Principles to Practices. ACM Computing Surveys. 2022 Aug:3555803. Available from: `https://dl.acm.org/doi/10.1145/3555803`.

[16] Strobel M, Shokri R. Data Privacy and Trustworthy Machine Learning. IEEE Security & Privacy. 2022 Sep;20(5):44-9. Available from: `https://ieeexplore.ieee.org/document/9802763/`.

[17] Kumar A, Braud T, Tarkoma S, Hui P. Trustworthy AI in the Age of Pervasive Computing and Big Data. In: 2020 IEEE International Conference on Pervasive Computing and Communications Workshops (PerCom Workshops); 2020. p. 1-6.

[18] Floridi L, Taddeo M. What is data ethics? Philosophical Transactions of The Royal Society A Mathematical Physical and Engineering Sciences. 2016 12;374:20160360.

[19] Hickok M. Lessons learned from AI ethics principles for future actions. AI and Ethics. 2021;1(1):41-7.

[20] Loi M, Heitz C, Christen M. A Comparative Assessment and Synthesis of Twenty Ethics Codes on AI and Big Data. In: 2020 7th Swiss Conference on Data Science (SDS); 2020. p. 41-6.

[21] Morley J, Elhalal A, Garcia F, Kinsey L, Mökander J, Floridi L. Ethics as a Service: A Pragmatic Operationalisation of AI Ethics. Minds and Machines. 2021.

[22] Ibáñez JC, Olmeda MV. Operationalising AI ethics: how are companies bridging the gap between practice and principles? An exploratory study. AI & SOCIETY. 2021.

[23] Fjeld J, Achten N, Hilligoss H, Nagy A, Srikumar M. Principled artificial intelligence: Mapping consensus in ethical and rights-based approaches to principles for AI. Berkman Klein Center Research Publication. 2020;(2020-1).

[24] Milossi M, Alexandropoulou-Egyptiadou E, Psannis KE. AI Ethics: Algorithmic Determinism or Self-Determination? The GPDR Approach. IEEE Access. 2021;9:58455-66.

[25] Floridi L, Cowls J, Beltrametti M, Chatila R, Chazerand P, Dignum V, et al. AI4People—an ethical framework for a good AI society: opportunities, risks, principles, and recommendations. Minds and Machines. 2018;28(4):689-707.

[26] Shneiderman B. Bridging the Gap Between Ethics and Practice: Guidelines for Reliable, Safe, and Trustworthy Human-Centered AI Systems. ACM Trans Interact Intell Syst. 2020;10(4).

[27] Middleton SE, Letouzé E, Hossaini A, Chapman A. Trust, regulation, and human-in-the-loop AI: within the European region. Communications of the ACM. 2022 Apr;65(4):64-8. Available from: https://dl.acm.org/doi/10.1145/3511597.

[28] Hanna R, Kazim E. Philosophical foundations for digital ethics and AI Ethics: a dignitarian approach. AI and Ethics. 2021.

[29] Ville Vakkuri, Kai-Kristian Kemell, Marianna Jantunen, Erika Halme, Pekka Abrahamsson. EC-COLA — A method for implementing ethically aligned AI systems. Journal of Systems and Software. 2021;182:111067. Available from: https://www.sciencedirect.com/science/article/pii/S0164121221001643.

[30] Zhou J, Chen F, Holzinger A. Towards Explainability for AI Fairness. In: Holzinger A, Goebel R, Fong R, Moon T, Müller KR, Samek W, editors. xxAI - Beyond Explainable AI. vol. 13200. Cham: Springer International Publishing; 2022. p. 375-86. Series Title: Lecture Notes in Computer Science. Available from: https://link.springer.com/10.1007/978-3-031-04083-2_18.

[31] Burkart N, Huber MF. A Survey on the Explainability of Supervised Machine Learning. J Artif Int Res. 2021;70:245-317.

[32] Kaur H, Nori H, Jenkins S, Caruana R, Wallach H, Wortman Vaughan J. Interpreting Interpretability: Understanding Data Scientists' Use of Interpretability Tools for Machine Learning. In: Proceedings of the 2020 CHI Conference on Human Factors in Computing Systems. CHI '20. New York, NY, USA: Association for Computing Machinery; 2020. p. 1-14.

[33] Choraś M, Pawlicki M, Puchalski D, Kozik R. Machine Learning – The Results Are Not the only Thing that Matters! What About Security, Explainability and Fairness? In: Krzhizhanovskaya VV, Závodszky G, Lees MH, Dongarra JJ, Sloot PMA, Brissos S, et al., editors. Computational Science – ICCS 2020. vol. 12140. Cham: Springer International Publishing; 2020. p. 615-28.

[34] Vellido A. The importance of interpretability and visualization in machine learning for applications in medicine and health care. Neural Computing and Applications. 2020;32(24):18069-83.

[35] Cheng L, Varshney KR, Liu H. Socially Responsible AI Algorithms: Issues, Purposes, and Challenges. J Artif Int Res. 2021;71:1137-81.

[36] Abolfazlian K. Trustworthy AI Needs Unbiased Dictators! In: Maglogiannis I, Iliadis L, Pimenidis E, editors. Artificial Intelligence Applications and Innovations. Cham: Springer International Publishing; 2020. p. 15-23.

[37] Bertino E. Privacy in the Era of 5G, IoT, Big Data and Machine Learning. In: 2020 Second IEEE International Conference on Trust, Privacy and Security in Intelligent Systems and Applications (TPS-ISA); 2020. p. 134-7.

[38] Singh R, Vatsa M, Ratha N. Trustworthy AI. In: 8th ACM IKDD CODS and 26th COMAD. CODS COMAD 2021. New York, NY, USA: Association for Computing Machinery; 2021. p. 449-53.

[39] Beckert B. The European way of doing Artificial Intelligence: The state of play implementing Trustworthy AI. In: 2021 60th FITCE Communication Days Congress for ICT Professionals: Industrial Data – Cloud, Low Latency and Privacy (FITCE); 2021. p. 1-8.

[40] Kaur D, Uslu S, Rittichier KJ, Durresi A. Trustworthy Artificial Intelligence: A Review. ACM Comput-ing Surveys. 2023 Mar;55(2):1-38. Available from: https://dl.acm.org/doi/10.1145/3491209.

[41] Yang G, Ye Q, Xia J. Unbox the black-box for the medical explainable AI via multi-modal and multi-centre data fusion: A mini-review, two showcases and beyond. Information Fusion. 2022 Jan;77:29-52. Available from: https://linkinghub.elsevier.com/retrieve/pii/S1566253521001597.

Information Modelling and Knowledge Bases XXXV
M. Tropmann-Frick et al. (Eds.)

doi:10.3233/FAIA231147

A Time-Series Semantic-Computing Method for 5D World Map System Applied to Environmental Changes

Yasushi KIYOKI[1,a,b,c] Asako URAKI[b] Shiori SASAKI[b,c] Yukio CHEN[d]

[a] *Graduate School of Media and Governance, Keio University, Japan*
[b] *Keio Research Institute at SFC, Keio University, Japan*
5322 Endo, Fujisawa, Kanagawa, http://gesl.sfc.keio.ac.jp/
[c] *Graduate School of Data Science, Musashino University, Japan*
[d] *Department of Information & Computer Sciences, Kanagawa Institute of Technology, Japan,*
kiyoki@sfc.keio.ac.jp, aco@sfc.keio.ac.jp,
ssasaki@musashino-u.ac.jp, chen@ic.kanagawa-it.ac.jp

Abstract. "Semantic space creation" and "distance-computing" are basic functions to realize semantic computing for environmental phenomena memorization, retrieval, analysis, integration and visualization. We have introduced "SPA-based (Sensing, Processing and Actuation) Multi-dimensional Semantic Computing Method" for realizing a global environmental system, "5-Dimensional World Map System". This method is important to design new environmental systems with Cyber-Physical Space-integration to detect environmental phenomena occurring in a physical-space (real space). This method maps those phenomena to a multi-dimensional semantic-space, performs semantic computing, and actuates the semantic-computing results to the physical space with visualizations for expressing environmental phenomena, causalities and influences. As an actual system of this method, currently, the 5D World Map System is globally utilized as a Global Environmental Semantic Computing System, in SDG14, United-Nations-ESCAP: (https://sdghelpdesk.unescap.org/toolboxes). This paper presents a semantic computing method, focusing on "Time-series-Analytical Semantic-Space Creation and Semantic Distance Computing on 5D World Map System" for realizing global environmental analysis in time-series. This paper also presents the time-series analysis of actual environmental changes on 5D World Map System. The first analysis is on the depth of earthquakes Earthquake with time-series semantic computing on 5D World Map System, which occurred around the world during the period from Aug. 23rd to Aug. 28th, 2014, and Jan 7th to Jan. 13th, 2023. The second is the experimental analysis of the time-series difference extraction on glacier melting phenomena in Mont Blanc, Alps, during the period from 2013 to 2022, and Puncak Jaya (Jayawijaya Mountains), Papua, during the period from 1991 to 2020 as important environmental changes.

Keywords. (1) Cyber & Physical Space Integration, (2) SPA-function, (3) Spatio-Temporal computing, (4) Semantic computing, (5) Environmental change analysis

---

[1] Corresponding Author, Yasushi Kiyoki, Keio University, Endo 5322, Fujisawa, Kanagawa, Japan; E-mail: kiyoki@sfc.keio.ac.jp.

1. Introduction

We have introduced the architecture of a global environmental system, "5-Dimensional World Map System" [3,4,6,10], to realize environmental knowledge memorization, sharing, retrieval, integration and visualization with semantic computing. The basic space of this system consists of a temporal (1st dimension), spatial (2nd, 3rd and 4th dimensions) and semantic dimensions (5th-dimension), representing a large-scale and multiple-dimensional semantic space. This space memorizes and recalls various environmental knowledge expressed in multimedia information resources with temporal, spatial and semantic correlation computing functions, and realizes a 5D World Map for dynamically creating temporal-spatial and semantic multiple views.

We have also proposed the concept of "SPA (Sensing, Processing and Analytical Actuation Functions)" for realizing a global environmental system, to apply it to our 5-Dimensional World Map System[10,11]. This concept is effective and advantageous to design environmental systems with Cyber-Physical integration to detect environmental phenomena as real data resources in a physical space (real space), map them to cyber-space to make analytical and semantic computing, and actuate the analytically computed results to the real space with visualization for expressing environmental phenomena, causalities and influences.

Semantic computing [1,2,5] is an important and promising approach to semantic analysis for various environmental phenomena and changes in a real world. This paper presents a new concept of *"Time-series-Analytical Semantic-Space and Computing for environmental phenomena"* to realize global environmental analysis [7,8,9,10,11,12,13,14]. This space and computing method are based on semantic space creation with time-analysis for analyzing and interpreting environmental phenomena and changes occurring in the world. We focus on semantic interpretations of time-series data, as an experimental study for creating *"Time-Series Analysis Semantic-Space for environment."*

2. Global Environmental Analysis with Semantic Computing

We have introduced "5D World Map System" with Spatio-Temporal and Semantic Computing in SPA, as the architecture of a multi-visualized and dynamic knowledge representation system [3,4,6,10]" applied to environmental analysis and semantic computing. The basic space of this system consists of a temporal (1st dimension), spatial (2nd, 3rd and 4th dimensions) and semantic dimensions (5th dimension, representing a large-scale and multiple-dimensional semantic space). This space memorizes and recalls various multimedia information resources with temporal, spatial and semantic correlation computing functions, and realizes a 5D World Map for dynamically creating temporal-spatial and semantic multiple views applied for various "environmental multimedia information resources."

2.1. Semantic Computing in 5D World Map System

We have presented the dynamic evaluation and mapping functions for multiple views of temporal-spatial metrics and integrate the results of semantic evaluation to analyze environmental multimedia information resources [3,4,6,10]. Our semantic computing system realizes the interpretations on "semantics" and "impressions" of environmental phenomena with multimedia information resources, according to "contexts"[1,2,5]. The main feature of this system is to create world-wide global maps and views of environmental situations expressed in multimedia information resources (image, sound, text and video) dynamically, according to user's viewpoints. Spatially, temporally, semantically and impressionably evaluated and analyzed environmental multimedia information resources are mapped onto a 5D time-series multi-geographical space. The basic concept of the 5D World Map System is shown in **Figures 1** and **2**. The 5D World Map system applied to environmental multimedia computing visualizes world-wide and global relations among different areas and times in environmental aspects, by using dynamic mapping functions with temporal, spatial, semantic and impression-based computations [3,4,6,10,11,13].

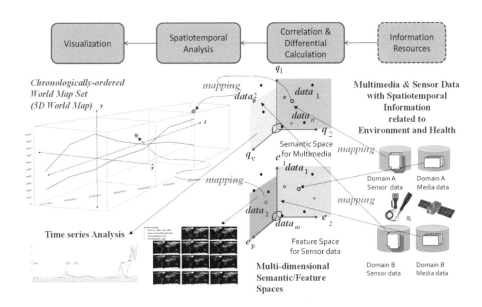

Figure 1. 5D World Map System for world-wide semantic computing for Global Environmental Analysis

2.2. SPA: Sensing, Processing and Analytical Actuation Functions in 5D World Map

"SPA" is a fundamental concept for realizing environmental systems with three basic functions of "Sensing, Processing and Analytical Actuation" for Physical-Cyber integration. "SPA" is effective and advantageous to detect environmental phenomena as real data resources in a physical space (real space), map them to the cyber-space to make analytical and semantic computing, and actuate the analytically computed results to the real space by visualization for expressing environmental phenomena with causalities and influence. This concept is applied to our semantic computing in 5D World Map System, as shown in **Figures 1, 2** and **3**.

The important application of the semantic computing system are "Global Environment-Analysis" for making appropriate and urgent solutions to global environment changes in terms of short and long-term changes. The "six functional-pillars" are essentially important with "environmental knowledge-base creation" for sharing, analyzing and visualizing various environmental phenomena and changes in a real world.

The 5D World Map System realizes Cyber-Physical Space-integration, as shown in **Figure 1**, to detect environmental phenomena with real data resources in a physical-space (real space), map them to the cyber-space to make knowledge bases and analytical computing, and actuate the computed results to the real space with visualization for expressing environmental phenomena, causalities and influences. The 5D World Map System and its applications create new analytical circumstance with the SPA concept (Sensing, Processing and Analytical Actuation) for sharing, analyzing and visualizing natural and social environmental aspects. This system realizes "environmental analysis and situation-recognition" which will be essential for finding out solutions for global environmental issues. The 5D World Map System collects and facilitates a lot of environmental information resources, which are characteristics of ocean species, disasters, water-quality and deforestation.

3. A Time-series Semantic Computing Method for Global Environmental Analysis

We introduce a concept of "time-series-context", as a context on time-series in semantic computing on a multi-dimensional space. The "time-series-context" is a data structure to specify dimensional projection (dimensional selection), that is, the projection (selection of dimensions) to be applied in "time-series semantic computing."

(1) One of the most important processes of multi-dimensional & time-series semantic computing is to define semantic "time-series-context".

(2) It is essential to compare between two different time-series on semantic features, expressing a time-series-context, for realizing semantic interpretations and predictions on natural environmental phenomena.

We define a multi-dimensional & time-series semantic computing method for time-series data in a time axis with the definition of time-series context.

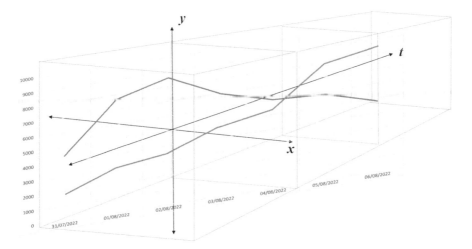

Figure 2. A Time-series Semantic-Computing Space for 5D World Map System

3.1. Basic data structures and operations

The basic data structures for time-series semantic computing are defined as follows:

(1) Space: Multi-Dimensional semantic space with time-axis
(2) Basic elements: point-series --> time-series (point-series along a time-series for expressing a phenomenon)
(3) Time-series-context: "time-series grain" & "time-interval"

3.2. Semantic computing process

To define a time-series-context, we express semantic meaning of temporal difference and its interpretations according to the time-series-context.
- If switching the N time-series-contexts for same data, we can obtain N different semantic meanings of temporal difference in each context.
- The definition of the time-series-context by the 3 steps is corresponding to set the closed world on time axis.

Step 1: Define semantic viewpoint to fix target axes, that are corresponding to multiple parameters as the semantic feature combination, reflecting expert-knowledge and viewpoint.
Step 2: Define semantic viewpoint to fix target time-series data to calculate semantic distances,

3.3. Semantic computing functions

In this section, we express the data structures and functions for "time-series stream-creation". The following 6 basic functions are defined to express the query-time-series, that creates time-series query expression as a new time-series stream:

(1) Time-series data structures

To realize "time-series stream-creation" (creating time-series stream), the following basic settings on time-series data structures are defined:

(1-1)   "time-granularity (granularity in time)" setting,
(1-2)   "time-interval" setting,
(1-3)   "time-grains-combination" setting,
(1-4)   "time-series-context" setting.

(2) Time-series stream

A time-series stream is defined with a basic-atomic-time-element, that is expressed:

(2-1) basic-atomic-time-element form: (time-i, (value-i-1, value-i-2, ---, value-i-m)).

(2-2) Time-series stream expression:

By combining basic-atomic-time-elements, any time-series stream is expressed and created. (time-grain setting, time-interval setting, time-grains-combination)

Time-series stream expressions:

Time-series-semantic-integration-method:
Temporal-Atomic-element:(time-series), as the time-grain setting:
((time-1, (value-1-1, value-1-2, ---, value1-m)) ,
(time-2, (value-2-1, value-2-2, ---, value-2-m)), ---,
(time-n, (value-n-1, value-n-2, ---, value-n-m))):

Atom-1:
((t-1,t-2,t-3)(v-1-i,v-2-i,v-3-i)) (The "i" is fixed with a "time-series context".)
Atom-2:
((t-1,t-2,t-3)(v-1-j,v-2-j,v-3-j))
Atom-3:
((t-1,t-2,t-3)(v-1-k,v-2-k,v-3-k))

(2-3) Time-series-semantic-integration (Time-series stream is expressed and created in the following basic structures): (time-grains-combination for time-interval setting,)

(2-3-1) Vertical integration for time-series stream:
(((t-1,t-2,t-3)(v-1-i,v-2-i,v-3-i)), ((t-1,t-2,t-3)(v-1-j,v-2-j,v-3-j)),
((t-1,t-2,t-3)(v-1-k,v-2-k,v-3-k))) - - -

(2-3-2) Horizontal integration for time-series stream:
((t-1,t-2,t-3) ((v-1-i,v-1-j,v-1-k), (v-2-i,v-2-j,v-2-k), (v-3-i,v-3-j,v-3-k)))

(2-3-3) Time-series stream integration:

$(((t-1,t-2,t-3), ((t-4,t-5,t-6)) (((v-1-i,v-1-j,v-1-k), (v-2-i,v-2-j,v-2-k),$
$(v-3-i,v-3-j,v-3-k))), ((v-4-i,v-4-j,v-4-k), (v-5-i,v-5-j,v-5-k),$
$(v-6-i,v-6-j,v-6-k)))$

(3) Geographical-time-series form:

Geographical time-series stream, as a time-series stream, is defined with a basic-geo-atomic-time-element, that is expressed:

(3-1) basic-geo-atomic-time-element form:

S1(place1) (time-1, (value-1-1, value-1-2, ---, value-1-m))
(time-2, (value-2-1, value-2-2, ---, value-2-m))
(time-3, (value-3-1, value-3-2, ---, value-3-m))

S2(place2) (time-4, (value-4-1, value-4-2, ---, value-4-m))
(time-5, (value-5-1, value-5-2, ---, value-5-m))
(time-6, (value-6-1, value-6-2, ---, value-6-m))

S3(place3) (time-7, (value-7-1, value-7-2, ---, value-7-m))
(time-8, (value-8-1, value-8-2, ---, value-8-m))
(time-9, (value-9-1, value-9-2, ---, value-9-m))

(4) Time-series-stream-comparison (semantic-distance computing between two time-series streams)

(4-a) distance of features (time-series-context features) between different timings in same time-series

(4-b) distance of features (time-series-context features) between different phenomena in different time-series

(4-c) distance of features (time-series-context features) between different places (geographical places) in the same phenomena in different time-series

The basic distance function between two time-series streams is defined in the following form:

Timeseries-streams-distance((t1, t2, ---, tn) (y1, y2, ---, yn) , (t1', t2', ---, tn')
(y1', y2' ---, yn')).

(4-1) Timeseries-streams-distance as the sum of each parameters' distances:

Timeseries-streams-distance-1((t1, t2, ---, tn) (y1, y2, ---, yn) , (t1', t2', ---, tn')
(y1', y2' ---, yn')) => $\Sigma(i=0, n) |yi - yi'|$

(4-2) Timeseries-streams-distance as distance-in-time-interval-normalization:

Timeseries-streams-distance-2((t1, t2, ---, tn) (y1, y2, ---, yn) , (t1', t2', ---, tn')

(y1', y2' ---, yn'))   =>
distance-in-time-interval-normalization ((t1, t2, ---, tn) (y1, y2, ---, yn) ,
(t1', t2', ---, tn') (y1', y2' ---, yn'))

(4-3)Timeseries-streams-distance as distance-in-start-time-normalization

Timeseries-streams-distance-3((t1, t2, ---, tn) (y1, y2, ---, yn) , (t1', t2', ---, tn')
(y1', y2' ---, yn'))   =>
distance-in-start-time-normalization ((t1, t2, ---, tn) (y1, y2, ---, yn) ,
(t1', t2', ---, tn') (y1', y2' ---, yn'))

(5) Geographical phenomenon-distance function form is defined for time-series
comparison between different places.

Geographical-timeseries-streams-distance((S1(place1),((time-1, (value-1-1, value-1-2, -
--, value-1-m)), (time-2, (value-2-1, value-2-2, ---, value-2-m)), (time-3, (value-3-1,
value-3-2, ---, value-3-m))), (S2(place2),(time-4, (value-4-1, value-4-2, ---, value-4-
m)), (time-5, (value-5-1, value-5-2, ---, value-5-m)), (time-6, (value-6-1, value-6-2, ---,
value-6-m))))

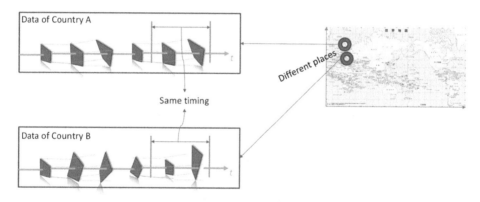

Figure 3. The Concept of a difference comparison with Time-series Semantic-Computing
with 5D World Map System

*3.4. Time-series semantic computing for phenomenon-prediction with time-interval
ratio*

We present a ratio computing method for phenomenon-prediction with time-interval
ratio between peak values. This method predicts the timing of future peak with
differential computing, according to "time-series-context".

The basic data structure of "time-series context" is defined in 6 Key elements:

- Original time-granularity (granularity in time) (OG)
- Target timing-granularity (TG)

- Feature extraction method (FEM)
- Focusing time-interval (FW) (time-interval)
- Differential computing method (DCM)
- Pivot extraction method on ITD (PEM)

Two time-series data (IRD, ITD) consists of time and its corresponding values expressed in target granularity in two different places, F and J. The ratio computing method is applied to three peaks of the corresponding values existing in IRD (FT1, FT2, FT3) in timing in the place F, and three peaks in ITD (JT1, JT2, "JT3(target for estimation)")) in the place J. Then, JT3 is computed as an estimated timing in the following process, as the timing when the situation corresponding to the third peak will occur in the future in the place J.

The important feature of this method is to define differential computing function as ratio computing between the timing of the peaks in time-series data to estimate the future peak.

Input data for analysis (IRD) = Time-series sequence of (parameter-value, time-point) for expressing the situation with the selected parameter in the place F:
- The number of confirmed-values in the place F.

Input data for prediction (ITD) = Time-series sequence of (parameter-value, time-point) for expressing the situation with the selected parameter in the place J:
- The number of confirmed-values in the place J.

The 6 key elements are defined to express time-series-context. The 6 key element-settings determine "time-series-context" to make common situations comparable between two different time-series.

The 6 key elements are expressed as a "time-series-context" for phenomenon-prediction with time-interval ratio between peak values.

The "time-series-context" definition is set in the following:
- Original time-granularity (granularity in time) = daily
- Target timing-granularity (TG) = peaks
- Feature extraction method (FEM) = time point of peaks
- Focusing time-interval (FW) = from first peak to the last peak 3 or more peaks that matched condition(condition :)
- Differential computing method (DCM) = ratio computing function for the number of days between the selected adjacent peaks, by applying average, difference, and other functions
- Pivot extraction method on ITD (PEM) = most recent 2 or more peaks that matched condition(condition :)

The prediction process with the differential computing method (DCM) is defined as the ratio computing function for computing the number of days between the selected adjacent peaks, by applying average, difference, and other operations.

The basic data structure for the prediction with the differential computing method is expressed:

FT1-3: time points at 3 peaks (FT1, FT2, FT3) timings, corresponding to top-three maximum parameter-values in the time-series sequence in the place F.
JT1-3: time points at 3 peaks (JT1, JT2, "JT3 (target for estimation)") timings, corresponding to top-three maximum parameter-values in the time-series sequence in the place J.

The process for the prediction with the differential computing method is expressed:

(Step-1) 3 peaks selection (FT1, FT2, FT3) in time series in IRD,
(Step-2-1) ratio computing in time-interval: (FT3-FT2)/(FT2-FT1),
(Step-2-2) average computing in time-interval: average((FT3-FT2), (FT2-FT1)),
(Step-2-3) differential computing in time interval: (FT3-FT2) => JT3-JT2 = (FT3-FT2)
(Step-3) (JT3-JT2)/(JT2-JT1) = (FT3-FT2)/(FT2-FT1) => JT3 is computed as an estimated time of peak-3 in this ratio computing if (2-1) is applied.

Then, JT3 is obtained as the prediction result of a next peak timing, occurring in the future.

4. Time-series semantic computing in 5D World Map System

We have integrated the time-series semantic computing method into the 5D World Map System. The following two cases (earthquake and glacier-melting analysis) are example targets of semantic computing in 5D World Map System with geographical time-series stream defined with a basic-geo-atomic-time-element in Section 3: Time-series semantic computing for Global Environmental Analysis.

4.1. Case I: Earthquake analysis with time-series semantic computing on 5D World Map System

This case shows the analysis of the depth of earthquakes, which occurred around the world during the period from Aug. 23rd to Aug. 28th, 2014, and Jan 7th to Jan. 13th, 2023. The target data is acquired from USGS Earthquake Hazard Program, Real-time Notifications Service [15]. The objective is the analysis of significant earthquakes in with time-series semantic computing to predict when and where significant earthquakes will occur especially in earthquake-prone countries and regions.

Figure 4 shows the visualization results of the time-series change of geographical distribution of the depth values of significant earthquakes with over 2.5 magnitude values in one week of August 2014. From the results, we can observe intuitively that there is a point where deep earthquakes had happened through the whole period (eg. Alaska), and there is an emergent timing that deep earthquakes happened in Fiji (2014/08/25) and consequently in Japan (2014/08/26). Also, **Figure 5** shows the visualization results of the depth values of significant earthquakes with over 2.5 magnitude values in one week of January 2023. We observe that there is a point where deep earthquakes had happened through the whole period (eg. New Zealand, Jan 7th, 9th, 10th and 13th).

In this case, the time-series query expression as a new time-series stream is created by the depth value of earthquake by 6 basic functions defined in Section 3 to express the query-time-series-stream for time-series semantic computing. In this case, the time-interval is set as 1 week, and the time-granularity is set as 1 day.

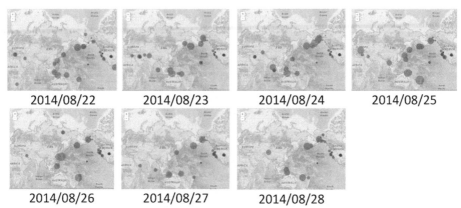

| 2014/08/22 | 2014/08/23 | 2014/08/24 | 2014/08/25 |

| 2014/08/26 | 2014/08/27 | 2014/08/28 |

Figure 4. Time-series change of geographical distribution of the depth values in significant earthquakes with over 2.5 magnitude values, which occurred around the world during the period from Aug. 23rd to Aug. 28th, 2014

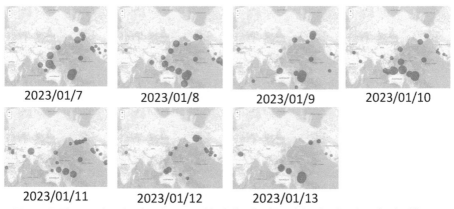

| 2023/01/7 | 2023/01/8 | 2023/01/9 | 2023/01/10 |

| 2023/01/11 | 2023/01/12 | 2023/01/13 |

Figure 5. Time-series change of geographical distribution of the depth values in significant earthquakes with over 2.5 magnitude values, which occurred around the world during the period from Jan. 7th to Jan. 13th, 2023

The following is an example of query creation and time-series-context settings for the analysis of significant earthquake and prediction with time-series semantic computing.

Input data for analysis (IRD) = time-series values of earthquake depth in two points
- Depth value of earthquake in Alaska
- Depth value of earthquake in New Zealand

Input data for prediction (ITD) = time-series values of earthquake depth in a target point
- Depth value of earthquake in Japan

As for the 6 key elements to express time-series-context, we can apply the followings.

6 Key elements for express time-series-context are:
- Original time-granularity (OG) = <u>daily</u>
- Target timing-granularity (TG) = <u>peaks of earthquake depth</u>
- Feature extraction method (FEM) = <u>time point of peaks</u>
- Focusing time-interval (FW) = <u>from first peak to the last peak 3 or more peaks that matched condition</u>
- Differential computing method (DCM) = <u>ratio computing function for, number of days between the selected adjacent peaks, by applying average, difference, and other functions</u>
- Pivot extraction method on ITD (PEM) = <u>most recent 2 or more peaks that matched condition</u>

4.2. Case II: Glacier melting analysis with time-series semantic computing on 5D World Map System

4.2.1. Case II-(1): Glacier melting in Mont Blanc, Alps, Europe

This case shows the analysis of the time-series difference extraction on glacier melting phenomena in Mont Blanc, Alps, Europe during the period from 2013 to 2022 for the analysis and prediction of time-series area-size change of other European countries' mountains' glaciers, when severe glacier melting has been reported in Mont Blanc area [16].

Figure 6 shows the original satellite images of Landsat 8 and 9 of the Mont Blanc area for Aug. 2013, 2015 and 2022, acquired from USGS EarthExplorer [17]. To detect the change in the same season with stable conditions, the RGB images in August (in summer, less cloud and no storms or snow falls) are obtained for each year.

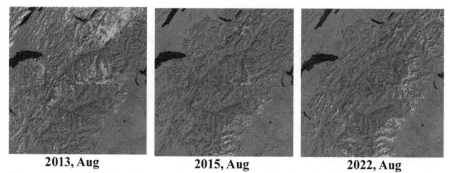

2013, Aug   **2015, Aug**   **2022, Aug**

Figure 6. Original RGB Landsat 8 & 9 satellite images in Mont Blanc, Alps, Europe of 2013, 2015 and 2022

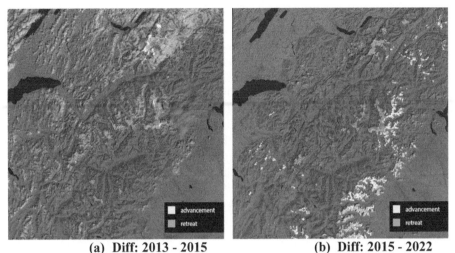

(a) **Diff: 2013 - 2015**   (b) **Diff: 2015 - 2022**

Figure 7. Difference extraction results from RGB Landsat 8 & 9 satellite images in Mont Blanc, Alps, Europe: (a) difference between 2013 and 2015, and (b) difference between 2015 and 2022

Figure 7 shows the difference extraction results by image processing: (a) difference between 2013 and 2015, and (b) difference between 2015 and 2022. The number of color clustering was set as 4 clusters. The focused colors are pale blue and gray which represent glacier area and cloud. In the results, retreated parts are represented in red color, and advanced parts are represented in yellow color. The results show that the glacier melting and retreating happened at the edges at the period between 2013 and 2015 (**Figure 7 (a)**), and the cloud increasing happened in the valleys at the foot of the mountain at the period between 2015 and 2022 (**Figure 7 (b)**).

Figure 8 shows the Normalized Difference Snow Index (NDSI) calculation results of each year, which indicate snow areas as bright white colors. In this experiment, we collected multispectral satellite images (Band 3 and Band 6 from Landsat 8 & 9 in USGS EarthExplorer [17]) by the following formula using Green (G) band and Short Wave Infra-Red (SWIR1) band.

$$NDSI = (G - SWIR1)/(G+SWIR1)$$

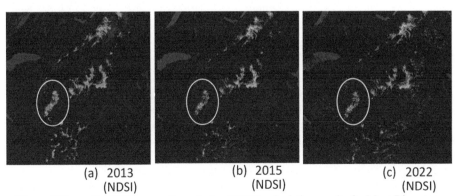

(a) 2013   (b) 2015   (c) 2022
(NDSI)   (NDSI)   (NDSI)

Figure 8 Normalized Difference Snow Index (NDSI) calculation results for Mont Blanc area: (a) 2013, (b) 2015 and (c) 2022 by using multispectral images (Band 3 and Band6 from Landsat 8 & 9)

As it is difficult to judge the glacier melting, whether it is increasing or not by these results. We examined the details to judge if these results mean that the speed of glacier melting is increased year by year or not, though in August 2021. Scientists reported that the danger of collapse due to rising temperatures threatens the lower valley on the Italian side of the Mont Blanc area [16].

In this case, to analyze and predict the time-series area size of glacier other European countries' mountains, the time-series query expression as a new time-series stream is created by the area size of glacier by the 6 basic functions defined in Section 3 to express the query-time-series-stream. In this case, the time-interval is set as 20 years, and the time-granularity in time-series-stream is set as 1 year.

The following is an example of query creation and time-series-context settings for the analysis of deforestation and prediction with time-series semantic computing.

Input data for analysis (IRD) = time-series values of area-size of glacier in Mont Blanc

- Area-size of glacier in Mont Blanc (4,808 m), Alps, Europe

Input data for prediction (ITD) = time-series values of area-size of glacier in other European countries' mountains with similar altitude

- Area-size of glacier in Matterhorn (4,478 m)
- Area-size of glacier in Aiguille du Midi (3,842 m)
- Area-size of glacier in Tsebrya Novitsa (4,485 m)

As for the 6 key elements to express the time-series-context, we applied the followings.

6 Key elements for express time-series-context are:
- Original time-granularity (OG) = yearly
- Target timing-granularity (TG) = peaks of glacier-melting ratio (speed)
- Feature extraction method (FEM) = time point of peaks
- Focusing time-interval (FW) = from first peak to the last peak or more peaks that matched condition
- Differential computing method (DCM) = ratio computing function for, number of years between the selected adjacent peaks, by applying average, difference, and other functions
- Pivot extraction method on ITD (PEM) = most recent 2 or more peaks that matched condition

4.2.2. Case II-(2): Glacier melting in Puncak Jaya, Papua, Indonesia

This case shows the analysis of the time-series difference extraction on glacier melting phenomena in Puncak Jaya (Jayawijaya Mountains) during the period from 1936 to 2020. Puncak Jaya is located in Indonesia's West Papua Province as the highest peak in Oceania, which has been noted to have glacier melting over the years due to rising temperatures and climate change. The objective is to acquire an up-to-date picture of the extent of melting of the glaciers in the region, which will completely disappear by 2026 in their models [18][19][20], and to predict the actual speed of their disappearance.

Figure 9 shows the target area images of peak in Puncak Jaya taken from Landsat 9. To detect the glacier area size by calculating NDSI (Normalized Difference Snow Index) in the same season (June to Aug., less clouds and no storm), the multispectral images are acquired from USGS EarthExplorer [16]. Because we need to calculate NDSI by Green and Short Wave Infra-Red (SWIR) bands, Band 2 and Band 5 of Landsat 5 for 1991, Band 2 and Band 5 of Landsat 7 for 2004, Band 3 and Band 6 of Landsat 8 for 2015 and 2020 were obtained and used.

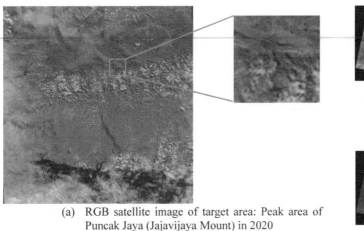

(b) Multispectral image (Band 3: Green, Landsat 9) in 2020

(a) RGB satellite image of target area: Peak area of Puncak Jaya (Jajavijaya Mount) in 2020

(c) Multispectral image (Band 6: SWIR1, Landsat 9) in 2020

Figure 9. Target area of Puncak Jaya, Papua, Indonesia in 2020: (a) RGB satellite image, (b) high-resolution multispectral images: (b) Green band and (c) SWIR1 band

Figure 10 shows the size of glacier in Puncak Jaya in 1991 by calculating NDSI (Normalized Difference Snow Index). NDSI is calculated by the following formula using Green (G) band and Short Wave Infra-Red (SWIR1) band.

$$NDSI = (G - SWIR1)/(G+SWIR1)$$

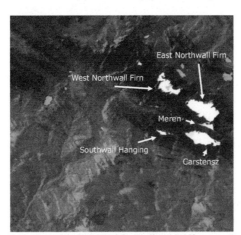

Figure 10. Calculation result of NDSI (Normalized Difference Snow Index) from multispectral images of Band 2 and Band 5 of Landsat 5 in 1991: Five original glaciers (East Northwall Firn, West Norththwall Firn, Meren Glacier, Southwall Hanging Glacier and Carstensz Glacier System) are observed.

Figure 10 is the NDSI calculation result using Band 2 (G) and Band 5 (SWIR1) of Landsat 5 for 1991. From **Figure 10**, five original glaciers (East Northwall Firn, West Norththwall Firn, Meren Glacier, Southwall Hanging Glacier and Carstensz Glacier System) are still observed.

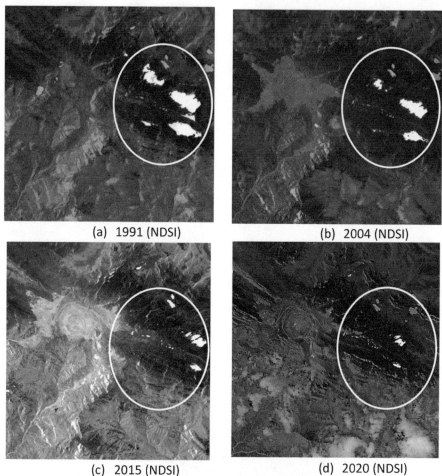

(a) 1991 (NDSI)   (b) 2004 (NDSI)

(c) 2015 (NDSI)   (d) 2020 (NDSI)

Figure 11. Calculation result of NDVI (Normalized Difference Snow Index) from 1991 to 2020 of Puncak Jaya glaciers: (a) 1991, (b) 2004, (c) 2015 and (d) 2020

Figure 10 and **Figure 11 (a)** show that five original glaciers (East Northwall Firn, West Norththwall Firn, Meren Glacier, Southwall Hanging Glacier and Carstensz Glacier System) are observed in 1991. In 2004, Meren glacier disappeared (**Figure 11 (b)**). In 2015, it is found that West Northwall Firn and South Hangging Glacier almost disappeared and the largest glacier, East Northewall Firn was split to three pieces (**Figure 11 (c)**). Actually, IKONOS satellite imagery studies indicate that the Eastern Northwall Firn lost an additional 4.5% of its surface area in the two years 2000-2002 [18][19], and another study by NASA Earth Observatory also reported that prior to 2017, West Northwall Firn had completely disappeared and the East Northwall Firn was broken up in three smaller patches [20]. In 2020, the East Northwall Firn was split to two smaller patches and Carstensz Glacier is shrined to a small piece (**Figure 11 (d)**).

To calculate the precise area size of glacier, we performed glacier area-size estimation by counting of the number of pixels with high NDSI values over a threshold based on the following formula:

$$A_{glacier} = L_{res}^2 * N_{pix}$$

where, $A_{glacier}$: Estimated size of glacier area [m^2]

L_{res}: Resolution of a target image [m/pix]

N_{pix}: Total number of pixels in the glacier area

In the case of using Landsat 5, 7, 8 & 9, the estimated size of the glacier area can be expressed by $A_{glacier} = 30^2 * N_{pix}$ because the resolution of G and SWIR of Landsat 5, 7, 8 and 9 is 30 [m/pix].

Table 1 shows the estimation results of area size of glacier by this study combined with the values acquired by other existing glaciology studies [18][19].

Table 1 Estimated area size (km^2) of the Pucak Jaya glaciers

Glacier area	1936	1972	1987	**1991**	2002	**2004**	**2015**	**2020**
West Northwall Firn	6.7	3.6	*1.3*	**0.8287**	*0.28*	**0.2142**	**0**	0
East Northwall Firn	1.6	1.1	N/A	**1.5266**	N/A	**1.088**	**0.4829**	**0.20768**
Meren Glacier	2.8	2.2	N/A	**0.1463**	N/A	**0**	**0**	0
Carstensz Glacier	1.6	1.2	*1.4*	**1.117**	*0.7*	**0.565**	**0.161**	**0.05219**
Southwall Hanging Glacier	0.3	0.2	*0.09*	**0.1178**	N/A	**0.009**	**0**	0
Total (Entire Puncak Jaya)	13	7.3	*5.09*	**3.7364**	*2.15*	**1.8766**	**0.643**	**0.25987**

Note: Bold values represent our estimated size by this study. Italicized values represent computed totals from published areas by glaciology studies (Kincaid and Klen, 2004) [18] and (Klein and Kincaid, 2017) [19]. Normal values were acquired during the field expeditions by experts in glaciology (Allison and Peterson, 1976, 1989, 1994)

In this case, to predict the time-series area size of existing glaciers in Puncak Jaya, the time-series query expression as a new time-series stream is created by the area size of glacier by 6 basic functions defined in Section 3 to express the query-time-series-stream. In this case, the time-interval is set as 10 years, and the time-granularity in time-series-stream is set as 1 year. The other parameters such as temperature, snowfall, depth of ice will be additional conditions for creating context to increase the precision of prediction.

The following is an example of query creation and time-series-context settings for the analysis of glacier melting and prediction with time-series semantic computing.

Input data for analysis (IRD) = time-series values of area-size of disappeared glaciers
- Area-size of West Northwall Firn
- Area-size of Meren Glacier
- Area-size of Southwall Hanging Glacier

Input data for prediction (ITD) = time-series values of area-size of existing glaciers
- Area-size of East Northwall Firn

- Area-size of Carstensz Glacier

As for the 6 key elements to express time-series-context, we apply the followings.

6 Key elements for express time-series-context are:
- Original time-granularity (OG) = <u>yearly</u>
- Target timing-granularity (TG) = <u>peaks of glacier-melting ratio (speed)</u>
- Feature extraction method (FEM) = <u>time point of peaks</u>
- Focusing time-interval (FW) = <u>from first peak to the last peak or more peaks that matched condition</u>
- Differential computing method (DCM) = <u>ratio computing function for, number of years between the selected adjacent peaks, by applying average, difference, and other functions</u>
- Pivot extraction method on ITD (PEM) = <u>most recent 2 or more peaks that matched condition</u>

Finally, **Figure 12** shows that the original satellite images with geo information, the difference-visualized images and calculated NDSI images are mapped onto 5D World Map System and visualized with other data such as sensor, statistic and multimedia data of weather which are related to glacier melting around the world. This visualization enables users to understand the complicated relations among various elements of environmental phenomena intuitively.

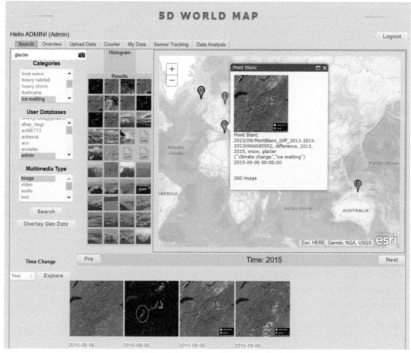

Figure 12. Mapping of an original satellite image with geo information, difference-images, NDVI calculation results of Mont Blanc, Europe and Puncak Jaya, Indonesia on 5D World Map System

5. Conclusion

We have presented a new concept of *"Time-series Semantic Computing"* for realizing global and temporal environmental analysis. The main feature of this system is to realize semantic time-series analysis in a multiple dimensional semantic space. This space is created for dynamically computing semantic relations between time-series data resources in different places and time. We have applied this method to time-series data resources in 5D World Map.

This system realizes a remote, interactive and real-time environmental research exchange among multiple and different remote spots in different areas. We have created a semantic-space for time-series analysis in environmental phenomena with multiple-dimensional axes along the time-axis. As the first step, this space is expandable to multiple spots to analyze and compare their time-series data in the global scope for environmental phenomena. We mapped them onto 5-Dimensional World Map System to make time-series semantic interpretations in those spots, as an international collaborative platform for environment analysis, to realize spatio-temporal and semantic interpretations.

As our future work, we will extend the *Time-series Semantic Computing"* realized onto 5-Dimensional World Map System to an international and collaborative research and education system for realizing mutual understanding and global knowledge-sharing on environmental issues in the world-wide scope.

Acknowledgement:

We appreciate *"5D World Map System Project"* members' significant discussions and experimental studies. We are also grateful to Dr. Petchporn Chawakitchareon and Dr. Sompop Rungsup for their active and collaborative research activities in environmental analysis.

References

[1] Yasushi Kiyoki and Saeko Ishihara: "A Semantic Search Space Integration Method for Meta-level Knowledge Acquisition from Heterogeneous Databases," Information Modeling and Knowledge Bases (IOS Press), Vol. 14, pp.86-103, May 2002.

[2] Yasushi Kiyoki, Xing Chen, "A Semantic Associative Computation Method for Automatic Decorative-Multimedia Creation with "Kansei" Information" (Invited Paper), The Sixth Asia-Pacific Conferences on Conceptual Modelling (APCCM 2009), 9 pages, January 20-23, 2009.

[3] Yasushi Kiyoki, Xing Chen, Shiori Sasaki, Chawan Koopipat, "A Globally-Integrated Environmental Analysis and Visualization System with Multi-Spectral & Semantic Computing in "Multi-Dimensional World Map", Information Modelling and Knowledge Bases XXVIII, pp.106-122,2017

[4] Yasushi Kiyoki, Shiori Sasaki, Nhung Nguyen Trang, Nguyen Thi Ngoc Diep, "Cross-cultural Multimedia Computing with Impression-based Semantic Spaces," Conceptual Modelling and Its Theoretical Foundations, Lecture Notes in Computer Science, Springer, pp.316-328, March 2012.

[5] Yasushi Kiyoki: "A "Kansei: Multimedia Computing System for Environmental Analysis and Cross-Cultural Communication," 7th IEEE International Conference on Semantic Computing, keynote speech, Sept. 2013.

[6]   Shiori Sasaki, Yusuke Takahashi, Yasushi Kiyoki: "The 4D World Map System with Semantic and Spatiotemporal Analyzers," Information Modelling and Knowledge Bases, Vol.XXI, IOS Press, 18 pages, 2010.

[7]   Totok Suhardijanto, Yasushi Kiyoki, Ali Ridho Barakbah: "A Term-based Cross-Cultural Computing System for Cultural Semantics Analysis with Phonological-Semantic Vector Spaces," Information Modelling and Knowledge Bases XXIII, pp.20-38, IOS Press, 2012.

[8]   Chalisa Veesommai, Yasushi Kiyoki, Shiori Sasaki and Petchporn Chawakitchareon, "Wide-Area River-Water Quality Analysis and Visualization with 5D World Map System", Information Modelling and Knowledge Bases, Vol. XXVII, pp.31-41, 2016.

[9]   Chalisa Veesommai, Yasushi Kiyoki, "Spatial Dynamics of The Global Water Quality Analysis System with Semantic-Ordering Functions". Information Modelling and Knowledge Bases, Vol. XXIX, 2018.

[10] Yasushi Kiyoki, Asako Uraki, Chalisa Veesommai, "A Seawater-Quality Analysis Semantic-Space in Hawaii-Islands with Multi-Dimensional World Map System", 18th International Electronics Symposium (IES2016), Bali, Indonesia, September 29-30, 2016.

[11] Yasushi Kiyoki, Petchporn Chawakitchareon, Sompop Rungsupa, Xing Chen, Kittiya Samlansin, "A Global & Environmental Coral Analysis System with SPA-Based Semantic Computing for Integrating and Visualizing Ocean-Phenomena with "5-Dimensional World-Map", INFORMATION MODELLING AND KNOWLEDGE BASES XXXII, Frontiers in Artificial Intelligence and Applications 333, IOS Press, pp. 76 – 91, Dec 2020.

[12] Shiori Sasaki and Yasushi Kiyoki, "Real-time Sensing, Processing and Actuation Functions of 5D World Map System: A Collaborative Knowledge Sharing System for Environmental Analysis", Information Modelling and Knowledge Bases, Vol. XXVIII, IOS Press, pp. 220-239, May 2016.

[13] Yasushi Kiyoki, Xing Chen, Chalisa Veesommai, Shiori Sasaki, Asako Uraki, Chawan Koopipat, Petchporn Chawakitchareon and Aran Hansuebsai, "An Environmental-Semantic Computing System for Coral-Analysis in Water-Quality and Multi-Spectral Image Spaces with "Multi-Dimensional World Map", Information Modelling and Knowledge Bases, Vol. XXVIII, 20 pages, March 2018.

[14] Sompop Rungsupa, Petchporn Chawakitchareon, Aran Hansuebsai, Shiori Sasaki and Yasushi Kiyoki, "Photographic Assessment of Coral Stress: Effect of Low Salinity to Acropora sp. Goniopora sp. and Pavona sp. at Sichang Island, Thailand", Information Modelling and Knowledge Bases, Vol. XXVIII, 20 pages, March 2018.

[15] USGS Earthquake Hazards Program, Real-time Norigication, Feeds, and Web service: https://earthquake.usgs.gov/earthquakes/feed/

[16] AFP/Andrea Bernardi with Alexandria Sage in Rome, "Experts eye unstable glacier within Italy's Mont Blanc", Planpincieux (Italy) (AFP), Issued on: 11/08/2021 - 19:16, Modified: 11/08/2021 - 19:14. https://www.france24.com/en/live-news/20210811-experts-eye-unstable-glacier-within-italy-s-mont-blanc

[17] USGS EarthExplorer: https://earthexplorer.usgs.gov/

[18] Kincaid, Joni L.; Andrew G Klein, "Retreat of the Irian Jaya Glaciers from 2000 to 2002", 61st Eastern Snow Conference. pp. 147-157, 2014.

[19] Andrew G. Klein and Joni L. Kincaid, "Retreat of glaciers on Puncak Jaya, Irian Jaya, determined from 2000 and 2002 IKONOS satellite images", Journal of Glaciology, Cambridge   University   Press,   September   8,   2017. https://www.cambridge.org/core/journals/journal-of-glaciology/article/retreat-of-glaciers-on-puncak-jaya-irian-jaya-determined-from-2000-and-2002-ikonos-satellite-images/5106CC4B3B1799DF722FAB5D59F984F7

[20] Kathryn Hansen, Glaciers in the Tropics, but Not for Long, at NASA Earth Observatory, February 13, 2018. https://earthobservatory.nasa.gov/images/91716/glaciers-in-the-tropics-but-not-for-long

Information Modelling and Knowledge Bases XXXV
M. Tropmann-Frick et al. (Eds.)
doi:10.3233/FAIA231148

Adaptive Charging and Discharging Strategies for Smart Grid Energy Storage Systems

Alexander DUDKO[a], Tatiana ENDRJUKAITE[b]

[a] *KEIO University, Graduate School of Media and Governance, Kanagawa, Japan*
[b] *Transport and Telecommunication Institute, Research Department, Riga, Latvia*

Abstract. The current state of energy generation and consumption in the world, where many countries rely on fossil fuels to meet their energy demands, poses significant challenges in terms of energy security and environmental degradation. To address these challenges, the world is shifting towards renewable energy sources (RES), which are not only environmentally sustainable but also have the potential to reduce dependence on fossil fuels. However, the intermittency and seasonality of RES arise new challenges that must be addressed. To overcome these challenges, energy storage systems (ESS) are becoming increasingly important in ensuring stability in the energy mix and meeting the demands of the electrical grid. This paper introduces charging and discharging strategies of ESS, and presents an important application in terms of occupants' behavior and appliances, to maximize battery usage and reshape power plant energy consumption thereby making the energy system more efficient and sustainable.

Keywords: Adaptive charging, Energy storage systems, Smart Grid, Energy, Renewable energy sources, Simulation, Occupants' behavior model.

1. Introduction

Many countries in the world rely heavily on oil, coal, and natural gas to meet their energy demands [1]. However, this reliance on fossil fuels presents two significant challenges from a perspective of energy security. Firstly, the import of fossil resources is subject to significant price swings, which can negatively impact the stability of a country's economy and make it difficult to predict the situation in regions that import these resources. Secondly, the use of fossil fuels leads to environmental pollution and the emission of greenhouse gases, such as carbon dioxide (CO_2), which contribute to the global warming problem.

Growing energy demands and fossil fuels depletion together with COVID-19, after-pandemic times, and global energy crisis in 2021-2022 force modern world to switch energy generation from fossil sources to renewable energy sources (RES) [2, 3]. Renewable energy has great potential to reduce prices and dependence on fossil fuels in the short and long term. On the other side, intermittency and seasonality of renewable energy makes RES hard to use. Although costs for new photovoltaic panels (PV) and wind installations have increased [4].

Some regions and countries are starting to introduce RES, but the intermittency of renewable energy is still covered by peak power plants burning oil and natural gas. To fully switch to renewables the generated energy has to be stored and used when renewable resources are not available. In such a case it is hard to underestimate the importance of energy storage systems (ESS) for modern world and smart grid (SG) systems.

Typically, a private house connected to the utility power line through a battery would have a solar panel array installed on the roof or elsewhere in the property. The solar panels would convert sunlight into direct current (DC) electricity, which would then be fed into an inverter.

The inverter would convert the DC electricity into alternating current (AC) electricity, which is compatible with the utility power grid. Also the DC electricity generated by the solar panels would be sent to a battery storage system, where it would be stored for later use. The battery storage system would be connected to the utility power grid, allowing the house to draw electricity from the grid when the battery is depleted and feed excess electricity back into the grid when the battery is charged.

A control system would be used to manage the flow of electricity between the battery, the solar panels, and the utility grid. This control system would monitor the electricity demand of the house and adjust the flow of electricity accordingly.

On the other side, energy storage system can have different goals [5]. For example, energy storage can be used to make renewable energy output more stable for bringing it to a combined energy mix for large regions. ESS can be used for energy shifting to make electricity availability supply curve meet the electricity demand curve. Another use case is voltage and frequency regulation which is a typical issue in Smart Grids with many distributed renewable sources such as PV installed locally at residential houses and residential wind turbines, and which feed the energy back to the grid.

Charging and discharging strategy can be optimized to solve a specific goal: maximize battery usage to reduce power plant (fossil fuels) energy consumption, and based on statistical data and probabilities decide when to charge and when to discharge, such as charge when grid frequency goes up and discharge when frequency goes down.

This paper introduces adaptive charging and discharging strategies based on energy availability data and energy demand data. We propose a model which controls battery use based on consumption demand and selected charging/discharging strategy represented in the form of a function of battery internal state. In a very simple case the battery is always used or a threshold value is defined. A more advanced case takes into account energy storage efficiency factor, capacity, charging and discharging speeds, and other characteristics.

This paper is organized as follows: Related work is presented in Section 2. Section 3 describes charging and discharging strategies. Experiments results and discussions are presented in Section 4. Section 5 gives conclusions and discusses a future work.

2. Related work

Over the past 20 years, researchers have been searching for new and alternative energy systems. There have been various attempts to develop concepts for distributed energy generation from renewable sources, as well as new designs for energy distribution and storage. Some researchers aim to make use of existing infrastructure and make the transition to a new system as seamless as possible, while others believe that starting from scratch with the option of integrating into the existing electrical grid is the best approach.

Rikiya Abe et al. in 2011 for the first time have presented an idea of a digital grid (IEEE Transactions on Smart Grid). They have been presented a new concept of a grid as a splitting electrical grid into cells and connect them with an electrical device to control the energy share between the cells. They have presented the design of the proposed system with very little details, lacking operation examples or simulations. At the same time the research also lacks analysis and integration overview from the penetration of RES into the digital grid [6].

The idea of grid digitalization was growing very fast in some smaller projects, such as an Open Energy System research in Okinawa Island in Japan [7]. There is a direct current (DC) based Open Energy System (DCOES) joint research project. This project was researching on a DC-based bottom-up system that generates, stores, and shares electrical energy. Annette Werth et al., in "Evaluation of centralized and distributed microgrid topologies and comparison to Open Energy Systems" (IEEE International Conference on Environment and Electrical Engineering 2015) study was examining microgrid topologies that combine solar panels and batteries for a community of 20 residential houses [8]. They consider a system with centralized PV and batteries that distributes energy to the 20 homes, they also consider 20 standalone homes with roof-top PV and batteries.

The virtual synchronous generator has gained significant interest as it operates similarly to a synchronous generator, making it a viable option for connecting distributed generation to the main power grid. However, the power and frequency output of a virtual synchronous generator can be unstable during significant power fluctuations in the distributed generation system. Fei Wang et al. studied how changes in parameters affect the active power and frequency of a virtual synchronous generator. They analyzed the impact of power fluctuations and developed a small-signal model to understand the dynamic behavior. Based on their research, they proposed a new adaptive control strategy and confirmed its effectiveness through experiments [9].

Hui Guo et al. published their research (IEEE Transactions on Industrial Informatics 2019) on the basis of bidding information. The real-time transaction was implemented to track the origin and destination of power transmission, as well as the amount and timing of power flow. To minimize losses from conversion and transmission, a minimum loss routing method was chosen for the transaction of power. The proposed optimization algorithm for selecting the minimum loss routing and managing congestion was confirmed through simulation results. [10].

Lijun Zhang et al. are researching on a novel matrix converter - based topology to be applied in smart transformers based on the concept of multiple modularity. The conventional smart transformer topology, which uses H-bridge modules and DC electrolytic capacitors, was replaced with a new design that utilizes two matrix modules for greater flexibility in AC-AC structures. This new design was thoroughly analyzed, including a detailed examination of the impact of switching sequences on capacitor voltages. To validate the proposed topology and its analysis, simulations and hardware-in-loop experiments were conducted. [11].

K. Chaudhari et al. proposed a hybrid optimization algorithm for energy storage management, which shifts its mode of operation between the deterministic and rule-based approaches depending on the electricity price band allocation. The cost degradation model for the energy storage system (ESS) and the levelized cost of photovoltaic (PV) power was applied to electric vehicle (EV) charging stations. The algorithm was divided into three parts: classifying real-time electricity prices into different categories, determining the real-time PV power from solar radiation data, and optimizing the operating cost of the EV charging station that combines PV and ESS to minimize expenses [12].

Another battery energy storage system based on direct method to control the power converter for fast compensation of grid voltage instability without energy management system has been proposed by D. -J. Kim et al. A new approach for improving the power quality at an electric vehicle charging station (EVCS) has been developed. This method uses a model predictive voltage control scheme that is based on a disturbance observer, and it operates without the need for communication infrastructure. The proposed controller takes into account parameter uncertainties and uses a systematic design procedure that includes stability analysis. The performance of the controller was verified through tests using a simulation testbed that was designed to closely resemble an actual EVCS. [13].

Daniel Kucevic's et al suggest a system for managing multiple battery energy storage systems located at electric vehicle charging stations within a distribution grid. The method involves linear optimization and time series modeling, with the goal of reducing peak power levels. A simulation tool was created to combine a power flow model with a battery energy storage system model to better understand the impact of storage systems on the distribution grid. [14].

Another research was done on occupant behavior data collection. This paper introduces a dataset of electricity usage in residential homes in Uruguay that was collected by the Uruguayan electricity company (UTE) and studied by Universidad de la República. The purpose of the dataset is to analyze consumer behavior and uncover patterns of energy consumption that can be used to improve electricity services. The dataset is publicly accessible and stored in a public repository. It is confirmed by three subsets that cover total household consumption, electric water heater consumption, and energy consumption by appliance, with sample intervals from 1 to 15 minutes. The total household consumption subset includes the total aggregated consumption of 110,953 households distributed in the 19 departments of Uruguay. On average, each household was monitored for 539.2 days and each day counts with 95.2 records [15].

Salvatore Carlucci and etl in their work on modeling occupant behavior in buildings studied reviews approaches, methods and key findings related to occupants' presence and actions (OPA) modeling in buildings. A comprehensive collection of research papers on the subject has been assembled and analyzed using bibliometric techniques. The initial review uncovered over 750 studies, with 278 selected for further analysis. These publications give a comprehensive overview of the progress and evolution of OPA modeling methods. The methods in the chosen literature have been divided into three categories: rule-based models, stochastic OPA modeling, and data-driven methods for modeling functions related to occupancy and the actions of occupants. [16].

Moreover, currently renewable energy generators have installation limitations in the modern power grid due to both technical and policy reasons, which further complicate the penetration of RES to energy mix models. Authors in [17] discuss the challenges of renewable energy penetration on power system flexibility.

3. Adaptive charging and discharging approach

Electrical energy storage in batteries is becoming a crucial thing in our life. We use batteries in mobile phones, watches, laptops, and headphones. Batteries have been used in cars for decades, but with the popularization of electric vehicles (EV) it has become especially important. Now we see more and more in-house appliances which benefit from utilizing batteries, such as electric toothbrushes, audio speakers, hair trimmer, cordless vacuum cleaner, and so on.

There are a number of benefits that can be achieved for an appliance when there is a battery, such as:

- less dependent on energy availability, for example when a solar panel was used to charge a device, the device can be further used when the sun no longer available;
- in case of short power outage times a device with a battery is still powered and ready for use;
- high power consumption of a device can be replaced with a lower charging power spread over longer time, so the power line to utility can be lower;
- the device becomes free from socket and wires, so it can be carried along with the user inside and outside of the house.

Even though batteries possess several advantages when utilized in appliances, it is important to acknowledge that there are also disadvantages and limitations associated with the usage of batteries as well:

- battery capacity is limited, so in some cases there may be insufficient amount of energy to complete a desired activity, other kinds of devices might be using too much energy that those can hardly be powered with a battery of reasonable size;
- batteries degrade over time, their capacity goes down, and may even have to be replaced in order to keep using the device;
- device with a battery is typically more complex and more expensive compared to similar analogues without a battery;
- devices with batteries usually are not able to share energy between each other, such that a mobile phone cannot be recharged from a cordless dust sucker;
- batteries have to be recharged from time to time to keep working, so the freedom from wires and sockets is limited.

In this work we consider a standalone energy storage device consisting of a battery and a Control Unit (CU). It can be plugged between the utility main line and any device. The layout for a customer can be set up as a single shared battery for the entire household as shown on **Figure 1**(a) or an individual battery per every appliance device as shown on **Figure 1**(b).

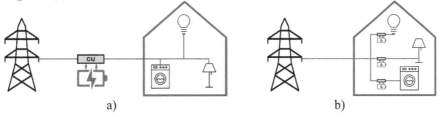

a)   b)

Figure 1. Setup layout options: a) one shared battery per customer, and b) individual battery per device.

There are advantages and disadvantages to both setup layouts. On one hand, installing a single large battery for a house looks reasonable and simpler. But on the other side, every device has its own usage pattern, power, and priority. So, it would make more sense to setup individual battery per appliance with proper characteristics matching the device electricity usage pattern.

Going further, combination of both options gives one more setup layout, where individual batteries work for targeted devices and a shared battery for the entire consumption of the customer. Also, when there is a shared energy storage system for a private house, there is also typically a private micro-generator installed in the system, such as a solar PV panel. **Figure 2** shows a more realistic setup.

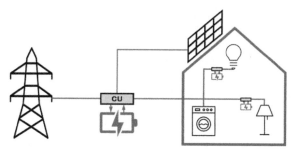

Figure 2. Mixed setup layout of batteries and use of private energy generation source, such as PV.

In a simple case we have a battery which is being used until fully discharges, and then the remaining part of the demand has to be covered from the utility line. This scenario is shown in **Figure 3**. Scenario, where battery is fully used until it gets totally discharged and the remaining time is covered by utility power line. This approach is good enough when battery capacity is large enough and periods of electricity demand by the consumer devices are short, so that battery capacity is larger than amount of electrical energy consumed during one session of device usage.

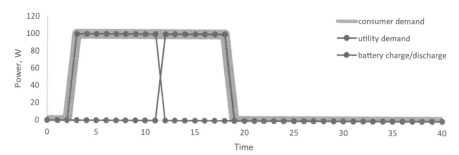

Figure 3. Scenario, where battery is fully used until it gets totally discharged and the remaining time is covered by utility power line.

In the scenario described in the **Figure 3**, the consumer device was fully supplied with the energy it needed. However, after the described case the battery is totally discharged, and it would not be possible to use it for the next session of consumer device usage. Battery charging has to happen along the way so that the overall process tends to optimize the battery usage.

Batteries, charging and discharging can happen in various ways. In this paper we do not touch the details of the technical differences of various types of batteries, as well as we do not target the differences in technical requirements of charging specific kinds of batteries.

In this paper a battery is conceptually viewed as an device for the storage of electrical energy that operates through the process of charging and discharging. The amount of stored capacity of a battery is increased through the charging process, which allows a predetermined amount of energy to be accumulated. This stored energy can be recovered upon demand through the discharge process. The fundamental properties of a battery are defined by a set of characteristic parameters:

- capacity,
- maximum charge power,
- maximum discharge power,
- storage efficiency.

The approach of determining when the battery has to take energy for charging, when the energy has to be given back, and by what power, depending on consumer demand, battery internal state, as well as other possible factors is called charging and discharging strategy.

We assume that energy demand can be covered not only from one of two sources, but also as an arbitrary mix of two of these sources. For example, 65% of energy is taken from a battery and the remaining 35% from utility line at any point of time. This can be achieved through various methods, such as by means of transformers, AC/DC converters, smart energy routers [18, 19], pulse-width modulation (PWM), etc. The efficiency and choice of the mix method is outside of the scope of this paper.

One of the options for taking the internal state of the battery into account is to discharge battery proportionally to the state of charge. In that case, when the battery is charged to 100% the consumption demand is fully covered by the battery. When at time t battery has 85% of its charge then only 85% of load power at time t will be covered by the battery and the other 15% should be taken from the utility. That way, battery use decreases exponentially over time which makes battery being used longer although covering only part of the demand power. At the same time, utility demand power is lower and increases gradually rather than as a step when the device is turned on. This case is displayed in **Figure 4**. This approach can be called discharge strategy S which is based on battery state of charge (SoC), and no charging was involved.

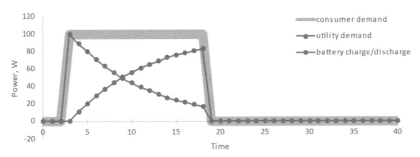

Figure 4. Scenario with proportional discharge strategy.

Calculation formulas for battery charge power P_{BC} and battery discharge power P_{BD} are as shown in (1.1) and (1.2). Where P_D is a consumer demand power, P_{CMAX} is maximum charge power, P_{DMAX} is maximum discharge power, F_C and F_D are charge and discharge strategy functions based on battery internal state.

$$P_{BC} = F_C(SoC) \times P_{CMAX} \tag{1.1}$$

$$P_{BD} = min(P_D \times F_D(SoC), P_{DMAX}) \tag{1.2}$$

That way we get battery power P_B as a difference between the discharge and charge power as shown in (2). When P_B is greater than zero, battery is discharging, when it is below zero it is charging.

$$P_B = P_{BD} - P_{BC} \tag{2}$$

Available capacity C_{AV} would be defined as differential equation as shown in (3.1) and which can be expanded in (3.2).

$$\frac{dC_{AV}}{dt} = -P_B = P_{BC} - P_{BD} \tag{3.1}$$

$$\frac{dC_{AV}}{dt} = F_C(SoC) \times P_{CMAX} - min(P_D \times F_D(SoC), P_{DMAX}) \tag{3.2}$$

Utility demand power P_U in turn is defined as a remaining power that is required to cover the consumer demand and battery charge, taking into account charge efficiency E_C, as shown in equation (4).

$$P_U = P_D - \frac{P_B}{E_C} \tag{4}$$

Charging and discharging strategies functions are defined as multiplier in range between 0 and 1. In the simplest case, these functions may always return 1 which would mean that the battery charges at the maximum possible power, as well as discharges at the maximum power according to demanded load.

Table 1. Charging and discharging strategies

Strategy	Function	Charge	Discharge
S_1	$f(x) = x$	CS_1 - Proportional	DS_1 - Proportional
S_2	$f(x) = x^k$	CS_2 - Optimistic	DS_2 - Wasteful
S_3	$f(x) = \sqrt[k]{x}$	CS_3 - Greedy	DS_3 - Economical
S_4	$f(x) = 1/\left(1 + e^{-k(x-0.5)}\right)$	CS_4 - Balanced	DS_4 - Balanced
S_5	$f(x) = 1$	CS_5 - Full charge	DS_5 - No use
S_6	$f(x) = 0$	CS_6 - No charge	DS_6 - Full use

In this paper we have taken 6 strategies for both charging and discharging to compare, so the overall battery available capacity over time depends on the battery state of charge (SoC), demand power, maximum charge power and maximum discharge power. The strategies are described in **Table 1**. The functions are represented in **Figure 5**.

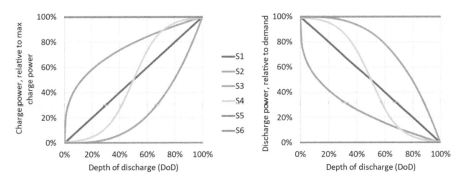

Figure 5. Charge and discharge strategies based on battery state of charge.

4. Experiments and Discussions

Residentials depend on electricity constantly, because a lot of appliances are working simultaneously, such as refrigerator, electrical heating, air conditioning, microwave, and so on. When an electrical issue arises, for example a power failure caused by a storm or there is a tripped breaker or any other problem with electricity in the circuit, the understanding of how an electrical system operates can be valuable in resolving the problem and restoring the power.

Experiments on Strategies. Comparison of the strategies is performed on reference demand signal which is 100 W consumption over 16 seconds. Battery capacity is set to be 0.25 Wh. The comparison results of strategies experiments $CS_1 - CS_6$ and $DS_1 - DS_6$ are presented in **Figure 6**.

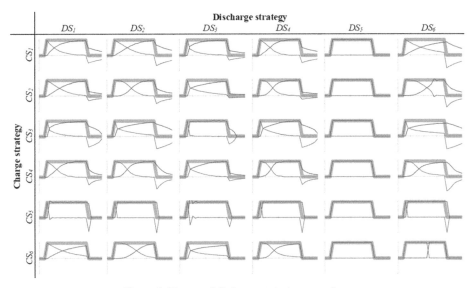

Figure 6. Charge and discharge strategies comparison.

In these experiments we can see that all cases with strategy DS_5 end up with the battery not involved in the process. A very similar situation can be seen with the charging strategy CS_5. At the beginning of the demand battery tries to cover the demand, but then battery usage is quickly reduced by the aggressive charge strategy, and even in some cases fading oscillations appear in front. Strategy CS_6DS_6 is identical to full use of battery until it is completely discharged and then the energy source is switched to utility line. All other strategies use battery and recharge it in different ways.

Strategies where discharging is DS_3 and where charging is CS_3 are mostly preserving the energy in the battery and it can be seen that utility demand quickly raises to power of the customer demand. In many cases we see that utility demand starts to raise immediately when the consumer demand increases. Although, there are several strategies, such as CS_2DS_2, CS_4DS_2, CS_2DS_4, CS_2DS_6, where utility demand stays close to zero for some time, so the device tries to cover the customer demand only by utilizing the battery.

Experiments on Capacity show that the system behavior was evaluated depending on various battery capacity sizes. In **Figure 7** are shown the results diagrams for the strategies CS_1DS_6 and CS_4DS_2 over battery capacities 0.25 Wh, 0.5 Wh, 1 Wh, 2 Wh, and 4 Wh. We can see that, when the capacity of the battery is getting bigger the strategies in both cases tend to use only battery power.

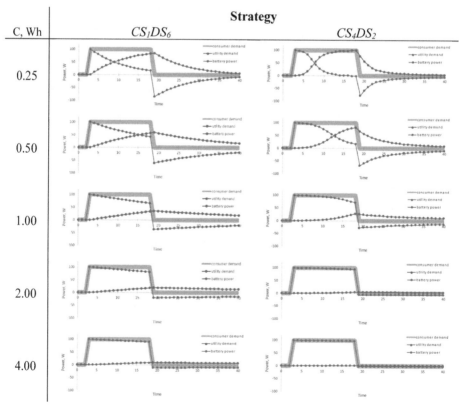

Figure 7. Comparison of strategies over battery capacity.

The main difference of the strategies plays a role when the consumer demand drains the battery significantly. Given the 100 W consumption over 16 seconds makes the total energy of the consumption demand data equal to 0.44 Wh. So, for the case of strategy CS_4DS_2 when the battery capacity is twice as much as the consumed energy of the customer, the power is almost fully covered by the battery.

Experiments on Power Limits. In these experiments, the system behavior was evaluated depending on reduced charge power and reduced discharge power options. In **Figure 8** the diagrams for the strategy CS_4DS_2 are shown. We can see that when only charge power is limited, it affects the result insignificantly. But when both charge power and discharge power are limited, the overall result becomes different to the initial setup.

The case when $P_{CMAX} = 20$ and $P_{DMAX} = 20$ shows that when limits are below the demand power and battery capacity is enough then the system behaves as a mechanism for utility line power reduction for a given margin.

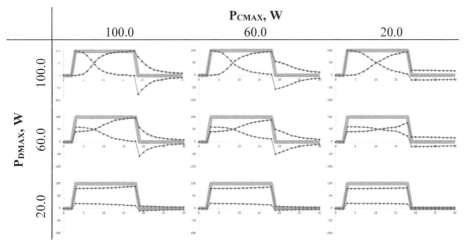

Figure 8. Comparison of strategy behaviors with limitations of maximum charge and discharge power.

Experiments on Demand Shape. During experiments on demand shape the system behavior was estimated on various kinds of consumer demand signal types. **Figure 9** shows the diagrams for the strategies CS_1DS_6 and CS_4DS_2 with battery capacity equal to 0.25 Wh, and charge/discharge limits of 100 W, which is above the demand power. Types of input signals included one-time session of demand, periodic load, increasing load as a step, and decreasing load as a step. In the considered cases strategy CS_1DS_6 provides a smoother utility demand power, because it utilizes battery more intensively.

The scenario of decreasing demand is quite a typical case when a device needs more power right after startup but then the demand decreases. Both strategies which are shown in the comparison results covered the front peak very well.

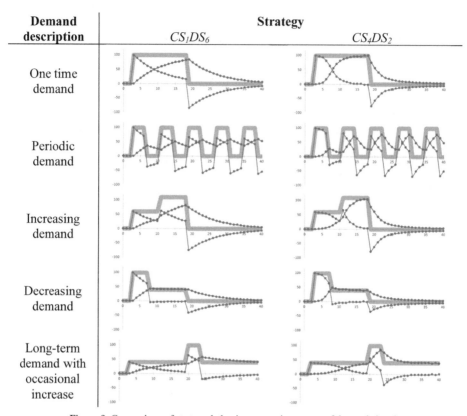

Figure 9. Comparison of strategy behaviors on various types of demand signal.

Experiments on Uruguay Dataset. In these experiments we have used data, which was collected during the research work on information on the behavior of electricity users. This research presented a dataset of electricity consumption in residential homes in Uruguay, collected by the Uruguayan Electricity Company (UTE) and analyzed by Universidad de la República [15, 20]. The goal of the dataset is to study occupants' behavior and discover patterns of energy consumption that can improve the electricity service. The dataset is open to the public and consists of three parts, which focus on overall household consumption, consumption by electric water heater, and energy usage by appliance, with time intervals ranging from 1 to 15 minutes.

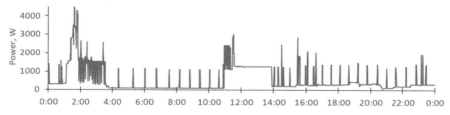

Figure 10. Load dataset example of one household (customer id 170004, date 2019-09-11).

The utility company is responsible for ensuring that electricity is supplied to residential properties. This includes maintaining the power lines up to the attachment point, which is referred to as the load side. From this point, the responsibility for ensuring that the electrical system functions properly falls on the homeowner. This includes addressing issues such as circuit overload, which can cause power outages. It is important for occupants to understand their responsibilities when it comes to the electrical system in their home in order to ensure that it operates safely and effectively.

A circuit overload means that there are too many high-powered appliances operating on the same electric circuit, for example hair dryer, air conditioner, washing or tumble-dryer machines, electric kettle, etc. An overloaded circuit means that occupants are using more electricity than the circuit is made for. In such a case the electrical system in a residence will experience a shutdown due to a circuit breaker in the service panel being triggered. Circuit breakers are a reliable solution for preventing electrical fires caused by overloads, but the safest approach is to manage electricity usage to avoid overloads in the first place. By taking proactive steps to control electricity usage and avoid overloading the system, homeowners can help ensure the safety and stability of their electrical system.

In this paper we have used the Disaggregated Energy Consumption by appliance dataset, which consists of two relevant data: the total aggregated consumption records of nine households in Montevideo, and the disaggregate consumption of a set of appliances in each household (e.g., lamps, fridges, air conditioner, etc.). The sampling interval is one minute, and the date range of consumption records is from 27th August 2019 to 16th September 2019. Appliances vary by customer and typically include dehumidifier, tumble dryer, microwave, electric oven, electric air heater, washing machine, fridge, electric water heater, and air conditioner.

The breakdown of the load demand data for customer id 170004 for entire day of 2019-09-11 is shown in **Figure 11**.

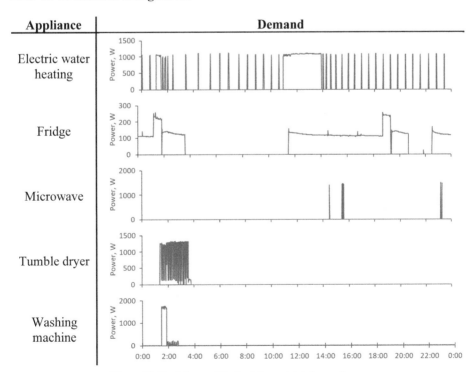

Figure 11. Breakdown of the load demand data by appliance.

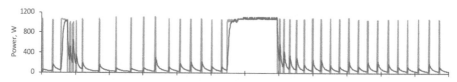

Figure 12. Electric water heating appliance demand with battery 250 Wh.

Figure 13. Fridge appliance demand with 300 Wh battery.

Figure 14. Microwave appliance demand with 500 Wh battery.

Figure 15. Tumble dryer appliance demand with 300 Wh battery.

Figure 16. Washing machine appliance demand with 1000 Wh battery.

Every appliance had its own individual battery. Its capacity was chosen individually based on the appliance demand. Capacity of batteries in the presented experiments make up a total of 2350 Wh. The same amount can be used as a single shared battery instead or can be shared between appliances in a different split in mixed layout. The details of the considered cases are presented in **Table 2**.

Table 2. Battery capacities split by appliances and by experiment cases.

Battery	Appliance	Capacity, Wh		
		Case 1	Case 2	Case 3
Individual	Electric water heating	0	250	250
Individual	Fridge	0	300	0
Individual	Microwave	0	500	500
Individual	Tumble dryer	0	300	0
Individual	Washing machine	0	1000	600
Shared	Entire household	2350	0	1000

The comparison of results is shown in **Figure 17**. We can see that all cases give relatively similar output. Although, many short-term load periods are smoothed out, the Case 2 where only individual batteries were involved, we can see that water heater battery capacity was not enough to avoid medium peaks. Those medium peaks are especially visible in the period between 14:00 and 16:00. Longer-term periods remain almost the same as in the original customer demand.

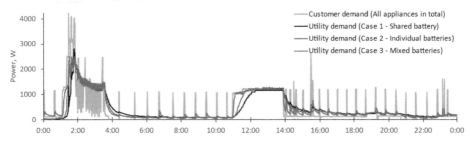

Figure 17. Comparison of results for shared battery, individual batteries, and mixed batteries layouts.

Various kinds of appliances have significantly different level of load power, however the importance and priorities of such appliances for the customer is very different. Therefore, mixed layout of batteries as in Case 3 becomes a good choice, and the battery sizes is the subject for configuration per customers individually based on appliances and their usage patterns.

In this set of experiments the overall peak was significantly lower for all cases with batteries compared to consumer demand. The comparison is given in **Table 3**. We can see that with the use of batteries, the peak power has decreased to approximately 60%. This is a significant value which contributes to reducing the utility power line and generation peaks which are in general more expensive.

Table 3. Peak power comparison for experiment cases 1-3.

Scenario	Peak power, W	Relative
Customer demand (All appliances in total)	4213.00	100.0%
Utility demand (Case 1 - Shared battery)	2817.06	66.9%
Utility demand (Case 2 - Individual batteries)	2484.16	59.0%
Utility demand (Case 3 - Mixed batteries)	2518.11	59.8%

5. Conclusions and future work

Energy generation and consumption in the world have significant challenges in terms of energy security and environmental degradation. Renewable energy sources help to address these challenges significantly and therefore have become very widespread in recent years. However, to fully switch to renewables the generated energy has to be stored and used when renewable resources are not available. In such a case it is hard to underestimate the importance of energy storage systems for the modern world and Smart Grid systems.

This paper introduces an adaptive charging and discharging approach with various strategies based on energy availability and energy demand. We propose a model which controls battery use based on consumption demand and selected charging/discharging strategy represented in the form of a function of battery internal state. In the model we take into account battery total capacity, available amount of energy in the battery in a given time, charging strategy, discharging strategy, energy storage efficiency factor, maximum charging and discharging power. Six strategies have been defined which can be applied for both charging and discharging.

The experiments present the comparison of adaptive energy storage system behavior depending on various setups of strategies, battery capacity, demand load signal, and power limits. Disaggregated energy consumption by appliance dataset of nine households in Montevideo from Uruguay was used in this paper. Three batteries setup layouts for a household were compared, which include the layout of individual batteries per appliance, single shared battery for entire household, and a mixed approach.

In the future work we plan to extend the strategies to take into account utility cost of electricity which varies during the day. We plan to include private microgeneration options as well as to explore in more details the optimal battery capacity split between appliances.

References

[1] Mayer, A. Fossil fuel dependence and energy insecurity. Energy, Sustainability and Society, 12, 27 (2022). https://doi.org/10.1186/s13705-022-00353-5
[2] World Energy Outlook 2022, IEA, Paris https://www.iea.org/reports/world-energy-outlook-2022, License: CC BY 4.0 (report); CC BY NC SA 4.0 (Annex A), 2022.
[3] Ozili, Peterson K and Ozen, Ercan, Global Energy Crisis: Impact on the Global Economy (January 2, 2023). Available at SSRN: https://ssrn.com/abstract=4309828 or http://dx.doi.org/10.2139/ssrn.4309828
[4] Renewable Energy Market Update - May 2022, IEA, Paris https://www.iea.org/reports/renewable-energy-market-update-may-2022, License: CC BY 4.0, 2022.
[5] H. Ibrahim, A. Ilinca, J. Perron. Energy storage systems – Characteristics and comparisons. Renewable and sustainable energy reviews 2008; 12(5): 1221-1250.
[6] R. Abe, H. Taoka, D. McQuilkin. Digital grid: communicative electrical grids of the future. IEEE Transactions on Smart Grid 2011; 2(2): 399–410.
[7] Okinawa Institute of Science and Technology, OIST Open Energy System Project, https://www.oist.jp/news-center/news/2015/2/17/energy-starts-home
[8] A. Werth, N. Kitamura, I. Matsumoto and K. Tanaka, "Evaluation of centralized and distributed microgrid topologies and comparison to Open Energy Systems (OES)," 2015 IEEE 15th International Conference on Environment and Electrical Engineering (EEEIC), Rome, Italy, 2015, pp. 492-497, doi: 10.1109/EEEIC.2015.7165211.
[9] F. Wang, L. Zhang, X. Feng and H. Guo, "An Adaptive Control Strategy for Virtual Synchronous Generator," in IEEE Transactions on Industry Applications, vol. 54, no. 5, pp. 5124-5133, Sept.-Oct. 2018, doi: 10.1109/TIA.2018.2859384.
[10] H. Guo, F. Wang, L. Li, L. Zhang and J. Luo, "A Minimum Loss Routing Algorithm Based on Real-Time Transaction in Energy Internet," in IEEE Transactions on Industrial Informatics, vol. 15, no. 12, pp. 6446-6456, Dec. 2019, doi: 10.1109/TII.2019.2904188
[11] Lijun Zhang, Alexandre Bento, Guilherme Paraíso, Pedro Costa, Sónia Ferreira Pinto, José Fernando Silva, Fei Wang. Multiple modularity topology for smart transformers based on matrix converters. IET Electric Power Applications. pp. 926-940, 2022. DOI: 10.1049/elp2.12200
[12] K. Chaudhari, A. Ukil, K. N. Kumar, U. Manandhar and S. K. Kollimalla, "Hybrid Optimization for Economic Deployment of ESS in PV-Integrated EV Charging Stations," in IEEE Transactions on Industrial Informatics, vol. 14, no. 1, pp. 106-116, Jan. 2018, doi: 10.1109/TII.2017.2713481.
[13] D. -J. Kim, B. Kim, C. Yoon, N. -D. Nguyen and Y. I. Lee, "Disturbance Observer-Based Model Predictive Voltage Control for Electric-Vehicle Charging Station in Distribution Networks," in IEEE Transactions on Smart Grid, vol. 14, no. 1, pp. 545-558, Jan. 2023, doi: 10.1109/TSG.2022.3187120.

[14] Daniel Kucevic, Stefan Englberger, Anurag Sharma, Anupam Trivedi, Benedikt Tepe, Birgit Schachler, Holger Hesse, Dipti Srinivasan, Andreas Jossen, Reducing grid peak load through the coordinated control of battery energy storage systems located at electric vehicle charging parks, Applied Energy, Volume 295, 2021, 116936, ISSN 0306-2619, https://doi.org/10.1016/j.apenergy.2021.116936

[15] Chavat, J., Nesmachnow, S., Graneri, J. et al. ECD-UY, detailed household electricity consumption dataset of Uruguay. Sci Data 9, 21 (2022). https://doi.org/10.1038/s41597-022-01122-x

[16] Salvatore Carlucci, Marilena De Simone, Steven K. Firth, Mikkel B. Kjærgaard, Romana Markovic, Mohammad Saiedur Rahaman, Masab Khalid Annaqeeb, Silvia Biandrate, Anooshmita Das, Jakub Władysław Dziedzic, Gianmarco Fajilla, Matteo Favero, Martina Ferrando, Jakob Hahn, Mengjie Han, Yuzhen Peng, Flora Salim, Arno Schlüter, Christoph van Treeck, Modeling occupant behavior in buildings, Building and Environment, Volume-174, 2020, 106768, ISSN:0360-1323, https://doi.org/10.1016/j.buildenv.2020.106768

[17] Semich Impram, Secil Varbak Nese, Bülent Oral, Challenges of renewable energy penetration on power system flexibility: A survey, Energy Strategy Reviews, Volume 31, 2020, 100539, ISSN 2211-467X, https://doi.org/10.1016/j.esr.2020.100539.

[18] Alexander Dudko, Tatiana Endrjukaite, and Leon R. Roose. 2020. Open Routed Energy Distribution Network based on a Concept of Energy Router in Smart Grid. In Proceedings of the 21st International Conference on Information Integration and Web-based Applications & Services (iiWAS2019). Association for Computing Machinery, New York, NY, USA, 483–491. https://doi.org/10.1145/3366030.3366036

[19] T. Endrjukaite, A. Dudko, and L. Roose. 2019. Energy Exchange Model in Routed Energy Distribution Network. In Proc. of the 6th ACM International Conference BuildSys '19. Association for Computing Machinery, New York, NY, USA, 393–394. https://doi.org/10.1145/3360322.3361017

[20] Chavat, Juan Pablo; Nesmachnow, Sergio; Graneri, Jorge; Alvez, Gustavo (2022): ECD-UY: Detailed household electricity consumption dataset of Uruguay. figshare. Collection. https://doi.org/10.6084/m9.figshare.c.5428608.v1

Information Modelling and Knowledge Bases XXXV
M. Tropmann-Frick et al. (Eds.)

doi:10.3233/FAIA231149

Data-Based Condition Monitoring and Disturbance Classification in Actively Controlled Laser Oscillators

Arne GRÜNHAGEN [a,b,c,1], Annika EICHLER [b,c] Marina TROPMANN-FRICK [a] and
Görschwin FEY [b]

[a] *Hamburg University of Applied Sciences, HAW, Germany*
[b] *Hamburg University of Technology, TUHH, Germany*
[c] *Deutsches Elektronen-Synchrotron DESY, Germany*

Abstract. The successful operation of the laser-based synchronization system of the European X-Ray Free Electron Laser relies on the precise functionality of numerous dynamic systems operating within closed loops with controllers. In this paper, we present how data-based machine learning methods can detect and classify disturbances to such dynamic systems based on the controller output signal. We present 4 feature extraction methods based on statistics in the time domain, statistics in the frequency domain, characteristics of spectral peaks, and the autoencoder latent space representation of the frequency domain. These feature extraction methods require no system knowledge and can easily be transferred to other dynamic systems. We combine feature extraction, fault detection, and fault classification into a comprehensive and fully automated condition monitoring pipeline. For that, we systematically compare the performance of 19 state-of-the-art fault detection and 4 classification algorithms to decide which combination of feature extraction and fault detection or classification algorithm is most appropriate to model the condition of an actively controlled phase-locked laser oscillator. Our experimental evaluation shows the effectiveness of clustering algorithms, showcasing their strong suitability in detecting perturbed system conditions. Furthermore, in our evaluation, the support vector machine proves to be the most suitable for classifying the various disturbances.

Keywords. Fault detection, Fault classification, Feature Extraction, Autoencoder

1. Introduction and Motivation

The European X-ray Free-Electron Laser (EuXFEL) [1] is a large-scale linear particle accelerator located in Hamburg, Germany. A 1.3 GHz Radio Frequency (RF) Main Oscillator (MO) is used to synchronize various components of the accelerator by distributing the RF signal as a timing reference. Since this electrical distribution via coaxial cables is heavily influenced by the environment (e.g. humidity, temperature, electromagnetic fields), an optical synchronization system is installed that is less vulnerable to these en-

---

[1]We acknowledge the support by DASHH (Data Science in Hamburg - HELMHOLTZ Graduate School for the Structure of Matter) with the Grant-No. HIDSS-0002.

vironmental condition changes [2]. This optical synchronization system provides ultra-stable reference timing information to the accelerator components and the experimental setups with an integrated timing jitter in the range of a few femtoseconds. The main component of this optical synchronization system is a mode-locked pulsed laser oscillator that is phase-locked to the MO delivering an ultra-stable optical reference used to locally resynchronize RF sources, to lock optical laser systems, and to diagnose the arrival time of the electron beam along various locations for fast beam based feedbacks.

Not only does the laser not produce a completely noise-free signal, but the emitted signal is also influenced by environmental disturbances (i.e., electrical, acoustical, mechanical, and optical) resulting in amplitude and phase fluctuations. To synchronize the laser oscillator to the MO, the relative phase error between a harmonic of the laser pulse repetition rate and the MO reference is determined and fed to a Proportional-Integral (PI) controller in a feedback loop. This controller acts on the laser oscillator cavity length to lock the laser oscillator repetition rate to the 1.3 GHz MO frequency with a loop bandwidth in the order of 1 kHz to 10 kHz [3]. Since the controller compensates for disturbances, the controller output signal is an ideal data source to detect potential disturbances that increase the integrated timing jitter and therefore decrease the synchronization performance.

The aim of this work is to detect and classify changes in the controller output signal which may indicate disturbances of the laser itself, disturbances in the internal detection chain, disturbances in the MO reference or environmental disturbances. This goal is achieved by realizing the fault analysis pipeline depicted in Figure 1. In the data preparation step, we extract the power spectral density (PSD) from the controller output signal using Welch's method [4] such that the fault analysis can be performed in the time and frequency domain. In the feature engineering step, we implemented three different methods to extract meaningful features to fit several fault detection models. The steps will be explained in detail in Sections 3 and 4.

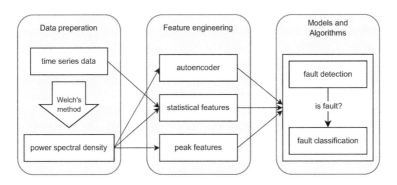

Figure 1. Fault Analysis Pipeline

In the following, we summarize related work in Section 2. Then we describe the data preparation and feature engineering steps in Section 3. Section 4 summarizes the methods selected for fault detection and fault classification and Section 5 gives a detailed overview on the experimental validation of the proposed fault analysis pipeline. We conclude this work highlighting specific findings and providing an outlook on future work in Section 6.

2. Related Work

Despite extensive literature about fault detection and anomaly detection in the area of manufacturing systems [5,6,7,8,9] only a few publications address fault detection and fault classification of dynamic systems in closed-loop control.

The authors of [10] use linear transfer functions to represent the actively controlled system under review and its controller. These models build the core of their fault diagnosis since they evaluate the discrepancy between the physical system output and the model output and the discrepancy between the physical controller output and the model output. In [11], the authors address control-loop data from a real system. They implement different fault detection mechanisms for different fault types, namely an oscillation detection based on an autocorrelation function, the detection of sluggish-tuned loops using the so-called idle index, quantization detection, and a saturation detection method. Both approaches require a deep system understanding for analyzing faulty system behavior.

In contrast to existing fault analysis targeting dynamic systems in closed loop control, we aim to develop a fault analysis pipeline that is purely based on historical data. Our fault diagnosis uses a combination of automatic feature extraction and data driven machine learning techniques. Feature engineering is addressed in different industrial sectors. The authors of [12,13,14] each extract different basic statistics in the time domain, like the mean, the maximum, the minimum, the root mean square, or the entropy. In [15,16], the authors analyze vibration signals in the frequency domain and decide on the system's health condition based on the values of domain-relevant frequency components. In [17] the authors combine both, statistics in the time domain and statistics in the frequency domain as features for fault analysis. In our research, we extract features from the controller output signal in the time and frequency domains and fit state-of-the-art data driven fault detection and fault classification algorithms to these features.

3. Data Engineering

In this section, we describe what kind of data is used and how the data is processed to build meaningful models that can describe the condition of laser oscillators.

Figure 2 shows a simplified version of the laser oscillator control loop. The input $e(t)$ to the PI controller is the difference between the reference signal $r(t)$, which in our case is the phase of the reference signal provided by the electrical timing information coming from the MO, and the measured phase $y_m(t)$ of the signal generated by the laser oscillator, affected by different disturbances $d(t)$. The phase $y(t)$ of the laser oscillator output signal $o(t)$ is determined by the phase detection. The output $u(t)$ of the PI controller feeding into the laser oscillator is a voltage that affects the cavity length of the laser oscillator and therby adjusting the phase of the laser signal. This outgoing signal, also called feedback signal, contains information about disturbances that the PI controller is processing and is therefore a valuable source of information for fault detection.

3.1. Time and Frequency Domain

The controller's output signal contains values in the range from 0 to 1 and is measured with a sampling rate of 0.32 MHz. To check what kind of disturbances affect the system, the operators of the optical synchronization system mainly study the PSD.

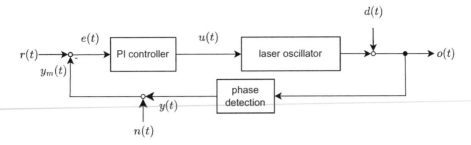

Figure 2. Overview of the Laser Oscillator Control Scheme

Figure 3 shows an examples of a feedback signal in time domain and the respective PSD in the frequency domain during healthy operation. The time series signal is an oscillating signal containing the adjustments to the cavity length of the laser oscillator. Due to the oscillating nature of the feedback signal in the time domain, single data points cannot reflect the entire state of the system and therefore it is mandatory to look at a series of data points. For our calculations, each series contains 30 000 datapoints, which is equivalent to 0.1 s.

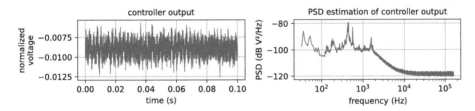

Figure 3. Example for time series signal and PSD during normal operation

We calculate the PSDs using Welch's method [4]. Welch's method divides the time series data into overlapping segments, computes a modified periodogram for each segment, and averages the periodograms to the resulting PSD. Our PSD calculation uses Hanning windows containing 10 000 data points with an overlap of 5000 datapoints. As a result, each PSD consists of 5000 datapoints. The shape of the PSD and its peaks at certain frequencies are characteristic of the current state of the system. For example, the increased power at 400 Hz comes from a mechanical disturbance of the laser oscillator and the peak at 60 000 Hz originates from the resonance frequency of the laser internal piezo actuator (see Figure 3).

In either case, considering the time-domain signals or the PSD in frequency domain, we work with a series of data points, also called frames. Depending on the frame size, the fault analysis algorithms may have to work with high dimensional data, which can lead to poor prediction performance. For this reason, we use several feature engineering techniques to reduce the dimensionality of the input data. In the following, we describe three feature engineering techniques applied to the controller data.

3.2. Statistical Feature Extraction

We use the *tsfresh* Python package [18] to calculate a set of statistics from the data frames. The selected statistics correspond to the most frequently used statistics in the field of feature extraction for fault analysis [19]. Table 1 gives an overview of the extracted statistics, a short description, and, if applicable, the corresponding parameter choices. These statistical features are extracted from the time frames and from the PSDs. In both cases, the resulting dataset contains 34 values for the time-domain frame or PSD, respectively.

Table 1. Summary of Extracted Statistics from Data Frame X Containing n Elements

Statistic	Description	Parameter values
maximum	$\max(X)$	-
minimum	$\min(X)$	-
mean	$\mu = \frac{\sum_{i=1}^n X_i}{n}$	-
absolute energy	$\frac{\sum_{i=1}^n X_i^2}{n}$	-
standard deviation	$std = \sqrt{\frac{\sum_{i=1}^n (X_i - \mu)^2}{n}}$	-
variation coefficient (cv)	$cv = \frac{std}{\mu}$	-
variance (σ)	$\sigma = (std)^2$	-
root mean square (rms)	$rms = \sqrt{\frac{1}{n}\sum_{i=1}^n X_i^2}$	-
skewness (sk)	$sk = \frac{\sum_{i=1}^n (X_i - \mu)^3}{n \cdot S^3}$	-
kurtosis ($kurt$)	$kurt = \frac{\sum_{i=1}^n (X_i - \mu)^4}{n \cdot S^4} - 3$	-
autocorrelation for lags	$R(l) = \frac{1}{(n-l)\sigma^2} \sum_{t=1}^{n-l} (x_t - \mu)(x_{t+l} - \mu)$	$l \in [0, 1, ..., 9]$
quantile	The quantile is the value that is greater than the q-th proportion of the values in X.	$q \in [0.1, 0.2, ..., 1]$
linear trend attributes	pvalue, rvalue, intercept, slope, stderr of the linear regression from X	-

3.3. Peak Feature Extraction

The peak feature extraction addresses data in the frequency domain. Peaks within a power spectrum are special characteristics since they show how much the PI controller was correcting and at which frequency. This behavior provides insights about possible disturbances. We define a potential peak as every point in a series of data points which has a value higher than both of its neighboring data points. We filter out the irrelevant peaks, i.e. peaks due to noise, by specifying that a peak should have a minimum prominence of 45 dbm and a minimum value of -105 dbm. The prominence of a peak is defined as the vertical distance to the highest valley. The minimum height and the minimum prominence are specific to the controller output signal. Based on this peak detection we implemented three feature extraction algorithms that identify peak related characteristics.

3.3.1. Number of Peaks per Area

We divided the frequency range in smaller regions, each covering 5000 Hz, and count the number of peaks. With a maximum frequency of 160000 Hz we have a total number of 32 features.

3.3.2. Characteristics of the Most Prominent Peaks

We identified the five most prominent peaks, from which we extract the prominence, the height, the width, and the frequency. While the prominence, the height, and the width are numerical values, the frequency is a categorical value because a higher frequency does not imply a worse or better system condition. Therefore, we again divided the frequency range into regions of 5000 Hz, and for each region we count the number of prominent peaks.

3.3.3. Peak Healthyness

This feature extraction method gives each extracted peak following our set of constraints a score between 0 and 1 that determines whether the peak belongs to a healthy or unhealthy operation. For that we acquired controller output data during healthy operation and extracted all peaks following our criteria from the PSDs. Based on these peaks we assigned each frequency f a healthyness score $healthyness(f) = \frac{\#peaks\,at\,f}{\#observed\,PSDs}$. The resulting distribution of healthy peaks is depicted in Figure 4.

In the feature extraction step, we identify the ten most prominent peaks and for each peak we take the healthyness score from the previously determined distribution as a feature.

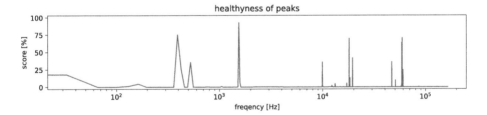

Figure 4. Probability Distribution of Frequencies Having a Healthy Peak

3.4. Autoencoder Latent Space

We use a feedforward AutoEncoder (AE) [20] trained on PSDs from healthy and disturbed operations. Using the AE's encoder, we transform a complete PSD into the AE latent space vector, which is used as a feature vector for fault detection methods. The basic structure of the AE is shown in Table 2. The AE consists only of fully connected layers and each layer, except for the output layer, is followed by the leakyRELU activation function.

Table 2. Overview Autoencoder

Layer	input	1. encoding	2. encoding	latent space	1. decoding	2. decoding	output
Dimension	5000	500	100	10	100	500	5000

4. Selected Models for Fault Detection and Fault Classification

The fault analysis pipeline depicted in Figure 5 is composed of two integral components: a semi-supervised fault detection algorithm based on healthy data and a supervised fault classification algorithm fitted on predefined classes. These algorithms are fed with input features extracted from 0.1 s snippets of the system's behavior. The fault detection performs an assessment of the system's condition, distinguishing between normal operation and states of malfunction or disturbance.

If the fault detection classifies a system state as faulty based on the input features, the same features are used as input for fault classification to distinguish between different system conditions. The supervised fault classification algorithms assigns a class score to each of the predefined predefined system conditions. This class score reflects the likelihood that the given 0.1 s snippet corresponds to a specific fault class. Through the synergistic operation of fault detection and fault classification, the pipeline enables the determination of the system's current health condition.

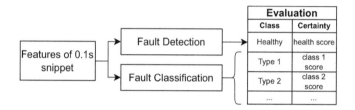

Figure 5. Fault Detection and Fault Classification

4.1. Fault Detection Algorithms

The fault detection algorithms are used to evaluate the features x extracted from a 0.1 s snippet of measurement data. For a vector x, the fault detector calculates a health score H, which quantifies the operational health of a system. This score ranges from 0 to 1, where 0 represents a highly faulty or disturbed state and 1 represents a completely healthy state.

4.1.1. Clustering Algorithms

Clustering algorithms aim to group data samples into classes with similar elements. Clustering requires the concept of a metric, which may differ from algorithm to algorithm [21]. For the purpose of fault detection, we assume that similar data samples belong to the same class. We use the following clustering algorithms:

- Balanced iterative reducing and clustering using hierarchies (BIRCH) [22]
- Clustering based local outlier factor (CBLOF) [23]
- Gaussian mixture model (GMM) [24]
- K-means clustering [25]

4.1.2. Outlier Detection Algorithms

Outlier detection algorithms aim to identify rare items or events that differ significantly from the rest of the dataset [26]. Assuming that faulty data samples can be classified as outliers compared to healthy data samples, we use the following outlier detection algorithms:

- Angle-based outlier detection (ABOD) [27]
- Connectivity-based outlier detection (COF) [28]
- Copula-based outlier detector (COPOD) [29]
- Empirical cumulative distribution outlier detection (ECOD) [30]
- Isolation-based outlier detection (IOF) [31]
- Kernel density estimation (KDE) [32]
- Kernel principal component analysis (KPCA) [33]
- K-nearest neighbor detection (KNN) [34]
- Linear model deviation-based outlier detection (LMDD) [35]
- Local outlier factor (LOF) [36]
- Minimum covariance determinant (MCD) [37]
- One-class support vector machine (OCSVM) [38]
- Principal component analysis (PCA) [39]
- Sampling [40]
- Stochastic outlier selection (SOS) [41]

In addition to the algorithms fitted on the feature dataset, we trained an AE with the structure shown in Table 2 on PSDs belonging to healthy system operation. Therefore, the AE only learns to reconstruct PSDs belonging to a healthy operation. The AE fault detector uses a threshold on the reconstruction loss, which is realized using the mean squared error (MSE) between the input PSD and the reconstructed PSD at the output layer. The fault detection is based on the assumption that PSDs belonging to healthy system operation have a low MSE, while PSDs belonging to poor system conditions have a high MSE.

4.2. Fault Classification

Fault classification is the process of categorizing a feature vector x into specific fault classes using algorithms that are built using labeled training data. For each fault class $C_1, C_2, ..., C_n$, the fault classifier assigns a feature vector x to the fault class C_i with the maximum likelihood $P(C_i|x)$:

$$C = \arg\max_i P(C_i|x)$$

The following supervised learning algorithms use feature vectors as input:

- Decision Tree (DT) [42]
- k-Nearest-Neighbor classifier (kNN) [43]
- Random Forest (RF) [44]
- Support Vector Machine (SVM) [45]

5. Experimental Evaluation

The experiments were performed using the Python libraries tsfresh [18], PyOD [46], and Scikit-learn [47]. The runtimes were measured on a Windows 11 operating system running Python 3.9 with a processor Intel(R) Core(TM) i7-1185G7 @ 3.00 GHz and 16 GB of RAM.

5.1. Dataset Summary

To evaluate the feature extraction techniques in combination with the fault detection and fault classification algorithms we generated disturbances at different frequencies by playing tones of single frequencies. The tones were played through a surface speaker mounted on the optical table directly next to the laser oscillator. Figure 6 shows exemplary the time series domain of the controller output and its corresponding PSD for a 1.0 kHz and a 2.0 kHz excitment. In total, we recorded 30 s of controller data for each excited frequency as summarized in Table 3.

Table 3. Summary of fitting dataset and validation dataset

Condition	Fitting data		Validation data	
	# Frames	Portion	# Frames	Portion
no disturbance	4208	60.49 %	231	7.97 %
0.5 kHz disturbance	305	4.38 %	296	8.97 %
1.0 kHz disturbance	305	4.38 %	296	8.97 %
1.5 kHz disturbance	306	4.4 %	296	10.22 %
2.0 kHz disturbance	305	4.38 %	296	10.22 %
2.5 kHz disturbance	305	4.38 %	296	10.22 %
3.0 kHz disturbance	305	4.38 %	231	10.25 %
3.5 kHz disturbance	306	4.4 %	296	10.22 %
4.0 kHz disturbance	306	4.4 %	296	10.22 %
4.5 kHz disturbance	306	4.4 %	296	10.22 %

For evaluating the combinations of feature extraction and fault analysis we recorded fitting data and validation data under the same environmental conditions (21 °C, 44 % relative humidity). From both, the time frames and the PSDs, we extracted the features as described in Section 3 and normalized the extracted features using Z-normalization [48]. The number of features per data frame depends on the feature extraction method and is shown in Table 4. The peak characteristic feature extraction leads to the highest dimension and the AE latent space feature extractor to the lowest.

Table 4. Numer of Features per Dataframe

Feature Extraction Method	statistics (time)	statistics (PSD)	peak characteristics (PSD)	AE latent space (PSD)
Number of extracted features	34	34	94	10

Figure 7 shows the four fitting data sets of the four different feature extraction methods (AE latent space, statistics in the time domain, statistics from PSDs, and peak fea-

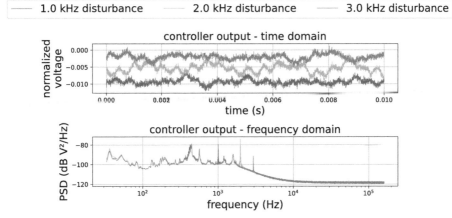

Figure 6. Controller output in time domain and frequency domain at 1.0 kHz, 2.0 kHz, and 3.0 kHz disturbances

tures). To represent the multidimensional feature datasets in a two-dimensional space, we used t-distributed Stochastic Neighbor Embedding (t-SNE) [49]. The visualization of the data is intended to provide a basis for evaluating the algorithms in Section 5.4.

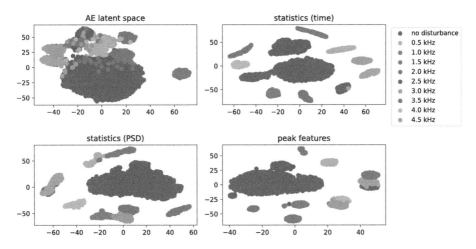

Figure 7. Feature Vizualization by t-SNE

The data points recorded under the same disturbances or no disturbance are clustered for all feature extraction methods. However, the clusters on the AE latent space dataset are significantly closer, sometimes even with an overlap, than the clusters on the other feature datasets. Since we are analyzing fault detection methods in this work, it is noteworthy that there is only an overlap between disturbed data points and undisturbed data points on the AE latent space dataset. In particular, the data from the 1.5 kHz disturbance have a strong overlap with the undisturbed data points. Using statistics from time series, statistics from PSDs, or peak features there are only overlapping clusters between data points of different disturbance types. Furthermore, it is noticeable that the undisturbed datapoints based on time statistics form two separate clusters rather than one cluster.

5.2. Algorithms Parameters

Most of the algorithms selected contain controllable parameters that influence different aspects of the algorithm. A summary of all the parameters used is given in Tables 5,6, and 7.

Table 5. Fault Detection Clustering Algorithms' Parameters

Algorithm	Parameter	Values
BIRCH	threshold	0.2, 0.4, ..., 3.8, 4.0
	branching factor	20, 40, 60, 80, 100
CBLOF	# clusters	2, 3, 4, 5, 6, 7, 8, 9, 10, 15
	alpha	0.5, 0.6, 0.7, 0.8, 0.9
	beta	1.5, 2, 5, 7, 10, 15
GMM	# components	2, 3, 4, 5, 6, 7, 8, 9, 10, 15
K-means	# clusters	2, 3, 4, 5, 6, 7, 8, 9, 10, 15

Table 6. Fault Detection - Outlier Detection Algorithms' Parameters

Algorithm	Parameter	Values
ABOD	# nearest neighbors	5, 10, ..., 95, 100
COF	# nearest neighbors	5, 10, ..., 95, 100
COPOD	-	-
ECOD	-	-
KDE	bandwith	0.2, 0.4, 0.6, ..., 3.8, 4.0
KNN	# nearest neighbors	5, 10, ..., 95, 100
KPCA	# components	1, 2, ..., 10
	kernel	linear, poly, rbf, sigmoid
LMDD	-	-
LOF	# nearest neighbors	5, 10, ..., 95, 100
MCD	-	-
OCSVM	kernel	linear, poly, rbf, sigmoid
PCA	# components	1, 2, ..., 10
Sampling	-	-
SOS	perplexity	5, 10, ..., 95, 100

5.3. Performance Criteria

We repeated the experiment under the same environmental conditions (21 °C, 44 % relative humidity) to verify the quality of the algorithms. The validation data again consists

Table 7. Fault Classification Algorithms' Parameters

Algorithm	Parameter	Values
DT	split criterion	gini, entropy, log-loss
kNN	# neighbors	5, 10, 50, 100, 500
	neighborhood weights	uniform, distance
	algorithm	ball-tree, kd-tree, brute
	distance metric	minkowski, cityblock, euclidean, manhattan
RF	# estimators	10, 50, 100, 200, 500
	split criterion	gini, entropy, log-loss
SVM	regularization parameter	0.25, 0.5, .., 2.0
	kernel	linear, poly, sigmoid, rbf

of 2896 data frames, each covering 0.1 s. A live fault detection or classification of a 0.1 s snippet can have a maximum inference duration of 0.1 s. To evaluate the system state at each point in time, it is necessary that the fault detection and classification algorithms operate at the same or higher speed. We evaluate this criterion by measuring the time it takes for each algorithm to classify the validation data samples and determine the inference speed by dividing the measured duration by the number of frames. Additionally, we measured the time each algorithm needs to be fitted.

To evaluate the feature extraction methods and algorithms qualitatively we are using the area under the receiver operating characteristic (AUROC) [50] as a performance metric. The AUROC score is defined as the area underneath the ROC curve and ranges between 0 and 1, where a score of 1 implies a perfect predictor, an AUROC score of 0 implies that the predictor gives always wrong predictions, and an AUROC score of 0.5 indicates that the predictor makes random guesses. We calculate the AUROC scores of both, the fitting dataset and the validation dataset.

The AUROC metric does not provide information on which of the disturbances are classified correctly and which of them are misclassified. Therefore, we also calculate the classification accuracy $\frac{True\,Predictions(condition)}{All\,Predictions(condition)}$ for each condition, either a disturbed frequency or undisturbed respectively.

We repeated the process of fitting and evaluation ten times with different random seeds and determined the mean value for each metric. In summary, we determined the mean values of the following metrics for each combination of feature extraction method and fault detection algorithm:

- Fitting duration (fitting dataset)
- Inference duration (validation dataset)
- AUROC score (fitting dataset)
- AUROC score (validation dataset)
- Condition specific accuracies (validation dataset)

5.4. Results

In this section, we describe the results of the algorithms applied to the experimental data. Combining the feature extraction methods and the different parameter choices, we built 3084 models on the different feature datasets (AE latent space, statistics from time series signals, statistics from PSDs, peak characteristics). We systematically traversed the parameters outlined in Tables 5, 6, and 7 in a nested loop iteration procedure.

The fitting durations of all algorithms related to the feature extraction method and the choice of parameters are depicted in Figure 8. The fitting durations only include the fitting of the algorithms and not the transformation of the recorded data into the features.

All clustering algorithms require very little time to be fitted for all feature extraction methods and all parameter choices. Among the outlier detection algorithms, the LMDD algorithm and ABOD have by far the longest fitting durations. Among the other algorithms, KPCA needs the longest time to be fitted for all feature extraction methods. It is noticeable that KPCA using the AE latent space features takes more than 100 seconds longer to be fitted than the other feature extraction methods.

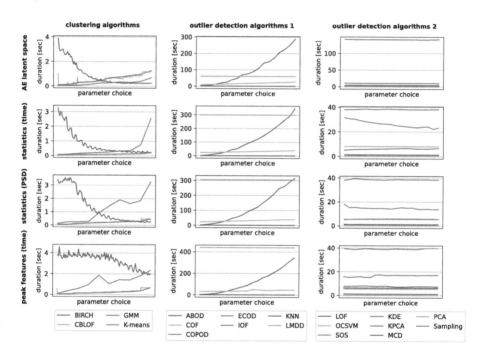

Figure 8. Fitting Durations

Figure 9 shows the duration needed by the algorithms to classify the validation data samples. The inference duration consists of both the feature extraction part and the algorithmic classification part.

The feature extraction methods are based on efficient signal processing algorithms, such as fast Fourier transforms or basic statistical calculations. Therefore, feature extraction has a small impact on the overall inference duration. The maximum allowed inference duration is 289.6 s. This criterion is fulfilled by all algorithms for all feature extraction methods and all parameter settings. All clustering algorithms perform particularly well, followed by the other algorithms and the outlier detection algorithms. For all feature extraction methods, ABOD has the worst inference duration when many nearest neighbors are used. The LMDD algorithm has the second highest inference duration.

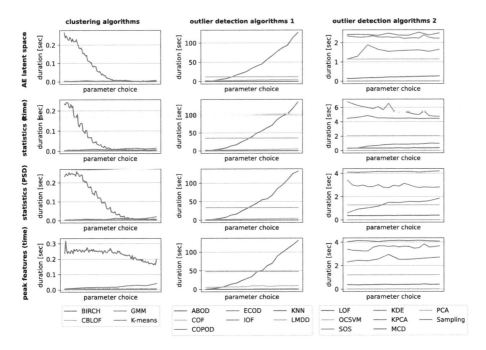

Figure 9. Fault Detection Algorithms Inference Durations

In the following, we describe the ability of the algorithms to classify disturbed data samples as disturbed and non disturbed data samples as normal. For both the fitting dataset and the validation dataset, we manually assigned a label to each data sample, either undisturbed or disturbed. The AUROC score is based on the manually assigned reference and the labels assigned by the fault detection algorithms.

5.4.1. Clustering Algorithms

The AUROC results and the condition specific accuracies of the clustering algorithms with respect to the feature extraction methods are depicted in Figure 10.

In general, features from the PSDs (statistics, and peak features) form a good basis for clustering algorithms to reliably identify disturbed laser oscillator feedback systems, since all clustering algorithms except the GMM achieve very good AUROC scores and high accuracies for all conditions. The GMM algorithm does not achieve satisfactory results for any combination of parameter setting and feature extraction method. It is noticeable that the condition specific accuracies obtained by GMM show that the GMM algorithm classifies all data samples as disturbed. From the results of the CBLOF algorithm, it can be seen that the fault detection quality is strongly dependent on the choice of input parameter. At an alpha of 0.5, the best AUROC scores of 1.0 are obtained on the fitting and validation dataset regardless of the choice of cluster number and beta for all feature extraction methods. Birch, and the K-Means algorithms achieve perfect results on the validation dataset for features from PSDs and the correct parameter choice.

The very good results of the clustering algorithms can be described with the help of the structure of the examined data. As the t-SNE embeddings of the data set already

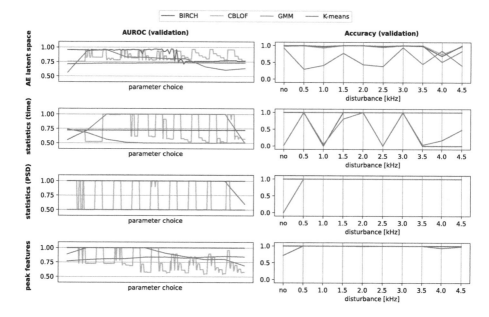

Figure 10. Results of clustering algorithms

indicate (see Figure 7), the data measured under similar conditions are positioned in cluster-like structures, especially using the PSD statistics and the peak features.

5.4.2. Outlier Detection Algorithms

The AUROC scores and the condition-dependent accuracies of the outlier detection algorithms are shown in Figure 11

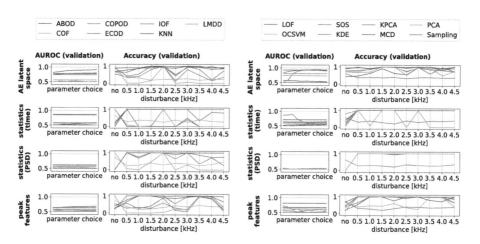

Figure 11. Results of the Outlier Detection Algorithms

In general, it can be seen that no combination of outlier detection algorithm and feature extraction method achieves a perfect AUROC score of 1.0. It is also noticeable that the choice of parameters for the outlier detection algorithms has no great influence on the result, because the maximum AUROC scores hardly differ from the minimum AUROC scores per algorithm. In contrast to the clustering algorithms, the outlier detection algorithms achieve very poor AUROC scores on the feature datasets that use PSDs as a basis. Among all outlier detection algorithms, KNN achieves the highest AUROC score of 0.9148 using the AE latent space as features. The corresponding condition specific conditions show that the data recorded under no excitation are correctly classified with an accuracy of 0.8788. The accuracies that KNN detects an excited system from the controller data are all higher than 0.9.

It is noticeable that all algorithms that were fitted with PSD statistics are predictors that classify all validation data as disturbed. This implies that the algorithms cannot generalize the error detection learned on the PSD statistics fitting dataset because not all data samples from the fitting data set are classified as disturbed. Furthermore, it can be seen that similar to the outlier detection algorithms, none of the other algorithms achieve a perfect AUROC score of 1.0 on the validation dataset.

For all feature extraction methods KPCA achieves the highest AUROC scores, with the highest value of 0.94 being achieved with the AE latent space as the feature. The number of principal components leading to the highest AUROC scores for the respective feature extraction methods differ. Therefore, there exists no correct choice of principal components such that KPCA can describe the error detection behavior for all feature datasets. The second highest AUROC score on the validation dataset is also achieved on the AE latent space by the MCD algorithm.

In addition, the AE fault detector achieves AUROC scores of 1.0 on both the fitting and validation datasets making it a perfect fault detector.

5.4.3. Fault Classification Algorithms

Figure 12 presents the classification results of the classification algorithms, each with various parameter combinations using the four different feature extraction methods. The outcomes are showcased through fitting duration, inference duration on the validation dataset, and AUROC scores on a validation dataset. It can be seen that the AE latent space, among all feature extraction methods, serves as the best input for the selected classification algorithms for achieving good AUROC scores (> 0.95).

When utilizing the sigmoid function as a kernel, the SVM exhibits the lengthiest fitting and inference durations across all feature extraction methods. However, these durations remain within the acceptable threshold of 289.6 s. Among all algorithms and feature extraction methods, SVM achieves the highest AUROC score of 0.967 when employing the radial basis function (rbf) kernel and the AE latent space as the feature extraction method.

Of all the algorithms and feature extraction methods tested, the decision tree performs the poorest, while the random forest classifier emerges as the second-best performer. Additionally, the k-nearest neighbor classifier demonstrates improved AUROC scores as the number of analyzed neighbors increases.

5.4.4. Summary

Table 8 gives an overview of the fault detection algorithms and their parameter configuration that achieve an AUROC score higher than 0.95 on the validation dataset. If an

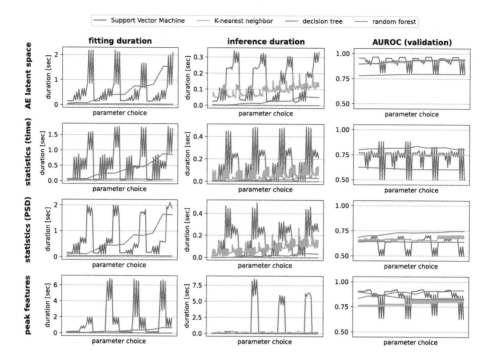

Figure 12. Results of the Fault Classification Algorithms

algorithm achieves such an AUROC score with multiple parameter combinations, we selected the parameter combination that gives the best AUROC score and the lowest inference duration.

The AE works directly on the PSDs. Therefore, no prior feature extraction is required. Among the algorithms that require prior feature extraction, only the clustering algorithms K-means clustering and CBLOF achieve very good AUROC scores on all validation datasets. Additionally, BIRCH achieves very good AUROC scores on the validation dataset using either the AE latent space, PSD statistics, or peak characteristics. Furthermore, it stands out that no algorithm which is fitted with the AE latent space achieves a perfect AUROC score. The best algorithms that do not belong to the clustering algorithms are KPCA having an AUROC score of 0.9368 and KDE with an AUROC score of 0.9436, both using the AE latent space as feature.

Table 9 shows for each feature extraction method the algorithm with the highest AUROC score on the validation dataset. The highest AUROC score is achieved by the SVM algorithm trained with the AE latent space. Statistics from PSDs do not provide a basis for reliable classification.

6. Conclusion

In this paper, we investigated the ability of data-based fault detection and fault classification algorithms in combination with four feature extraction methods to model the condition of an actively controlled phase-locked laser oscillator and determined the best methods and parameters for detecting and classifying disturbances that affect the healthy

Table 8. Best Fault Detection Results on the Validation Dataset

Feature	Algorithm	Parameter	AUROC	Inference duration in s
-	AE	-	**1.0**	0.1335
AE latent space	BIRCH	threshold: 2.4 branching factor: 80	0.9726	0.007
	K-means	# clusters: 4	0.9559	0.0014
	CBLOF	# clusters: 10 alpha: 0.5 beta: 5	0.9667	0.0018
statistics (time)	CBLOF	# clusters: 9 alpha: 0.6 beta: 1.5	**1.0**	0.002
	K-means	# clusters: 4	**1.0**	0.002
statistics (PSD)	BIRCH	threshold: 3.8 branching factor: 20	**1.0**	0.0019
	CBLOF	# clusters: 2 alpha: 0.5 beta: 1.5	**1.0**	**0.0018**
	K-means	# clusters: 5	**1.0**	0.0019
peak characteristics	BIRCH	threshold: 4.0 branching factor: 40	**1.0**	0.1606
	CBLOF	# clusters: 2 alpha: 0.7 beta: 1.5	**1.0**	**0.0018**
	K-means	# clusters: 6	**1.0**	0.0036

Table 9. Best Fault Classification Results on the Validation Dataset

Feature	Algorithm	Parameter	AUROC	Inference duration in s
AE latent space	svm	regularization parameter: 2 kernel: rbf	**0.9674**	0.2029
statistics (time)	svm	regularization parameter: 1 kernel: sigmoid	0.8811	0.2475
statistics (PSD)	RF	# estimators: 200 split criterion: entropy	0.7463	0.0362
peak characteristics	svm	regularization parameter: 1 kernel: poly	0.9246	0.0333

operation of the synchronization system. The fault detection methods were validated experimentally by disturbing the system acoustically. We evaluated the classification performance for each combination of feature extraction, machine learning algorithm, and algorithmic-specific parameters using the fitting duration, inference duration, and AUROC scores as quality measures.

From the fault detection results, we can conclude that very good prediction results can be obtained without deep system expertise. Comparing the prediction results of the different types of algorithms, we notice that clustering algorithms achieve the best results regardless of the feature extraction methods. Moreover, there is no combination of an algorithm not belonging to the clustering algorithms and a feature extraction method that achieves a perfect AUROC score on the validation dataset. Additionally, there is no combination of a fault detection algorithm and the AE latent space as a feature extractor that achieves a perfect AUROC score on the validation dataset. With an AUROC score of 1.0 and a inference duration of 0.0018 s when applied to the validation dataset, the combination of CBLOF and peak characteristics or the combination of CBLOF and statistics from PSDS achieve the best results. However, we would like to draw particular attention to the performance of the AE fault detector, as it does not require prior feature extraction and can thus be applied directly to any dynamic system controlled in a closed loop. In addition, the inference time for the validation dataset is below the maximum acceptable threshold for real-time fault detection.

The results of fault classification highlight the impressive predictive capabilities of data-driven approaches. Notably, all algorithms have their best predictive performance when using the AE latent space feature extraction, a contrast to the fault prediction outcomes. The support vector machine trained on the AE latent space representation of the PSD emerges as the most effective classification algorithm among them.

In this paper, we compared the performance of the four feature extraction methods separately from each other. It would make sense to merge these feature extraction methods and train machine learning models on a combined feature dataset. The experimental evaluation used in this work is based on the excitation of different frequencies at the same level by a surface loudspeaker. For future work, we plan to investigate what minimum interference intensity must be present for a fault detection algorithm to be effective and to extend the fault detection mechanism to a predictive maintenance module that can predict when the next faulty operating point will occur.

References

[1] Sobolev E, Zolotarev S, Giewekemeyer K, Bielecki J, Okamoto K, Reddy HKN, et al. Megahertz Single-Particle Imaging at the European XFEL. Communications Physics. 2020;3(1).
[2] Schulz S, Czwalinna M, Felber M, Fenner M, Gerth C, Kozak T, et al., editors. Few-Femtosecond Facility-Wide Synchronization of the European XFEL: JACoW Publishing, Geneva, Switzerland; 2019.
[3] Heuer M. Identification and Control of the Laser-Based Synchronization System for the European X-ray Free Electron Laser [doctoralThesis]. Technische Universität Hamburg-Harburg; 2018.
[4] Welch P. The Use of Fast Fourier Transform for the Estimation of Power Spectra: A Method Based on Time Averaging Over Short, Modified Periodograms. IEEE Transactions on Audio and Electroacoustics. 1967;15(2):70-3.
[5] Zheng H, Wang R, Yin J, Li Y, Lu H, Xu M. A New Intelligent Fault Identification Method Based on Transfer Locality Preserving Projection for Actual Diagnosis Scenario of Rotating Machinery. Mechanical Systems and Signal Processing. 2020;135:106344.
[6] Siahpour S, Li X, Lee J. Deep Learning-Based Cross-Sensor Domain Adaptation for Fault Diagnosis of Electro-Mechanical Actuators. International Journal of Dynamics and Control. 2020;8(4):1054-62.

[7]   Bagheri M, Zollanvari A, Nezhivenko S. Transformer Fault Condition Prognosis Using Vibration Signals Over Cloud Environment. IEEE Access. 2018;6:9862-74.

[8]   Gamal M, Donkol A, Shaban A, Costantino F, Di G, Patriarca R. Anomalies Detection in Smart Manufacturing Using Machine Learning and Deep Learning Algorithms. In: Proceedings of the International Conference on Industrial Engineering and Operations Management, Rome, Italy; 2021. p. 1611-22.

[9]   Lopez F, Saez M, Shao Y, Balta EC, Moyne J, Mao ZM, et al. Categorization of Anomalies in Smart Manufacturing Systems to Support the Selection of Detection Mechanisms. IEEE Robotics and Automation Letters. 2017;2(4):1885-92.

[10]   Quevedo J, Puig V, Escobet T. Model Fault Detection of Feedback Systems: How and Why to Use the Output of the PID Controller? IFAC Proceedings Volumes. 2000;33(4):319-24. IFAC Workshop on Digital Control: Past, Present and Future of PID Control, Terrassa, Spain, 5-7 April 2000.

[11]   Bauer M, Auret L, Bacci di Capaci R, Horch A, Thornhill NF. Industrial PID Control Loop Data Repository and Comparison of Fault Detection Methods. Industrial & Engineering Chemistry Research. 2019;58(26):11430-9.

[12]   Wang Q, Liu J, Wei B, Chen W, Xu S. Investigating the Construction, Training, and Verification Methods of k-Means Clustering Fault Recognition Model for Rotating Machinery. IEEE Access. 2020;8:196515-28.

[13]   Duong BP, Kim JM. Non-Mutually Exclusive Deep Neural Network Classifier for Combined Modes of Bearing Fault Diagnosis. Sensors. 2018;18(4).

[14]   Kim D, Heo TY. Anomaly Detection with Feature Extraction Based on Machine Learning Using Hydraulic System IoT Sensor Data. Sensors. 2022;22(7).

[15]   Li H, yun Xiao D. Fault Diagnosis Based on Power Spectral Density Basis Transform. Journal of Vibration and Control. 2015;21(12):2416-33.

[16]   Wang Z, Yang J, Li H, Zhen D, Xu Y, Gu F. Fault Identification of Broken Rotor Bars in Induction Motors Using an Improved Cyclic Modulation Spectral Analysis. Energies. 2019;12(17).

[17]   Sundaram S, Zeid A. Smart Prognostics and Health Management (SPHM) in Smart Manufacturing: An Interoperable Framework. Sensors. 2021;21(18).

[18]   Christ M, Braun N, Neuffer J, Kempa-Liehr AW. Time Series FeatuRe Extraction on basis of Scalable Hypothesis tests (tsfresh – A Python package). Neurocomputing. 2018;307:72-7.

[19]   Grünhagen A, Tropmann-Frick M, Eichler A, Fey G. Predictive Maintenance for the Optical Synchronization System of the European XFEL: A Systematic Literature Survey. In: BTW 2023. Bonn: Gesellschaft für Informatik e.V.; 2023. p. 1023-45.

[20]   Tschannen M, Bachem O, Lucic M. Recent Advances in Autoencoder-Based Representation Learning. arXiv preprint arXiv:181205069. 2018.

[21]   Xu R, Wunsch D. Survey of Clustering Algorithms. IEEE Transactions on Neural Networks. 2005;16(3):645-78.

[22]   Zhang T, Ramakrishnan R, Livny M. BIRCH: An Efficient Data Clustering Method for Very Large Databases. SIGMOD Rec. 1996 jun;25(2):103-14.

[23]   He Z, Xu X, Deng S. Discovering Cluster-Based Local Outliers. Pattern Recognition Letters. 2003;24(9):1641-50.

[24]   Reynolds DA. Gaussian Mixture Models. Encyclopedia of biometrics. 2009;741(659-663).

[25]   Hartigan JA, Wong MA. Algorithm AS 136: A K-Means Clustering Algorithm. Journal of the Royal Statistical Society Series C (Applied Statistics). 1979;28(1):100-8.

[26]   Singh K, Upadhyaya S. Outlier Detection: Applications and Techniques. International Journal of Computer Science Issues (IJCSI). 2012;9(1):307.

[27]   Kriegel HP, Schubert M, Zimek A. Angle-Based Outlier Detection in High-Dimensional Data. In: Proceedings of the 14th ACM SIGKDD International Conference on Knowledge Discovery and Data Mining. KDD '08. New York, NY, USA: Association for Computing Machinery; 2008. p. 444-52.

[28]   Wang Y, Li K, Gan S. A Kernel Connectivity-based Outlier Factor Algorithm for Rare Data Detection in a Baking Process. IFAC-PapersOnLine. 2018;51(18):297-302. 10th IFAC Symposium on Advanced Control of Chemical Processes ADCHEM 2018.

[29]   Li Z, Zhao Y, Botta N, Ionescu C, Hu X. COPOD: Copula-Based Outlier Detection. In: 2020 IEEE International Conference on Data Mining (ICDM); 2020. p. 1118-23.

[30]   Li Z, Zhao Y, Hu X, Botta N, Ionescu C, Chen G. ECOD: Unsupervised Outlier Detection Using Empirical Cumulative Distribution Functions. IEEE Transactions on Knowledge and Data Engineering. 2022:1-1.

[31]   Liu FT, Ting KM, Zhou ZH. Isolation-Based Anomaly Detection. ACM Trans Knowl Discov Data. 2012 mar;6(1).

[32]   Parzen E. On Estimation of a Probability Density Function and Mode. The Annals of Mathematical Statistics. 1962;33(3):1065 1076. Available from: https://doi.org/10.1214/aoms/1177704472.

[33]   Hoffmann H. Kernel PCA for Novelty Detection. Pattern Recognition. 2007;40(3):863-74.

[34]   Angiulli F, Pizzuti C. Fast Outlier Detection in High Dimensional Spaces. In: European conference on principles of data mining and knowledge discovery. Springer; 2002. p. 15-27.

[35]   Arning A, Agrawal R, Raghavan P. A Linear Method for Deviation Detection in Large Databases. In: Proceedings of the Second International Conference on Knowledge Discovery and Data Mining. KDD'96. AAAI Press; 1996. p. 164-9.

[36]   Breunig MM, Kriegel HP, Ng RT, Sander J. LOF: Identifying Density-Based Local Outliers. SIGMOD Rec. 2000 may;29(2):93-104.

[37]   Rousseeuw PJ, Driessen KV. A Fast Algorithm for the Minimum Covariance Determinant Estimator. Technometrics. 1999;41(3):212-23.

[38]   Schölkopf B, Williamson R, Smola A, Shawe-Taylor J, Platt J. Support Vector Method for Novelty Detection. In: Proceedings of the 12th International Conference on Neural Information Processing Systems. NIPS'99. Cambridge, MA, USA: MIT Press; 1999. p. 582-8.

[39]   Shyu ML, Chen SC, Sarinnapakorn K, Chang L. A Novel Anomaly Detection Scheme Based on Principal Component Classifier. Miami Univ Coral Gables Fl Dept of Electrical and Computer Engineering; 2003.

[40]   Sugiyama M, Borgwardt K. Rapid Distance-Based Outlier Detection via Sampling. Advances in neural information processing systems. 2013;26.

[41]   Janssens J, Huszár F, Postma E, van den Herik H. Stochastic Outlier Selection. Tilburg centre for Creative Computing, techreport. 2012;1:2012.

[42]   Kingsford C, Salzberg SL. What are Decision Trees? Nature biotechnology. 2008;26(9):1011-3.

[43]   Aha W, Kibler D, Albert M. Instance-Based Learning Algorithms. Machine Learning. 1991 01;6:37-66.

[44]   Breiman L. Random forests. Machine learning. 2001;45:5-32.

[45]   Platt J, et al. Probabilistic Outputs for Support Vector Machines and Comparisons to Regularized Likelihood Methods. Advances in large margin classifiers. 1999;10(3):61-74.

[46]   Zhao Y, Nasrullah Z, Li Z. PyOD: A Python Toolbox for Scalable Outlier Detection. Journal of Machine Learning Research. 2019;20(96):1-7.

[47]   Pedregosa F, Varoquaux G, Gramfort A, Michel V, Thirion B, Grisel O, et al. Scikit-learn: Machine Learning in Python. Journal of Machine Learning Research. 2011;12:2825-30.

[48]   Goldin DQ, Kanellakis PC. On Similarity Queries for Time-Series Data: Constraint Specification and Implementation. In: Montanari U, Rossi F, editors. Principles and Practice of Constraint Programming — CP '95. Berlin, Heidelberg: Springer Berlin Heidelberg; 1995. p. 137-53.

[49]   Van der Maaten L, Hinton G. Visualizing Data Using T-SNE. Journal of machine learning research. 2008;9(11).

[50]   Fawcett T. An Introduction to ROC Analysis. Pattern Recognition Letters. 2006;27(8):861-74. ROC Analysis in Pattern Recognition.

Information Modelling and Knowledge Bases XXXV
M. Tropmann-Frick et al. (Eds.)
doi:10.3233/FAIA231150

'Anywhere to Work'
A Data Model for Selecting Workplaces According to Intents and Situations

Hitoshi KUMAGAI[a,1], Naoki ISHIBASHI[a], Yasushi KIYOKI[a]

[a]Graduate School of Data Science, Musashino University

Abstract. In this paper, we proposed a new workplace data model and its calculation method. The method was designed to calculate appropriate workplace according to the intents (activities) and situations of a worker. The data model was designed as a semantic space with three knowledge bases: 'Activity-affecting', 'Place-determining', and 'Activity and Place'. Experiments were conducted to show the different results depending on activities and the contexts of the workplace and presented the feasibility of the proposed data model and calculation method.

Keywords. Workplace, Active Based Working, Hybrid work, Semantic Computing, Information modelling

1. Introduction

1.1. 'Workplace': research definition

'Workplace', where the present study focuses on. It is also called 'office'. However, recently, the term; 'workplace' is often used with winder means as a place to work. A typical person who uses the workplaces can be 'knowledge workers', Drucker [1] coined this term and defined it as 'high-level workers who apply theoretical and analytical knowledge, acquired through formal training, to develop products and services. For knowledge creation, Nonaka [2] developed the 'SECI model', and divided it into four-dimensions; each dimension was called 'Ba', which means 'place' in Japanese. Nonaka notes that knowledge creation is a spiral through the 'Ba' with some human interactions. 'Ba' does not necessarily mean physical place, although each 'Ba' can be connected to certain workplace (**Figure 1**).

The number of knowledge workers has increased, and a research firm has been estimated to have more than one billion workers [3]. Hence, 'knowledge workers' are the key players in economic society, and the preparation of the workplace becomes more important.

---

[1] Corrsponding Author: Hitoshi Kumagai, Graduate School of Musasino University, 3-3-3, Ariake, Koto-ku、Tokyo, Japan: e-mail:g2251001@stu.musashino-u.ac.jp

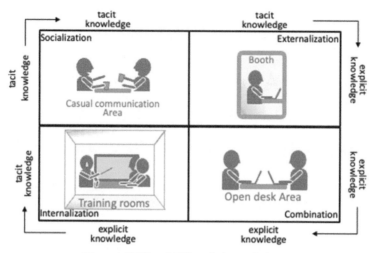

Figure 1. SECI model [2] applied to workplaces

Here we defined several terms in this study as follows;

- **Workplace**: Places where 'workers' are working, which includes conventional 'centre office', 'home office' (work from home), and the '3rd place'

- **Workers**: People who are knowledge workers, but not limited to these, which includes people whose jobs are information processing and do not have essential reason to use any physical place.

- **Centre office**: Physical workplaces (offices) of the organisations of the "workers"

- **Home office**: the home of the worker from where they can work.

- **The 3rd place**: An alternative workplace besides the centre and home offices, such as, a shared service office, café, library or anywhere to work.

- **Functional spaces**: Components of physical workplaces, such as desks (workstations), open communication spaces, meeting rooms, phone booths, or others.

- **Workplace services**: Services that are provided to the workers in workplaces, such as reception, beverages, canteens, or others.

- **Workplace settings**: Features of a workplace, which comprises a set of 'functional spaces' and 'workplace services'.

1.2. Recent workplace problems

In the three years since the emergence of COVID-19, workplace circumstances have changed drastically. The term 'hybrid work' has become common, which refers to the combination of working at the centre office and remotely, particularly from home. Although the movement for flexible working from anywhere appeared 20 years ago, as mentioned in Chapter 2, it had been adopted by only a few advanced technology companies. However, during the COVID-19 pandemic, many workers were forced to work from home, with many organisations rapidly introducing remote communication tools, and workers having to acquire remote communication literacy faster than in the last decade. However, whether workers can work from anywhere or should come to centre offices still remains controversial. The ZOOM CEO, Eric Yuan wants the employees to come to the office[4], as well as the GAFA executives have called for employees to return to the centre office over their resistance, despite the fact that their company appears to be better able to utilise IT tools for remote working. [5]. The hybrid work model, which is a compromise or mixture of working from centre office and from anyplace, seems to be the new normal for workplaces.

Workers have now become more flexible for anywhere to work, however, this means that they must select more appropriate workplace for their productivity in complex situations. Exectives, such as the ZOOM CEO, want to attract employees to comet to office. In addition, facility managers who are responsible for planning, implementing, and maintaining the workplace of an organisation, have more difficulties in planning the size, or workplace settings (**Figure 2**).

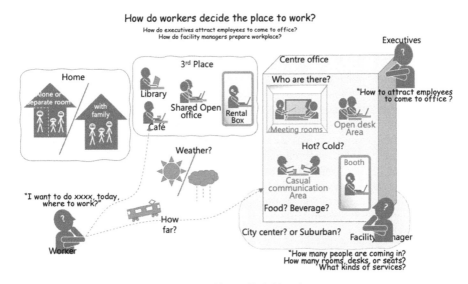

Figure 2. Problems of hybrid work.

1.3. research journey and scope of the proposal of this study

Investment in a new workplace (physical centre office) is immense. Therefore, improving workplaces using the 'trial and error' approach is difficult. The current planning of physical workplaces has been a conceptual approach; some experienced and knowledgeable designers define a concept for a new workplace with a small study of the current work situations of the organisation. Although this study could predict the volume of each functional facility in current settings, it cannot predict changes in a new setting. For example, the concept might state that 'The workers should communicate casually in open spaces rather than talk formally in a meeting room', and recommend that the client prepare some open communication spaces. However, the study, if the current setting of the client does not have such spaces, then an estimated number of workers will use such an open communication space cannot be made. In other word, explanatory variables of conventional mathematical method, such as operations research, might not be provided in current workplace planning practice. In addition, we must have challenged to treat multiple and complex contexts of the workplace to solve the problems in hybrid work situation as mentioned in previous section. Although, collecting multiple and complex data is still difficult, many sensors, including social sensors, are emerging and those will help us to collect the data in the near future.

Therefore, a data model that describes behaviours and preferred workplaces of the workers must be constructed. An indication for the future of this model is the digital twin of self-driving cars. Data collection is no longer being conducted in the real world but in digital twins where virtual drivers drive with virtual cars in virtual towns. The future objective of this research is to establish a workplace digital twin, where virtual workers work in a virtual workplace setting, which can predict the comfort and productivity of the workers.

This study is the first step of the entire journey for a workplace digital twin and proposes a data model in which a worker can find an appropriate place to work in complex situations.

2. Discussion and research

2.1. Discussions in workplace

Over the last 20 years, workplace-setting trends have been changed slightly. As knowledge workers have become the core human-capital of an economic society, some people, particularly executives of advanced technology companies, believe that the workers must be more communicable to the knowledge creation spiral reported by Nonaka et al [2]. However, knowledge workers must transform tacit knowledge into explicit knowledge. As a result, workers must concentrate to create knowledge. Therefore, knowledge workers must engage in contradictory activities, such as communication and concentration.

In 2004, a Dutch consultant Veldhoen [6] coined the term 'activity based working (ABW)'. His established company, Veldhoen + Company, notes that: 'ABW creates a space that is specifically designed to meet the physical and virtual needs of individuals and teams'. [7] The ABW concept has become popular among facility managers particularly in Northern Europe, Australia, and Japan.

The COVID-19 pandemic accelerated this movement; however, the situation has become more complicated with hybrid work. Workers and facility managers obtained more options regarding work location. Thus, several data models and calculation methods are required, which allow workers to select a workplace.

2.2. Research for data model of intent of people based on situation

Workers and workplace settings may vary, and a single type does not seem to be present in the open world. Thus, the workplace data model of should be treated as a closed-world assumption.

Research conducted by Yokoyama et al. [8] proposes an 'information-ranking method' of facilities and services based on the dynamic contexts (intent/situation) of train passenger with a semantic space model. They had presented a method that calculate the appropriate facility or service in complex situation by using semantic space model. The setting of their study was similar to that reported in this study, in which a place based on dynamic and static contexts of a person is selected. We assumed that the semantic space model could be applied to workplace data modelling. If the contexts of the workplace could be defined, we could calculate the behaviours of the workers.

3. Proposed data model and calculation method of 'Anywhere to work'

3.1. Data model aim

The aim of the data model proposed in this study is to calculate appropriate workplaces based on the context of the workplace, and the intentions and situations, of a worker using knowledge bases. In this study, as the first step, we aimed to calculate a single appropriate workplace for a worker in a set of their situations. Then we will aim to calculate the work journey of the workers in the future. Therefore, in this study, we set the workplace as the objective variable and the other parameters for the context of the workplace as the explanatory variables.

3.2. Approach

The process through which workers select their workplace must be determined. The ABW concept recommends that workers select an appropriate place depending on their 'activity', such as solo work, casual communication, or official meetings. Therefore, 'activity', one of a dynamic intent of a worker, can be the primary context of a workplace. Traditionally, in workplace planning, facility managers use their knowledge to correlate the activities of the workers and functional places. If workers had to work daily at only their centre office, this primary correlation could be sufficient. However, more complex contexts have recently emerged for hybrid work situation.

In this study, we raised contexts of workplace in 'Dynamic/Static' and 'Intention/Situation' categories, based on the study by Yokoyama et al. [8]. We then divided the contexts of workplace into 'Personal/Interpersonal' and 'Environmental (Place-oriented/General)'. This scheme made it easier to raise some context in the determination of workplaces by the workers; however, the manner in which a worker decides on a place to work in these contexts remains complicated. Finally, we found another axis: the 'Activity-affecting' and the 'Place-determining' contexts. (**Figure 3**) .

Activity-affecting contexts: Affects the productivity of the intent ('Activity') or motivation of a worker for doing an activity (intent) such as, psychological safety level, attendees (who will be) in the centre office, or indoor quality (such as temperature and humidity).

Place determining context: Affects directory the determination of a **worker** for a place, such as the weather and access (commuting) to the centre office or area of the centre office.

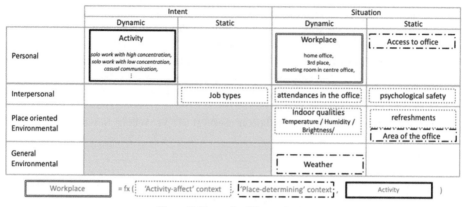

Figure 3. Example of the contexts

3.3. 'Tri-knowledge-base with personal context vectors model': Proposed data model concept

In this study, we set the possible 'Workplace' options into vector y (**Table 1 lists** all symbols of this proposed model). The proposed model calculated that the more appropriate workplace y_i will be the bigger in a set of workplace contexts. We set the possible activity options into vector x. When a worker wanted to do x_i (an activity), the value of x_i was set to '1' and all other items x_j were set to '0'. If we could define the correlation between in matrix M, we can calculate $y=Mx$.

Findings mentioned in the previous section noted 'Activity' as the primary context, as well as the 'Activity-affecting' and 'Place-determining' contexts as complementary contexts, allowing us to describe the relationship among the contexts of workplace into three correlations. Consequently, we easily defined each correlation as a knowledge base.

Primary knowledge base M_{ap}: Correlation between 'Activity and Place'

Complementary knowledge bases:

- o M_a: Correlation between 'Activity' and 'Activity-affecting' context
- o M_p: Correlation between 'Place' and 'Place-determining' context

We set the complementary contexts of workplace as vector c_a for 'Activity-affecting', and c_p for 'Place-determining' context. Subsequently, we adopted the result of the calculation: $x'=c_{ai}M_ax$ as the adjusted value of x, and in the same way, $y'=c_{pi}M_p$ adjusted the value of y. Then, we formulated:

$$y= y'M_{ap}x'= (c_{pi}M_p)M_{ap}(c_{ai}M_ax)$$

These correlations might differ depending on the worker. However, significant efforts were made to prepare knowledge base for each worker. To simplify this problem, we adopted the personal context vector v (v_{ai} for c_{ai}/v_{pi} for c_{pi}). It weighed the extent to which each complementary workplace context affected the results of choosing a place. For a worker, weighting the personal context vectors for each context of the workplace (c_a, c_p) was easier. Therefore, $c_{ai}v_{ai}$ was applied instead of c_{ai}, similarly, $c_{pi}v_{pi}$ was applied instead of c_{pi}. Consequently, we calculated the proper workplace y as follows (**Figure 4**).

$$y=\{(c_{ai}v_{ai})\, M_p\}M_{ap}\{(c_{ai}v_{ai})M_ax\}$$

Table 1. Definitions of proposed data model symbol

Symbol	Definition	Explanation	Example
y	Workplace: Objective variable (vector)	Result of the more proper workplace yi will be the bigger in a context	y_1:home office, y_2:3rd place, y_3:meeting room in centre office, $\vdots$
x	Activity: Primary explanatory variable (vector)	Activity which a worker is intent on doing	x_1:solo work with high concentration, x_2:solo work with low concentration, x_3:casual communication, $\vdots$
c_{ai}	Activity-affecting context (vector)	Affects the productivity of the intent ('activity') or motivation of worker for an 'activity'	c_{a1}: psychological safety level, c_{a2}: attendances in the centre office, c_{a3}: temperature (indoor), $\vdots$
c_{pi}	Place-determining context (vector)	Affects directory the determination of a worker for a place	c_{p1}: weather, c_{p2}: access to the centre office, $\vdots$
M_{ap}	Primary knowledge base (Matrix)	Correlation between 'Activity and Place' the larger is the more related	y_1:home office to x_1:solo work with lower concentration = 1.0, y_3:meeting room in centre office to x_3:formal communication = 0.4, $\vdots$
M_a	Complementary knowledge bases (Matrix)	Correlation between 'Activity' and 'Activity-affecting' contexts the larger is the more related	x_1:solo work with lower concentration to c_{a2}: attendances in the center office = 0.4, x_3:casual communication to c_{a1}:psychological safety level =1.0, $\vdots$
M_p	Complementary knowledge bases (Matrix)	Correlation between 'Place' and 'Place-determining' contexts the larger is the more related	y_1:home office to cp1:weather =1.0, y_3:meeting room in centre office to c_{p2}:access to the centre office =0.6, $\vdots$
V_{ai}	Context vector for Activity-affecting context	Each worker weights the "Activity affecting contexts"	v_{a1}= 0.5 then x_3 to c_{a1} is adjusted as 1.0*0.5=0.5
V_{pi}	Context vector for "Activity affecting contexts"	Each worker weighs the Activity-affecting context	v_{p1}=0 then y_1 to c_{p1} = is adjusted as 1.0*0=0

4. Prototype system implementation

4.1. Assumed applicable area

In this study, we conducted calculations using sample data to confirm that the working the model. We assumed a simple organisation in Tokyo, Japan, with simple workplace settings in the summer season.

4.2. Functional overview 3-Type / 4-module

We designed a prototype system based on Tri-knowledge-base. In practice with the assumed the contexts of workplace, two types of 'Activity-affecting' contexts were observed; one type was not dependent on any place, while the other was dependent on the centre offices. Therefore, we divided the 'Activity-affecting' contexts calculation into two. As a result, the system had four modules in three types (**Figure 5**).

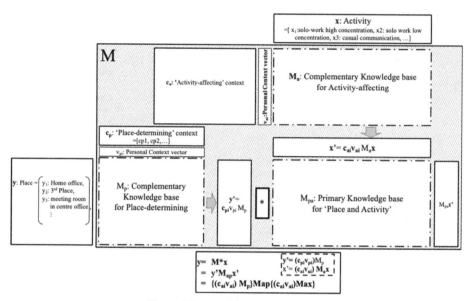

Figure 4: Proposed data model structure
'Tri-knowledge-base with personal context vectors model'

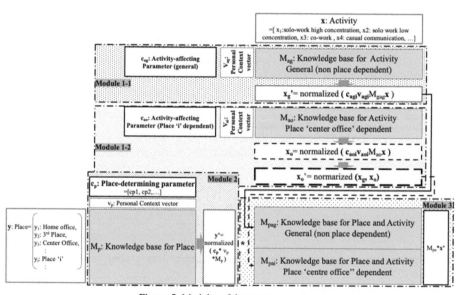

Figure 5: Modules of the prototype system

- Module 1 (1-1, 1-2) 'Activity-affecting' context calculation

    The first module calculated **x'**: 'Activity-affecting' context and divided it into two sub-modules.

    o Module 1-1: General (none place dependent)
      This module calculated 'General (none place dependent)' context. We defined the parameters of the context as c_{ag} and knowledge base as M_{ag}. The

result: x_g' was normalised and applied to the final calculation 'Activity and Place General (none place dependent)' with knowledge base M_{apg} in Module 3.

o   Module 1-2: Place dependent
    In this experiment setting, some 'Activity-affecting' contexts which depended on the place 'centre office'. We defined the parameters of the contexts as c_{ao}, and knowledge base as M_{ao}. The result: x_o was normalised in these contexts, added to x_g,' and then normalised to x_o'. The result: x_o' was applied to the calculation only for 'Activity and Place' knowledge base 'centre office' dependent M_{apg} in Module 3.
    Another intermediate calculation: x_o, might occur in other place-dependent workplace contexts.

- Module 2: 'Place-determining' context calculation

  Module 2 calculated 'Place-determining' context. We defined c_p as the context parameter, and M_p as the knowledge base. Result: y' was normalised.

- Module 3: 'Activity and Place'

  The final module calculated 'Activity and Place' with the primary knowledge base M_{ap}. In this experiment, the knowledge base was divided into 'none place dependent' (M_{apg}) and 'centre office dependent' (M_{apo}), and applied to the results of Module1 (1-1, 1-2) and Module 2.

- Personal context vectors

  We defined one personal context vector item as a parameter of the complementary context of the workplace, c_a and c_p. The context vector v_i was set by each worker, in advance, who was the system user. In addition, we set different context vectors for different options of a parameter if it could vary from person to person. For example "Indoor temperature", was set basically 22 to 28°C as the comfortable range. However, the feeling of 'Indoor temperature' might vary depending on the person. Therefore, we divided the range into three, 22-24/24-26/26-28, and applied to same correlation to the knowledge base. If a worker felt uncomfortable in the band of 22-24, the person could weigh lower on their context vector, such as 0.5 or 0. Thus, personal preferences could be included in the personal context vector.

4.3. Parameter, correlation, and normalisation range

In this experiment, all complementary contexts (c_{ai} and c_{pi}) were defined from '0' to '1'. If several options were available for a parameter, such as very good/good/neutral/bad/very bad in 'Psychological safety level', they were divided into exclusive options; only the value of selected option became '1' and rest were set to '0'.
    In addition, we set the range of correlations in the knowledge bases from zero to one. Therefore, multiple results of one parameter (the context of the workplace) and correlation (knowledge base) fell within the range of 0 to 1.

Finally, we normalised the matrix product by the average and divided the matrix product by the number of parameters. Consequently, the objective variable y_i fell within the range of 0 to 1.

5. Experiment

5.1. Experimental context parameters and knowledge bases

For the experiment, we defined the workplace options, activity options and complementary contexts of workplace parameters and personal context vectors, as shown in **Table 2**, and knowledge bases, as shown in **Figure 6-9**.

Table 2. the parameters of the experiment.

Symbol	definition	Options	Actual value	Context Vector
y	Workplace: the objective variable (vector)	y_1: home office; Live alone or separate room y_2: home office; Live with family y_3: 3rd place; Café or Library y_4: 3rd place; Shared open office y_5: 3rd place; Rental Bos y_6: Centre office; Booth y_7: Centre office; Open desk y_8: Centre office; Open communication small y_9: Centre office; Open communication small y_{10}: Centre office; Meeting room	Results can vary depends on the context	Not applied
x	Activity: primary explanatory variable (vector)	x_1: solo work; high concentration, x_2: solo work; low concentration, x_3: co-work x_4: casual communication x_5: formal communication	exclusive options	Not applied
'Activity-affecting contexts': c_a				
- General (none place dependent): C_{ag}				
c_{ag1}	Job type	c_{ag11}: Administration c_{ag12}: Coordinator c_{ag13}: Business planning c_{ag14}: R&D c_{ag15}: Sales	Percentage (total 100%)	One for all options
c_{ag2}	Psychological safety level	c_{ag21}: Very good c_{ag22}: Good c_{ag23}: Neutral c_{ag24}: Bad c_{ag25}: Very bad	exclusive options	One for all options
- Place 'centre office' dependent				
c_{ao1}	Attendances	c_{ao1}: preferable people is there	0/1	Applied one
c_{ao2}	Attendances	c_{ao2}: dislike people is not there	0/1	Applied one
c_{ao3}	Attendances	c_{ao3}: Team member(s) be there	0/1	Applied one
c_{ao4}	Indoor quality; temperature	c_{ao42}: 22-24°C c_{ao43}: 24-26°C c_{ao44}: 26-28°C	exclusive options	One for each option
c_{ao5}	Indoor quality; humidity	c_{ao52}: 35-45% c_{ao53}: 45-55% c_{ao54}: 55-65%	exclusive options	One for each option

c_{ao6}	Indoor quality; CO_2(ppm)	c_{ao6}: ppm	1-([actual ppm]-1000)/1500	Applied one
c_{ao7}	Indoor quality; Brightness on desktop	c_{ao71}: Less 300Lx c_{ao72}: 300-600Lx c_{ao73}: Over 600Lx	exclusive options	One for each option
c_{ao8}	refreshment	c_{ao8}: Drink	0/1	Applied one
c_{ao9}	refreshment	c_{ao9}: Snack	0/1	Applied one
c_{ao10}	refreshment	c_{ao10}: Meal	0/1	Applied one
'Place-determining contexts': c_p				
c_{p1}	Weather: Rain chance forecast at last 21pm	c_{p11}: 0% c_{p12}: 10-40% c_{p13}: 50% c_{14}: 60-90% c_{p15}: 100%	exclusive options	One for all options
c_{p2}	Area of the office	c_{p21}: Central 3-wards Tokyo c_{p22}: Central 5-ward c_{p23}: Dedicated Big Cities c_{24}: Others	exclusive options	One for all options
c_{p3}	Commuting time	c_{p31}: In 30-mins c_{p32}: 30 - 60 mins c_{p33}: 50% c_{p34}: 60-120 mins c_{p35}: Over 120 min	exclusive options	One for all options

	x1: solo work; high concentration,	x2: solo work; low concentration,	x3: co-work	x4: casual communication	x5: formal communication
y1: home office; Live alone or separate room	1.0	0.8	0.0	0.2	0.8
y2: home office; Live with family	0.6	0.6	0.0	0.2	0.2
y3: 3rd place; Café or Library	0.6	0.6	0.0	0.0	0.0
y4: 3rd place; Shared open office	0.4	0.6	0.4	0.2	0.6
y5: 3rd place; Rental Bos	0.6	0.4	0.0	0.0	0.4
y6: centre office; Booth	0.8	0.2	0.0	0.0	0.0
y7: centre office; Open desk	0.6	0.8	0.6	0.4	0.2
y8: centre office; Open communication small	0.4	0.6	1.0	0.8	0.2
y9: centre office; Open communication small	0.0	0.8	0.8	1.0	0.4
y10: centre office; Meeting room	0.0	0.0	0.2	0.4	1.0

Figure 6. Knowledge base; M_{ap}: 'Activity and Place'

		x1: solo work; high concentration,	x2: solo work; low concentration,	x3: co-work	x4: casual communication	x5: formal communication
Job type	c_{ag11}: Administration	0.4	0.6	0.4	0.4	0.8
	c_{ag12}: Coordinator	0.4	0.6	0.6	0.4	1.0
	c_{ag13}: Business planning	1.0	0.8	0.8	1.0	0.4
	c_{ag14}: R&D	1.0	0.8	1.0	1.0	0.4
	c_{ag15}: Sales	0.6	1.0	0.6	0.8	0.6
psychological safety level	c_{ag21}: Very good	0.4	0.6	0.8	1.0	0.6
	c_{ag22}: Good	0.4	0.6	0.6	0.8	0.6
	c_{ag23}: Neutral	0.4	0.4	0.4	0.4	0.4
	c_{ag24}: Bad	0.2	0.2	0.2	0.2	0.4
	c_{ag25}: Very bad	0.2	0.2	0.2	0.0	0.2

Figure 7. Knowledge base; M_{ag}: 'Activity-affecting' General, none place dependent

		x1: solo work; high concentration,	x2: solo work; low concentration,	x3: co-work	x4: casual communication	x5: formal communication
Attendances	c_{ao1}: preferable people is	0.4	0.8	0.8	1.0	0.6
	c_{ao2}: dislike people is not	0.0	0.6	0.4	1.0	0.2
	c_{ao3}: Team member(s) be	0.4	0.6	0.6	0.6	0.8
Indoor quality; temperature	c_{ao42}: 22-24°C	0.8	0.8	0.6	0.8	0.4
	c_{ao43}: 24-26°C	0.8	0.8	0.6	0.8	0.4
	c_{ao44}: 26-28°C	0.8	0.8	0.6	0.8	0.4
Indoor quality; humidity	c_{ao52}: 35-45%	0.8	0.8	0.6	0.8	0.4
	c_{ao53}: 45-55%	0.8	0.8	0.6	0.8	0.4
	c_{ao54}: 55-65%	0.8	0.8	0.6	0.8	0.4
Indoor quality; CO2(ppm)	1-([actual ppm] -1000)/1500	1.0	0.8	0.6	0.6	0.6
Indoor quality; Brightness on desktop	c_{ao71}: Less 300Lx	0.2	0.2	0.2	0.6	0
	c_{ao72}: 300-600Lx	0.8	0.8	0.6	0.8	0.8
	c_{ao73}: Over 600Lx	0.2	0.2	0.4	0.2	0.6
refreshment	c_{ao8}: Drink	0.6	0.8	0.6	1.0	0.2
	c_{ao9}: Snack	0.4	0.4	0.4	1.0	0.0
	c_{ao10}: Meal	0.4	0.4	0.4	0.8	0.0

Figure 8. Knowledge base; M_{ao}: 'Activity-affecting' Place, centre office dependent.

	Rain chance forecast at last 21pm					Area of the office				Commuting time			
	0%	10%-40%	50%	60-90%	100%	Central 3-wards	Central 5-ward	Dedicated Big Citis	Others	In 30-mins	30 - 60 mins	60-120 mins	Over 120 min
y_1: home office; Live alone or separate room	0.4	0.4	0.6	0.8	1.0	0.2	0.6	0.8	1.0	0.4	0.6	0.8	1.0
y_2: home office; Live with familiy	0.4	0.4	0.6	0.8	1.0	0.0	0.4	0.6	0.8	0.4	0.6	0.8	1.0
y_3: 3rd place; Café or Library	0.4	0.4	0.4	0.2	0.2	0.2	0.2	0.4	0.6	0.0	0.2	0.4	0.6
y_4: 3rd place; Shared open office	0.4	0.4	0.4	0.2	0.2	0.2	0.4	0.6	0.8	0.2	0.4	0.6	0.8
y_5: 3rd place; Rental Bos	0.4	0.4	0.4	0.2	0.2	0.2	0.4	0.6	0.8	0.2	0.4	0.6	0.8
y_6: centre office; Booth	0.5	0.5	0.5	0.3	0.0	0.8	0.5	0.3	0.0	0.8	0.6	0.2	0.0
y_7: centre office; Open desk	0.5	0.5	0.5	0.3	0.0	0.8	0.5	0.3	0.0	0.8	0.6	0.4	0.2
y_8: centre office; Open communication small	0.5	0.5	0.5	0.3	0.0	0.8	0.5	0.3	0.0	0.8	0.8	0.6	0.4
y_9: centre office; Open communication small	0.5	0.5	0.5	0.3	0.0	0.8	0.5	0.3	0.0	1.0	0.8	0.6	0.4
y_{10}: centre office; Meeting room	0.5	0.5	0.5	0.3	0.0	0.8	0.5	0.3	0.0	0.6	0.4	0.2	0.0

Figure 9. Knowledge base; M_p: 'Place-determining'

5.2. Visualization of Results

We prepared sample data that can show the features of the model. The system lists the two results in a line graph; the dashed line describes the results of the primary knowledge base for 'Activity and Place', and the solid line describes the results of the complementary contexts of the workplace. A place with a higher value is preferable to other places in the workplace.

5.3. Experiment

5.3.1. Result for different activities

First, we created three sample datasets and set activities differently but the same for all other complementary contexts of the workplace (**Figure 10**). The shapes of the results for both the primary knowledge base (dashed line) and with-contexts-of-workplace (solid line) were similar. However, some points of with-contexts-of-workplace (circles in the graphs) differed from the primary points. This indicates that the context of the workplace affects differently.

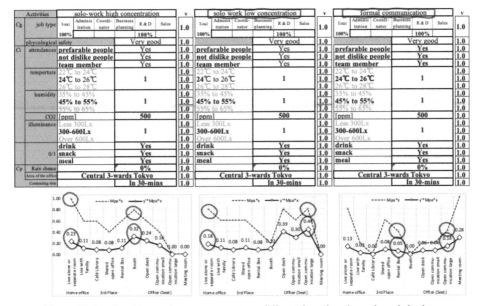

Figure 10: Results with complementary context are different from the primary knowledge base

5.3.2. Results for different complementary contexts

Second, we prepared three sample datasets and set either different 'Activity-affecting context' or different 'Place-determining context' for the same activity (**Figure 11**). Both types of workplace contexts generated different preferences.

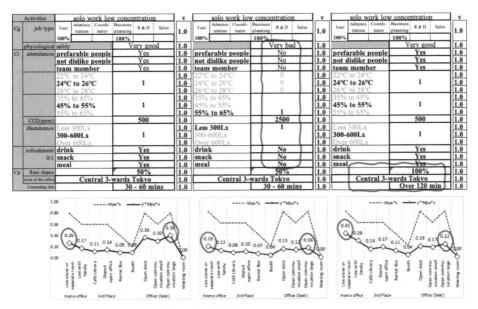

Figure 11: Results for different complementary context

5.3.3. Results for different personal context vectors

We prepared three sample datasets and set the same activity and complementary contexts for the workplace, but with different personal context vectors (see **Figure 12**). The results were not much different from each other, but slightly changed the rank of preferability (circles in the graphs).

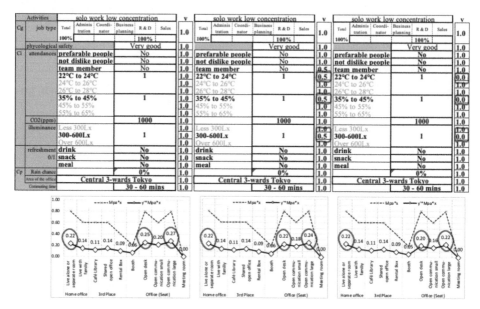

Figure 12: Results for different personal context vector

5.3.4. Results of appropriate activity per workplace

The primary aim of this prototype system was to identify appropriate workplaces for a single activity of a user in a set of the contexts of workplace. Furthermore, our prototype system can show which activity is suitable for a workplace in a set of the context of the workplace. As we mentioned in the introduction section, some executives want to attract employees to come to office, and some universities' lecturers also want the students to come to their campus. The result of this additional experiment can show the executives (lecturers) what is appropriate activity at their centre office, then they can suggest their employees (students) to come to the centre office (campus) and appropriate activities.

We prepared four different sets of contexts combined by two sets of data for both activity-affecting contexts and place-determining contexts (Figure 13-14.) In this experiment, we want to show just the characteristics mainly of centre office, therefore, we showed, first, the averages of remote work (home-office and 3rd place) and centre office. Then, show each detail workplace in centre office, and we did not to change personal context vectors to avoid complexity.

As the results, we found significantly appropriate to do "casual communication" at "open communication small" area in a set situation shown in the left chart of Figure 13. The appropriate level is much different from other places such as "Booth" even in the centre office comparing to the other situation as right chart of Figure 13. Facility managers collect significant cases for working at centre office, they can suggest it to their employees to come to office.

Even some sets of contexts seem to be better to work remotely (comparing averages between remote work and working at centre office), appropriate levels of a certain activity and a workplace in the centre office is higher than the average of remote work (Figure 14.) the fact also allows the facility manager to attract their employees to come to the centre office.

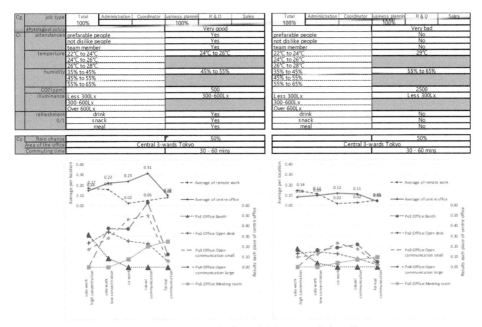

Figure 13: Results for activities per workplace (1)

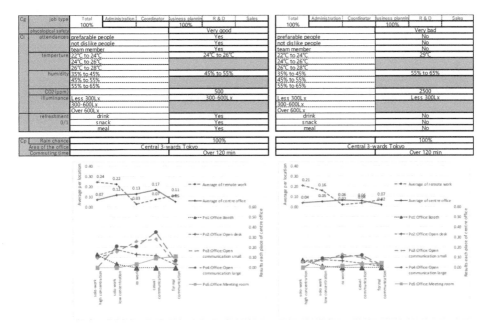

Figure 14: Results for activities per workplace (2)

6. Conclusions and further scope

Herein, we proposed a data model and calculation method with three knowledge bases and the contexts of workplace and showed the possibility of selecting appropriate workplaces. The system afforded different results with the complex contexts of workplace from the result with only 'Activity and Place' knowledge base, which has been used for traditional workplace planning. In addition, in supplementary experiment we could show the characteristics of workplaces in several sets of contexts. However, several practical issues remain unresolved.

6.1. Is there sufficient context?

Some readers of this paper may state that they have different contexts to decide the workplace. Particularly, 'activities' as the primary context, must be well modeled. In this study, we prioritized the method to calculate in complex workplace context. However, we must define the activity model for more practical situations. Furthermore, we believe that the contexts of the workplace and knowledge bases might be different from a set of organisational and workplace settings. In our prototype system, we manually set up the contexts of the workplace and knowledge base. Therefore, the system must be improved to easily establish context and knowledge bases.

6.2. Are the 'Activity-affecting' and 'Place-determining' contexts related each other?

Here, we have determined that 'Activity-affecting' and 'Place-determining' contexts are related each other. Therefore, the result: $\mathbf{x'}$ of 'Activity-affecting' context has multiplied by the results: $\mathbf{y'}$ of 'Place-determining' context as $\mathbf{y} = \mathbf{y'M_{pa}x'}$. If there is no relationship between 'Activity-affecting' and 'Place-determining', we can add $\mathbf{y'}$ to $\mathbf{M_{pa}x'}$; as $\mathbf{y} = \mathbf{y'} + \mathbf{M_{pa}x'}$. The formula means that the 'Place-determining' context will less affect, if the result; $\mathbf{x'}$ of 'Activity-affecting' context becomes larger. We aim to investigate this relationship by applying it to actual settings in the future.

6.3. How should the value be normalised?

Here, we used the average to normalise the results. Although a strategy for normalization is currently unavailable, we aim to investigate the normalization way in the next step.

6.4. How can the future prediction of the contexts of workplace be collected?

Some workplace contexts include future prediction, such as attendance of other people, indoor quality (temperature/humidity) of tomorrow. Each workplace context cannot be collected by any sensor and must be predicted using two types of method.
1) Using some other prepared information, e.g., for attendances context, due to COVID-19, some organisations adopted 'Office access control'. The organisations ask the workers to book in advance to come to office. The system can provide future attendance for a person.
2) Alternatively, the system may make inferences using knowledge bases and past data.

6.5. How should the personal information be protected?

There is an attention that personal information, such as attendant place of a person, should not be revealed to another person. In practice, complementary contexts can be hidden and only show the appropriate workplace to the users of the system. Furthermore, each user can choose not to be chased their attendant place, or not to be revealed even though they allow to be chased. Furthermore, the users can choose whether to reveal their attendance at any time or some occasion when they want to be found by their colleagues.

7. Future possibility and Next steps

7.1. Future possibility of the proposed model

The calculations were conducted manually and individually using the prototype system. If implemented as a real-time online system in an actual setting, the model can serve as a personal assistance tool for workers. This tool, which connects to schedule organising applications, can make workers more productive and comfortable in complex workplace contexts.

If the system can handle multiple data simultaneously, facility managers can use it as a simulator to plan workplace settings. A facility manager can set functional spaces and workplace services in several options, and then simulate the occupancy rate of the virtual centre office and estimate the excess or deficiency.

7.2. Next step of the research

In the next step, we plan to prepare a more practical system and apply it to an actual setting. Subsequently, we aim to evaluate the functionality of the model, contexts of the workplace, and knowledge bases.

However, the study encounters a challenge; therefore, we aim to collect more dynamic intent (activity) data and the feelings of workers. Currently, we can collect such intent data from only a few questionnaires. However, we desire to have more continuous and extensive data to improve this model. Therefore, we aim to develop service applications, such as the personal assistance mentioned in the previous section.

References

[1] Peter F. DRUCKER (1959), *Landmarks of Tomorrow*, Harper colophon books
[2] Ikujiro NONAKA, (1990). Management of Knowledge Creation. Tokyo: Nihon Keizai Shinbun-sha.
[3] Craig ROTH (2019, December 11), *2019: When We Exceeded 1 Billion Knowledge Workers, Gartner Blog Network*, https://blogs.gartner.com/craig-roth/2019/12/11/2019-exceeded-1-billion-knowledge-workers/#:~:text=At%20some%20point%20this%20year,many%20knowledge%20workers%20in%20history, Retrieved December 21st 2022
[4] Abe Asher, (2023, August 26), "Zoom CEO raises eyebrows by saying people need to go back to the office" https://www.independent.co.uk/news/world/americas/zoom-ceo-return-to-office-b2399155.html, Retrieved August 27th 2023.
[5] Jack KELLY, (2021, April 1), *Google Wants Workers To Return To The Office Ahead Of Schedule: This Looks Like A Blow To The Remote-Work Trend*, Forbes, https://www.forbes.com/sites/jackkelly/2021/04/01/google-wants-workers-to-return-to-the-office-

ahead-of-schedule-this-looks-like-a-blow-to-the-remote-work-trend/?sh=43dec3c11575,   Retrieved December 21st 2022

[6]   Erik VELDOHOEN (2004), The Art Of Working, Academic Service
[7]   Veldhoen + Company,   *Rethink   the   way   we   work   Activity   Based   Working,* https://www.veldhoencompany.com/en/activity-based-working/, Retrieved December 21st 2022
[8]   Yokoyama, M., Kiyoki, Y., & Mita, T. (2019). A Correlation Computing Method for Integrating Passengers and Services in Semantic Anticipation. Information Modelling and Knowledge bases XXX, 312, 435., IOS Press

Information Modelling and Knowledge Bases XXXV
M. Tropmann-Frick et al. (Eds.)

133

doi:10.3233/FAIA231151

An Implementation Method of *GACA*: Global Art Collection Archive

Yosuke TSUCHIYA [a,b1] and Naoki ISHIBASHI [a]

ª *Graduate school of Data Science, Musashino University*
ᵇ *IT System Group, Ishibashi Foundation*

Abstract
In this paper, an implementation method of GACA, Global Art Collection Archive, is proposed. Each museum maintains their own archives of art collections. GACA dynamically integrate those collection data of artworks in each museum archive and provide them with REST API. GACA works as a integrated data platform for various kinds of viewing environment of artworks such as virtual reality, physical exhibitions, smartphone applications and so on. It allows users not only to view artworks, but also to experience the creativity of artworks through seeing, feeling, and knowing them, inspiring a new era of creation.

Keywords. museum database, open data, multidatabase system

1. Introduction

In recent years, many museums put large efforts to establish digital archives of their art collections. Some museums such as the Metropolitan Museum of Art in New York[1], the Paris Musées[2], and the Louvre Museum[3], provide their archives on art collections as open data. These archives contain various types of information (such as information about the collections and exhibitions) in various media formats (such as text, images, video, audio, and 3D models). The archives of these museums consist of different media and different genres of artworks, and multidatabase system approach [4,5,6,7] that seems applicable to integrate such heterogeneous archives. *Artizon Cloud*[8] is a multidatabase system that integrates various archives of art collection data and enables them to use inside the museum and public areas while properly handling issues such as copyrights.

By integrating collection data, new types of art experience could be implemented in both physical and virtual spaces. Art Sensorium Project[9], as shown in Figure 1, was launched in Musashino University with focusing on two key technologies as follows: 1) a multidatabase system architecture to integrate multiple art collections, 2) virtual space design and implementation for the Data Sensorium[10]. In particular, personalized art exhibitions where artworks are selected from a museum archive and displayed based on the viewer's tastes and viewing tendencies could be implemented [11].

---

¹ Corresponding Author: Yosuke Tsuchiya, Graduate School of Musashino Unviersity, 3-3-3, Ariake, Kotoku, Tokyo, Japan: E-mail: g2251002@stu.musashino-u.ac.jp

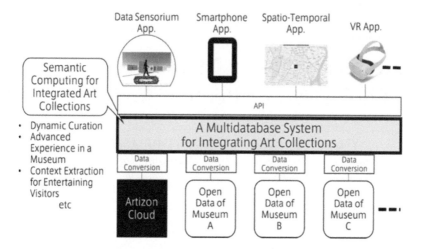

Figure 1. A System Architecture of Art Sensorium Project

The primary focus of the Art Sensorium Project is the design and implementation of a multidatabase system that integrates art collections. Therefore, in this paper, an implementation method of *GACA*, Global Art Collection Archive, is proposed. Each museum creates its own archives of art collections, then GACA integrates these archives and provides appropriate data for use in virtual reality, Data Sensorium, personal fabrication[12], and other applications. The structure of the paper is as follows: Section 2 reviews related researches and highlights the challenges that need to be addressed. Section 3 outlines the GACA architecture, designed to integrate with an arbitrary number of museum archives. Section 4 details the implementation of GACA, focusing on its integration with three specific museum archives. Section 5 presents two experiments conducted to verify the system's functionality and effectiveness.

2. Related Researches

There are several existing integrated archives of art collections, including Japan Search[13] and the Heritage Connector[14] in the UK. These archives receive government subsidies and contain art collections from museums within their respective countries. Google Arts & Culture [15] is another example of an integrated archive. It provides art collections and connects them to other web services provided by Google such as Geo Locations and Augmented Reality. These existing integrated archives of art collections have issues in terms of data heterogeneity and collection coverage.

The first issue is data heterogeneity, which can manifest in two ways: the heterogeneity of the data structure and the heterogeneity of the data notation. In terms of data structure, art collection data of each museum are typically organized according to each own rules. This results in missing data items (e.g., an item that exists in one museum but not in another) and non-uniform data types (e.g., a serial ID of a work may be an integer in one museum but a string in another).

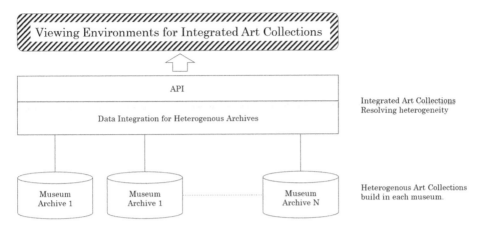

Figure 2. Idea of GACA

The other is about the heterogeneity of data notation, such as the language notation of the artist's name, unit of artwork size, and so on. For example, the same "artist name" may be listed in multiple languages in one museum, while in another museum, only listed in the local language. Additionally, the size of a work may be listed in centimeters in one museum, but in inches in another.

The second issue is collection coverage. Covering art collections from all over the world is a challenging task. To achieve this, an environment should be created where art collection data from each museum can be easily shared online. Japan Search and the Heritage Connector are federally subsidized integrated collection archives that provide collection data from museum archives via API linkage or CSV. However, their coverage is limited to data from domestic museums.

Google Arts & Culture is a cloud service provided by Google. Museums can choose to manually register their collections with Google Arts & Culture, which can then be linked to other Google services such as Google Maps and AR. However, not all museums provide all of their collection data to Google Arts & Culture (although some, such as the MET, do provide API integration). Many museums register their collections with Google Arts & Culture for public relations purposes, such as showcasing famous painters. This means that less famous, but still significant and important artworks are not accessible.

Our goal is to create a viewing environment that allows users not only to see famous artworks, but also to experience the creativity of artworks through seeing, feeling, and knowing them, inspiring a new era of creation. To achieve this, GACA is designed as a data platform that integrates various archives of art collection data maintained by each museum, making them accessible through a range of devices and applications (as shown in Figure 2). To facilitate seamless integration and use of these data within the devices and applications, GACA will be implemented as a multidatabase system that addresses the previously mentioned issues of heterogeneity and collection coverage.

3. GACA Architecture

GACA is designed as shown in Figure 3 to address the issues with existing integrated archives, such as data heterogeneity and collection coverage. Specifically, GACA

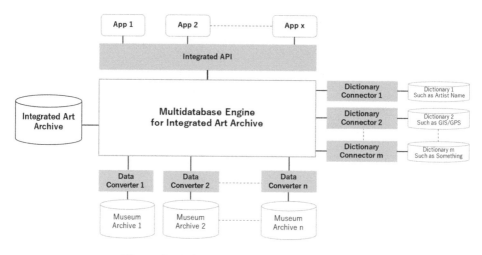

Figure 3. A System Architecture of GACA

consists of five main components, Multidatabase Engine for Integrated Art Archive, Integrated Art Archive, Data Converters, Dictionary Connectors and Integrated API.

3.1. Multidatabase Engine for Integrated Art Archive

The Multidatabase Engine for Integrated Art Archive serves as the core of GACA. It incorporates various curatorial functions of data from the Integrated Art Archive, utilizing methods such as image recognition, machine learning, spatial and temporal operations and so on. Multidatabase Engine sends requests based on those methods to the Integrated Art Archive, and receive integrated art collection data of each museum as response from the archive.

3.2. Integrated Art Archive

The Integrated Art Archive serves as a central location where art collection data from various museum archives are stored. As described below, Data Converters are used to store the art collection data of each museum with converting to a common schema. Dictionary Connector adds a unique key to those art collection data to connect it to the dictionary. The Integrated Art Archive utilizes these unique keys to provide the integrated art collection data in response to requests from the Multidatabase Engine.

3.3. Data Converters

The Data Converters convert the data schema of the art collections in each museum archive into a common data schema. Each museum builds its own archive, so each museum has a different schema for its collection data. For example, in one museum archive, artwork and artist information are maintained in separate tables, and each assigned a unique ID. In contrast, another museum archive maintains artworks and artists on the same table but does not assign a unique ID to artists. Additionally, each museum retains different types of media data. For instance, regarding multimedia data in a

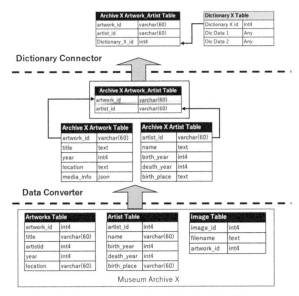

Figure 4. A Data Flow in GACA

collection, one museum may only have images, while another may also manage audio and video in addition to images.

To address this heterogeneity among museum archives, GACA converts the collection data schema of each archive into a common collection data schema and stores it in the GACA Integrated Archive, as shown in Figure 4. The Data Converters generate three tables for managing collection data: a table of artworks, a table of artists, and a table of correspondence between artworks and artists. This allows the collection data from each archive to be combined at the meta-level, providing a comprehensive overview of the collections in the GACA Integrated Archive.

3.4. Dictionary Connectors

Dictionary Connectors obtain information on references (dictionary information) and assign unique information for data retrieval in GACA. Collection data contains a variety of information. For example, artist information includes the artist's name, place of birth, date of birth, and date of death. Artwork information includes the name of the work, year of creation, place of creation, materials, techniques, and dimensions. While this information is useful for searching collections, the notation and units differ within each museum's archives. For example, names may be written in the native language of the museum, and the locations and units of measurement for dimensions of works may vary (e.g., inches or centimeters). These differences make it difficult to search and compare information across different museums' archives.

To address the issue of heterogeneity of data notation, the Dictionary Connector connects to relevant dictionary databases, including artist notations, dimensions, time, and location data. The Dictionary Connector also generates a unique key for the art collection data from the dictionary database. It assigns this unique key to the collection data of each archive, connecting to the dictionary data. This enables cross-search and information extraction within the GACA.

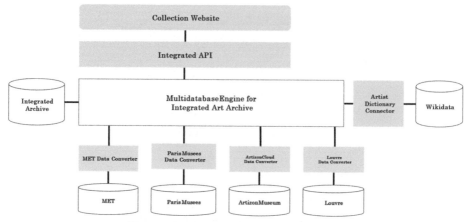

Figure 5. An Implementation of GACA

By implementing Dictionary Connector and Data Converter, GACA enables to integrate of each museum archive dynamically, without selecting and limiting the collection data. The museum archives which store huge amounts of collection data could also easily be integrated into GACA by implementing the data converter. As a result, the GACA addresses the issue of collection coverage.

3.5. Integrated API

Integrated API works as the interface between Multidatabase Engine for Integrated Art Archive and various types of application such as virtual museum, Data Sensorium and so on. Integrated API designed as RESTful API with implementing a token authentication. When the Integrated API receives a request with a search key via GET or POST, API send the search key to Multidatabase Engine and receive the matching collection data. Integrated API return the collection data to the application with formatted in a supported data format such as JSON, CSV, or XML.

4. An Implementation of GACA

A GACA prototype system was implemented as shown in Figure 5. It is connected to four museum archives: the MET Collection, the Paris Musées Collection, the Artizon Cloud, and Louvre Collection. These archives are independently implemented and some of them offer open data with REST API. In addition, GACA is connected to an artist dictionary on Wikidata[16], which includes notation of artist names in five different languages: English, French, Chinese, Korean, and Japanese. As a result, GACA has integrated approximately over one million art collections from the four archives.

4.1. MET Data Converter

As shown in Figure 4, the role of data converters is to generate three tables with a common schema. The Metropolitan Museum of Art (MET) in New York City has approximately 480,000 artworks, documents, and other materials available as open data. This data can be accessed through REST API or CSV. However, the MET's collection data is organized into a single table with both artist information and artwork information. Each artwork is given a local unique ID (Object ID), but the artists do not have IDs. On the other hand, each artist information includes a Wikidata URL, which has an Entity ID that uniquely identifies the artist information in Wikidata. To convert this data structure, the Data Converter for the MET Collection follows these steps:

1. Separate the data about the artwork and the artist from the collection CSV file.
2. Create a table of artworks using Object ID of the artworks as a key.
3. Extract Entity IDs from the Wikidata URLs of the artists.
4. Create a table of artist data using the Entity ID extracted in step 3 as a key.
5. Create a table of correspondence between the Entity ID of the artist and the Object ID of the artwork.

4.2. Paris Musées Data Converter

Paris Musées is a public organization that oversees 14 museums in the city and has made the collections of approximately 360,000 items housed in these institutions available as open data. The collection data is shared among the 14 museums and can be accessed via a JSON-formatted API. In contrast to the MET API, which is based on RESTful, a GraphQL query must be generated to retrieve the collection data from Paris Musées. Each artwork and artist in the collection has a unique ID, and the artwork is also associated with the ID of the museum that owns it. To convert this data structure, the Data Converter for Paris Musées follows these steps:

1. Submit a GraphQL query to obtain information on the 14 museums in the Paris Musées network and retrieve the data in JSON format.
2. Using the ID of each museum as a key, submit a GraphQL query to retrieve the collection data stored in each museum and obtain the data in JSON format.
3. Separate the data related to artworks and artists from the data obtained in step 2.
4. Create an artwork table using the unique ID of each artwork as the key.
5. Create an artist table using the unique ID of each artist as the key.
6. Create a table of correspondences between the unique ID of each artwork and artist.

4.3. Artizon Cloud Data Converter

The Bridgestone Museum of Art, which was founded in 1952, was reopened in 2020 as the Artizon Museum[17]. Artizon Cloud is a multidatabase system that contains various data archives related to artworks owned by the Artizon Museum. These archives include basic information of collection, evidential documents, multimedia (including images and sound), text, and event archives. Artizon Cloud controls the scope of collection offerings through three layers (Private Zone, Museum Zone, Public Zone) and rights relations. The Artizon Cloud Data Converter converts the data structure of the collection data published in the Public Zone of Artizon Cloud using the following steps:

1. Separate the data about artworks and the data about artists from the Artizon Cloud art collection.
2. Create a table of artworks using the artwork IDs as keys.
3. Create a table of artists using the artist's ID as a key.

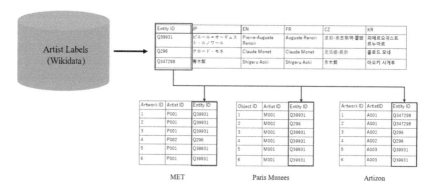

Figure 6. A Workflow of Dictionary Connector

4. Create a table of correspondences between the unique ID of each artwork and artist.

4.4. Louvre Converter

Louvre Museum is one of the largest museums in the world, and Louvre manages a large number of favored artworks. Louvre provide metadata of their artworks under the Etalab Open License[18], and they provide it with JSON format. Also, they provide the list of artworks by categories in CSV that includes their own identification numbers of each artwork. Therefore, the Louvre converter converts the data structure of the Louvre collection data using following steps:

1. Download CSV files in each category of the artworks (Painting, Sculptures, Drawing, etc), and extract the Arkid (that uniquely identified the artworks).
2. Then, download metadata in JSON format of each artwork with using Arkid.
3. Create a table of artworks using the Arkid as keys.
4. Create a table of artists using the artist's ID as a key.
5. Create a table of correspondences between the artworks and the artists.

4.5. Artist Dictionary Connector

In this prototype system, Wikidata was utilized as the reference dictionary for artist notation. Wikidata is a collaborative, open data database that is compiled and normalized by volunteers. It is freely available to the public and has gained a reputation for credibility, receiving the Open Data Publisher Award in 2014. Additionally, its open-source nature has made it a central hub for datasets from various institutions, including libraries and museums.

Figure 6 demonstrates the process of creating the artist notation dictionary data from Wikidata. The MET have already used Wikidata URLs as references for artist information in its collection data, and the MET Data Converter employs Wikidata Entity ID as the artist ID of MET. Thus, the Dictionary Connector first uses this Entity ID to obtain the notation of the relevant artist in five languages and create a basic dictionary table. It then searches the basic dictionary data table for the artist notations of Paris Musées, Artizon Cloud and Louvre Museum, querying Wikidata for any artist notations that do not match. These notations are obtained in the five languages and added to the basic dictionary table. Finally, the Dictionary Connector searches the respective Artwork-Artist tables generated by the Data Converter and assigns the corresponding artist a Wikidata Entity ID. This connects the artist information in each museum collection with the information in the notation dictionary, using the Wikidata Entity ID as the key.

4.6. Integrated Art Archive

Integrated Art Archive is implemented with a relational database management system (PostgreSQL version 12.3). As shown in Figure 3, art collection data, which is converted to a common data schema by Data Converter, are stored in artworks tables and artist tables. Also, Wikidata Entity ID of the artist's name is added to the artwork-artist table. Integrated Art Archive receives the query by SQL from Multidatabase Engine and returns the result set.

4.7. Multidatabase Engine for Integrated Art Archive

As a prototype of multidatabase engine for the Integrated Art Archive, a method to search art collections by the different languages of artist names was implemented. It works as following steps to retrieve the art collection data from Integrated Art Archive.

1. Receive all or a part of an artist's name from the Integrated API. The artist's name can be in any five languages (Japanese, English, French, Chinese, and Korean), obtained from the Dictionary Connector.
2. Search the received artist name in the Artist Dictionary to obtain the Wikidata Entity ID and notation of the artist name by five languages of the artist.
3. Submit a query to the Integrated Art Archive using the artist's Wikidata Entity ID obtained in step 2 as a key to retrieve the relevant artist's collection data. The query is submitted by SQL.
4. Receive the result set (integrated art collection data) from the Integrated Art Archive and return it to the Integrated API.

4.8. Integrated API

In this prototype, the Integrated API was implemented using Python 3.6.8 and the Flask framework for a web application. At this point, two endpoints have been implemented as follows: 1) an endpoint for artist name, which returns a set of Wikidata Entity ID and the artist's name in five languages from the Artist Dictionary, 2) an endpoint for Wikidata Entities ID, which returns a list of art collection data from the Multidatabase Engine for the Integrated Art Archive.

5. Experiments

To confirm that the system is functioning as intended, two experiments were conducted: one to test the integrated search capabilities of the collections, and the other to test the operation of the Integrated API.

Artworks of Pierre-Auguste Renoir

Name: ピエール＝オーギュスト・ルノワール,Pierre-Auguste Renoir,Auguste Renoir,皮耶-奧古
Birth; 1841 Death: 1919

API	Title	BeginYear	EndYear
LOUVRE	10 mai 1912, Les Collettes, Cagnes, à Théodore Duret	1912	
LOUVRE	(14 janvier 1882), sans lieu, à X	1882	
LOUVRE	Pièce autographe		
met	Young Girl in a Blue Dress	1890	1890
met	Two Young Girls at the Piano	1892	1892
LOUVRE	La Danse à la campagne		

(omitted)

LOUVRE	Femme assise dans un intérieur, entourée de personnages		
ATZ	Nude		
Paris	Femme debout	1906	
met	A Young Girl with Daisies	1889	1889
ATZ	Terrace at Cagnes		
LOUVRE	Feuille d'études		

Figure 7. A Result of Integrated Search by Artist name

5.1. Experiment of Integrated Collection Search

An experiment was conducted to test the integrated search functionality of the system. During the experiment, it was confirmed that the following two points were working as expected: 1) searches for artists could be performed in five languages, and 2) the results showed that the works of the corresponding artists were retrieved from all four archives and displayed in a single list. Figure 7 shows some of the results, with works from the Metropolitan Museum of Art, Paris Musées, Artizon Cloud and Louvre displayed in the same list.

5.2. Experiments of Integrated API

As a test of the Integrated API, we created a simple artwork viewer in Python that displays images of artworks corresponding to the artist's search. This application displays images of the artist's artwork according to the following procedure:

1. The user send the Entity ID of the artist in the form at the top of the application.
2. The application accesses the API based on the Entity ID entered and obtains the JSON data of the list of works.
3. The application accesses the image URL of the artwork using JSON data.
4. The application download image of artworks and displays them.

Figure 8. Artwork Viewer from Integrated API

Figure 8 shows the artworks of Auguste Renoir displayed in the simple image viewer we created. Note that the API only includes images that are in the public domain, and only the corresponding artworks are displayed on the viewer[2].

5.3. Observations and Future Issues

During the experiment, several issues became apparent. The first issue concerns the Integrated Collection Search, where some artworks—particularly those attributed to "anonymous"—could not be retrieved. Additionally, if the relevant artist's name was not available in a particular language on Wikidata, it would not appear in the search results. These problems could be resolved by integrating other dictionaries, such as those for geolocation, size units, or alternative artist databases. Further, more advanced methods for retrieving artworks, such as ontological modeling, should be explored.

The second issue relates to the application that uses the Integrated API. Given that GACA operates on a distributed system architecture, data retrieval can be unstable. This instability is exacerbated by the fact that GACA maintains URLs for images within each collection's data. These URLs must be accessed and downloaded each time. To correspond this issue, the Integrated Archive should store cached versions of artwork image files in various sizes (Small/Medium/Large).

6. Conclusion

In this paper, the system architecuture for integrating heterogeneous art archives, Global Art Collection Archive (GACA), was proposed. GACA integrates approximately over one million artworks of four archives so far, and it provides accessibility via REST API. The most significant future effort is to create a viewing environment based on

---

[2] Images are cited from Met Collection: https://www.metmuseum.org/art/the-collection, and Paris Musées Collection: https://www.parismuseescollections.paris.fr/en (2022).

GACA that allows users to experience the creativity of artworks. We envision this environment not just as a place to view artworks, but as a space where users can fully engage with and be inspired by the artworks through seeing, feeling, and knowing them. We hope that this challenging effort will open a new era of creativity and innovation.

Acknowledgment

Without collaborative research partnership between Musashino Unviersity and Ishibashi Foundation, this research would not even exist. We would like to express our utmost gratitude to Hiroshi Ishibashi, Taiji Nishijima, Kazunori Yamauchi, Takeshi Szuki, Shoji Kometani and Tomohiro Kawasaki of Ishibashi Foundation for their great cooperation and support throughout the project period.

References

[1] The Metropolitan Museum of Art: The Met Collection, available via WWW, https://www.metmuseum.org/art/collection (2022)

[2] Paris Musées: Les collections en ligne des muse´es de la Ville de Paris , available via WWW, https://www.Paris Muséescollections.paris.fr/ (2022).

[3] Muse´e du Louvre: Atlas database of exhibits, available via WWW, http://cartelen.louvre.fr/ (2021).

[4] Kitagawa, T. and Kiyoki, Y.: "The mathematical model of meaning and its application to multidatabase systems," Proc. 3rd IEEE Int. Workshop on Research Issues on Data Engineering: Interoperability in Multidatabase Systems, p.130–135 (1993).

[5] Kiyoki, Y. and Kitagawa, T.: "A metadatabase system supporting interoperability in multidatabases", Information Modeling and Knowledge Bases, Vol.5, pp.287–298 (1993).

[6] Kiyoki, Y., Kitagawa, T. and Hitomi, Y.: "A fundamental framework for realizing semantic interoperability in a multidatabase environment", Journal of Integrated Computer-Aided Engineering, Vol.2, No.1, pp.3–20 (1995).

[7] Kiyoki, Y., Hosokawa, Y. and Ishibashi, N.: "A Metadatabase System Architecture for Integrating Heterogeneous Databases with Temporal and Spatial Operations," Advanced Database Research and Development Series Vol. 10, Advances in Multimedia and Databases for the New Century, A Swiss/Japanese Perspective, pp.158–165, World Scientific Publishing (1999).

[8] Ishibashi, N.: "*Artizon Cloud:* A Multidatabase System Architecture for an Art Museum," Information Modelling and Knowledge Bases XXXIII, pp.323-331 (2022).

[9] Ishibashi, N., Fukuda, T., Tsuchiya, Y., Enzaki, Y., Iwata H.: "*Art Sensorium Project:* A System Architecture of Unified Art Collections for Virtual Art Experiences," *33rd International Conference on Information Modelling and Knowledge Bases EJC 2023.* (2023) (submitted)

[10] Iwata, H., Sasaki, S., Ishibashi, N., Sornlertlamvanich, V., Enzaki, Y., Kiyoki, Y.: "Data Sensorium: Spatial Immersive Displays for Atmospheric Sense of Place," Information Modelling and Knowledge Bases XXXIV, IOS Press, pp.247-257. (2022).

[11] Fukuda, T., and Ishibashi, N: "Virtual Art Exhibition System: An Implementation Method for Creating an Experiential Museum System in a Virtual space", Information Modelling and Knowledge Bases XXXIV, IOS Press, pp.38-47.(2022).

[12] Gershenfeld, N., Gershenfeld,A. and Cutcher-Gershenfeld, J.:"Design Reality: How to Survive and Thrive in the Third Digital Revolution", Basic Book (2017).

[13] Japan Search, available via WWW, https://jpsearch.go.jp/ (2022).

[14] Heritage Connector, available via WWW, https://www.sciencemuseumgroup.org.uk/project/heritage-connector/ (2022)

[15] Google Arts & Culture, available via WWW, https://artsandculture.google.com/ (2022).

[16] Wikidata, available via WWW, https://www.wikidata.org/ (2022).

[17] Artizon Museum, available via WWW, https://www,artizon.museum (2022).

[18] Etalab Open License, available via WWW, https://www.etalab.gouv.fr/wp-content/uploads/2018/11/open-licence.pdf

Information Modelling and Knowledge Bases XXXV
M. Tropmann-Frick et al. (Eds.)
doi:10.3233/FAIA231152

Art Sensorium Project: A System Architecture of Unified Art Collections for Virtual Art Experiences

Naoki ISHIBASHI [a,b,1], Tsukasa FUKUDA [b], Yosuke TSUCHIYA [b], Yuki ENZAKI [a] and Hiroo IWATA [a,b]

[a] *Faculty of Data Science, Musashino University*
[b] *Graduate School of Data Science, Musashino University*

Abstract.

This paper introduces *Art Sensorium Project* that is founded in Asia AI Institute of Musashino University. A main target of the project is to design and implement a system architecture of unified art collections for virtual art experiences. To provide art experiences, a projection-based VR system, called Data Sensorium, is used to stage art materials in a form of real-sized virtual reality. Furthermore, a system architecture of a multidatabase system for heterogeneous art collection archives is presented, so a set of integrated art data is applied to Data Sensorium for newly generated art experiences.

Keywords. museum systems, multidatabase systems, multimedia databases, immersive image, projection-based VR

1. Introduction

A term virtual museum has been widely discussed for a long time. A definition of virtual museums is as follows: "a collection of digitally recorded images, sound files, text documents and other data of historical, scientific, or cultural interest that are accessed through electronic media[1]." It could include various digital archives, databases, applications, digital gadgets and so on, so applying digital technologies to the area of art seems matching to the definition. To design and to implement virtual museums, there are many technologies expected to apply. In [2], seven technologies are mentioned useful to implement virtual museums as follows: 1) High Resolution Images, 2) Web3D, 3) Virtual Reality, 4) Augmented Reality, 5) Mixed Reality, 6) Haptics, 7) Handheld Devices.

In recent years, many museums have worked to construct digital archives of their art collections such as Louvre Museum[3]. In addition, some museums have published their digital data archives as open data[4,5]. These open data are provided through Web API, so many kinds of digital innovation are expected to come in the area of art. As a commercial activity, Google Arts & Culture[6] is an widely-used example that presents

---

[1]Corresponding Author: Naoki Ishibashi, Faculty of Data Science, Musashino University, 3-3-3, Ariake, Kotoku, Tokyo, Japan; E-mail:n-ishi@musashino-u.ac.jp.

master pieces of art museums in forms of mobile applications or virtual reality on a screen.

Governmental activities are also very active recently and globally. United Kingdom has launched a national project to establish a national collection with digital technologies, and it also targets to establish innovation using data of cultural heritages[7]. In Japan, some public services have been established such as Cultural Heritage Online[8] that integrates information of cultural heritages across many museums in Japan, and Art Platform Japan[9] that provides information of contemporary Japanese artworks.

The services like [6,8] provide accessibility to masterpieces of museums by integration, but a system framework to stage any artwork by integrating various digital archives is not proposed.

Museums, in general, provide art exhibitions designed with knowledge, experiences and inspirations of curators to provide art experiences for visitors. The actual museums provide exhibitions in common to all visitors since exhibitions are real and static. However, a virtual museum in a virtual reality environment could provide a personal exhibition with dynamic curation according to visitor's favour.

The primary purpose of the art experience in this research is to stimulate the user's intellectual curiosity, appeal to his/her emotions, and provoke an emotional response through the provision of various art data. Furthermore, the art experience includes cross-cultural exchange, such as the visualization of different subjectivities through an environment that brings people into contact with art from all over the world, and the inspiration for the creation of new art.

In this paper, we would like to introduce *Art Sensorium Project* that dynamically integrates multiple art collection archives to stage art experiences in Data Sensorium.

2. Data Sensorium

Data Sensorium is a conceptual framework of systems providing physical experience of contents stored in database[10], and Data Sensorium consists of spatial immersive display in a form of room-like display, various sensors that detect behaviour of users, and mechanical subsystems that provide haptics.

A prototype system of the Data Sensorium was implemented with four 120-inch screens and corresponding projectors, and Torus Treadmill[11] as shown in Fig.1.The Torus Treadmill is a locomotion interface that creates sense of walking.

3. Art Sensorium Project

Art Sensorium Project started to stage art experiences in Data Sensorium. The Art Experience is an essential term in this research, meaning the experience given to the user by representing art in a virtual space, and is intended to stimulate physical, emotional, and intellectual curiosity through the experience and to make art more enjoyable. When we started the project, we considered the possibility of applying Data Semsorium to the field of art in order to A) transcend inter-museum barriers, B) transcend time constraints, C) express differences in sensibility, and D) transcend spatial constraints, and Fig.2 shows early sketches of the project to study expected applications of Data Sensorium in the area of art as follows:

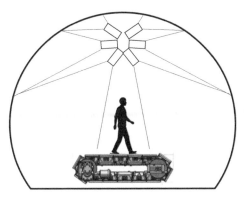

Figure 1. Data Sensorium

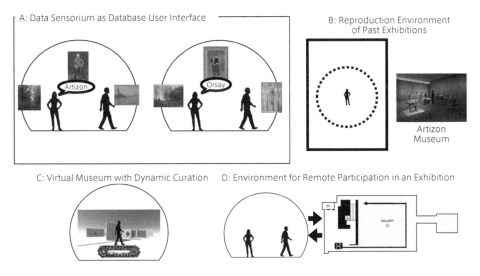

Figure 2. Early Sketches of Art Sensorium Project

A: Data Sensorium as Database User Interface

Visitors are expected to interactively search the integrated art collection to explore artworks such as searching artworks according to an artist, a museum, a motif, etc in Data Sensorium. Therefore, this application could realize inter-museum exhibitions.

B: Reproduction Environment of Past Exhibitions

As mentioned above, art exhibitions are intellectual product of curators to stage actual artworks in a specific space, however the exhibition disappears when the exhibition finishes. Virtual reality, especially Data Sensorium, could be a candidate technology to restore any exhibition in the past.

C: Virtual Museum with Dynamic Curation

Functionalities of dynamic curation are essential to automatically generate art exhibitions, and also very challenging. Knowledge base approaches such as [12,13]

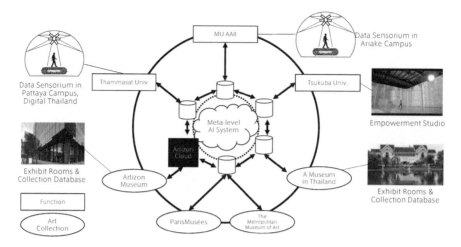

Figure 3. A Collaboration Scheme of Art Sensorium Project

or machine learning approaches are currently under discussion to realize the dynamic curation as well as detecting user's favour or emotion using variuos sensors.

D: Environment for Remote Participation in the Exhibition

Data Sensorium could be used as a remote controller for a robot with an omni-directional camera, and such combination could make it possible to remotely attend an actual art exhibition in Data Sensorium. Especially, this type of application could be suitable under circumstances like pandemic, because it makes possible to virtually and remotely participate an art exhibition with Data Sensroium.

A current collaboration scheme is shown in Fig.3. So far, a data set of Artizon Museum[14] is connected using Artizon Cloud[15], as well as the open-data of The Metropolitan Museum of Art[4] and Paris Musées[5]. Prototype systems of Data Sensorium in Musashino University as well as Thammasat University are already implemented, and Empowerment Studio of Tsukuba University is also discussed for the connection.

4. A System Architecture for Art Sensorium Project

A system architecture of Art Sensorium is composed by two essential parts. Firstly, art data of each museum are integrated in a multidatabase system as Fig.4. Secondly, Data Sensorium Applications receive the integrated data to stage virtual exhibitions.

4.1. A Multidatabase System for Art Sensorium Project

An system architecture of the multidatabase system is shown in Fig.5. There are many approaches to design and implement multidatabase systems[16,17,18,19]. However, the meta-level system approach[20,21,22,23], seems applicable for the Art Sensorium Project by following reasons:

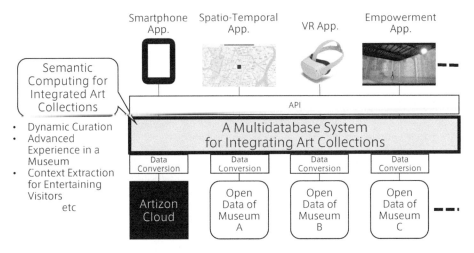

Figure 4. A System Structure of Art Sensorium Project

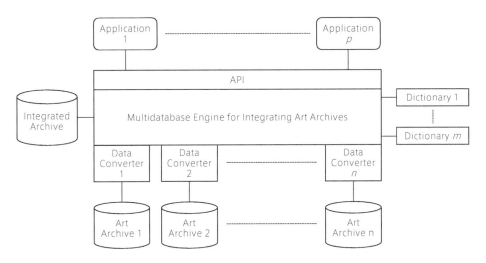

Figure 5. A Multidatabase System Architecture of Art Sensorium Project

1. Flexibility to solve heterogeneity of local database structures and their access methods is a top priority, and the simple architecture to implement the multidatabase system is very important.

2. Solving heterogeneity in data formats and languages comes as a second issue, and flexibility is again very important to solve the problem for heterogeneity among various museums.

3. Semantic computing to realize the dynamic curation will be a critical issues to come, and the meta-level system approaches are observed as a good solution[12, 13,24].

To match such requirements, local data archives are connected to the multidatabase engine through corresponding data converters. There are many reasons for heterogenuity

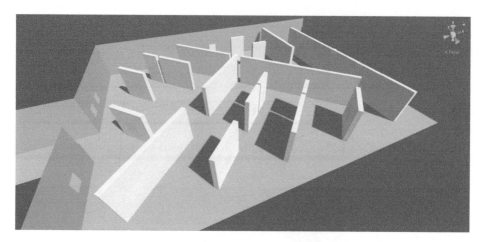

Figure 6. An Example Floor of a Data Sensorium Application

of data such as languages and local policies for text or mumerical data, formats and resolution for photographs. Especially for the heterogeneity of text data, such as artwork names of artist names, are converted using dictionaries. By applying the data converters, each data archive is stored in the integrated archive as shown in Fig.5. More details of an implementation method of the multidatabase system is described in [25].

4.2. Data Sensorium Applications

To design and implement Data Sensorium Applications, two key aspects are involved as follows:

1. Designs and implementations of gallery floors
2. Curation functions to stage artworks in 1

As Data Sensorium Applications, two prototype applications have been implemented. Dynamic generation of the gallery floor is quite challenging, so these prototype systems use static gallery floors. However, artwork data are delivered through the multidatabase engine, so artworks are dynamically staged in Data Sensorium. All these applications are implemented with Unity[26].

4.2.1. Reproduction Environment of Past Exhibitions

For a reproduction environment of a past exhibition, a floor layout of an exhibition "Inaugural Exhibition Emerging Artscape: The State of Out Collection", that was held 18/Jan./2020-31/Mar./2020 at Artizon Museum[14], was virtually reproduced as show in Fig.6.

A list of artworks corresponding to each wall is stored in the multidatabase system, and URLs of artwork images are transmitted to each wall as shown in Fig.7.

4.2.2. A Virtual Museum with Dynamic Curation

As a prototype application of a virtual museum with dynamic curation, $10m$ x $10m$ a cube shaped gallery was constructed in Unity, and 2 planes on a wall are assigned to stage each artwork as shown in Fig.8.

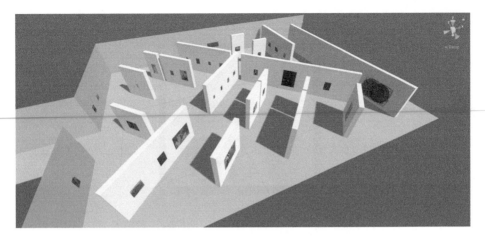

Figure 7. Representing a Past Exhibition in the Data Sensorium

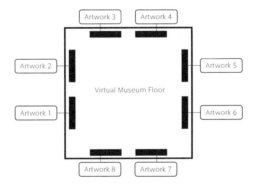

Figure 8. A Virtual Exhibition Room

The prototype system of Data Sensorium consists of the spatial immersive display and Torus Treadmill, but it does not have any other sensor. Therefore, invisible spheres have been set according to each plane for an artwork to detect if an user is close to the artwork as shown in Fig.9.

Once an user enters the virtual gallery, 8 artworks are randomly selected and staged from a set of artworks that are staged in actual Artizon Museum at the same time. Then, the user takes a look on each artwork, and the most interested artwork is extracted by using times spent in each invisible spheres. Furthermore, 8 newly selected artworks are staged relating to the previously selected the most interested artwork when the user reloads the gallery as shown in Fig.10.

Some example screenshots of the gallery is shown in Fig.11, and more details for the implementation method for creating the gallery is presented in [27].

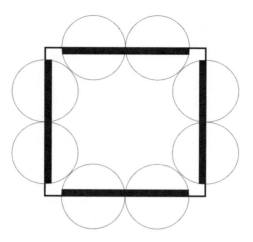

Figure 9. Invisible Spheres to Detect a Visitor

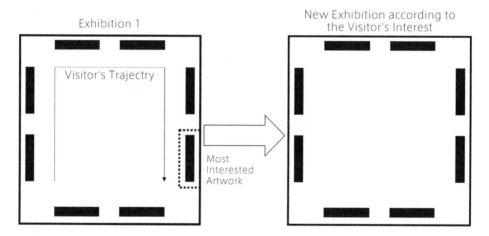

Figure 10. A Transition of Virtual Exhibition Rooms

5. Conclusion

In this paper, *Art Sensorium Project* was introduced. The main target of the project is to design and implement the system architecture of unified art collections for virtual art experiences. The system architecture of the multidatabase system that integrates various digital art archives was proposed, as well as the Data Sensorium applications were mentioned.

For the future issues, there could be many strategies for the dynamic curation. The knowledge of curators should be treated as knowledge bases for generating an exhibition, or physical/logical perspective of artworks could be computed to generate an exhibition in a form of machine learning. Sensing techniques for one's emotion or interest is also an issue. Above all, a system architecture that provides capabilities to implement such variety of strategies for dynamic curation is strongly needed in the collaboration scheme.

Figure 11. An Example of a Virtual Exhibition

Acknowledgment

This research is founded in Asia AI Institute of Musashino University, and supported by Musashino University, JSPS KAKENHI Grant Number JP22511707, Consortium for Advanced Service Implementation Industry-Government-Academia of Tokyo Metropolitan Government, and Artizon Museum. We would like to express our sincere gratitude to all organizations above.

References

[1] Britannica, The Editors of Encyclopaedia: "virtual museum", Encyclopedia Britannica, https://www.britannica.com/topic/virtual-museum. Accessed 26 January 2023.

[2] Styliani, S., Fotis, L., Kostas, K. and Petros, P.: "Virtual museums, a survey and some issues for consideration", Journal of Cultural Heritage, Vol.10, No.4, pp.520–528. (2009)

[3] Musée du Louvre: *Atlas database of exhibits*, available via WWW, http://cartelen.louvre.fr/. Accessed 26 January 2023.

[4] The Metropolitan Museum of Art: *The Met Collection*, available via WWW, https://www.metmuseum.org/art/collection. Accessed 26 January 2023.

[5] Paris Musées: *Les collections en ligne des musées de la Ville de Paris* , available via WWW, https://www.parismuseescollections.paris.fr/. Accessed 26 January 2023.

[6] Google LLC: "Google Arts & Culture", available via WWW, https://artsandculture.google.com. Accessed 26 January 2023.

[7] Arts and Humanities Ressearch Council: "Towards a National Collection", available via WWW, https://www.nationalcollection.org.uk. (2023)

[8] The Agency for Cultural Affairs: "Cultural Heritage Online", available via WWW, https://bunka.nii.ac.jp. Accessed 26 January 2023.

[9] The Bunka-cho Art Platform Japan Project: "Art Platform Japan", available via WWW, https://artplatform.go.jp. Accessed 26 January 2023.

[10] Iwata, H., Sasaki, S., Ishibashi, N., Sornlertlamvanich, V., Enzaki, Y and Kiyoki Y.: "*Data Sensorium-Spatial Immersive Displays for Atmospheric Sense of Place*", Information Modelling and Knowledge Bases XXXIV, pp.247–257. (2023)

[11] Iwata,H.: "The Torus Treadmill: Realizing Locomotion in VEs", IEEE Computer Graphics and Applications, Vol.19 No.6, pp.30-35. (1999)

[12] Kiyoki, Y., Sasaki, S., Nhung Nguyen Trang and Nguyen Thi Ngoc Diep: "Cross-cultural Multimedia Computing with Impression-based Semantic Spaces", Conceptual Modelling and Its Theoretical Foundations, Lecture Notes in Computer Science, Springer, pp.316-328. (2012)

[13] Itabashi, Y., Sasaki, S. and Kiyoki, Y.: "An explorative cultural-image analyzer for detection, visualization, and comparison of historical-color trends", Information Modeling and Knowledge Bases XXVI, IOS Press, pp.152–171. (2014)

[14] Artizon Museum: *Artizon Museum,* available via WWW, `https://www.artizon.museum/en/`. Accessed 26 January 2023.

[15] Ishibashi, N.: "*Artizon Cloud*: A Multidatabase System Architecture for an Art Museum", Information Modelling and Knowledge Bases XXXIII, IOS Press, pp.323–331. (2022)

[16] Batini, C., Lenzerini, M. and Navathe, S.B.: "A comparative analysis of methodologies for database schema integration", ACM Computing Surveys, Vol.18, No.4, pp.324–364 (1986).

[17] Litwin, W., Mark, L. and Roussopoulos, N.: "Interoperability of Multiple Autonomous Databases", ACM Comp. Surveys, Vol.22, No.3, pp.267-293 (1990).

[18] Sheth, A.P. and Larson, J.A.: "Federated database systems for managing distributed, heterogeneous, and autonomous databases," ACM Computing Surveys, Vol.22, No.3, Special issue on heterogeneous databases, pp.183–236 (1990).

[19] Zhang, J.: "Classifying approaches to semantic heterogeneity in multidatabase systems," Proceedings of the 1992 conference of the Centre for Advanced Studies on Collaborative research - Volume 2, pp.153–173 (1992).

[20] Kitagawa, T. and Kiyoki, Y.: "The mathematical model of meaning and its application to multidatabase systems," *Proc. 3rd IEEE Int. Workshop on Research Issues on Data Engineering: Interoperability in Multidatabase Systems*, p.130–135 (1993).

[21] Kiyoki, Y. and Kitagawa, T.: "A metadatabase system supporting interoperability in multidatabases", Information Modeling and Knowledge Bases, Vol.5, pp.287–298 (1993).

[22] Kiyoki, Y., Kitagawa, T. and Hitomi, Y.: "A fundamental framework for realizing semantic interoperability in a multidatabase environment", Journal of Integrated Computer-Aided Engineering, Vol.2, No.1, pp.3–20 (1995).

[23] Kiyoki, Y., Hosokawa, Y. and Ishibashi, N.: "A Metadatabase System Architecture for Integrating Heterogeneous Databases with Temporal and Spatial Operations," Advanced Database Research and Development Series Vol. 10, Advances in Multimedia and Databases for the New Century, A Swiss/Japanese Perspective, pp.158–165, World Scientific Publishing (1999).

[24] Sasaki, S., Takahashi, Y. and Kiyoki, Y.: "The 4D World Map System with Semantic and Spatiotemporal Analyzers, " Information Modelling and Knowledge Bases, Vol.XXI, IOS Press, pp.1–18, 2010.

[25] Tsuchiya, Y. and Ishibashi, N.: "An Implementation Method of *GACA*: Global Art Collection Archive", *33rd International Conference on Information Modelling and Knowledge Bases EJC2023.* (2023) (submitted)

[26] Unity: available via WWW, `https://unity.com/`. Accessed 26 January 2023.

[27] Fukuda, T. and Ishibashi N.: "*Virtual Art Exhibition System*: An Implementation Method for Creating an Experiential Museum System in a Virtual space", Information Modelling and Knowledge Bases XXXIV,pp.38–47. (2023)

Information Modelling and Knowledge Bases XXXV
M. Tropmann-Frick et al. (Eds.)
doi:10.3233/FAIA231153

A Cross-Cultural Analysis of COVID-19 Coverage in American, German and Japanese Daily Newspapers: Actors, Topics, and Values

Yukiko SATO [a,1] and Stefan BRÜCKNER [b,2]

[a] *Sophia University, Faculty of Foreign Studies*
[b] *Toyo University, Faculty of Business Administration*

Abstract. Throughout the COVID-19 pandemic, the news media played a crucial role in disseminating information to the public and influencing public opinion, such as governmental responses to the outbreak. The way the pandemic and pandemic-related news were handled varied across different countries and regions. This study analyzes a random selection of newspaper articles from three different sources: the German Bild, the Japanese Yomiuri Shimbun, and the American USA Today. The aim is to shed light on how these newspapers reported on COVID-19 during its initial stages, from January to March 2020. The study presents initial findings from comparing the coverage of these three newspapers with respect to (1) mentioned actors, (2) depicted regions, and (3) mentioned themes. In addition, we compare the results of our analysis with cultural values and discuss how the cultural context influences the coverage. Japan's Yomiuri Shimbun places more emphasis on the government's response to the pandemic, while Germany's Bild and America's USA Today focus more on how the pandemic has affected the lives of citizens and the individual measures taken to deal with the virus. The results show the contrast between the cultural values of individualism and uncertainty in the media coverage of the pandemic.

Keywords. COVID-19 and news media, cross-cultural analysis, computer assisted text analysis, cultural values.

1. Introduction

The global trend shows a decline in new cases and deaths of COVID-19, with the virus now being considered endemic in many countries [1]. However, as of August 2023, the National Institute of Infections Disease of Japan reported a rise in new cases since April and that the numbers could rise due to the weakening immunity [2]. Despite Japan downgrading COVID-19's status to be on par with influenza and measles in May 2023 [3], the increasing numbers indicate that COVID-19 still poses various challenges to

---

[1] Yukiko Sato, Sophia University, Faculty of Foreign Studies, 7-1 Kioi-cho, Chiyoda-ku, Tokyo, 102-8554 Japan; E-mail: yukisato@sophia.ac.jp.

[2] Stefan Brückner, Toyo University, Faculty of Business Administration, 5-28-20 Hakusan Bunkyo-ku, Tokyo, 112-8606 Japan; E-mail: brueckner@toyo.jp.

society. This has resulted in uncertainty within Japan, leading to instances of discrimination against foreigners and the continuation of antivirus measures, such as wearing face masks [4].

Following the WHO's official designation of COVID-19 as a global pandemic in 2020, many countries, including Japan, implemented non-pharmaceutical interventions (NPIs) to control or prevent the spread of the virus [5]. On May 18th, the WHO designated Public Health and Social Measures (PHSM) such as mask-wearing, restrictions on social gatherings, closure of schools and businesses, limitations on domestic and international travel, as well as testing and quarantine, as a global guideline for NPIs [6]. Simultaneously, governments worldwide introduced policies to combat the virus, while individuals adapted to these new rules and guidelines, or autonomously adopted new behaviors meant to safeguard themselves and their communities. The current situation in Japan highlights the ongoing challenges in finding solutions for a society prone to COVID-19, as well as calming citizens' anxieties.

Countries and their citizens responded to the virus's spread with varying measures, influenced by differences in political and economic systems, legal frameworks, and cultural norms [7]. For instance, in countries like South Korea and Japan, the use of face masks in public, a pre-existing practice, faced little resistance. In contrast, many Western nations witnessed protests against mask mandates, leading to a decline in mask usage once guidelines were relaxed [8]. Travel restrictions also exhibited significant disparities, with some countries keeping borders open and others imposing diverse forms of quarantine, testing, vaccination, or complete bans on international travel [9].

During the initial phase of the pandemic, news media played a crucial role in disseminating information about COVID-19 and government measures, while also shaping the national and international discourse on pandemic response [10]. Media coverage not only influenced public understanding but also had an impact on the decision-making processes of politicians, corporations, and scientists [11]. Given the proliferation of diverse media outlets and the rapid spread of false or misleading information, referred to by the WHO as an "infodemic"[12], people (re)turned to traditional news sources like television and newspapers for reliable information[13]. To comprehend the varying responses to COVID-19 across countries, and to contrast different methods of disseminating information during crises like the current pandemic, it is essential to analyze how the media portrayed the pandemic and related measures, recognizing the disparities between countries and media outlets.

Previous comparative studies on the media coverage of COVID-19 tend to focus either on quantitative (monolingual) comparisons [10, 14, 15] or have narrow thematic scopes [16-18] often neglecting changes in coverage over time. In contrast, this study examines how COVID-19 was portrayed in the most widely circulated national newspapers in Germany, Japan, and the United States of America (see Figure 1) in their respective original languages. We analyze the period from January to March 2020 to elucidate differences in newspaper coverage both within each selected newspaper and over time.

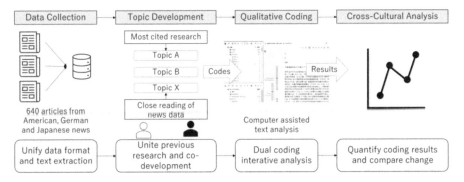

Figure 1. Overview of research

In our study, we first concentrated on the highest-circulated newspapers in Germany, Japan, and the USA. We gathered a random sample of newspaper articles (n=600) containing the term COVID-19 or its synonyms from Bild (Germany), Yomiuri Shimbun (Japan), and USA Today (USA) for January, February, and March 2020. By combining categories derived from prior studies and conducting thorough examinations of the collected data, we established 45 categories to discern (1) who, (2) where, and (3) what is mentioned in the news articles, and how this evolves from January to March 2020. Through a comparative analysis of mentioned or cited actors, observed locations, and discussed subjects in the newspaper articles, we gain insight into the distinct national discourses surrounding the pandemic, its portrayal in the media, and the dissemination of information and opinions from various sources. This offers valuable perspectives on how disparities in media coverage reflect (or influence) diverse responses to the pandemic and contributes to discussions on the effective communication of public health and policy-related information. Additionally, we juxtapose our analysis results with previously examined cultural values and consider how the unique cultural contexts of Germany, Japan, and the USA influence the reporting in news media during the pandemic. This paper serves as an initial step in a broader project towards a comparative analysis of discourses and cultural difference in global crises.

2. Background

As of January 2023, there are more than 5 million research articles on COVID-19 indexed on Google Scholar, with more than 2 million also including the term "news". While unsurprisingly, Kousha and Thelwall [19] identify clinical and medical studies on COVID-19 as the most cited research items in the beginning of the pandemic, COVID-19 has provided an incentive for research in various fields.

Researchers' focusing on media content in specific countries have investigated how news related to the virus are framed in different types of media [14, 20-23], what kind of health, medical, and political information the media covered [24-27], the sentiment of the news [15], as well as a quantitative analysis of online news coverage through text mining, topic analysis, and sentiment analyses [10]. Others analyzed the coverage of COVID-19 in relation to specific themes, such as "tourism", "digital contact tracing", "residential care" or "older people" [16-18, 28]. Analyzed languages and regions include English (USA, UK, Canada, New Zealand, Australia), Chinese, German (Germany,

Austria, Switzerland), Korean and Spanish. Most studies focus on one or two regions/languages, while broader comparative studies either are limited to English material or focus on a narrow topic, such as the portrayal of German chancellor Angela Merkel, and former and current Presidents of the United States Donald Trump and Joe Biden [10, 20]. Through these approaches key themes to examine the coverage on COVID-19 have become evident.

For example, Hubner [23] categorized 10 news source categories by recording individuals and their organizations, along with 27 news topics, each supported by 5 to 6 keywords, in American news media. Gozzi et al. [29] compared the differences in multiple topics on Reddit and traditional media. Ophir et al. [22] presented 12 topic labels along with top 10 key words by investigating COIVD-19 in Italian media. Mach et al. [27] conducted a cross-cultural study of news on public health and policy information by comparing 5 major topics in American, British and Canadian news media. However, while the development of labels to understand the news coverage on COVID-19 is a necessary endeavor to clarify what is reported in the news and how, these categories are usually not connected or utilized for further, in particular cross-regional comparative research. As such, this paper reports on a comparative content analysis to clarify how topics in the COVID-19 related news coverage vary in different regions, by investigating news articles in national daily national newspapers, from Germany, Japan, and the USA in their original language. In a previous report [30], Sato shows that the threat of the virus was downplayed in the three newspapers in early January. By extending the scope of analysis until March 2022, we can examine and compare the changes in news coverage with the growing awareness of the extent of the virus' spread.

Furthermore, the relation between news coverage and cultural values was largely disregarded in previous research. However, differing cultural values can precipitate differing perspectives on events, differing reactions, and solutions, as well as differing modalities of reporting. To begin addressing this gap in research, we aim to explore how previously established dimensions of cultural values at a national level can be applied and elucidated within the findings of our analysis. We draw upon Hofstede's widely used six cultural dimensions [31], which are based on an extensive analysis of 74 countries and regions. These dimensions consist of:

- Small Power Distance vs. Large Power Distance: the difference in how organizations and institutions accept and expect power distribution.
- Weak Uncertainty Avoidance vs. Strong Uncertainty Avoidance: the difference in how a society tolerates ambiguity.
- Individualism vs. Collectivism: the difference in how individuals integrate into groups.
- Masculinity vs. Femininity: the extent to which a culture supports a traditional view of masculine and feminine traits.
- Long-Term vs. Short-Term Orientation: whether a culture is rather oriented towards the future, or the past/present.
- Indulgence vs. Restraint: whether a culture endorses or disapproves of the free gratification of needs.

3. Method

We collected all newspaper articles including the term COVID-19 or a synonym published in the German Bild, the Japanese Yomiuri Shimbun, and the American USA Today between January 1 to March 31, 2020. In consideration of feasibility, we then drew a simple random sample for each newspaper and month (see Table 1) for the analysis. The three newspapers were chosen to represent each region, as, at the time of data collection in April 2022, they were the most widely circulated daily national newspapers in Germany, Japan, and the USA respectively [32-34]. Data was collected from Nexus Uni and the Yomiuri Database Service and compiled into a spreadsheet. We utilized the search query "covid OR coronavirus OR (corona AND virus)" in English and German, and "'*corona uirusu*' [in Japanese characters] OR COVID" in Japanese. Data collected includes the year, month, and day it was published, page number, section, author, title and sub-title, and finally the article's main text. We chose the period from January to March 2020 to examine how the media covered the spread of the virus from the initial outbreak in January 2020, up until the WHO declared COVID-19 a "Global Pandemic" in March 2020.

Table 1. Overview of the collected data

Newspaper		**Bild**	**Yomiuri Shimbun**	**USA Today**	
Country		Germany	Japan	USA	TOTAL
No. of articles	1/2020	11	129	13	153
	2/2020	52	801	45	898
	3/2020	247	1,778	445	2,470
	Total	310	2,708	503	3,521
Random Sample	1/2020	11	70	12	93
	2/2020	39	127	35	201
	3/2020	94	139	113	346
	Total	144	336	160	640

The articles were imported into the qualitative data analysis software MAXQDA. MAXQDA is a tool for conducting computer-assisted qualitative and mixed-method data analysis, that enables researchers to intuitively create, assign, organize, and count codes and categories representing a segment of text (see Figure 2). It also provides an environment for collaboration between researchers during the coding of data.

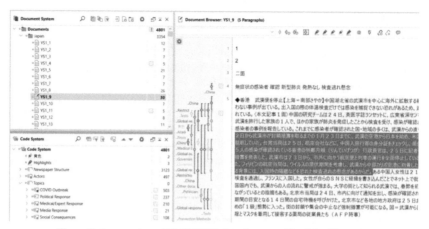

Figure 2. An overview of MAXQDA's interface we utilized for this paper.

Through a first round of close readings of the articles in the sample and based on a synthesis of previous studies [22, 23, 27, 29] we then developed a set of 45 categories to analyze (1) which actors (see Table 2) are mentioned in the articles, (2) which regions are discussed in the articles (see Table 3) and (3) what topics are mentioned (see Table 4). The authors, fluent in English, German and Japanese then assigned these categories to each news article in a second round of close readings. Discussion between the authors ensured that the same criteria were used to code all articles during the analysis, revising the code system when necessary. Similar to content analysis [35], we then counted the frequency with which each category was applied to the articles, counting each category only once per article.

Table 2. Overview of actor categories.

Actor Category	Definition
WHO	The World Health Organization and its staff
Media	Media organizations
Academica	Researchers, scholars, and experts with affiliation to academic institutions
Politicians	Politicians not directly part of the government
Government	Government, ministries, and their staff
Industry	Companies, industry organizations, their staff
NGOs	Think tanks, public interest groups, foundations
Medical Experts	Persons affiliated with medical institutions
Health Officials	Public health agencies or institutions
Sports	Sport clubs, sport-related organizations (e.g., UEFA) and their staff
Celebrities	Celebrities, e.g., actors, singers, etc., including royalty
Citizens	Ordinary citizens

Table 3. Overview of location categories.

Region Category	Definition
Response Reports	Regional responses reported in the news articles
Japan	Responses in Japan
USA	Responses in the USA
Germany	Responses in Germany
China	Responses in China
WHO	Responses by the WHO
Others	Responses in other countries

Outbreak Reports	Reports on the COVID-19 outbreaks
Japan	Outbreak in Japan
USA	Outbreak in the USA
Germany	Outbreak in Germany
China	Outbreak in China
Cruise Ship	Outbreaks on cruise ships
Others	Outbreaks in other countries

Table 4. Overview of topic categories.

Topic Category	Definition
Cases and deaths	Infection numbers and deaths, portrayal of cases
Restrictions	Travel restrictions and lockdowns
Political Response	**Responses of the government and political leaders**
Leaders' Response	Actions of political leaders directed at the person (e.g., Angela Merkel)
Governmental Response	Actions of governmental departments and staff
Financial Support	Governmental financial support plans and actions
Medical/Health	**Medical handling of COVID-19**
Preventing Spread (Official)	Political actions to prevent COVID-19
Preventing Spread (Personal)	Wearing masks, washing hands, social distancing
COVID Tests	Virus tests on COVID-19
Treatment	Treatments of patients in hospitals and patients
Research	Research on virus and vaccines
Role of the Media	**Function of the Media during the pandemic**
Explaining COVID	Providing information on symptoms, how the virus spreads, etc.
Chinese Censorship	Chinese governmental control of information
Information Accuracy	Issues on accurate information and misinformation
Social Effects	**Effects on the society**
Public Events	Cancelation or restrictions on social events
Work	Effects on working and workplace
Education	Effects on education
Olympics	Issues regarding the Tokyo Olympics
Daily Lives	Effects on daily lives of the people
Economic Effects	**Economic effects of COVID-19**
Economy	Effect on economy
Business	Effect on industry and companies
Stock Markets	Effect on financial markets

4. Results

Below, we detail the results of our analysis. Figures 3-5 depict heat maps, based on the frequency of assigned categories per newspaper and month. The heatmaps are calculated per column, that is, red indicates a high frequency of a category within that particular newspaper and month. Overall, a higher number of articles in the Japanese Yomiuri Shimbun, particularly in January and February, reflects a greater geographical proximity to the original outbreak of the virus.

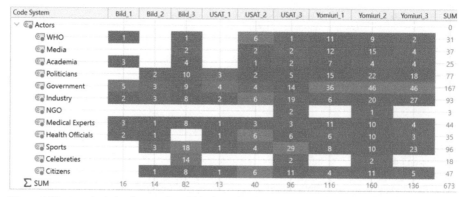

Code System	Bild_1	Bild_2	Bild_3	USAT_1	USAT_2	USAT_3	Yomiuri_1	Yomiuri_2	Yomiuri_3	SUM
⌄ Actors										0
WHO	1		1		6	1	11	9	2	31
Media			2		2	2	12	15	4	37
Academia	3		4		1	2	7	4	4	25
Politicians		2	10	3	2	5	15	22	18	77
Government	5	3	9	4	4	14	36	46	46	167
Industry	2	3	8	2	6	21	4	20	27	93
NGO							2	1		3
Medical Experts	3	1	8	1	3	3	11	10	4	44
Health Officials	2	1		1	6	6	6	10	3	35
Sports		3	18	1	4	29	8	10	23	96
Celebreties			14			2		2		18
Citizens		1	8	1	6	11	4	11	5	47
Σ SUM	16	14	82	13	40	96	116	160	136	673

Figure 3. Heatmap depicting frequencies within the categories for "actors", between the Bild, USA Today, and Yomiuri Shimbun, from January (1) to March (3).

Figure 3 depicts the frequency with which a particular actor was mentioned in the news coverage per newspaper and month. In all three newspapers, mentioning governmental institutions was most frequent in the Japanese Yomiuri Shimbun, as members of the government are often cited when reporting on the spread of the virus and possible and actual countermeasures. Politicians aside from members of the government are also frequently mentioned in the same light. While industry actors were mentioned in all three newspapers, usually in concert with depicting the economic outfall of the pandemic, this was comparatively more frequent in the USA Today, especially in March. In contrast, the categories "Sports" and "Celebrities" were most frequent in the German Bild, possibly indicating a stronger focus on human interest stories. Health officials are not mentioned frequently in the Bild, although academics are mentioned in a similar function to the mention of health officials in the other two newspapers, that is to provide expertise on the spread of the virus. In March 2020, the USA Today mentions the WHO comparatively frequently, regarding the designation of COVID-19 as a global pandemic.

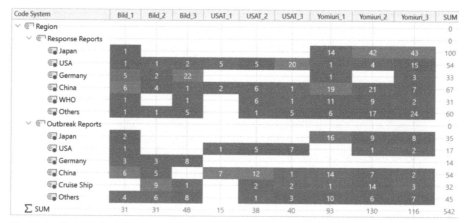

Code System	Bild_1	Bild_2	Bild_3	USAT_1	USAT_2	USAT_3	Yomiuri_1	Yomiuri_2	Yomiuri_3	SUM
⌄ Region										0
⌄ Response Reports										0
Japan	1						14	42	43	100
USA	1	1	2	5	5	20	1	4	15	54
Germany	5	2	22				1		3	33
China	6	4	1	2	6	1	19	21	7	67
WHO	1		1		6	1	11	9	2	31
Others	1	1	5		1	5	6	17	24	60
⌄ Outbreak Reports										0
Japan	2						16	9	8	35
USA	1			1	5	7		1	2	17
Germany	3	3	8							14
China	6	5		7	12	1	14	7	2	54
Cruise Ship		9	1	2	2	1		14	3	32
Others	4	6	8		1	3	10	6	7	45
Σ SUM	31	31	48	15	38	40	93	130	116	542

Figure 4. Heatmap depicting frequencies within the categories for "regions", between the Bild, USA Today, and Yomiuri Shimbun from January (1) to March (3).

The heatmap in figure 4 depicts the frequency with which a particular region was mentioned in the news coverage of each newspaper in each month. Broadly speaking, aside from reporting on the outbreak and response within the country they are based in, each newspaper also reported on the original outbreak in China and the response of the Chinese government. The USA Today in particular mentions the outbreak in China in reports on US citizens stranded there. In comparison to the Bild and USA Today, the Japanese Yomiuri Shimbun reported more frequently on how other countries responded to COVID-19, including Germany and the USA. As citizens of the respective country were involved, the Yomiuri and Bild more frequently mentioned COVID-19 outbreaks in cruise ships.

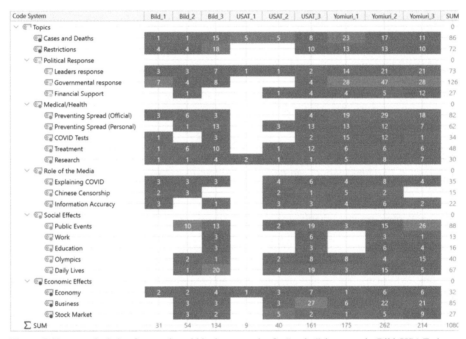

Code System	Bild_1	Bild_2	Bild_3	USAT_1	USAT_2	USAT_3	Yomiuri_1	Yomiuri_2	Yomiuri_3	SUM
∨ Topics										0
Cases and Deaths	1	1	15	5	5	8	23	17	11	86
Restrictions	4	4	18			10	13	13	10	72
∨ Political Response										0
Leaders response	3	3	7	1	1	2	14	21	21	73
Governmental response	7	4	8			4	28	47	28	126
Financial Support	1			1	4	4	5		12	27
∨ Medical/Health										0
Preventing Spread (Official)	3	6	3			4	19	29	18	82
Preventing Spread (Personal)		1	13		3	13	13	12	7	62
COVID Tests	1		3			2	15	12	1	34
Treatment	1	6	10		1	12	6	6	6	48
Research	1	1	4	2	1	1	5	8	7	30
∨ Role of the Media										0
Explaining COVID	3	3	3		4	6	4	8	4	35
Chinese Censorship	2	3			2	1	5	2		15
Information Accuracy	3		1		3	3	4	6	2	22
∨ Social Effects										0
Public Events		10	13		2	19	3	15	26	88
Work			3			6		3	1	13
Education			3			3		6	4	16
Olympics		2	1		2	8	8	4	15	40
Daily Lives		1	20		4	19	3	15	5	67
∨ Economic Effects										0
Economy	2	2	4	1	3	7	1	6	6	32
Business		3	3		3	27	6	22	21	85
Stock Market	3		2		5	2	1	5	9	27
∑ SUM	31	54	134	9	40	161	175	262	214	1080

Figure 5. Heatmap depicting frequencies within the categories for "topics", between the Bild, USA Today, and Yomiuri Shimbun from January (1) to March (3).

Figure 5 shows the code frequencies of three newspapers in the Topic category from January to March. Common topics throughout the three periods and newspapers were reports on the number of infections and deaths, as well as research on the virus and its effect on the economy. Restrictions, discussed and gradually put in place over the early stages of the pandemic, were frequently mentioned in Germany, especially in March, whereas they were not mentioned in the USA Today and comparatively less frequently in the Yomiuri Shimbun. The effects of the pandemic on work and education did not receive widespread attention until March. In comparison to the Bild, the Yomiuri and USA Today more frequently mentioned the fallout of the pandemic in respect to the overall economy, specific businesses, and the stock market. Each newspaper shows a specific tendency to focus on particular topics throughout the three months observed. The Bild frequently reported on public events and the restrictions placed on them, as well as the daily lives of citizens during the pandemic. The USA Today less frequently mentions official efforts to prevent of the virus, but in turn, more frequently reports on how to prevent a further spread or infection through personal measures such as wearing a mask or disinfection. The Yomiuri focuses more strongly the response of the Japanese government and officially introduced methods of prevention.

5. Discussion and Conclusion

This study conducted an analysis of news articles from three major newspapers: the German Bild, the Japanese Yomiuri Shimbun, and the American USA Today and compared the mentioned actors, localities, and topics. The analysis aimed to clarify the differences across newspapers and over time during the beginning of the pandemic from January to March 2020.

During this period, all three newspapers reported extensively on the COVID-19 outbreak. The Japanese Yomiuri Shimbun placed a significant emphasis on conveying the actions and measures taken by the Japanese Government. In contrast, the German Bild and the American USA Today focused more on the pandemic's impact on individual citizens' lives. Notably, the USA Today even provided advice to its readers on how to navigate the challenges posed by the pandemic.

When arguing within the framework of Hofstede's cultural dimensions, these differing levels of attention on government responses in the Yomiuri Shimbun compared to the other two newspapers can be attributed to cultural values, particularly the contrast between Individualism and Collectivism [31]. Western countries place greater value in individual self-sufficiency, whereas Japan, problems are often delegated to groups that provide protection in exchange for loyalty. Additionally, the topic analysis revealed that the Japanese Yomiuri and the German Bild reported more extensively on official responses compared to the USA Today. This discrepancy reflects the variance in cultural values related to Uncertainty Avoidance [31], with Japanese and German-speaking regions exhibiting higher levels of uncertainty avoidance, as uncertainty is viewed negatively, that is as a threat that requires the formulation of rules and a strong authority to enforce them.

Moreover, in contrast to Bild, both USA Today and Yomiuri Shimbun frequently address the pandemic's impact on businesses. In contrast, Bild leans more towards human interest stories. This discrepancy can be attributed to the different target audiences and editorial approaches of these newspapers. Bild, being a tabloid, places a stronger emphasis on the social repercussions of the pandemic, while particularly Yomiuri Shimbun caters more to a business-oriented readership.

In general, despite confirmed cases of COVID-19 in each country by March 2020, newspapers tended to focus less on the specific health risks associated with the pandemic. Instead, there was a greater emphasis on the economic and societal consequences. Additionally, even as the virus continued to spread, the frequency of articles providing the public with concrete information regarding the virus's transmission, potential symptoms, and available treatments did not noticeably change over time.

6. Limitations, Further Work and Reflections on Methodology

This paper presents initial findings from a cross-regional analysis of COVID-19 news coverage in three prominent newspapers: the German Bild, Japanese Yomiuri Shimbun, and the American USA Today. We randomly selected articles from the period of January to March 2020, which, though providing valuable insights, does impose some limitations on the depth of our analysis. Our approach affords us the opportunity to identify prominent disparities in news coverage, yet it may not fully capture the quantitative aspects of our coding analysis. Furthermore, by focusing on the most widely circulated newspaper in each country, our sample of articles may be narrower due to differences in journalistic approach, target audience, and political leaning.

The next step in our study involves expanding our analysis to encompass all articles published throughout 2020 and incorporating a broader selection of newspapers. This expansion aims to provide a comprehensive and quantitatively interpretable comparison of COVID-19 news coverage. Our initial step of using a random sample and qualitative analysis was pivotal in establishing foundational codes and thematic categories. This groundwork will serve as the basis for implementing automatic coding, wherein a set of search terms linked to codes and categories will be applied to the entire corpus. Subsequently, we will conduct a qualitative in-context analysis of these automatically coded text segments, integrating both qualitative and quantitative approaches. Unlike text mining or topic modeling, our method allows for a more theoretically grounded and interpretable examination of textual data, with applicability beyond the context of newspaper articles.

Acknowledgement

This work was supported by JSPS KAKENHI Grant Number 21K13444. I would like to thank my research project members at Keio University, Japan, as well as researchers and faculty members who shared their valuable insights and comments for this project.

References

[1] World Health Organization. WHO Coronovirus (COVID-19) Dashboard 2023 [Available from: https://covid19.who.int/.

[2] National Institute of Infectious Diseases. Shingata koronauirusu kansenshōno chokkinno kansenjōkyōtō [Recent infection status of new coronavirus infection]: National Institute of Infectious Diseases, Japan; 2023 [updated August 4 2023. Available from: https://www.niid.go.jp/niid/ja/2019-ncov/12188-covid19-ab124th.html.

[3] Ministry of Health Labour and Welfare. Response to COVID 19 (Novel Coronavirus) after the classification change: Ministry of Health, Labour and Welfare; 2023 [Available from: https://www.mhlw.go.jp/stf/covid-19/kenkou-iryousoudan_00006.html.

[4] Otake T. Rise in new COVID-19 cases in Japan shows little sign of abating: The Japan Times; 2023 [Available from: https://www.japantimes.co.jp/news/2023/07/18/national/covid-cases-rise-continues/.

[5] European Centre for Disease Prevention and Control. Non-pharmaceutical interventions against COVID-19 2021 [updated Nov. 23 2021. Available from: https://www.ecdc.europa.eu/en/covid-19/prevention-and-control/non-pharmaceutical-interventions.

[6] World Health Organization. Overview of public health and social measures in the context of COVID-19 2020 [Available from: https://apps.who.int/iris/bitstream/handle/10665/332115/WHO-2019-nCoV-PHSM_Overview-2020.1-eng.pdf.

[7] Wang D, Mao Z. A comparative study of public health and social measures of COVID-19 advocated in different countries. Health Policy. 2021;125(8):957-71.

[8] Offeddu V, Yung CF, Low MSF, Tam CC. Effectiveness of masks and respirators against respiratory infections in healthcare workers: a systematic review and meta-analysis. Clinical Infectious Diseases. 2017;65(11):1934-42.

[9] sherpa. Travel requirements map. Where's open, what's required? [Available from: https://apply.joinsherpa.com/map?affiliateId=sherpa&language=en-US.

[10] Krawczyk K, Chelkowski T, Laydon DJ, Mishra S, Xifara D, Gibert B, Flaxman S, Mellan T, Schwämmle V, Röttger R, Hadsund JT, Bhatt S. Quantifying online news media coverage of the COVID-19 pandemic: Text mining study and resource. Journal of Medical Internet research. 2021;23(7):e31544.

[11] Schwitzer G, Mudur G, Henry D, Wilson A, Goozner M, Simbra M, Sweet M, Baverstock KA. What are the roles and responsibilities of the media in disseminating health information? PLoS Med. 2005;2(7):e215.

[12] World Health Organization. Infodemic 2023 [Available from: https://www.who.int/health-topics/infodemic#tab=tab_1.

[13] Ali SH, Foreman J, Tozan Y, Capasso A, Jones AM, DiClemente RJ. Trends and predictors of COVID-19 information sources and their relationship with knowledge and beliefs related to the pandemic: nationwide cross-sectional study. JMIR Public Health and Surveillance. 2020;6(4):e21071.

[14] Xu Y, Yu J, Löffelholz M. Portraying the Pandemic: Analysis of textual-visual frames in German news coverage of COVID-19 on Twitter. Journalism Practice. 2022:1-21.

[15] de Melo T, Figueiredo CM. Comparing news articles and tweets about COVID-19 in Brazil: Sentiment analysis and topic modeling approach. JMIR Public Health and Surveillance. 2021;7(2):e24585.

[16] Amann J, Sleigh J, Vayena E. Digital contact-tracing during the Covid-19 pandemic: An analysis of newspaper coverage in Germany, Austria, and Switzerland. Plos one. 2021;16(2):e0246524.

[17] Chen H, Huang X, Li Z. A content analysis of Chinese news coverage on COVID-19 and tourism. Current Issues in Tourism. 2022;25(2):198-205.

[18] Allen LD, Ayalon L. "It's pure panic": The portrayal of residential care in American newspapers during COVID-19. The Gerontologist. 2021;61(1):86-97.

[19] Kousha K, Thelwall M. COVID-19 publications: Database coverage, citations, readers, tweets, news, Facebook walls, Reddit posts. Quantitative Science Studies. 2020;1(3):1068-91.

[20] Ogbodo JN, Onwe EC, Chukwu J, Nwasum CJ, Nwakpu ES, Nwankwo SU, Nwamini S, Elem S, Ogbaeja NI. Communicating health crisis: A content analysis of global media framing of COVID-19. Health Promotion Perspectives. 2020;10(3):257-69.

[21] Gabore SM. Western and Chinese media representation of Africa in COVID-19 news coverage. Asian Journal of Communication. 2020;30(5):299-316.

[22] Ophir Y, Walter D, Arnon D, Lokmanoglu A, Tizzoni M, Carota J, D'Antiga L, Nicastro E. The framing of COVID-19 in Italian media and its relationship with community mobility: a mixed-method approach. Journal of Health Communication. 2021;26(3):161-73.

[23] Hubner A. How did we get here? A framing and source analysis of early COVID-19 media coverage. Communication Research Reports. 2021;38(2):112-20.

[24] Su Z, McDonnell D, Wen J, Kozak M, Abbas J, Šegalo S, Li X, Ahmad J, Cheshmehzangi A, Cai Y, Yang L, Xiang Y. Mental health consequences of COVID-19 media coverage: The need for effective crisis communication practices. Globalization and Health. 2021;17:4.

[25] Basch CH, Hillyer GC, Meleo-Erwin Z, Mohlman J, Cosgrove A, Quinones N. News coverage of the COVID-19 pandemic: Missed opportunities to promote health sustaining behaviors. Infection, Disease & Health. 2020;25(3):205-9.

[26] Moon H, Lee GH. Evaluation of Korean-language COVID-19–related medical information on YouTube: cross-sectional Infodemiology study. Journal of Medical Internet research. 2020;22(8):e20775.

[27] Mach KJ, Reyes RS, Pentz B, Taylor J, Costa CA, Cruz SG, Thomas KE, Arnott JC, Donald R, Jagannathan K, Kirchhoff CJ, Rosella LC, Klenk N. News media coverage of COVID-19 public health and policy information. Humanities and Social Sciences Communications. 2021;8(1):220.

[28] Morgan T, Wiles J, Williams L, Gott M. COVID-19 and the portrayal of older people in New Zealand news media. Journal of the Royal Society of New Zealand. 2021;51(sup1):S127-S42.

[29] Gozzi N, Tizzani M, Starnini M, Ciulla F, Paolotti D, Panisson A, Perra N. Collective response to media coverage of the COVID-19 pandemic on Reddit and Wikipedia: Mixed-methods analysis. Journal of Medical Internet Research. 2020;22(10):e21597.

[30] Sato Y. Cross-cultural analysis of the American, German, and Japanese newspaper coverage on COVID-19. 2022 International Electronics Symposium (IES). 2022:595-600.

[31] Hofstede G. Dimensionalizing cultures: The Hofstede model in context. Online Readings in Psychology and Culture. 2011;2(1):8.

[32] Cision Media Research. Top 10 U.S. Daily Newspapers 2019 [Available from: https://web.archive.org/web/20190722203322/https://www.cision.com/us/2019/01/top-ten-us-daily-newspapers/.

[33] deutschland.de. Most read German newspapers deutschland.de 2020 [Available from: https://www.deutschland.de/de/topic/wissen/ueberregionale-zeitungen.

[34] The Bunka News. ABC kyōkai shimbunhakkōsha repōto 2022 nen kamihanki heikinbusū [ABC Association Newspaper Publishers Report Average circulation in the first half of 2022] 2022 [Available from: https://www.bunkanews.jp/wp-content/uploads/2022/09/a3da7b4446fd290fea90591f28e7e09a.pdf.

[35] Bengtsson M. How to plan and perform a qualitative study using content analysis. NursingPlus Open. 2016;2:8-14.

Information Modelling and Knowledge Bases XXXV
M. Tropmann-Frick et al. (Eds.)
doi:10.3233/FAIA231154

How to Incorporate Accessibility to Design Principles for IS Artefacts?

Juho-Pekka MÄKIPÄÄ[a,1] and Tero VARTIAINEN[a]

[a] *School of Technology and Innovations, Computing Sciences Department,*
University of Vaasa, Finland
ORCiD ID: Juho-Pekka Mäkipää https://orcid.org/0000-0002-2757-8609,
Tero Vartiainen https://orcid.org/0000-0003-3843-8561

Abstract. Design principles are used to specify design knowledge and describe the aim of artefact instantiation. Accessibility research aims to create artefacts that can be used by all users. However, schemes for design principles lack the tools to define accessibility explicitly. This study proposes extensions to scheme design principles for accessibility-related design science research. We draw accessibility domain-specific characteristics from the literature to include accessibility in design principles for Human-Computer Interaction (HCI) instantiations. We extended the components of design principles with the following attributes: HCI Artefact Features; Contextual factors; Computer Input Modalities; Computer Output Media; Human Sensory Perception; Human Cognition; Human Functional Operations. We devised a checklist for researchers to follow the variations in accessibility. The extensions are intended to foster researchers to incorporate accessibility in producing a more accurate formulation of design principles.

Keywords. Accessibility, Design Principles, Design Science Research

1. Introduction

Accessibility is a research topic often categorized as a sub-subject of the Human-Computer Interaction (HCI) discipline [1]. Accessibility research is interdisciplinary in nature and has domain-specific characteristics that are needed to address in research. In general, accessibility-related research is attempting to identify issues in the HCI within a wide spectrum of human abilities and aims to discover solutions to information and system quality that enables users' autonomy use of information and information technology (IT) [2]. Simply to say, in practice, accessibility aims to create artefacts that can be used by all users. Accessibility, therefore, represents the extent to which users with their variable abilities in perception, cognition, and action can interact and operate with a system without external assistance (secondary users or assistive technology) [2]. In contrast, the goal of HCI research is to attempt to build and evaluate new behavioural solutions with a focus on interactions that increase human capabilities to interact with information, technologies, and tasks [3,4]. HCI research is focusing advancing the knowledge base with descriptive knowledge by explaining human cognition, affect, and behaviour in interaction with technology. Secondly, HCI research is providing

---

[1] Corresponding Author: Juho-Pekka Mäkipää, juho-pekka.makipaa@uwasa.fi

prescriptive knowledge for IT system design and human process and interaction artefacts presented in a form of design theories and/or design entities [4].

According to Adam et al., (2021) [3:4], Design Science Research (DSR) can support three modes of HCI research: (1) 'how to construct an HCI artefact for a given problem space.' (2) 'how individuals use the artefact in its environment,' and (3) 'building and evaluating novel composite solutions that improve synergies between technologies and human behaviour'. Mäkipää et al., (2022) [2], identified four domains in IT artefact development, the factors within them, and their roles and actions that influence the realization of accessibility. The domains are (1) user, (2) management (3) developers, and (4) features of IT artefact. The factors within these domains and the relationships between the domains should all be concerned to ensure the realization of accessibility. However, accessibility research barely uses design science as a research method even though it is promising for HCI research [5].

Gregor et al., (2020) [6] derived a schema for researchers to specify a design principle for IT-based artefacts. The schema aids researchers to formulate design principles components and define who is implementer, in what context, by what mechanisms, for what purpose, for whom, and why the instantiation is intended. The components include aim, implementer, user, context, mechanism, and rational. It clarifies the general role of the actors (implementer, users, and enactors) who are involved with the use of the design principle. In psychology and cognitive science, a schema is defined as a concept that describes a pattern of thought or behaviour that organizes categories of information and the relationships among them [7]. Schema is, in psychology, an internal model of the mental structure from the real world. People organize information into schemes and schema is used to understand added information. For example, a builder of an artefact (IT developer, researcher etc.) has a schema about the user, that is, an idea of what the user is like. This schema, however, allows the builder to identify different users as the same user type (c.f. user groups which are categorized based on certain characteristics). The schema also includes activities such as how artefacts is used by users i.e., designers' assumptions. These assumptions are needed to convert to realization by observing real-world interaction behaviour of users. In accessibility research, this means that we need to focus on user abilities. However, user ability is a variable that depends on the individuals. The nature of human abilities, severity, and their mixture is complex. Moreover, due to assistive technology, potential accessibility barriers become even more complex to understand [8]. Gregor et al., (2020) [6] addressed the lack of 'people aspect' of design principles and devised a design theory to make design principles more understandable and useful in real world design contexts. Accessibility is therefore also one criteria of reusability of design principles [9]. Addressing the lack of a more accurate description of the attributes of the components in the design principle scheme would enable accessibility researchers to incorporate accessibility to design principles. Therefore, we addressed this issue by asking: **How to incorporate accessibility to design principles for IS artefacts?**

In this paper, we continue the work and propose an extension to the scheme presented by Gregor et al., (2020) [6]. The goal of this study is to extend the scheme for design principles with attributes of human aspect factors in use of HCI artefact including: HCI artefact features; variables of the context; mechanisms in HCI; and variables in user abilities. In this study, we draw upon theories related to the components of design principles and accessibility domain specific characteristics that should be included and addressed in design principles for HCI instantiations. This paper is organized as follows. The next section describes the theoretical foundation of DRS as well as DSR in HCI research. Then, we present research methods which is followed by the proposal of theoretical extensions. Finally, we propose future research directions to complement and justify the extensions.

2. Theoretical Foundation

2.1. Design Science Research

The goal of DSR is to generate prescriptive knowledge about the design of IS artefacts like software, methods, models, and concepts [10]. The design of the artefact, its precise definition and the evaluation of its usefulness are the most central issues of DSR [11]. Design research differs from design in general by focusing more on generating and developing new knowledge, while design in general focuses on using existing knowledge [12]. Therefore, the design must combine behavioural and organizational theories to develop an understanding of business problems, context, solutions, and evaluation methods [11].

For strategies to be implemented in the business infrastructure effectively, it requires organizational designing activities as well as information system designing activities [11]. These design activities are interdependent, and they reflect the most central research subjects in the field of IS. To be more precise, design activities show the relationship of business strategies and IT strategies to the infrastructures of the organization and information systems [11]. The design activities contain a sequence of activities that produces an innovative product, i.e., an artefact. The evaluation of the artefact produces feedback, based on which both the design process and the artefact and their quality can be developed. This type of iteration between build and review is typical before the final version of the artefact is complete. In design science, one contradiction must be accepted. Design means both process and product (artefact) – in other words, design means both doing and a thing [13]. Researchers must therefore consider both the design process and the artefact itself as part of the research [11]. March and Smith (1995) [14], indicated two types of design activities (construction and evaluation), and four types of artefacts (constructs, models, methods, and instantiations) produced by design scientists in IS studies. Construction refers to the process of constructing an artefact for a specific purpose. Construction is guided by the question of whether the artefact is feasible. Thus, the artefact itself becomes a research object that must be evaluated scientifically [14]. Evaluation is the process of deciding how well an artefact performs its task [14]. Evaluation requires developing metrics and measuring the artefact against those metrics. Metrics also determine what the artefact is trying to achieve. If the metrics have not been defined or the testing was not successful, it is impossible to scientifically prove the usefulness of the artefact.

Hevner et al. (2004) [11] further emphasized that, it is important to separate routine design work from design research. Routine design refers to the utilization of existing knowledge in the solution of the organization's known problems [15]. The key distinction between routine design and design science research is that it is precisely recognized what contribution the research makes to current knowledge, both in terms of basic knowledge and the methodological part [15]. Maedche et al., (2021) [12] proposed a reference framework for design research activities to help researchers position their own work and justify the type of contribution they want to make. The framework includes two dimensions between which design-oriented research varies. The first dimension includes the researchers' explanation of their contribution to current knowledge and tells whether the explanation is prescriptive or descriptive. The second dimension comprises the role of researchers in relation to the artefact and shows whether researchers are creating a new artefact (Creation) or examining an existing artefact (Observation) [12].

2.2. Design Science in Human Computer Interaction Research

HCI research focus on producing information about how people interact with information, technology, and tasks [3,4]. Design research and HCI research streams can be seen inherently related and highly overlapping [4]. The knowledge produced in HCI research can be classified as either descriptive knowledge aimed at explaining human behaviour and cognition with technology or as prescriptive knowledge aimed at guiding how IT systems should be constructed [3].

Adam et al., (2021) [3] presented three modes that DSR can focus in HCI. First, they called 'interior mode' as such research that focuses on IT system design technically and aim to solve problems on how to build and design an interface that enhance human performance. These HCI artefact constitutes constructs, model, methods, and instantiations for an interface design. Second, 'exterior mode' focuses on the use of artefact in its environment. Researchers focus on how individuals use the artefact by observing and analysing existing real-world use cases. Researchers primarily evaluate how effectively users interact with the IT system interface basing the observations to qualitative and/or quantitative evidence to produce both prescriptive and descriptive knowledge around human behaviours [3]. Third, some research projects that integrate both interior and exterior modes Adam et al., (2021) [3] called 'gestalt mode'. Gestalt mode type of research focuses on synergistic design of human behaviour and IT systems to improve human performance. In such projects selected evaluation methods should cover both systems performance and human performance so that the improvements to the HCI application can be justified. These types of research projects contribute to guiding design theories to achieve synergies between people and systems between socio-technical systems and technical components [3].

Hevner and Zhang, (2011) [4] indicated that it is crucial to identify what constitute an HCI artefact in design research. They categorized examples of HCI artefacts within DSR artefact types: construct, model, method, or instantiations [14]. Constructs in HCI are defined as 'vocabulary and symbols used to define design problems and solutions that provide a means to represent design ideas' [4:58]. Examples of construct-type HCI artefacts included metaphors, constructs of interaction, visualization, and organization (layouts of HCI). Models in HCI are '...sensemaking arrangements of constructs that allow exploration of abstract design' [4:58]. Examples of these type of HCI artefacts are such as graphical models, card stacks, 3D models, cognitive maps, etc. [4]. Methods-type HCI artefacts are defined as 'processes that provide guidance on how to solve problems and exploit opportunities' [4:58]. Examples of these types of HCI artefacts are well-established participatory design, collaboration processes, human-centred design, and value sensitive design [4]. Lastly, instantiations in HCI represents the 'implementation of an artefact in a working system,' 'demonstrates feasibility and value,' or 'provides ability to study uses and impacts on embedded system' [4:58]. Instantiation-type of artefacts in HCI are websites, user interfaces, input/output devices, avatars, etc. [4].

2.3. Accessibility Domain Specific Characteristics in Design Activities

The domain of accessibility contains basically three points of knowledge of accessibility that can be considered as field specific characteristics that are required for successfully design an accessible HCI artefact: (1) assumptions about users' abilities, that is developers should consider human senses one by one and assume that users may lack one of abilities; (2) users' actual need, that is developers should elicit users' requirements related to task and context of HCI artefact that is a target of development. (3) factors in value chain that are related to management and development of the artefact and have influence on accessibility [2].

Assumptions about users' abilities contain the mindset that user lack some human abilities therefore multimodal interaction should be provided. Users' actual needs are detected in the collaboration with users. Collaboration with users is the process of planning a partnership. Since its introduction, the method has been adapted and extended in the field of HCI. Similarly, the participatory design approach consists of a set of theories, practices, and studies related to end-user participation in technology development and design [16]. User participation and experimental research are also getting increasingly important in IS research to study decision-making processes and user behaviour [17]. Overall, user participation as an approach contains several methods that can be used in various parts of the value chain such as brainstorming, direct observation, activity diaries, cultural probes, surveys and questionnaires, interviews, group discussion, empathic modelling, user trials, scenarios and personas, prototyping, cooperative and participatory design, etc. [16]. To achieve a diverse view of users' needs, user participation should be including users with different disabilities as a representative. However, some of the user participation methods have limitations to adopted into user requirements elicitation with certain users [16]. From these methods and techniques direct observation, scenarios, personas, and prototyping are evaluated to be appropriate as such for use with user groups with motion, vision, hearing, or cognitive and communication disabilities [16]. However, the information derived from observation, scenarios, and personas is mostly produced by the researcher, which means that only the use of a prototype can be classified as one that produces user-oriented information and can be used with users with disabilities without adjustment. Factors in the value chain refer to the accessibility implementation process that includes different stakeholders and their input to the realisation of accessibility.

3. Design Science Research Methodology

We designed our study based on design science research process model by Peffers et al. (2007) [18] (see Figure 1.). Present study focuses on extending a scheme for design principles proposed by Gregor et al. (2020) [6]. Thus, we started with the objective-centred solution entry point [18]. We aimed to improve [15] existing scheme [6] with the relevance that makes the scheme more accurate and adaptable for accessibility-related DSR. Therefore, we first defined objectives of a solution.

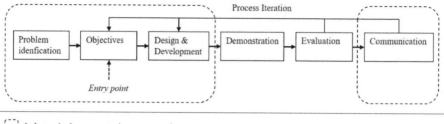

Figure 1. Research Process Model (Adopted from Peffers et al. 2007 [18]).

To define objectives, we performed a literature search to draw accessibility domain specific characteristics that should be included and addressed in design principles for HCI instantiations. We adopted kernel theories such as the International Classification of Functioning, Disability and Health (ICF) agreed upon by the World Health Assembly [19], which helped us to identify variations in human abilities. ICF is commonly used by disability experts in governments and other sectors [20]. Then, we based the search within the lens of the following components of the design principle scheme [6]: instantiation, context, mechanism, enactor, and user. We reasoned and drawn attributes related to the interaction with an HCI artefact. In this paper, we conducted three first step in design science research process: problem identification; definition of objectives; and design and development [18]. We adopted existing knowledge [11], and constructed the first version of the extensions. We also included the communication phase to the present study as we developed the first proposal based on peer-reviewing process [18]. In Demonstration, and Evaluation phase, we will apply and demonstrate the results with focus group including accessibility researchers and evaluate the feasibility by interviewing accessibility researchers.

4. Theoretical Extensions to the Scheme for Formulating Design Principles in Accessibility-Related DSR

In this section we illustrate the extensions to a scheme for design principles. The knowledge i.e. building blocks of the extensions are draw from the following kernel theories: Studies [21,22] related to HCI artefact features; [23–27] related to Contextual factors; [6,28] related to Computer Input Modalities; [28] related to Computer Output Media; [20,28,29] related to Human Sensory Perception; and [29–33] related to Human Cognition. The extensions are intended for accessibility-related research to incorporate accessibility to produce more accurate design principles. Figure 2. illustrate the components of design principles [6] and indicates our proposed attributes of these components that should be specified in a case of formulating design principles in accessibility-related DSR.

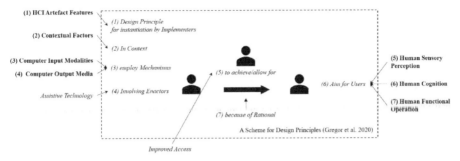

Figure 2. Extensions for Components for Design Principles (area inside the dotted line is adopted from Gregor et al. 2020 [6])

Extensions for the components for design principles are described as follow:

(1) HCI Artefact Features: We extended the component "Design Principles for instantiation by Implementers" [6] with features that HCI artefact instantiation include. HCI artefact instantiations such as websites and user interfaces can be sorted into specific features, where users interact with the artefact trough the content, presentation style, functionality, interaction style, and structure [21,22]. For example, text is one of the presentation styles that include its formatting such as font style and size. The text content contains a message that its provider wants to convey. This also include presentation style such as use of plain language. Users construct their own conceptual version of the nature of an artefact with their personal judgment. This judgment is influenced by emotional consequences such as pleasure, satisfaction, etc. as well as behavioural consequences, such as the time spend with artefact [21].

(2) Contextual factors: The context of use can affect users' abilities. The context of use may vary due to environmental factors, including users' emotional state, sociocultural factors, socio-technical factors, whereby cultural, political, sociological, and historical aspect of context [23–26] etc. Moreover, user expectations of artefact behaviour often rely on past experiences, prejudice, evoked memories, unmet expectation, and conviction that strongly influences how users perceive and experience the accessibility [27]. Furthermore, the expectations are related to the history of context and the emotional state.

(3) Computer Input Modalities: Mechanisms, such as acts, activities, and processes [6] in a case of HCI artefact relate to mechanisms how user interact with the HCI artefact. This differs from HCI artefact features and describes factors related to human. Referring to the basic model of HCI by [28], human (user) mechanisms include modalities that the user uses to interact with HCI artefact: movements, force, sound, and images [28]. For example, the user can access the interface by pressing buttons, producing sound, or showing an image to the interface e.g. QR code (quick-response code).

(4) Computer Output Media: Once the computer has received the input from the user, it processes the input data and gives the user an output that should be able to be received by some human senses or a combination of them. These channels can be visual, auditive, tactile, olfactory, gustatory, as well as vestibular [28]. A description of the mechanism by which the HCI artefact should be designed should include descriptions of the input modalities and output medias to ensure that the user has access to the HCI artefact even in cases where the user lacks any ability.

(5) Human Sensory Perception: We extended the component "Aim for Users" [6] with an features that human user may have. The specification of the users' abilities should include variables in human sensory perception, cognition, and functional operations. Human sensory perceptions can differ in terms of abilities in sight, hearing, touch, smell, taste, and balance [20,28,29].

(6) Human Cognition: Cognitive abilities are different for everyone [32,33]. It is therefore necessary to consider each specific cognitive deficit rather than considering cognitive matters as a whole [33]. Cognitive abilities includes possible variations in focusing attention, memory, thinking and speed of processing, reading and writing, mental functions of language, calculating and quantitative knowledge, solving problems, making decisions and reaction speed, psychomotor functions and sequencing complex movements and speed, emotional functions, perceptual functions, higher-level cognitive functions and domain specific knowledge, experience of self and time functions, and comprehension-knowledge [29–31]. The awareness of individuals' cognitive abilities to perform tasks in HCI artefact and the adoption of this knowledge into the design activities are crucial for creating a successful interaction.

(7) Human Functional Operations: Human outputs for HCI artefacts, such as typing with a keyboard and using pointing devices, touch screens and others, require at least one human functional ability [34]. Human functional abilities can be classified as follows: voice and speech functions (voice functions, articulation functions, fluency and rhythm of speech functions, alternative vocalisation functions) and neuromusculoskeletal and movement-related functions (functions of the joint and bones, muscle functions, movement functions) [29]. As the interaction with HCI artefact can also be considered social interactions [35], factors related to human abilities for social interaction, such as abilities for interpersonal interactions, relationships, and communication (receiving and producing, conversation, and use of communication devices and techniques) should be considered in designing for accessibility [29].

The component "Involving Enactors" in the original scheme for design principles [6] are extended with the considerations of possible use of assistive technology as one part of enactor. Assistive technology refers to technologies assisting the user to perceive the information or interact with a computer e.g., the use of screen readers. However, assistive technology as an external source should not be treated as a solution that provides the access since access should be designed for the HCI artefact itself.

The component "to achieve/allow for" [6], describes the extent that the current design principles are aiming for or endorse. In a case of accessibility this means the access to the information or ability to interact with the HCI artefact. Therefore, we extended this component with a goal "Improved Access" as it is a goal that accessibility design principles should endorse.

The component "because of Rationale"[6], states the theoretical or empirical justification that employing mechanisms described in the principles will achieve the defined aim. Design principles in accessibility-related DSR should be justified in the same way as the other topics therefore we did not extend this component.

Summing up the extensions, we devised a demonstration of a checklist for researchers to incorporate accessibility into design principles (Table 1.).

Table 1. A Checklist to Incorporate Accessibility in Design Principles

HCI Artefact Features	Context	Computer Input Modalities	Computer Output Media	Human Sensory Perception	Cognition	Human Functional Operation
What feature are you addressing?	What are contextual factors influencing your target?	In what way the computer will take the input from user?	How is the information presented?	With what sense the user receives the information?	What human cognitive abilities are addressed?	How the user performs the action?
☐ Content	☐ Environmental	☐ Movements	☐ Text	☐ Sight	☐ Focusing attention	☐ Movement
☐ Presentational style	☐ User's emotional state	☐ Force	☐ Image	☐ Hearing	☐ Memory	☐ Voice
☐ Functionality	☐ Socio-cultural	☐ Sound	☐ Video	☐ Touch	☐ Thinking and speed of processing	☐ Sight
☐ Interactional style	☐ Socio-technical	☐ Images	☐ Graphs	☐ Smell	☐ Reading and writing	
☐ Structure	☐ Cultural	☐ other…	☐ Tables	☐ Taste	☐ Mental functions of language	
☐ other…	☐ Political		☐ Sound	☐ Balance	☐ Calculating and quantitative knowledge	
	☐ Sociological		☐ other…		☐ Solving problems	
	☐ Historical				☐ Making decisions and reaction speed	
	☐ other…				☐ Psychomotor functions and sequencing complex movements and speed	
					☐ Emotional functions	
					☐ Perceptual functions	
					☐ Higher-level cognitive functions and domain specific knowledge	
					☐ Experience of self and time functions	
					☐ Comprehension-knowledge	

The checklist in Table 1. is not, however, comprehensive. The checklist does not separate different severity levels in human abilities. Moreover, all variables in computer input modalities, computer output media, and in contexts are not presented. However, the checklist is intended to provide help for researchers in accessibility-related research to incorporate a wide aspect of accessibility and improve accuracy by identifying attributes relate to context, human abilities, and interaction. For example, studies exploring IT use of blind individuals often ignore the fact that these same individuals may have variations in cognitive abilities. The checklist therefore helps to specify more accurately what human factors the design principles intend to cover.

5. Discussion

Our contribution provides a tentative description of the extensions to a scheme for design principles. Our extensions are intended for accessibility-related research to incorporate accessibility into the design of systems and to produce a more accurate formulation of design principles. We aim to contribute improvements to a scheme for design principles presented by [6] so that they are more adaptable to accessibility-related DSR. We provided seven attributes to extend the components of design principles and devised a checklist for researchers to incorporate accessibility in design principles. We conducted three first steps of the design science research process: problem identification; definition of objectives; and design and development.

This paper has the following implications for research and practice. The research will continue with the evaluation of proposed extensions. We will apply the Demonstration, and Evaluation phase [18], and include accessibility researchers to evaluate the usefulness of the extensions. In addition, our research process generated an important research avenue: Adoption of the design principles for accessibility should be studied. The adoption process is likely dependent on the business benefit and social responsibility of a firm. There might be other factors affecting the adoption process. Identification of factors might affect the formulation of design principles. The design principles are meant for the practitioners in accessibility to develop better information technology artefacts for everyone's use. We encourage practitioners to adopt the principles and further tailor them in their organizations to suit better the needs of single businesses. We also recommend practitioners assess the consequences of adoption and tailor the principles accordingly.

References

[1]   S. Lewthwaite, and D. Sloan, Exploring pedagogical culture for accessibility education in computing science, in: Proceedings of the 13th International Web for All Conference, Association for Computing Machinery, New York, NY, USA, 2016: pp. 1–4. doi:10.1145/2899475.2899490.

[2]   J.-P. Mäkipää, J. Norrgård, and T. Vartiainen, Factors Affecting the Accessibility of IT Artifacts: A Systematic Review, CAIS. 51 (2022) 666–702. doi:10.17705/1CAIS.05129.

[3]   Marc.T.P. Adam, S. Gregor, A. Hevner, and S. Morana, Design Science Research Modes in Human-Computer Interaction Projects, THCI. (2021) 1–11. doi:10.17705/1thci.00139.

[4]   A. Hevner, and P. Zhang, Introduction to the AIS THCI Special Issue on Design Research in Human-Computer Interaction, THCI. 3 (2011) 56–61. doi:10.17705/1thci.00026.

[5]   K. Mack, E. McDonnell, D. Jain, L. Lu Wang, J. E. Froehlich, and L. Findlater, What Do We Mean by "Accessibility Research"? A Literature Survey of Accessibility Papers in CHI and ASSETS from 1994 to 2019, in: Proceedings of the 2021 CHI Conference on Human Factors in Computing Systems, Association for Computing Machinery, New York, NY, USA, 2021: pp. 1–18. http://doi.org/10.1145/3411764.3445412 (accessed January 8, 2022).

[6]   S. Gregor, L. Chandra Kruse, and S. Seidel, The Anatomy of a Design Principle, Journal of the Association for Information Systems. 21 (2020) 1622–1652. doi:10.17705/1jais.00649.

[7]   P. DiMaggio, Culture and Cognition, Annual Review of Sociology. 23 (1997) 263–287. doi:10.1146/annurev.soc.23.1.263.

[8]   B. Vollenwyder, G.H. Iten, F. Brühlmann, K. Opwis, and E.D. Mekler, Salient beliefs influencing the intention to consider Web Accessibility, *Computers in Human Behavior.* **92** (2019) 352–360. doi:10.1016/j.chb.2018.11.016.

[9]   J. Iivari, M.R.P. Hansen, and A. Haj-Bolouri, A proposal for minimum reusability evaluation of design principles, *European Journal of Information Systems.* **30** (2021) 286–303. doi:10.1080/0960085X.2020.1793697.

[10] J. vom Brocke, and A. Maedche, The DSR grid: six core dimensions for effectively planning and communicating design science research projects, *Electron Markets.* **29** (2019) 379–385. doi:10.1007/s12525 019 00358 7.

[11] A.R. Hevner, S.T. March, J. Park, and S. Ram, Design Science in Information Systems Research, *MIS Quarterly.* **28** (2004) 75–105.

[12] A. Maedche, S. Gregor, and J. Parsons, Mapping Design Contributions in Information Systems Research: The Design Research Activity Framework, *CAIS.* **49** (2021) 355–378. doi:10.17705/1CAIS.04914.

[13] J.G. Walls, G.R. Widmeyer, and O.A. El Sawy, Building an Information System Design Theory for Vigilant EIS, *Information Systems Research.* **3** (1992) 36–59. doi:10.1287/isre.3.1.36.

[14] S.T. March, and G.F. Smith, Design and natural science research on information technology, *Decision Support Systems.* **15** (1995) 251–266. doi:10.1016/0167-9236(94)00041-2.

[15] S. Gregor, and A.R. Hevner, Positioning and Presenting Design Science Research for Maximum Impact, *MIS Quarterly.* **37** (2013) 337–355.

[16] C. Stephanidis, ed., The Universal Access Handbook, CRC Press, Boca Raton, 2009. doi:10.1201/9781420064995.

[17] A. Greif-Winzrieth, A. Maedche, and C. Weinhardt, Designing a Public Experimental Terminal for Citizen Engagement, (2021) 11.

[18] K. Peffers, T. Tuunanen, M.A. Rothenberger, and S. Chatterjee, A Design Science Research Methodology for Information Systems Research, *Journal of Management Information Systems.* **24** (2007) 45–77. doi:10.2753/MIS0742-1222240302.

[19] World Health Organization, Towards a Common Language for Functioning, Disability and Health ICF. (WHO/EIP/GPE/CAS/01.3),   (2002). https://www.who.int/classifications/icf/icfbeginnersguide.pdf?ua=1.

[20] World Health Organization, How to use the ICF: A practical manual for using the International Classification of Functioning, Disability and Health (ICF), (2013).

[21] M. Hassenzahl, The Thing and I: Understanding the Relationship Between User and Product, in: M.A. Blythe, K. Overbeeke, A.F. Monk, and P.C. Wright (Eds.), Funology, Springer Netherlands, Dordrecht, 2003: pp. 31–42. doi:10.1007/1-4020-2967-5_4.

[22] W3C, Web Content Accessibility Guidelines (WCAG) 2.1, (2018). https://www.w3.org/TR/WCAG21/ (accessed June 14, 2020).

[23] K. Lyytinen, and M. Newman, Explaining information systems change: a punctuated socio-technical change model, *European Journal of Information Systems.* **17** (2008) 589–613. doi:10.1057/ejis.2008.50.

[24] J. McKay, P. Marshall, and R. Hirschheim, The Design Construct in Information Systems Design Science, *Journal of Information Technology.* **27** (2012) 125–139. doi:10.1057/jit.2012.5.

[25] G. Meiselwitz, B. Wentz, and J. Lazar, Universal Usability: Past, Present, and Future., *Foundations and Trends in Human-Computer Interaction.* **3** (2010) 213–333.

[26] H. Sharp, N. Lotz, L. Mbayi-Kwelagobe, M. Woodroffe, D. Rajah, and R. Turugare, Socio-cultural factors and capacity building in Interaction Design: Results of a video diary study in Botswana, *International Journal of Human-Computer Studies.* **135** (2020) 102375. doi:10.1016/j.ijhcs.2019.102375.

[27] A. Aizpurua, M. Arrue, and M. Vigo, Prejudices, memories, expectations and confidence influence experienced accessibility on the Web, *Computers in Human Behavior.* **51** (2015) 152–160. doi:10.1016/j.chb.2015.04.035.

[28] L. Schomaker, and K. Hartung, A Taxonomy of Multimodal Interaction in the Human Information Processing System, *Rep. Esprit Proj.* **8579** (1995).

[29] WHO, ICF Browser, (n.d.). https://apps.who.int/classifications/icfbrowser/ (accessed March 24, 2021).

[30] J. Carroll, Human-computer interaction: Psychology as a science of design, *Annual Review of Psychology.* **48** (1997) 61–83. doi:10.1146/annurev.psych.48.1.61.

[31] K.S. McGrew, CHC theory and the human cognitive abilities project: Standing on the shoulders of the giants of psychometric intelligence research, *Intelligence.* **37** (2009) 1–10. doi:10.1016/j.intell.2008.08.004.

[32] G. Berget, F. Mulvey, and F.E. Sandnes, Is visual content in textual search interfaces beneficial to dyslexic users?, *International Journal of Human-Computer Studies.* **92–93** (2016) 17–29. doi:10.1016/j.ijhcs.2016.04.006.

[33] J. Sevilla, G. Herrera, B. Martínez, and F. Alcantud, Web accessibility for individuals with cognitive deficits: A comparative study between an existing commercial Web and its cognitively accessible equivalent, *ACM Trans. Comput.-Hum. Interact.* **14** (2007) 12-es. doi:10.1145/1279700.1279702.

[34] J.B. Carroll, Human Cognitive Abilities: A Survey of Factor-Analytic Studies, Cambridge University Press, Cambridge, 1993. doi:10.1017/CBO9780511571312.

[35] K.M. Lee, and C. Nass, Designing social presence of social actors in human computer interaction, in: Proceedings of the SIGCHI Conference on Human Factors in Computing Systems, Association for Computing Machinery, New York, NY, USA, 2003: pp. 289–296. doi:10.1145/642611.642662.

Information Modelling and Knowledge Bases XXXV
M. Tropmann-Frick et al. (Eds.)

doi:10.3233/FAIA231155

Thammasat AI City Distributed Platform: Enhancing Social Distribution and Ambient Lighting

Virach SORNLERTLAMVANICH[a,b,1],

Thatsanee CHAROENPORN[a,2], and Somrudee DEEPAISARN[c,3]

[a]*Asia AI Institute (AAII), Faculty of Data Science, Musashino University, Japan.*
[b]*Faculty of Engineering, Thammasat University, Thailand.*
[c]*Sirindhorn International Institute of Technology, Thammasat University, Thailand.*
ORCID ID: Virach SORNLERTLAMVANICH https://orcid.org/0000-0002-6918-8713
ORCID ID: Thatsanee CHAROENPORN https://orcid.org/0000-0002-9577-9082
ORCID ID: Somrudee DEEPAISARN https://orcid.org/0000-0001-7647-6345

Abstract. The Thammasat AI City distributed platform is a proposed AI platform designed to enhance city intelligent management. It addresses the limitations of current smart city architecture by incorporating cross-domain data connectivity and machine learning to support comprehensive data collection. In this study, we delve into two main areas, that is, monitoring and visualization of city ambient lighting, and indoor human physical distance tracking. The smart street light monitoring system provides real-time visualization of street lighting status, energy consumption, and maintenance requirement, which helps to optimize energy consumption and maintenance reduction. The indoor camera-based system for human physical distance tracking can be used in public spaces to monitor social distancing and ensure public safety. The overall goal of the platform is to improve the quality of life in urban areas and align with sustainable urban development concepts.

Keywords. AI City, smart city, social distribution, city ambient lighting, AI platform

1. Introduction

As cities continue to grow and become more connected, there is an increasing need for advanced technologies such as artificial intelligence (AI) to manage and optimize the complex systems that make up a modern city. One area where AI can have a significant

---

[1] Corresponding Author: Virach Sornlertlamvanich, Asia AI Institute (AAII), Faculty of Data Science, Musashino University, 3-3-3 Ariake Koto-ku, Tokyo, 135-8181, Japan; and Faculty of Engineering, Thammasat University, 99 Moo 18, Paholyothin Road, Klong Nueng, Klong Luang, Pathumthani 12120, Thailand; E-mail: virach@musashino-u.ac.jp

[2] Thatsanee Charoenporn, Asia AI Institute (AAII), Faculty of Data Science, Musashino University, 3-3-3 Ariake Koto-ku, Tokyo, 135-8181, Japan; E-mail: thatsane@musashino-u.ac.jp

[3] Somrudee Deepaisarn, School of Information, Computer, and Communication Technology, Sirindhorn International Institute of Technology, Thammasat University, 99 Moo 18, Paholyothin Road, Klong Nueng, Klong Luang, Pathumthani 12120, Thailand; E-mail: somrudee@siit.tu.ac.th

impact is in the field of smart cities, where AI can be applied to improve the quality of life for residents and make cities more efficient and sustainable. As technology advances and the cost of sensors and network devices decreases, the concept of the Internet of Things (IoT) is becoming more feasible. Cities are able to use digital infrastructure and high-speed communication to connect various devices and systems, allowing for greater data collection and analysis, and improved efficiency and decision-making. This is the place where artificial intelligence and machine learning come into play to maximize data's value. Machine learning can be used to process the large amounts of data generated by connected devices in the IoT which can lead to more efficient and effective decision-making. Machine learning can also be used to optimize the performance and energy efficiency of connected devices and systems, and to improve the accuracy and reliability of their data. In conjunction with the data streaming from various possible sources including IOT devices, to a platform and the analytic results from machine learning, the data-driven artificial intelligence is well-suited to form the analytical foundation of the AI City.

Thammasat AI City initiative is an determined program that aims to establish a resilient AI platform at the Rangsit campus of Thammasat University. The initiative focuses on four key domains, including elderly and healthcare, mobility, environment, and economy. It is designed to identify the opportunities and challenges of AI disruption and to create a role model for the full activation of data and physical availability. The Rangsit campus location is an ideal setting for the project as it allows for testing AI solutions in a real-world scenario and involving multiple stakeholders. The initiative aligns with the societal changes and technology trends that have emerged in the wake of the COVID-19 pandemic, namely distributed city, human traceability, new reality, home-office integration, contactless technology, digital lending, and frugal innovation. The goal of the initiative is to create a model for a smart city that is efficient, sustainable, and responsive to the needs of its citizens.

The remainder of the paper is organized as follows. Section 2 discusses the issues in the challenges of urbanization. Section 3 explains the architecture and design of the AI City initiatives. Section 4 elaborates on the AI City domain specific connectivity with the proposed technologies. And the conclusion in Section 5.

2. The Challenges of Urbanization

Thammasat University, Rangsit Campus is one of the leading universities in Thailand, known for its research and education programs in various fields including agriculture, economy, politics and science. The Rangsit campus is situated in Pathum Thani province, a city near Bangkok, where covers an area of 1,526 square kilometers. The city has a population of 985,643 according to a 2020 report of the National Statistical Office of Thailand. It serves as an important hub for higher education, hosting ten renowned universities, Thailand Science Park and seven mega economic areas which includes shopping malls and agricultural markets. And 35.11 percent of the total land area are the agriculture area.

Similar to many cities in Thailand, Pathum Thani Province is facing a rising population situation. This increase in population is accompanied by a number of urbanization problems, such as insufficient elderly care facilities, environmental deterioration, and traffic congestion. These issues can have a negative impact on the overall quality of life for the inhabitants of the province. With the reference of the

Pathum Thani City Planning 2018 – 2022 by The Pathum Thani Provincial Office (2018) [1], the urbanization of Pathum Thani brings with it the potential for a surge in various issues and hurdles. These encompass challenges like heightened traffic congestion and road safety concerns, a rise in environmental issues, economic and tourism-related troubles, as well as shifts in lifestyle patterns. To address their challenges, it is important for the local government and community to work together to develop sustainable solutions that balance the needs of the growing population with the preservation of the environment and quality of life for residents. This may include efforts to improve public transportation, promote sustainable development, and increase access to healthcare and other services. Additionally, encouraging the creating an efficient solid waste management system, developing of the capabilities of the target industries, social development and basic security of the people can help to mitigate the negative impacts of urbanization on the environment and economy.

3. AI City Initiatives

The Thammasat University's AI City networking in RUN project is an initiative to model AI capacity on a city scale within the Rangsit campus, which is 2.8112 square kilometers in size. The project aims to address the current limitations of AI research caused by the insufficiency and diversity of data. Reliable and connected data will be collected and made available to demonstrate AI's capabilities in real-life applications fully. The project functions as a based-platform [2] for four high-impact domains in Rangsit city, including healthcare, environment, mobility, and economy. The project is equipped with various AI-enabled devices namely healthcare monitoring devices [3], noninvasive bed sensors [4], environmental sensors, video analytics cameras, street lights, indoor tracking devices [5], and drones for aerial photography. Figure 1 depicts the architecture of the AI City platform and its cross-domain connectivity.

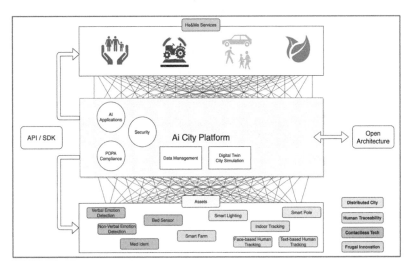

Figure 1. AI City platform architecture and cross-domain connectivity.

In order to make the data from several sources available for modeling, the data is stored and sent to the cloud services using low energy mesh network (6LoWPAN protocol in case of smart lighting, Bluetooth low energy (BLE) in case of indoor positioning and bed sensor, etc.). To reduce the high bandwidth consumption devices such as video streaming of surveillance cameras, LAN connectivity, and several techniques[2] (steady state at rest, motion detection, etc.) are introduced. In addition, bed sensors for elderly care systems, the detection of types of on-bed position is localized not only to realize the real-time warning but also to conserve the bandwidth by sending the compressed results to the cloud.

The AI City Project is a comprehensive approach to integrate AI into city operations and infrastructure through four main layers: the accumulation layer, the knowledge layer, the understanding layer, and the decision-making layer, as illustrated in Figure 2. Data from IoT devices is analyzed and connected to produce models and prediction results in four targeted domains. The primary layer is the layer of accumulating physical raw data through various sensor network devices as the foundation for the subsequent layers. The next layer is data extraction into knowledge and once the knowledge has been created with new coming data, we can make good understanding and provide good decision at the final layer by the advance of deep learning, neural network and machine learning. Model training for specific tasks is conducted in the understanding layer. The appropriate machine learning paradigms are introduced and evaluated to produce the results in the decision-making layer. The connectivity and selection of the data from various sources are crucial to implementing in the city-scale AI platform development. The platform composes of health & aging care platform, environment platform, mobility platform and economy platform [6].

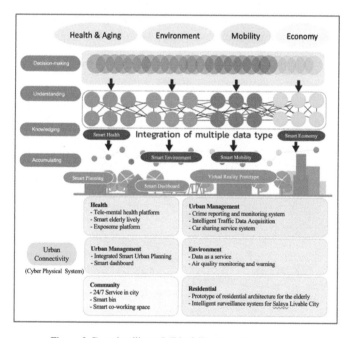

Figure 2. Deep intelligent IoT in fully connected network.

---

[2] https://info.verkada.com/surveillance-features/bandwidth/

3.1. Smart Health and Aging Care Platform

As Thailand transitions into a fully aged society, with 10% of its population being over 60 years of age, significant demographic changes are underway. The project aims to address the growing burden of caring for the elderly. It seeks to improve the quality of life and access to health care services for communities near Thammasat University, focusing on five areas: social, activity, health, medicine, and sleep condition. The project involves the development of a technology-based health platform for the aging population, consisting of five main components. Those are the sleep quality analysis system, the medicine identification system, the indoor positioning and services system, the daily health monitoring system, and the elderly follow-up and care robotic system.

3.2. Smart Mobility Platform

Centered around the Thammasat University Rangsit Campus and Pathum Thani Province, this platform holds the objective of elevating mobility, curbing air pollution, enhancing safety, and fostering tourism through the analysis of travel trends and the provision of comprehensive insights. The platform encompasses three key components: an intelligent traffic data acquisition system, a car sharing service system, and a crime reporting and monitoring system.

3.3. Smart Environment Platform

The smart environment platform is strategically designed to tackle environmental challenges and contribute to the overarching objective of smart city development. This platform harnesses the capabilities of IoT technologies and AI systems to vigilantly monitor the urban environment. Anchored in the principles of urban environment monitoring, the platform encompasses pivotal systems including the monitoring of air pollution levels, a weather forecasting system, and a vehicle front camera-based inspection system designed to identify suspicious objects.

3.4. Smart Economy Platform

The Thammasat University Rangsit Campus and Pathum Thani Province are home to various educational and research organizations, including AIT and NSTDA, that conduct research in various fields. However, there is a lack of promotion and connection between these organizations and the private sector. Thus, a Smart Economy Platform is being developed to connect these organizations and bring research results to real-life applications. This will involve collaboration between research universities and researchers to improve innovation and foster cross-disciplinary and geographic cooperation. Leveraging the power of big data and Deep Learning, this platform is poised to analyze and process information. Its core objective is to facilitate collaboration between the public and private sectors. Moreover, it aspires to enhance the domain specific service value and productivity, cultivate specialized industries and services, and bolster local entrepreneurship. This comprehensive approach involves integrating research with real-world challenges, aiming to bring about tangible advancements.

4. AI City Domain Specific Connectivity

Regarding to the domain specific connectivity, there are four types of technology that we focus on, namely distributed city, human traceability, contactless technology and frugal innovation. In this paper, we will mainly focus on the distributed city and the contactless technology.

As countries around the world try to admit that the Covid-19 has evolved a strain to survive, to be able to spread easily and quickly until eventually many countries have to accept that COVID-19 is an endemic disease. From trying to block the border to minimize the spread. As well as efforts to eradicate this disease within a limited time at the cost of enormous social and economic losses. Finally, we have to adapt and learn to live safely with COVID-19 and have as much balance in life as possible. From the concept of new normal that our way of living moved to relied on the online communities, it was currently changed to the next normal. Although epidemic prevention measures are sparse, the lives of people have changed a lot from the original.

Covid-19 changes our behaviors and attitudes in life, especially the exposure to technology including the online platforms which meets the needs of convenience, safety, and hygiene. These behaviors are leading to the next normal way of living which impact to the economy and environment in the future. People are aware of safety, stability, and more flexibility in living and of a greater understanding that health is fundamental to life. The stay-at-home economy, touchless society, physical distancing, and elevating health and wellness concern are concrete examples of the next normal.

Although the situation has improved. But there is still no vaccine that is 100 percent effective in preventing infection. This allowed people to maintain their distance and avoid entering the areas where people are crowded. However, job duties or social contact is sometimes difficult to avoid being in the public areas. Contactless or touchless society then shifted into account. The focus is on adopting technology and practices that allow social and economic activities to continue while minimizing the risk of disease transmission through physical contact. This can include contactless payment systems, virtual meetings, facial recognition technology, and the use of robots for tasks that would normally require human contact. The goal is to reduce the spread of disease while maintaining as much normalcy and efficiency as possible in daily life.

The contactless approach to internet of thing and wearable medical technology emphasizes the need for comfort and ease of use, while also respecting privacy and avoiding interference with daily activities. Following the contactless approach, we aim to create systems that can provide medical monitoring and care without the need for invasive or uncomfortable devices, through the use of contactless technology such as sensors and platforms. These systems include health monitoring, elderly care, and medicine identification, which are designed to provide medical personnel with the information they need to ensure the well-being of their patients.

4.1. Indoor Camera-Based System for Human Physical Distance Tracking

The proposed method for determining physical distance in indoor environments introduces the use of end-to-end cameras to track a person's position, movement direction, and seat activity. The system does not identify individuals, but instead records their location for the purpose of monitoring physical distancing. The research mainly focuses on two main aspects: detecting a person's location and detecting seat positions [7].

4.1.1. Seat Detection

The seat detection in the proposed system uses contour color extraction [8] on the top part of the seat or table. It extracts unique contour shape as a feature, as shown in Figure 1. The results indicate that contour detection works well for the first rows of seats, but may have difficulties detecting seats in the rest of the rows.

The perspective transformation [9], [10] has been applied to changes the original image projection into a new visual plane for system requirements using Equation (1).

$$[x', y', w'] = [u, v, w] \begin{bmatrix} a_{11} & a_{12} & a_{13} \\ a_{21} & a_{22} & a_{23} \\ a_{31} & a_{32} & a_{33} \end{bmatrix} \tag{1}$$

For improving the seat detection ability, we apply the perspective transformation with the selection of the top seat area in the room as the region of interest (ROI), before seat contour detection. The process allows the system to accurately detect the seats in the room.

4.1.2. Person Detection

The proposed system detects a person in the specified area using YOLOv3 algorithm, which uses trained weights and data sets to detect objects. The pre-trained model and function selected specifically for human body detection were utilized in the algorithm. as illustrated in Figure 3.

Figure 3. Human body detected using YOLOv3 in green boxes, and the image reference frame in black line.

In the standard pre-trained YOLOv3 [11],[12], the bottom center of the detection box is used as the reference point for a person's location. The proposed system improves person location reference point by first calculating the height-to-width ratio of the detected human object and rounding it, which better appropriate for the indoor environment being monitored. The ratio is denoted as $QBox = hBox/wBox$. Where $hBox$ and $wBox$ represent the height and the width of the box, respectively.

The classification of standing and sitting is based on the ratio of $QBox$, which is calculated as the height of the box ($hBox$) divided by its width ($wBox$) ($QBox = hBox/wBox$). And it can be concluded that

- if the value of $QBox$ >= (greater than or equal) 1.6, refers to a standing person in the box
- if the value of $QBox$ < 1.6, refers to a sitting person in the box

$$c = \begin{cases} 0.775; & \text{if } Q_{\text{Box}} \geq 1.6 \\ 0.675; & \text{otherwise} \end{cases} \tag{2}$$

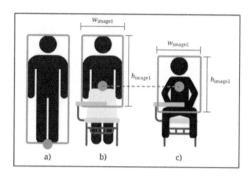

Figure 4. Illustration of human body detection reference point (green). (a) original approach (at the bottom-middle point of the green box), (b) a person standing between seats (77.5% of vertical proportion from the top-middle point as $h_{\text{image}_1}/w_{\text{image}_1} \geq 1.6$), (c) a person sitting on the seat (67.5% of vertical proportion from the top-middle point as $h_{\text{image}_2}/w_{\text{image}_2} < 1.6$).

The distinction between standing and sitting scenarios is illustrated in Figure 4 (b) and 4 (c) compared to Figure 4 (a) which shows the conventional algorithm for determining the reference location of a person. Here, the location of the person in each frame is identified using a modified algorithm. The conventional point at the bottom-middle of the detected human body has been replaced with a reference point c, which can take the values 0.775 or 0.675 for a standing or sitting person, respectively. The reference points for standing and sitting cases are calculated using Equation (2) and this approach was used to improve the accuracy of location of persons in a room environment.

4.1.3. Physical Coordinate Calculation

The reference point coordinates for seats and persons were determined and used to calculate physical coordinates by converting the image coordinates to physical coordinates using two reference parameters from the room's physical dimensions, including the real size of the room and the pixel size of the region of interest in the image frame. The ratio between image and room size was calculated using Equation (3).

$$Q_{\text{Physical}} = \frac{ImageSize}{RoomSize} \tag{3}$$

4.1.4. Performance Evaluation and Discussion

The proposed system uses seat contour detection to initiate seat positioning in a room. Nonetheless, the accuracy of the detection decreases in the back rows according to constraints from further seats. To improve the detection ability for the back row seats, a perspective transformation is proposed. This transformation increases the ability of the seat detection algorithm to detect seats in the back rows.

For physical distancing monitoring, the system uses the upper left-hand corner of the seat boundary area after the perspective transformation as the reference point. This point is used to transform the image space into a bird-eye view, allowing for calculation of physical locations of seats and people [13]. While the system can estimate actual distances in real-world units, there may still be errors from the transformation, which have been studied in various related researches [14], [15], [16]. To improve the accuracy of image-based distance measurement, we need to select the proper area of interest and algorithm to calibrate the image-physical distance.

A camera-based system was implemented to determine the physical locations of seats and people in a room. The average error of seat location determined by the system was ±5.25 cm. with a standard deviation of 4.64 cm. The small error suggests the overall performance of the system in determining real-world locations. The system can accurately determine whether people are at an appropriate physical distance (180 cm.) apart from others for COVID-19 prevention, and the uncertainty of 5.25±4.64 cm. has a small effect on the scale of distancing. The system is reliable in providing proper physical distancing suggestions.

To classify whether a person is sitting or standing, we used the height-to-width ratio of the area surrounding a detected person as the criteria. Based on this classification, an appropriate reference point was determined to represent the spatial location of the person in the room space. The maximum boundary for a person sitting on a seat was found to be 46x87 cm., which is reasonable according to seat dimensions. The system is able to accurately determine whether a seat is occupied or available This method solved the problem of the hidden part of the human body behind the seat, allowing for more precise location identification. The improvement of the body reference point shows the potential for developing a more precise location identification system in the future. Figure 5 illustrates the system workflow of the camera-based indoor physical distancing log recording system.

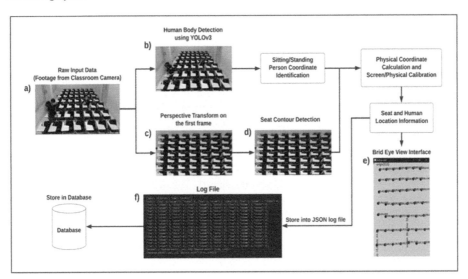

Figure 5. The system workflow for camera-based indoor physical distancing log recording system.

4.2. Smart Street Light Monitoring and Visualization Platform

Smart lighting is a concept that utilizes artificial intelligence (AI) and the Internet of Things (IoT) technology to manage and control lighting systems in cities. The implementation of smart lighting has become a popular trend in modern cities as it enables efficient and effective management of lighting equipment, reduces energy consumption and costs, and enhances the overall safety and security of the city. Smart lighting has been implemented in many major cities worldwide as an important solution for smart city management. The ability to monitor and control lighting equipment in real-time, collect and analyze data from devices and sensors, and the ease of use of the platform make it a convenient solution for managing and improving the lighting systems in cities.

The Smart Lighting project at Thammasat University, Rangsit Campus, is an example of the implementation of this concept. The project involves the development of a web application on a cloud platform that serves as a central control system for monitoring, controlling, and collecting data from lighting equipment and sensors in the university campus in real-time. The platform provides a user-friendly interface for monitoring and controlling the lighting equipment, and it also visualizes the data collected from the devices and sensors in the area, making it easier for users to analyze and understand the information, and for the efficient maintenance by campus staff as well. The platform, moreover, this platform aims to improve energy efficiency and align with Thammasat University's sustainable development goals through monitoring and data analysis for optimal energy consumption [17].

For the first phase, the 167 smart light poles, equipped with LED lamps and adjustable dimming levels were installed. The pole-to-pole separation of approximately 20 meters ensures optimal coverage with the general regulation of street light in Thailand and provides a more efficient and effective lighting solution.

4.2.1. Smart Street Light Installation

In collaboration with the Minebea Mitsumi Inc., of Japan, smart street lights and environmental sensors are installed in six zones on five roads within the Rangsit campus. The project equipment consists of 167 controllable lighting devices with brightness sensors attached to each lighting device, environment station including weather condition and light sensors, three gateways for connecting all equipment to an external control system.

As depicted in Figure 6, the smart LED lights and their associated illuminance sensor are connected to the control node and CMS Neptune SC-v6.0.3 platform operated by the manufacturer (Paradox Engineering, Switzerland). The API can be accessed via REST (the Representa- tional State Transfer) over HTTP (Hypertext Transfer Protocol) to collect data and control the local device. The backend of the system must be able to send HTTP requests and receive responses from the CMS API. The front-end visualization is presented as a web application, which also connected to the lighting system via the CMS API, accessible from any devices with a web browser, and can display received data and device status. Advantageously, the web application can be accessed from anywhere at any time.

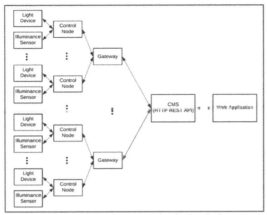

Figure 6. Device connection in the platform.

4.2.2. Development of Back-end and Front-end System

To develop the web application, it is necessary to establish both the back-end or the server-side and the front-end or the client side of the application. Node.js, a JavaScript runtime environment, is used in web application development as it allows JavaScript to run on both ends. [18]. On top of node.js, the Express.js web framework module is introduced because of its highly configurable nature, thus allowing for more customization on the web application development [19].

Express.js provides a robust and convenient routing system that allows developers to create custom API endpoints to handle HTTP requests and send responses. The Axios module [20] makes it easy to send HTTP requests and receive responses, which is useful when connecting to third-party APIs like the CMS API. For security, it's common to implement authentication and authorization mechanisms to protect the API and its resources. The use of cookies to store user tokens can help to improve the performance of the authentication process by reducing the number of requests to the CMS server. By using these technologies, developers can create a back-end application that integrates with the CMS API and provides a secure and efficient way for users to access and control devices through the CMS. The back-end application communicates with the CMS API to retrieve data from lighting devices and environmental sensors. It processes and reformats the data received from the API and sends it as an HTTP response in JSON format to the front-end application, making it easier to display and use. The API also provides additional information, such as device information and status, to support the monitoring system on the front-end. The process in the back-end application is illustrated in the provided Figure 7.

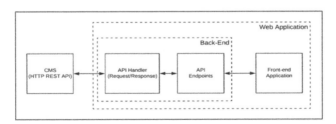

Figure 7. The connection between CMS API and the back-end processing of the web application.

The front-end web application is designed to be user-friendly and accessible via the internet or cellular network using HTTP protocol. To ensure that the web application behaves the same across all devices, including mobile and desktop devices, responsive web application design with Bootstrap is implemented. This allows for fast and optimized rendering of web pages on devices with different screen sizes, improving the user experience on mobile devices.

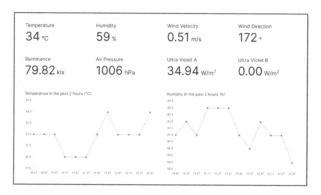

Figure 8. The dashboard interface used in the web application.

Chart.js, an open source JavaScript library [21], is used for data visualization on the dashboard. The library provides a wide range of customization options and is used in the web application to display data from environmental sensors including temperature and humidity from the past 2 hours, in the form of line graphs. The numerical data of illuminance, Ultra Violet A and B indices, wind velocity, wind direction, and air pressure are updated every 10 minutes. The dashboard interface is displayed in Figure 8.

Finally, the device location is displayed on an interactive map using Leaflet.js [22]. The interactive map provides real-time information on the device information and precise location. The web application, a combination of front-end and back-end development, s deployed on Microsoft Azure App Service [23], which supports Node.js applications and has a streamlined deployment process. After deployment, a public URL is available for accessing the web application to monitor the smart lighting system and retrieve data from environmental sensors.

4.2.3. Illumination Data Analytics and Prediction Models

Figure 9 illustrates the results of the first set of analyses, which focuses on examining the hourly average illuminance values over a period of nine months (February to October 2022). It was observed that the natural light illuminance in Thailand exhibited a predictable pattern of increasing from 06:00, peaking during midday, and declining to zero at approximately 18:00. Additionally, a correlation matrix was analyzed, as shown in Figure 10, to assess the relationship between the selected dataset features. The results indicated that Ultraviolet A and Ultraviolet B were highly correlated with illuminance values.

Figure 9. The hourly average of illuminance values over the period of nine months, covering February to October 2022.

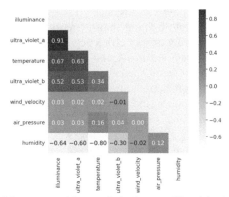

Figure 10. Investigation of the strong positive correlation between Ultraviolet A and illuminance values by generating a correlation matrix for every pair of variables.

Machine learning algorithms were implemented to forecast future illuminance timestamps in this study. The correlation matrix showed a significant correlation between Ultraviolet A and Ultraviolet B with illuminance values; therefore, they were eliminated from the dataset to prevent overfitting. Five environmental parameters, namely humidity, temperature, air pressure, illuminance, and wind velocity, were retained as input parameters. Date and time were also included as parameters during training. The performance of each model was assessed using a correlation coefficient metric by comparing the predicted values with the actual values. Table 1 presents the results of experiment, which compared the performance of four different machine learning models, including Gradient Boosting, XGBoost, Random Forest, and Decision Tree, across different analysis window sizes (3, 4, 5, 6, and 7 days) for predicting illuminance values in the environmental dataset.

Table 1. Evaluation of correlation coefficient between predicted and actual illuminance values on test data using varied machine learning models and window sizes.

Window size / Models	3 Days	4 Days	5 Days	6 Days	7 Days
Gradient Boosting	0.918	0.914	0.919	0.912	0.912
XGBoost	**0.922**	**0.920**	**0.920**	**0.919**	**0.903**
Random Forest	0.919	0.917	0.918	0.915	0.918
Decision Tree	0.839	0.840	0.848	0.838	0.840

Typically, a model is deemed better if it has a higher correlation coefficient between predicted and actual values. According to the results in Table 1, the optimal machine learning model varied based on the size of the analysis window. For a 3-day window size, the XGBoost model had the highest correlation coefficient of 0.922, making it the best-performing model among the selected ones.

5. Conclusion

The Thammasat AI City platform stands as a visionary solution for advancing urban management through the integration of cross-domain data connectivity and machine learning, enabling comprehensive data collection. Within this study, we have validated the platform's effectiveness in two vital domains: the monitoring of street lights and the tracking of indoor human physical distance. The street light monitoring system empowers real-time insights into lighting status, energy consumption, and maintenance requirements, thereby optimizing energy efficiency and cost reduction. Simultaneously, the camera-based indoor system ensures social distancing adherence for public safety. As we look to the future, potential avenues for further exploration could involve expanding the platform's applications to encompass additional urban challenges, optimizing data analysis techniques, and fine-tuning the integration of AI-driven insights for more precise decision-making. Ultimately, the Thammasat AI City platform remains dedicated to enhancing the quality of urban life while aligning seamlessly with the principles of sustainable urban development.

Acknowledgement

This work was supported by the Thailand Science Research and Innovation Fundamental Fund, Contract Number TUFF19/2564 and TUFF24/2565, for the project of "AI Ready City Networking in RUN", based on the RUN Digital Cluster collaboration scheme.

References

[1]   Klaylee J, Iamtrakul P, Kesorn P. Driving Factors of Smart City Development in Thailand. In: Proceedings of International Conference and Utility Exhibition on Energy, Environment and Climate Change (ICUE); 2020, p. 1-9. doi: 10.1109/ICUE49301.2020.9307052
[2]   Ota N. Create Deep Intelligence TM in the Internet of Things; 2014. URL http://on-demand.gputechconf.com/gtc/2015/presentation/S5813-Nobuyuki-Ota.pdf
[3]   Singh KK, Singh A, Lin J-W, Elnger A. Deep Learning and IoT in Healthcare Systems. Paradigms and Applications: CRC Press; 2021 Dec.
[4]   Viriyavit W, Sornlertlamvanich V. Bed Position Classification by a Neural Network and Bayesian Network Using Noninvasive Sensors for Fall Prevention. Journal of Sensors: Hindawi. 2020 Jan; Volume 2020, Article ID 5689860. p. 1-14. https://doi.org/10.1155/2020/5689860
[5]   Kovavisaruch L, Sanpechuda T, Chinda K, Kamolvej P, Sornlertlamvanich V. Museum Layout Evaluation based on Visitor Statistical History. Asian Journal of Applied Sciences. 2017 Jun;5(3). p. 615-622.
[6]   Virach Sornlertlamvanich, Pawinee Iamtrakul, Teerayuth Horanont, Narit Hnoohom, Konlakorn Wongpatikaseree, Sumeth Yuenyong, Jantima Angkapanichkit, Suthasinee Piyapasuntra, Prittipoen Lopkerd, Santirak Prasertsuk, Chawee Busayarat, I-soon Raungratanaamporn, Somrudee Deepaisarn, and Thatsanee Charoenporn. Data Analytics and Aggregation Platform for Comprehensive City-Scale AI Modeling, Proceedings of the 32nd International Conference on Information Modelling and Knowledge Bases (EJC2022), Hamburg, Germany, May 30 - June 3, 2022, pp. 97-112.
[7]   Somrudee Deepaisarn, Angkoon Angkoonsawaengsuk, Charn Arunkit, Chayud Srisumarnk, Krongkan Nimmanwatthana, Nanmanas Linphrachaya, Nattapol Chiewnawintawat, Rinrada Tanthanathewin, Sivakorn Seinglek, Suphachok Buaruk, and Virach Sornlertlamvanich, "Camera-Based Log System for

Human Physical Distance Tracking in Classroom," Proceedings of 2022 APSIPA Annual Summit and Conference, Chiang Mai, Thailand, November 7-10, 2022.

[8]   S.-W.HongandL.Choi,"Automatic recognition of flowers through color and edge based contour detection," in *2012 3rd International conference on image processing theory, tools and applications (IPTA)*, pp. 141–146, IEEE, 2012.

[9]   N. I. Hassan, N. M. Tahir, F. H. K. Zaman, and H. Hashim, "People detection system using yolov3 algorithm," in *2020 10th IEEE international conference on control system, computing and engineering (ICCSCE)*, pp. 131–136, IEEE, 2020.

[10] I. Ansari, Y. Lee, Y. Jeong, and J. Shim, "Recognition of car manufacturers using faster r-cnn and perspective transformation," *Journal of Korea Multimedia Society*, vol. 21, no. 8, pp. 888–896, 2018.

[11] N. I. Hassan, N. M. Tahir, F. H. K. Zaman, and H. Hashim, "People detection system using yolov3 algorithm," in *2020 10th IEEE international conference on control system, computing and engineering (ICCSCE)*, pp. 131–136, IEEE, 2020.

[12] P. Gupta,V.Sharma,andS.Varma,"People detection and counting using yolov3 and ssd models," *Materials Today: Proceedings*, 2021.

[13] J. C. Marutotamtama and I. Setyawan, "Physical distancing detection using yolo v3 and bird's eye view transform," in *2021 2nd Interna- tional Conference on Innovative and Creative Information Technology (ICITech)*, pp. 50–56, IEEE, 2021.

[14] S.-F. Lin, J.-Y. Chen, and H.-X. Chao, "Estimation of number of people in crowded scenes using perspective transformation," *IEEE Transactions on Systems, Man, and Cybernetics-Part A: Systems and Humans*, vol. 31, no. 6, pp. 645–654, 2001.

[15] J. Yu, N. Gao, Z. Meng, and Z. Zhang, "High-accuracy projector calibration method for fringe projection profilometry considering perspective transformation," *Optics Express*, vol. 29, no. 10, pp. 15053–15066, 2021.

[16] V. Kocur and M. Fta´cˇnik, "Detection of 3d bounding boxes of vehicles using perspective transformation for accurate speed measurement," *Machine Vision and Applications*, vol. 31, no. 7, pp. 1–15, 2020.

[17] Somrudee Deepaisarn, Paphana Yiwsiw, Chanon Tantiwattanapaibul, Suphachok Buaruk, and Virach Sornlertlamvanich, "Smart Street Light Monitoring and Visualization Platform for Campus Management," 2022 17th International Joint Symposium on Artificial Intelligence and Natural Language Processing (iSAI-NLP), Chiang Mai, Thailand, November 5-7, 2022, pp. 1-5, doi: 10.1109/iSAI-NLP56921.2022.9960257.

[18] N. Chhetri, *A Comparative Analysis of Node.js (Server-Side JavaScript)*. Master's thesis, St. Cloud State University, 2016.

[19] A. Mardan, "Using express.js to create node.js web apps," *Practical Node.js*, pp. 51–87, 2018.

[20] "Axios.". Available at https://axios-http.com/, 2022.

[21] H. M. Millqvist and N. Bolin, A comparision of performance and scalability of chart generation for Javascript data visualisation libraries: A comparative experiment on Chart.js, ApexCharts, Billboard, and ToastUI. Bachelor's thesis, University of Sko¨vde, 2022.

[22] V.Agafonkin, "Leaflet-anopen-sourceJavascriptlibraryforinteractive maps." https://leafletjs.com/, 2022.

[23] V. P. Desai, K. S. Oza, P. P. Shinde, and P. G. Naik, "Microsoft azure: Cloud platform for application service deployment," *International Journal of Scientific Research in Multidisciplinary Studies*, vol. 7, no. 10, pp. 20–23, 2021.

Information Modelling and Knowledge Bases XXXV
M. Tropmann-Frick et al. (Eds.)
doi:10.3233/FAIA231156

Digital Modeling of the Impact of Energy Sector Transformations on the Economic Security of the EU

Olena KHADZHYNOVA[a]; Žaneta SIMANAVIČIENĖ[a]; Oleksiy MINTS [b,1];
Kateryna POLUPANOVA [a]
[a] *Mykolas Romeris University, Vilnius (Lithuania)*
[b] *SHEI "Pryazovskyi State Technical University", Dnipro (Ukraine)*
ORCiD ID: Olena KHADZHYNOVA https://orcid.org/0000-0002-7750-9791,
Žaneta SIMANAVIČIENĖ https://orcid.org/0000-0001-5689-4355,
Oleksiy MINTS https://orcid.org/0000-0002-8032-005X,
Kateryna POLUPANOVA https://orcid.org/0000-0001-7310-0596

Abstract. The energy security of the EU is a current issue for all member countries. The EU's energy policy aims for diversification of energy resources and energy independence. After 2022, this issue has worsened. The article analyzes the main risks to the energy security of EU countries and industries located in these countries. The dynamics of energy consumption by different sectors of the EU economy are considered and the impact of changes in the energy sector on the economic security of businesses is evaluated. Approaches to modeling the impact of transformations in the energy sector on the economic security of businesses are discussed. A simulation model of a three-sector energy market has been developed. The driver of changes in the model is the minimization of carbon emissions. Experiments were conducted to simulate the development of the energy market from 2012 to 2052. Digital modeling showed that in a case of "gas blackmail" the most probable scenario means increasing of dirty energy sources with high carbon emission.

Keywords. economic security, energy security, enterprises, industry, modeling, European Union

1. Introduction

The energy sector is a vital component of the European Union's economy and plays a significant role in ensuring economic security for enterprises. In recent years, the EU has undergone significant transformations in its energy sector, aimed at reducing its dependence on fossil fuels, increasing the use of renewable energy sources, and enhancing energy efficiency.

The shift towards cleaner energy sources has led to the creation of new business opportunities and the expansion of existing ones, particularly in the renewable energy and energy efficiency sectors. The increased investment in these areas has created jobs,

---

[1] Corresponding Author, e-mail: mints_a_y@pstu.edu

stimulated innovation, and helped drive economic growth.

However, the transformation of the energy sector also presents challenges for enterprises. The transition to new energy sources and technologies can result in changes to traditional business models, leading to increased competition and reduced profits. It can also cause uncertainty for companies that are heavily invested in fossil fuels, leading to potential job losses and financial instability.

To mitigate these risks, the EU has implemented various measures, including providing financial support to companies, encouraging the development of new technologies, and promoting the adoption of energy-efficient practices. These initiatives aim to support enterprises in the transition to a more sustainable energy future and ensure their long-term economic security.

The EU is heavily dependent on energy imports from other countries, particularly for oil and natural gas. This dependence on energy imports leaves the EU vulnerable to price fluctuations and supply disruptions, which can have significant impacts on the economy and individual enterprises.

During a long time Russian Federation perceived as a reliable supplier of natural gas. However, 2022 marked the beginning of a hybrid economic war between the Russian Federation and the EU, during which the probability of a complete cessation of natural gas supplies from the Russian Federation to the EU increases significantly.

The war between Ukraine and the Russian Federation has already led to significant transformations in the energy sector of the European Union. Moreover, this process continues and the final configuration of the energy sector of the EU is still difficult to predict. But it is already clear that the energy sector transformations will greatly affect the economic security of industrial enterprises in Europe.

The main purpose of this article is to consider the prerequisites for modeling the impact of EU energy sector transformations on the economic security of enterprises. In order to accomplish this objective, we will conduct a literature review on the topic of the economic security of the EU, trends in the development of the European energy sector, and the modeling of their interrelationships. Subsequently, we will analyze the development of the energy infrastructure of the EU, and examine trends in the dynamics of energy consumption by the industrial sector. Based on the findings, we will identify approaches to model the transformations of the EU energy sector and their impact on the economic security of enterprises. In this regard, we will consider possible methods within the framework of inductive and deductive approaches.

2. Literature review

The close relation between the energy and economic security of the EU countries has been evident for a long time. Although the need for a dramatic transformation of the energy sector became critical only in 2022, the prerequisites for modeling such a situation were considered in the works of many scientists.

The authors (Sharples, 2013; Smiech, 2013) show the key aspects of economic security for the EU energy in the context of climate change. Their articles deal with the concept of energy security and economic problems for the EU countries. The problem of natural gas consumption as a 'green fuel' for Europe is considered.

The other group of authors (Jonsonn et al., 2015; Sytailo & Okhrimenko 2020) defines the key security indicators of the EU energy market in the next aspects: energy security, security of supply, security of demand and revenue, other political, social, technical and environment risk factors. Therefore, energy consumption in the context of low-carbon energy transitions described as not only technological problem, but also the consideration of market supply and demand aspects.

An important component of the economic security of the EU energy consumption is the development and implementation of renewable energy sources (Zherlitsyn et al., 2020). The authors consider the economic aspects of the implementation of the appropriate technological solutions, evaluate the forecasting and economic efficiency models for such projects.

The relationship between the EU foreign policy and energy strategies is the other part of economic security aspect (Youngs, 2020). In particular, the factors exogenous to energy policy can be significant and how these can contain contestation as well as generate it. These aspects have become key in 2022. Contemporary works show what the EU economic security needs to improve its external energy security. The author (Misik, 2022) shows that the EU's response in energy security policy have been rather slow and mainly towards the revision of the Union's internal mechanisms rather than the common external energy policy creation.

The study by Perdana et al. (2022) examines the economic repercussions of a complete ban on fossil fuel imports from Russia to European energy producers. Of particular interest is the analysis of the effects of cutting off energy imports from Russia for each individual EU country. Another study by Chachko and Linos (2022) evaluates the EU's energy consumption and identifies security and defense strategies in response to Russia's invasion of Ukraine. The outcome of the crisis revealed a lack of attention paid to the economic security aspects in the EU's energy sector.

As a result, early 21st-century authors placed a significant emphasis on the promotion of "green fuel" and diversification of energy sources for EU countries. Nonetheless, the outcome of partial and total embargoes on fossil fuel imports from Russia in 2022 exposed a deficiency of economic security in the energy sector for EU.

3. Results and discussion

Energy security is considered to be an important aspect of ensuring a stable and reliable energy supply for individuals, businesses, and governments. This includes ensuring the availability of resources such as oil, natural gas, and coal, as well as promoting the use of renewable energy sources and reducing dependence on single sources of energy. Energy security also involves protecting energy infrastructure and addressing potential risks such as supply disruptions, price volatility, and environmental impacts. Thus, energy security is an important part of economic security.

Energy security refers to the availability, reliability, and affordability of energy supplies, as well as the stability of the energy systems and infrastructure that support them. It involves ensuring a consistent and sufficient supply of energy to meet the needs of individuals, businesses, and governments, while also mitigating the risks and impacts of energy production and consumption, such as price volatility, supply disruptions, and environmental degradation. The goal of energy security is to ensure a stable and sustainable energy system that supports economic growth and protects national economic security.

From the perspective of enterprises, energy security is the assurance that they have access to a reliable and cost-effective supply of energy to meet their operational needs and support their business goals. It involves minimizing the risks and uncertainties associated with energy prices and supply, and ensuring the resilience of the energy infrastructure that supports their operations. Companies may adopt strategies to improve their energy security, such as diversifying their energy sources, implementing energy-efficient technologies, and investing in renewable energy. In the economical context the ultimate goal for companies is to minimize their exposure to energy price volatility and supply disruptions, while ensuring the sustainability of their energy consumption and supporting their bottom line.

Energy security is a key concern for the European Union, as the bloc relies heavily on imported energy, particularly oil and natural gas. The EU has taken various steps to improve its energy security by diversifying its energy mix and reducing its dependence on single sources of energy. This includes promoting the use of renewable energy sources, such as wind and solar power, and increasing energy efficiency through the implementation of policies and regulations.

The EU has also established a number of initiatives aimed at improving energy security and the stability of the energy market. For example, the EU has established a single energy market, which facilitates the flow of energy between member states and helps to reduce dependence on single sources of energy. The bloc has also established a number of interconnections between its national energy grids, which help to increase the security of energy supply and reduce the impact of disruptions.

The EU is also working to improve the security of its energy infrastructure, particularly in the context of increasing concerns about cyber security threats. The EU has established various initiatives aimed at enhancing the resilience of its energy systems, including the development of a comprehensive framework for the security of the electricity grid and the strengthening of emergency response mechanisms.

Overall, energy security is a high priority for the EU, and the bloc is taking a multi-faceted approach to address the challenges it faces in ensuring a secure, reliable, and sustainable energy supply, which is confirmed by the analysis below.

To assess the impact of changes in the energy sector structure on the economic security of enterprises, the dynamics of energy consumption by various sectors of the economy should be considered (Fig. 1).

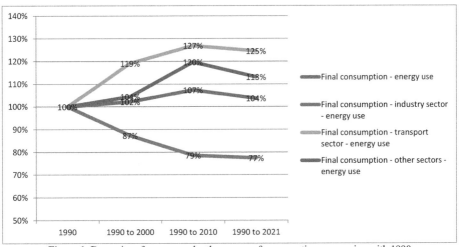

Figure.1. Dynamics of energy use by the groups of consumption, comparing with 1990
Source: [authors' estimations and (Eurostat, 2022)]

The decline in energy consumption by the industrial sector, as shown in Fig. 1, is a noteworthy trend in the EU's economy. The reduction in energy consumption compared to 1990 levels, where the industrial sector consumed 79% of energy, to 77% in 2021 highlights the efforts made by the EU to improve energy efficiency and reduce its carbon footprint. The decrease in energy consumption in the industrial sector can be attributed to the implementation of energy-saving technologies, as well as increased awareness about the environmental impact of energy consumption.

On the other hand, the data in Fig. 1 shows that the other sectors of the EU economy have experienced a steady increase in energy consumption until 2006-2010. The subsequent decrease in energy consumption after this period can be attributed to the implementation of energy-efficient technologies and practices, such as the use of renewable energy sources and the development of more efficient buildings and appliances.

The changes in energy consumption by the industrial sector of EU countries began much earlier and can be traced back to the early 1990s. Fig. 2 provides a more detailed look at these changes, highlighting the specific industries that have seen the greatest reductions in energy consumption. Understanding the changes in energy consumption by industry is crucial for policymakers, as it provides valuable insights into the effectiveness of energy efficiency policies and the areas where additional efforts are needed to reduce energy consumption.

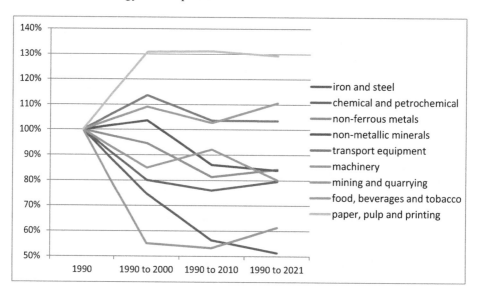

Figure.2. Dynamics of energy consumption by the groups of industries,
comparing with 1990
Source: [authors' estimations and (Eurostat, 2022)]

The data shown in Fig.2 reveals that most industries have experienced a decrease in energy consumption. However, the printing, food, and transport industries show an exception, yet they have either seen a decrease or no increase in energy consumption since 2000.

Such dynamics, in the context of an increase in GDP in EU countries, could indicate that industrial enterprises had two main opportunities: or become more energy efficient or shutting down. An additional analysis of industrial production statistics showed that most industries have seen an increase in production over the period under review. This is even true for energy-intensive industries such as metal production (with a 5% increase from 1991 to 2021), motor vehicle production (with a 47% increase over the same period), mining, and others (Eurostat, 2022).

Let's consider the approaches to modeling the transformations of the EU energy sector and its impact on the economic security of enterprises. The positive influence in this case is the availability of sufficient statistical data reflecting the dynamics of the development of various industries in the EU and their energy consumption, including a breakdown by types of fuel used (Eurostat, 2022). This allows for sufficient use of such inductive models:

Statistical models, that use historical data to estimate the relationship between energy sector transformations and economic security can be used to make predictions about the future. This type of model can be used to estimate the impact of changes in energy prices, energy mix, and energy efficiency on the economy and individual enterprises.

Input-output models: This type of model looks at the flow of goods and services between different sectors of the economy, including the energy sector. By analyzing the interconnections between different sectors, input-output models can be used to estimate the indirect and spillover effects of energy sector transformations on the economy and individual enterprises.

Using inductive models allows us to establish and statistically confirm the main trends and interrelations in the transformation of the energy sector of the EU, which have historically arisen over the past decades. Unfortunately, inductive models cannot adequately predict the reaction of the research object in case of sharp changes in external conditions. This is the situation that arose in 2022 when the EU countries were forced to sharply restructure the chains of energy carriers supplies and the structure of the energy market due to the start of the war in Ukraine and the "gas blackmail" by the Russian Federation. To model the transformations of the energy sector of the EU and their impact on the economic security of enterprises in this case, the following models based on a deductive approach can be used:

Scenario analysis: This type of analysis considers different future scenarios for the energy sector, taking into account different policy interventions and technological developments. Scenario analysis can be used to explore the potential impact of energy sector transformations on the economy and individual enterprises, allowing for a more comprehensive understanding of the risks and opportunities associated with the transition to a more sustainable energy future.

Simulation modeling: It's a broad class of models that includes system dynamics models, agent-evolutionary models, service system models, and others. The use of simulation models involves formulating assumptions about the structure, properties, and internal relationships of the modeled objects. By constructing virtual representations of real-world phenomena, simulation models enable us to experiment with different scenarios, identify cause-and-effect relationships, and make informed decisions about how to optimize and manage these systems. Based on these assumptions, the behavior of the object (energy sector, or industry) in the future is calculated, taking into account both random and planned deviations in its conditions of existence.

The deductive approach to modeling the impact of bifurcation changes in the energy sector on the economic security of enterprises does not exclude the use of inductive methods of modeling to confirm specific trends in the economies of EU countries. Economic development processes are to a sufficient degree inertial and it should be expected that even in the conditions of global catastrophes, the main vector of development will remain unchanged.

Even a cursory analysis of statistics and literary sources allows us to note that the use of "green energy" and high energy efficiency in production is characteristic for EU countries. However, additional research is needed to more accurately establish the impact of these factors. Fig. 3 illustrates the changes in the EU energy market by selected energy sources, such as Solid fuels, Natural gas and Renewable energy. The choice of these energy sources is made in accordance with the level of carbon emissions.

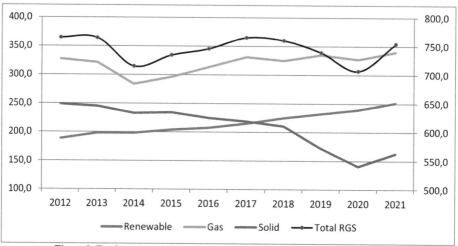

Figure 3. Total energy supply by the Renewable energy, Natural gas and Solid fuel
Source: [authors' estimations and (Eurostat, 2022)]

The graph shows a significant decrease in the usage of dirty fossil fuels, an increase of renewable energy supply, and mostly growing trend towards the use of clean fossil fuels.

Based on the identified trends, it can be assumed that the carbon emission level significantly impacts the energy sector structure of EU countries. Priority directions of development include minimizing carbon emissions and maximizing renewable energy sources. Moreover, the interconnections between changes in various segments of the energy market can be represented in a causal relationship diagram (Fig. 4).

The model's operation can be described as follows: In the first stage of the cycle, the growing energy production from fossil sources leads to increasing carbon emissions. Since this contradicts the goals declared by the EU, in the second stage, such an increase eventually results in higher investments in renewable energy sources. Funding can include collected fines, government subsidies, and preferential credit programs. In the third stage, the increased production of energy from renewable sources alters the energy market balance and leads to a reduced demand for fossil fuels energy, consequently reducing production.

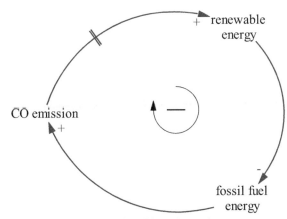

Figure 4. A causality model for carbon-driven changes in energy sector structure.
Source: [authors' own estimations]

Based on this cause-and-effect diagram, a simulation model of the development of a three-sector energy market was built (Fig. 5).

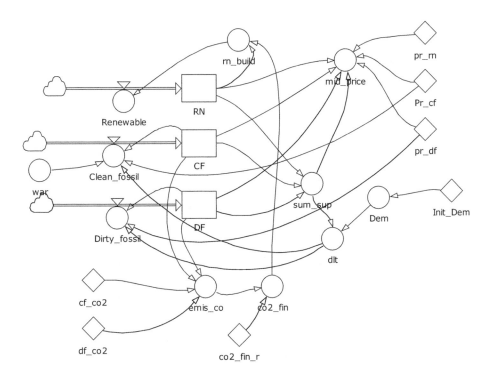

Figure 5. Simulation model of three sectors energy market.
Source: [authors' own estimations]

The driver of changes in the model is the minimization of carbon emissions. An increase in emissions leads to increased investments in renewable energy sources. However, the effectiveness of these investments decreases as the renewable segment requires specific conditions for growing the solar, wind, or hydroelectric power plants. Therefore, the number of suitable locations for their deployment is limited. In the remaining energy production sectors, preference is given to the use of clean fossil fuel sources, while the remaining market needs are met through the utilization of dirty fossil fuels.

In the next part of the article, we will present the results of experiments with the developed simulation model. Real data were used to set critical model parameters, but some data were assumed. Some parameters, such as energy demand or energy prices, are set constant to simplify the model. The initial modeling period roughly corresponds to the real year 2012.

The Fig. 6 presents the results of the energy sector's development simulation over a 40-year period.

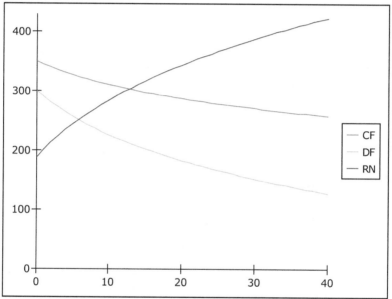

Figure 6. Simulation results for a 40 years period.
Source: [authors' own estimations]

From the graph, it can be observed that despite a significant decrease in energy generation from fossil fuel sources, their complete cessation was not achieved. The use of dirty fossil fuels decreased much more than the using of natural gas, but it did not completely cease due to the relatively high gas prices. Generation from renewable energy sources increased by more than twice.

Fig. 7 shows the results of simulating an external impact on the system, specifically a reduction in energy generation from clean fossil fuels by 100 units (equivalent to the share of Russian Federation in the natural gas market of the EU). This simulates a situation of "gas blackmail" in the 2022.

From the graph (Fig. 7), it can be observed that there is an energy deficit in the system for a certain period of time, which is compensated (supposably) by using other energy sources, mainly dirty fossil fuels. However, the energy system's balance is eventually restored. In particular, alternative channels for the supply of natural gas are may established.

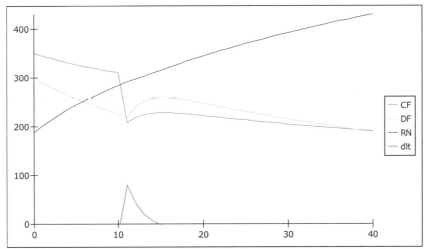

Figure 7. Simulation results with a shock in a Clean fossil fuels supply at a 10`s period
Source: [authors' own estimations]

The modeling results demonstrate that the energy system have a self-balancing properties and can adapt even to strong negative influences. However, this adaptation occurs through an increase in energy production from dirty sources, which has a negative impact on the achievement of the EU's sustainable development goals.

It is important to note that these models are just a tool and the results they provide should be interpreted with caution. The results are strongly influenced by the assumptions made, data used, and methodologies employed. Indeed, it seems that in the long term, the shock caused by the gas blackmail situation could lead to an acceleration of transformations in the energy sector and to increase in its autonomy.

4. Conclusion

The transformation of the EU energy sector presents both opportunities and challenges for enterprises. While the shift to cleaner energy sources offers new business opportunities, it also requires companies to adapt to changes in the market and the energy sector. Through various measures and initiatives, the EU is working to ensure that enterprises can thrive in a changing energy landscape and contribute to a more sustainable and economically secure future.

It is currently impossible to accurately predict all the consequences of the transformation of the EU's energy sector as a result of the military conflict between Ukraine and Russia. Industrial enterprises in the EU have long been focused on improving energy efficiency, which has helped to bolster their economic security against energy threats from Russia. The potential physical shortage of natural gas supply is driving the EU to increase its use of renewable energy and electric vehicles. But digital modeling showed that in a case of "gas blackmail" the most probable scenario means increasing of dirty energy sources with high carbon emission.

References

[1] Chachko, E., & Linos, K. (2022). Ukraine and the Emergency Powers Of International Institutions. American Journal of International Law, 116(4), 775-787. Doi:10.1017/ajil.2022.57

[2] Eurostat (2022) Energy statistics - an overview. Eurostat https://ec.europa.eu/eurostat/statistics-explained/index.php?title=Energy_statistics_-_an_overview#

[3] Jonsson, D. K., Johansson, B., Mansson, A., Nilsson, L. J., Nilsson, M., & Sonnsjo, H. (2015a). Energy security matters in the EU Energy Roadmap. Energy Strategy Reviews, 6, 48-56. doi:10.1016/j.esr.2015.03.002

[4] Misik, M. (2022). The EU needs to improve its external energy security. Energy Policy, 165, 5. doi:10.1016/j.enpol.2022.112930

[5] Perdana, S., Vielle, M., & Schenckery, M. (2022). European Economic impacts of cutting energy imports from Russia: A computable general equilibrium analysis. Energy Strategy Reviews, 44, 15. doi:10.1016/j.esr.2022.101006

[6] Sharples, J. D. (2013). Russian approaches to energy security and climate change: Russian gas exports to the EU. Environmental Politics, 22(4), 683-700. doi:10.1080/09644016.2013.806628

[7] Smiech, S. (2013). Some aspects of energy security in the EU member countries in the period 2000-2010. Proceedings of the 7th Professor Aleksander Zelias International Conference on Modelling and Forecasting of Socio-Economic Phenomena, 157-164.

[8] Sytailo, U., & Okhrimenko, O. (2020). Evaluating the level of economic security of the EU energy markets. Eastern Journal of European Studies, 11(2), 353-377.

[9] Youngs, R. (2020). EU foreign policy and energy strategy: bounded contestation. Journal of European Integration, 42(1), 147-162. doi:10.1080/07036337.2019.1708345

[10] Zherlitsyn, D., Skrypnyk, A., Rogoza, N., Saiapin, S. & Kudin, T. (2020). Green tariff and investment in solar power plants. Studies of Applied Economics. Vol 38 (4). Doi: http://dx.doi.org/10.25115/eea.v38i4.3994

Sources of funding for research presented in a scientific article or scientific article itself: This research is/was funded by the European Social Fund under the No 09.3.3-LMT-K-712-23-0211 "Transformation of the economic security system of enterprises in the process of digitalization" measure.

Information Modelling and Knowledge Bases XXXV
M. Tropmann-Frick et al. (Eds.)

doi:10.3233/FAIA231157

Enhancing Collaborative Prototype Development: An Evaluation of the Descriptive Model for Prototyping Process

Janne HARJAMÄKI [a,1], Mika SAARI [a], Mikko NURMINEN [a], Petri RANTANEN [a],
Jari SOINI [a] and David HÄSTBACKA [a]

[a] Tampere University, Pori, Finland

Abstract.

In this article, the ongoing research on collaborative prototype development between university and enterprises is presented. The study of project featured numerous pilot cases and prototypes, executed in collaboration with organizations to address real-world challenges. This article assesses the appropriateness of the Descriptive Model for Prototyping Process (DMPP) for research project applications. We delve into two primary facets: the synergy between universities and enterprises, and the potential for artifact reusability within the DMPP. The article presents various pilot cases from the KIEMI project, highlighting the DMPP's role in each. Furthermore, the paper evaluates the model, sets forward the challenges faced, and, finally, discusses topics for future research.

Keywords. Artifact, Reusability, Collaboration, Descriptive Model for Prototyping Process, DMPP, Prototyping, Iterative design, Process model

1. Introduction

Universities and other research organizations produce research results, typically in the form of publications, such as papers and technical reports. In addition, applied research produces prototypes with proofs of concept (PoC). This study presents the outcome of one university project, where proofs of concept were mainly implemented by building data-gathering prototypes.

The focus of this study is on the findings of the KIEMI project ("Vähemmällä – Kohti Kiinteistöjen Energiaminimiä", or "Less is More: Towards the Energy Minimum of Properties" in English). The aim of the project was to develop proof-of-concept demonstrations and prototype applications that illustrate how cost-effective, open, and modular solutions could be utilized to improve the energy efficiency of existing, older buildings [1]. The KIEMI project was selected for analysis in this paper because of its large number of pilot use cases.

---

[1] Corresponding Author: Mika Saari, mika.saari@tuni.fi

The goal of the KIEMI project was to save energy, and we worked towards this goal by developing and constructing data-gathering IoT sensor systems. We used the developed SW/HW framework [2] and the formerly developed descriptive model for the prototyping process (DMPP) [3]. The SW/HW framework generalizes prototype development into a group of necessary components and even more precisely the framework defines guidelines for constructing prototype systems to collect data for different purposes by reusing the required software and hardware components [2]. The DMPP was developed to guide the IoT prototype development process and can be used as a guideline when building a prototype. The DMPP contains the prototype development practices that have been applied in research projects between our university and enterprises. With these developed IoT prototypes, developers can receive valuable feedback on the possibility of implementing the application [3].

The following research questions were formulated during the project work. In a previous study, [4] we sought to gain insights into the following topics:

- RQ1: Collaboration. How was university-enterprise collaboration executed in practice using the DMPP?
- RQ2: Reusability. How did the reusability of the artifacts in the DMPP steps support the workflow of the pilot cases?

The additional research question extends the scope of the previous study to analyze the results of enterprise-university collaboration gained during the project and to inform future projects:

- RQ3: Collaboration. How the DMPP process usage can be improved for the enterprise-university collaboration?

University-enterprise collaboration (part of universities' third mission [5], [6]) has been used in previous projects and the DMPP model was developed into its current format based on the pilot cases of these previous projects. The KIEMI project also aimed to build prototypes in collaboration with companies for IoT type data gathering. Since we already had a completed process template, it was decided to put it to good use in this project as well, and RQ1 looks at the success of this issue.

Further, RQ2 focuses on the operation of DMPP sub-processes and how templates were created from them. The use of templates was intended to accelerate the operation. At the beginning, their significance was not understood, but by following the model the usefulness of the templates was noted. The same practices were observed when using the process model, so reuse was included in the review. The benefit and reusability of templates created specifically from reporting was monitored as it was expected to speed up the implementation of some steps.

RQ3 continues analyzing usage of the DMPP process in enterprise-university collaboration, with a particular focus on understanding enterprise-side motivations for collaborative activities. We aim to identify common factors that may influence the success of collaboration efforts with enterprises, as only a limited number of executed pilot cases were able to achieve a high level of collaboration.

The structure of this paper is as follows: In Section II, we review the related research about universities' third mission, industry collaboration. Also the background of the KIEMI project is explained. In Section III, we introduce the DMPP and its connections with project work. Further, the implementation of university-enterprise collabora-

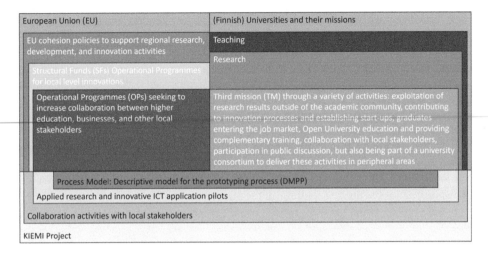

Figure 1. Third mission concept with the KIEMI project

tion in prototype development is described by means of process modeling notation in Section IV.

Moving forward, Section V delves into a description of the prototyping pilot cases conducted as part of the KIEMI project, and Section VI undertakes the analysis of collaboration activity features. Section VII evaluates the usability of DMPP in the KIEMI project highlighting results of the project and pilot cases. Section VIII summarizes the study, and includes a discussion and suggestions for future research on the topic.

2. Background

2.1. Third mission

It is a common conception that the modern university serves three main purposes: teaching, research, as well as a broader social function. The latter of these functions, commonly dubbed "The Third Mission" [5], [6], is regarded as including measures contributing to social impacts and interaction.

Industry-academia collaboration benefits those organizations that do not have their own R&D facilities. For example, companies can utilize the resources of a university to understand their modern-day software engineering problems. Industry has realized that it can support innovation and development processes when collaborating with researchers. [7]

Figure 1 illustrates how the process model approach can be used to align European Union policy and Finnish universities' missions in the form of applied research and collaboration.

The EU cohesion policy and EU Structural Funds (SF) are used through Operational Programmes (OPs) to make it possible to create innovative collaboration projects for local stakeholders. Finnish universities have extended their traditional teaching and research activities within the third mission (TM) to exploit research results for peripheral areas, i.e., in the form of collaboration with local stakeholders. [8]

The University Consortium of Pori (UC Pori) has longstanding and specialized experience of creating collaboration with local stakeholders using the EU SF and OPs through university facilities and resources [8]. The KIEMI project represents a continuation of the series of OPs executed at UC Pori in recent years.

In collaboration, the transfer of technology is an important part, because it innovates development processes and innovative products achieve improved business competitiveness. In the study by [9], innovation is considered as a process consisting of two phases: technology creation and technology transfer.

As seen in Figure 1, the KIEMI project was a framework for implementing collaboration and applied research methods in the form of innovative ICT application pilot cases for local stakeholders. The descriptive model for the prototyping process (DMPP) was the spearhead of the process, pulling all the pieces together.

2.2. Collaboration channels for interactions

Interaction between public research organizations and industry can be implemented through many kinds of collaboration channels. One way to classify collaboration channel types was done in [10], where channels were divided into four groups: traditional, services, commercial, and bi-directional. In this paper, collaboration in SF OPs can be seen as bi-directional collaboration between university and industry, where both parties benefit from the acquisition and development of the technological know-how necessary for the prototype. In addition to the technical content, the prototype usage must take into account the development of interconnections necessary for university-enterprise collaboration and their impact on future cooperation activities.

2.3. Innovation models for collaboration

In projects like KIEMI, collaboration activities are done several times; mostly each time with different SMEs or public organizations (or some unit or department from their organization). To simplify this for the reader, we use the term industrial development (ID) for these collaboration parties or stakeholders. In addition, in case some ID has their own research group or department or if there is a CEO with a researcher's mindset, their staff can be referred to as industrial research (IR). Similarly, the university research unit, as in the KIEMI project, can be defined as academic research (AR).

For successful collaboration management between ID and AR, it is useful to have a framework or process model to ensure that the collaboration and innovation activities inside it create solutions and PoC along with pilot cases and receive strong support from all parties from the very beginning.

In the study by Punter[9], two main stakeholder groups were identified: researchers and industrial practitioners, where the former (AR) act as a technology provider and the latter (ID) as a technology receiver. They also pointed out that AR and ID may have completely different values and targets for technology and collaboration activities. AR is interested in proving concepts for technology via pilot cases during projects. ID is looking for a statement or evaluation of the business benefits and costs of the technology and may see AR's PoC as a technology study without the necessity for proof, i.e., a production proof version.

With an EU OP (such as KIEMI), the ID types of collaboration are predefined in the OP requirements. The same set of requirements also contains targets for project results which can be related to certain products or services through ID or a target may be related to co-creation activities or to research and development activities between AR and ID. in this project, a production proof version is not included, only PoCs. It is assumed that ID will continue the production proof version from the results of the project.

The model used should take different types of ID into account. It should also take into consideration the fact that innovation activities and technology transfer may happen in all phases or steps. As an example, Punter [9] highlights a case where design work was able to add value for ID. Similarly, in projects, value can be produced in cases where some commercial product, already designed for a certain usage, has been applied in a new environment through pilot case activities.

Naturally, activities to develop a suitable collaboration model fall mostly to the party responsible for the project, as here on the AR side. The model and its efficiency define success for current and future collaboration between AR and ID.

A study by [11] presents the Certus model, which was developed at a Norwegian research-based innovation center. Their needs for a collaboration model contained similar elements to the DMPP model. They required deeper research knowledge of co-creation activities via problem definition and solving tasks and more active dialog between researchers and practitioners to align their expectations. They also wanted to ensure that the results and outputs from research projects that are created have practical relevance and benefit for their partners and that the results can be transferred and exploited effectively by their partners.

The Certus model [11] contains seven phases, from problem scoping to market research. Whereas the first four phases (problem scoping, knowledge conception, knowledge and technology development, and knowledge and technology transfer) can be regarded as similar to proof-of-concept development, the following three phases (knowledge and technology exploitation, organizational adoption, and market research) are more related to production proof activities.

2.4. The KIEMI project

The reduction of greenhouse gas emissions is one of the most challenging global objectives of the near future. Low carbon emissions, energy savings, a climate-friendly approach, and ecologically sustainable choices require new and innovative services, solutions, and products. One of the biggest potential areas where savings can be made is energy use in properties in Finland. The KIEMI project, carried out by Tampere University Pori unit, designed and developed methods and technologies that aid in finding and achieving the property- and situation-specific "energy minimum", i.e., a situation where the minimum amount of energy is used while still preserving a comfortable environment within the building. In the KIEMI project, the primary focus was not on new properties or so-called "smart buildings", but on older buildings and apartments that do not contain modern automatic and intelligent devices commonly used for controlling the quality of the living and working environment.

Proof-of-concept demonstrations and prototype applications were developed in the KIEMI project that illustrate how cost-effective, open, and modular solutions can be utilized to improve the energy efficiency of buildings. Further, a decrease in overall energy usage will lead to cost savings related to energy expenses and reduce the carbon footprint caused by, for example, the heating, cooling, and air conditioning of buildings.

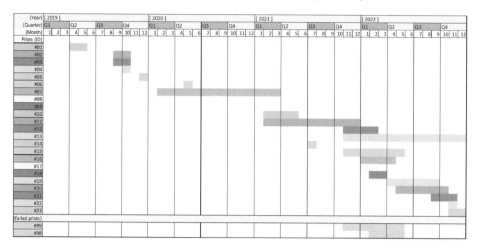

Figure 2. Timeline of pilots in KIEMI.

In the present world situation in 2023, the theme of the project, energy savings, is especially topical, at least in Europe. The KIEMI project partners consisted of organizations and companies who were able to take part in the pilot cases implemented during the project by providing properties, equipment, sensors, and measurement data or by acting as experts. The results of the project can be utilized by all those involved with the energy and resource efficiency of properties and housing-related wellbeing as well as the relevant private (companies) and public bodies (municipalities).

The commitment of the project partners to the project activities was based on the DMPP collaboration model developed in previous projects. In the KIEMI project, the focal point of the partner-specific co-operation varied, depending on how the partner wished to participate, and how they were able to contribute to the research. Collaboration and contribution to the project pilot cases took place roughly according to the following breakdown:

1. Identifying premises for use in the project (condition measurements in the properties)
2. Handing over existing property data for use in the project (interfaces with existing property measurement systems)
3. Determining measurement needs and planning pilot cases together (tailored needs for condition measurement of the target)
4. General development of condition measurement (developing sensor and measurement systems in collaboration with project partner)

During the project a total of 23 different types of pilot cases were carried out related to the energy efficiency and condition measurement of properties. The pilot cases conducted during the KIEMI project as well as the prototype systems developed for them and the technology testing have been reported extensively in the form of scientific articles (several internationally peer-reviewed research publications). Figure 2 shows the schedule of pilot case implementation by month and quarter over the duration of the project. For interrupted pilot cases, the timetable describes the time interval during which discussion and reflection took place.

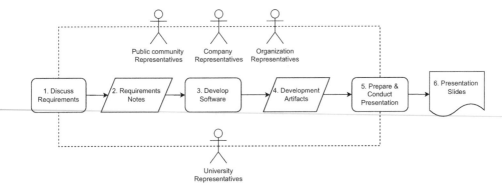

Figure 3. Process model for prototype development. Adapted from [3].

3. Process model for prototyping: Descriptive model for the prototyping process (DMPP)

The purpose of this section is to present how the selected process model has supported the work within the projects. Our descriptive software process model for IoT prototyping was introduced in [3]. The DMPP was developed during a previous project where the prototyping focused on one area. The DMPP was developed using the descriptive process model (DPM) approach [12]. The basic concepts related to processes are role, activity, resource, and artifact. The example is illustrated by a developer (role) involved in software development (activity) using a programming tool (resource). The activity produces some software (artifact) used in a prototype system. The process data for the model is collected through interviews with the developers involved in the four different prototype development processes. Four prototype development projects and their outcomes were reported in several studies [13], [14], [15], [16]. The common factor in all of the studies is that they present developed IoT prototype systems that gather data.

When the KIEMI project started, we noticed that this DMPP could be an acceptable way to approach the subject. During the project, we actively searched for pilot cases (Step 0) where previously collected knowledge about prototyping IoT data-gathering systems could be used. Figure3 presents the DMPP [3] including steps one to six. The pilot case starts with an issue related to a suitable situation for the research group. The pilot case ends after it has been presented to the customer and other reports have been published. After the pilot case, there is also the possibility to add step 7 (Production proof mentioned in 2.3) which consists of following up the procedure, e.g., client or someone outside of the original pilot case group wishes to utilize the prototype or parts of it. The second possibility is that the developed prototype system goes into production and needs further support (this kind of situation is reported in [15]).

Figure 3 presents the DMPP model. The model includes six steps and the roles, activities, and artifacts can be described as followed using the SW/HW framework [3] and the DMPP [2]:

1. The first step starts from the requirements definition, a collaborative discussion between the developers and the client. The client defines what kind of data would be useful. The developer group starts to define the hardware and overall architecture of the system and how the data will be collected by the software. The

selected hardware mostly determines the software environment and tools used. Benefit - Clarification of the problem item together with the customer. Limitation - Does the development team have sufficient expertise in the subject area?

2. The outcome of the discussion is the first artifact: for example, the prototype system requirements in the discussion notes. The developer group constructs the first architecture model of the component interconnections. For example, in IoT systems, we describe the practice of how to define a system by reusing the system definitions of previous prototypes. Light documentation has been found to speed up stage completion, but may cause problems later if the system is put into production.

3. The third step is the software/hardware prototype development made by the research group including the project manager and SW/HW developers. The IDs' representatives are involved in the development process in the role of instructor. In this step, the SW/HW framework is used as the guideline for selecting the components for the prototype. The SW/HW framework gives guidelines and speeds up development when the operating process of suitable components has at least partially been thought through in advance. Reuse of components also makes it easier when the number of background studies decreases.

4. The fourth step introduces the working prototype artifact, which consists of the developed software and hardware components. Also, the interconnections of the components are tested. The testing process overall is usually only the functional testing of the prototype system. Additionally, the gathered data is inspected and if possible, compared to the expected results. Another notable issue is the fact that, if the system is later put into production, testing must be carried out more thoroughly.

5. The fifth step includes preparing the outcome of the development process. Further, this step includes presenting the prototype and its functionality to the ID. The SW/HW framework can be complemented if necessary.

6. The sixth step is to publish the results, for example, the prototype system, collected data, and analysis of the project. For example, in a university environment, the the publication of results is important for supporting future research projects.

The process model in Figure 3 is a simplified presentation of the prototype development process. It gives abstract instructions for the operation with defined steps to implement the pilot case from start to finish. If all of the steps are performed, the level of the outcome is predictable. The model is sufficient for developing a prototype, and also makes it possible to add more activities if needed. For example, procedures such as iterations, testing, and customer testing could be included in the process. Further, because the model is developed from university pilot cases, it combines two factors: software/hardware prototype development and collaboration with customers. Both of these are discussed in the following section when the usability of the DMPP in the KIEMI project is evaluated.

4. DMPP utilization in the KIEMI project and technology transfer

The purpose of this section is to describe how the DMPP model was utilized in the work process of the KIEMI project. This section also describes how different parties were involved in the project, what kind of collaboration actions were taken during the DMPP steps, and which technology transfer actions occurred during the work process. Figure 4 presents an overall picture of the project, collaboration, and DMPP process in the form of the Business Process Model and Notation (BPMN, [17]).

4.1. Project partners

In the overall picture (in Figure 4) four groups can be recognized in their own swimlane:

1. EU OP and its program documents and goals (via OP documents and goals) must be taken into account for project content and implementation.
2. University within its third mission (TM) and its strategy (via University Strategy) which gives guidelines for research group activities and publishing of project work.
3. Project (like KIEMI) activities are carried by project team members (academic researchers, AR) and activities can be divided into three sub categories:
    (a) Project management (Management) is responsible for implementation of the project plan (Project Plan) and reporting project results to the funding representatives of EU OP (OP supervision) as well keeping track of research publications for university representatives (Research supervision). Project management also acts as the selector of new prototypes in the form of collaboration and pilot case actions.
    (b) DMPP process (DMPP) and its six steps (1-6), which are linked to each other and to collaborative actions with IDs via prototype and pilot case actions.
    (c) Collaboration and Piloting (Collaboration/Piloting) which contains actions and paths supporting DMPP process steps.
4. Collaborative Organization(s) are representatives of collaborating IDs and with whom the content of prototypes and usage via pilot cases is co-created and co-developed.

Technology transfer (and technology creation) takes place between AR and ID via project work and the work process used in it.

4.2. The work process

In Figure 4 the work process of project work can be divided into the following actions (one to eight):

1. The project starts when the project administration (Management) is organized. The project administration defines/selects an appropriate pilot case (Select New Pilot Case), the resources and actions required for the content, and launches the pilot case (Start Pilot Case).
2. From the point of view of the project, a single collaborative pilot case starts (in Collaboration/Piloting) with the invitation of the collaborator (Collaboration Call) and the agreement on cooperation (Collaboration Ignition). For pilot cases #17, #18, #19, and #23, invitations to collaboration IDs were sent via a 3rd party. Using 3rd party for invitations allows project to reach more extended range of organizations compared to its usual collaborative communes.

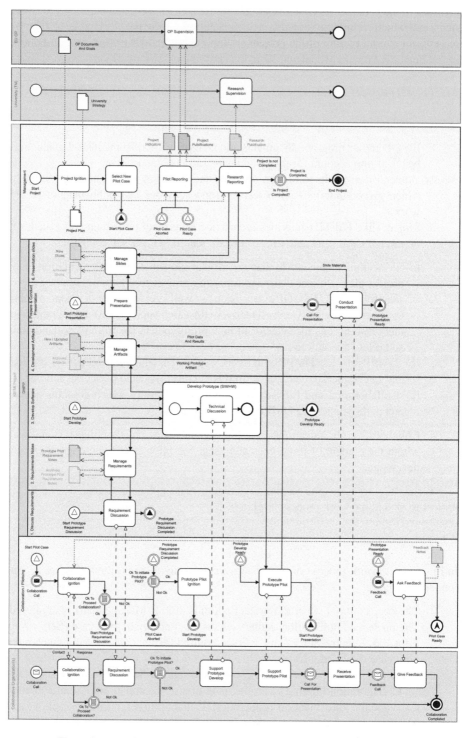

Figure 4. Technology transfer in the Kiemi project. (The figure is available in [18])

3. The first phase of the DMPP process (Discuss Requirements) starts when the project has established contact with the collaborator (ID) and the actual discussion of requirements and objectives begins (Requirement Discussion). For pilot cases #17, #18, #19, and #23, we also received positive responses to collaborate. In beginning of the project discussion base is more informal and results may vary a lot. While piloting evolves the project utilizes the discussion base created in previous discussions (Achieved Prototype Pilot Requirement Notes) as a basis for a new discussion. This allows discussion to move forward more efficient. ID brings their views (needs and support and available partners or technical vendors (TV)) to the discussion. For example, needs can be related to certain sensors or measurements and support can be related to the facilities where measurements are made. This starts technology transfer actions between AR and ID/TV. The discussion will result in a decision to continue cooperation and (in a positive decision) the content of the next phase of the DMPP process, namely the requirement notes (Prototype Pilot Requirement Notes).

   As the discussion produces a positive decision (OK To Initiate Prototype Pilot?), a pilot case (Prototype Pilot Ignition) and the third phase of the DMPP process (Develop Software) will begin (Start Prototype develop). On the ID side, the corresponding decision (OK To Initiate Prototype Pilot?) to proceed initiates support for prototype development and supports prototype piloting activities. In the event of a discussion producing a negative decision (or cooperation ending without successful agreement), the pilot case is reported to the administration as interrupted (Pilot Case Aborted), which then processes the interruption result. Most of pilot cases succeeded to move into third phase. For pilot cases #98 and #99, collaboration was ended in the first phase of the DMPP process (Discussion).

4. In the third phase of the DMPP process (Develop Software), the prototype artifacts (software and hardware) needed in the pilot case are developed. The development of the prototype (Develop Prototype (SW/HW)) is guided by the requirements recorded in the previous phase (Prototype Pilot Requirement Notes in Requirement Notes) and utilizes any artifacts (Development Artifacts) that may have been generated in previous cases. Prototype development involves discussions and exchanges of information (Technical Discussion) with the ID and TV brought into the pilot case. New and advanced artifacts resulting from the prototype development phase are introduced to artifact management (Manage Artifacts in Development Artifacts), representing the fourth stage of the DMPP process. Pilot case #11 was an example of a case where both technology creation and technology transfer occurred between AR and ID. Also pilot case #12 and #13 had activities for technology creation part but for case #12 technology transfer collaboration was not that active.

5. The completion of the prototype development phase (Prototype Develop Ready) initiates the prototype pilot case execution phase (Execute Prototype Pilot in Collaboration/Piloting), where pilot case data and results are collected from the use of the prototype at the pilot case site (received from ID). The data collected in the prototype pilot case is included/added to the Development Artifacts (via Manage Artifacts) generated in the third step (Development Software).

   The piloting of a single prototype could take several weeks. Time period needed relates on environment and how quickly it reaches its different situations and brings them on to be measured. For most of pilot cases time period was from 4 week to 8 weeks. For pilot case #19, data was collected for a period of several months and data collection was monitored online. On the other hand, pilot case #13 contained data for a period of over one year and data was collected afterwards from ID's database. The latter case also contained technology transfer between AR and ID to tune up ID's interface about database metadata information.

6. At the end of the prototype pilot case (Start Prototype Presentation), the penultimate stage of the DMPP process, the preparation phase for the presentation of the results is initiated. In this phase (Prepare Presentation in Prepare & Conduct Presentation), the artifacts generated during the prototype pilot case are compiled (via Manage Artifacts in Development Artifacts) into presentation materials for the final stage of the DMPP process (via Manage publications in Presentation Slides) and the presentation of the materials to ID (Conduct Presentation in Prepare & Conduct Presentation). In the preparatory phase, previous presentation materials (Archieved Slides via Manage Slides) can be utilized. The presentation schedule is discussed with ID (Call For Presentation) who gathers their team and TV for the meeting (Receive Presentation in Collaborative Organizations(s)). The presentation ends steps five and six of the DMPP process for collaboration tasks (Prototype Presentation Ready). Pilot cases #17, #18, #19, and #23 were examples of technology transfer via a presentation and delivered report documents. Case #23 also included a representative from ID's TV side. For many of pilot cases presentation content was shared only to ID and documents were kept as internal.

7. There is usually a feedback discussion (Ask Feedback/Give Feedback in Collaboration/Piloting) following the presentation (Prototype Presentation Ready) on the results obtained from the use of the prototype and the implementation of its piloting, as well as on the success of the collaboration. Feedback processing concludes the collaborative pilot case (Pilot Case Ready) and technology transfer actions between AR and ID/TV. Pilot case #10 contained a feedback discussion where ID felt that the collaboration was very successful and they requested another pilot case (#16 in the list) after the issue for the target facility had been solved thanks to the first pilot case. As mentioned with discussion activities also feedback process and its content evolves during project. Feedback from first pilot cases works as inputs for setting up next collaboration.

8. At the end of the pilot case (Pilot Case Ready), the information is sent to the administration (Pilot Reporting), which records the project indicators and progress (via Project Indicators) for reporting to the EU OP financier (OP Supervision) on the pilot case. The administration is also responsible for sharing the research results (Research Reporting) through communication channels (via Project Publications) and to the university (Research supervision via Research Publications). Actions for communication tasks are also reported to the EU OP financier (OP Supervision).

   Artifacts and publication slides generated in the DPMM process may be published or distributed in connection with the news blog. Pilot cases #17, #18, and #19 were examples of (one way) technology transfer via news blogs for any other ID or individual interested in the topic.

When a single collaborative pilot case has ended, management decides on the need for another pilot case (Is Project Completed?). Once the required number of prototypes and their piloting work have been completed (or project time is coming to an end, it leads to the final tasks and the end of the project.

5. Pilot cases in KIEMI

The purpose of this section is to present the background or characteristics related to the pilot cases (comparison table) as well as to compare the activity levels of collaboration associated with the pilot cases.

Table 1 contains pilot case specific reference parameters. **Pilot cases** are numbered with a running identification number according to their starting time (see pilot case time-line in Figure 2). Comparative data has been compiled for each pilot case using six parameters. The **User Group** parameter describes the classification of the piloting target. Options include company (A), public operator (B), entity (C), and others (D). The **Stakeholders** parameter describes the classification of parties who joined the piloting target. Alternatives include subscriber (E), users (F), technical vendor (G), and developer (H). Several parties may have been involved in the piloting. The **DMPP usage** parameter describes the number of steps in the DMPP process utilized at the piloting site. Each pilot case may have utilized one or more, or even all of the steps. The **OTS used** parameter contains information on whether off-the-shelf components were used in the pilot case. The **Publish content** parameter includes information on whether the results of the pilot case were released in a transparently available format through a research publication (X) or project news blog (Y) or both. Some pilot case results were only handled internally. The **Collaboration activity level** parameter describes the collaboration activity of ID during the work process (in Fig. 4). For a couple of pilots some information was not yet available during the writing of this paper and that information is marked with (*).

5.1. Pilot cases with high-level collaboration

In high-level collaboration, the counterpart (ID) demonstrates active cooperation at all stages of the work process. ID brings to the discussion stage a view of the features required for the prototype and its operating environment. ID also demonstrates its interest in the technical content of the prototype resulting from the development phase and is involved in the processing of observations made during the pilot case phase. In high-level cooperation, ID shows interest in the content of the results (report) and highlights their views on the exploitation of the results. It is clear that ID benefits from high-level collaboration in many ways.

Pilot case #10 is a good example of high-level collaboration. The target was a day-care center, which had received feedback about poor air quality inside the building. The first target was to measure the temperature, humidity, and CO_2 values at different times and report the readings to the partner. The first results showed that at certain moments the temperature and CO_2 values had risen. During the early phase meeting where the results were shown, we decided with the partner(ID) to continue and expand the pilot case. Expansion meant contacting the air conditioning equipment supplier(TV). This gave us an interface with the air conditioning system. In addition, they expanded the sensor number

Table 1. Properties of pilot cases in the KIEMI project

Pilot case	User group (A/B/C/D)	Stakeholders (E,F,G,H)	DMPP usage (1-6 / 6)	OTS used (Yes/No)	Published content (-,X,Y)	Collaboration activity level (Low/Mid/High)
#01	B	E	3	No	-	LOW
#02	B	E	3	No	-	LOW
#03	B	E	5	Yes	X	LOW
#04	B	E	3	Yes	-	LOW
#05	B	E	5	Yes	-	LOW
#06	D	E	3	Yes	-	LOW
#07	B	E+G	3	No	Y	LOW
#08	D	E	5	Yes	-	MID
#09	D	-	6	No	X	LOW
#10	B	E+F+G	6	Yes	X+Y	HIGH
#11	B	E+G	6	No	X+Y	HIGH
#12	A	E+F+G	5	No	Y	MID
#13	A	E+G	5	No	Y	MID
#14	D	E	5	Yes	-	MID
#15	B	E+F+G	5	Yes	X	LOW
#16	B	E+F+G	6	Yes	X	LOW
#17	C	E	5	Yes	Y	LOW
#18	C	E	5	Yes	Y	LOW
#19	C	E	5	Yes	Y	MID
#20	A	E	6	Yes	-	MID
#21	A	E	3 (*)	Yes	- (*)	? (*)
#22	D	E+F	4	Yes	-	LOW
#23	A	E+F	5	Yes	Y (*)	MID
(failed pilots)						
#99	A	E+G	2	N/A	-	-
#98	A	E+G	2	N/A	-	-

and type to collect data that was more specifically environmental. Our project team also used the previously developed visualization tool to this pilot case.

Outcome: This was the widest pilot case with several partners(TV and ID), using previously used and developed components.

Pilot Case #11 serves as another example of high-level collaboration, involving an investigation into a university of applied science building. This pilot case was carried out in partnership with a property maintenance organization (ID) and focused on testing a new prototype of a water leak indicator. ID had a problem with water leaks caused by users (such as leaving water faucets open). Those are a significant concern, particularly in large public buildings. Potential solution emerged through monitoring water temperature in pipes. The equipment was developed in collaboration with a water leak detector supplier (TV). Both ID and TV expressed keen interest in the outcomes of the pilot case.

5.2. Pilot cases with mid-level collaboration

In mid-level collaboration, the counterpart (ID) is involved at the beginning and end of the work process and in some way also involved in the development content of the work process. ID support may be required, particularly in situations where part of the prototype content is sourced from an ID-managed data source. In general, ID benefits from mid-level collaboration, at least from the perspective of external testing obtained for its own functions.

Pilot case #13 can be used as an example of mid-level collaboration. In this case ID had a vast amount of facilities at their disposal and they had already implemented a data sensor system and were using data analysis tools via their TV. For the pilot case, ID allowed AR to use their data (collected by ID's TV) for AR's tools to produce another kind of analysis from the data. ID did not participate in the actual SW development, but the use of data via ID's API during piloting required technical discussions. .

Pilot Cases #19 and #23 also fall into the category of mid level collaboration, each with distinct characteristics. The first case involved a building used by a local choir group. While the building had a recently upgraded air ventilation system, there was some uncertainty among customers renting the facilities regarding its proper use. To address this, the property maintenance organization (ID) was tasked with gathering additional data on facility usage, while data on temperature and humidity were collected using pilot equipment. Through this collaboration, the results of the pilot case helped clarify guidelines for the air ventilation system. The second case focused on a building used as a local machine workshop. This building also featured an air ventilation system, but its ability to respond to factors like opening doors for cargo transportation during the winter period was uncertain. Similar to the previous case, this pilot case required the property maintenance organization (ID) to collect additional data on facility usage, while temperature and humidity data were collected using pilot equipment. Once again, collaboration played a pivotal role, as the results of the pilot case shed light on the behavior of the air ventilation system.

Outcomes: The benefits for the collaborative organizations (IDs) resulting from these pilot cases were related to the experience gained in working with their API, understanding the behavior of their air ventilation systems, and the overall knowledge acquired through the pilot case reports.

5.3. Pilot cases with low-level collaboration

In low-level collaboration, the counterpart (ID) is involved in the work at the beginning (Discuss Requirements) and end of the process (Presentation Slides). In these cases, the project team has most often conducted a search for actors interested in collaboration and provided the test target, giving the ID the opportunity to obtain new information about its application through the report. Thus, AR also provides technology transfer to ID. For a project, low-level collaboration can also be beneficial. Piloting over a longer time period does not necessarily burden the project staff and the results obtained from the pilot case can be very useful for demonstrating the functionality of the prototype.

Pilot cases in the beginning of project have been identified into category of low-level collaboration. This may have relation with DMPP utilization and the evolution of each phase content. For example discussion for possible pilot case requirements with ID is not so efficient if the knowledge for the ability of equipment for different measurements is limited. When amount of knowledge and results from measurements increases, it allows also better ground for new discussion.

Low-level collaboration is also no obstacle to publicizing the results of the project - on the contrary, for example pilot cases #17 and #18 (entities as user groups) and the disclosures generated from their results have contributed to the local visibility and reputation of the project. The presentation materials have also been utilized to obtain new, higher-level collaborative cases.

5.4. Failed pilot cases

In addition to the above levels of collaboration, it is also useful to point out exceptions where piloting collaboration ended or was interrupted. In the work process, piloting can usually be interrupted only in its initial stages.

The reason may be ID's reluctance (or resource shortage) to initiate collaboration. ID is not interested even in free piloting if it does not promise immediate benefit; in practice, however, that requires some involvement. Piloting may involve TV on ID's part, which is necessary but TV is reluctant (similar to ID's own reluctance).

Another reason may be that something comes up during the discussion stage (Discuss Requirements) that makes it impossible to continue or not meaningful to continue the piloting.

Even after progressing to the technical stage of the DMPP process (Develop Software), a situation may arise where a developed prototype is found to be unworkable. From the point of view of collaboration, the work process is interrupted, although from the point of view of research, a non-working prototype is also part of the results of the research. If the idea works, the hardware can be replaced with more suitable hardware in the next iteration round.

Pilot cases #98 and #99 are examples of cases where collaboration was interrupted. In case #99, ID was interested in collaboration, but access to required data was managed via ID's TV's API and TV had little or no interest in collaboration. For case #98, ID was also interested in collaboration. During the discussion stage AR noticed that it would be too difficult to produce data in such a form that would work for ID's needs. In both cases proceedings (in discussion stage) were paused and finally project management decided to shelve the piloting case.

It is worth mentioning that in the work process there were also some cases where project management was asked to help to communicate with ID to make sure that the collaboration would continue. Interruptions in collaboration cause serious harm to the work process. For example, due to material limitations, when the test equipment is reserved at one site, the next piloting target cannot be handled.

6. Common features for collaboration activity

The purpose of this section is to compare the characteristics of collaboration activities related to the pilot cases (using a comparison table) and to investigate the factors influencing the selection of a collaboration organization.

Upon examining Table One, it becomes evident that out of the twenty-five listed pilot cases, only nine managed to achieve mid-level collaboration, with only two of those progressing to high-level collaboration. One might consider excluding the influence of specific user groups or stakeholders on the success factors, but the background data presented in Table One suggests that this approach may not be applicable. High-level collaboration involves user group B (public operator) with stakeholders E (subscriber) and G (technical vendor, TV), yet the same combination can also be found in low-level collaboration cases. Therefore, a more detailed examination of the DMPP process and the KIEMI project may be necessary.

In the described work process, the first phase of the DMPP process involves discussions about requirements. Within this work process, it's apparent that the collaborative organization (ID) for requirement discussions is determined as a result of collaboration calls and collaboration ignition. This raises questions about the content of these collaboration calls and ignitions and their impact on the risk of low-level collaboration or collaboration interruption. Given that the EU OP imposes limits on available time and resources, there is only a finite number of collaboration attempts that can be made. Consequently, every collaboration call holds significant importance. It's worth noting that, from a research perspective, even a non-working prototype can be considered a result. However, from an enterprise standpoint, the motivation to continue collaboration for a non-working prototype may diminish.

It is evident that high-level collaboration necessitates success in prototype development. Success with prototypes, in turn, hinges on successful development and requirement discussions. To achieve these, a project requires a collaboration with organizations (ID/TV) where their demand and interest align with the content of the EU OP. Regrettably, from the developer enterprise's (TV) standpoint, this might lead to a very limited set of development options. If this realization comes too late, particularly in the DMPP development phase, collaboration interruption becomes imminent.

Upon closer examination of the pilot cases, it becomes apparent that the search for a potential collaboration organization (ID) primarily focused on the owners or users of the buildings (stakeholders E and F). The idea within the KIEMI project was to demonstrate how to measure and improve the working environment for better energy efficiency to these target groups. These groups have the influence to demand better air quality and more economical heating costs through their voices. Unfortunately, the necessary technological improvements are closely tied to the building technology provided by their vendors (TVs).

While some TVs participated in the pilot cases, our main contacts were not directly with them, making it challenging to involve TVs in the development process. TV often raised questions about the new business value of the proposed solution and the cost of developing the technology. We had limited or no answers to these questions as our primary focus was not to deliver a business plan to TV. This frequently resulted in a situation where TV's participation in the process was very limited.

Pilot cases with high or mid-level collaboration typically included TV with an interest in developing new measurement equipment or enhancing their systems for handling measurement data. In some cases, the original organization (ID) was able to improve the efficiency of their current systems based on user guides (for users, F) derived from measured data. In these pilot cases, there was a clearer connection between the development process and its impact on ID's business. On the other hand, pilot cases with low-level collaboration mainly involved subscribers (E). For low-level collaboration cases with TVs, the target buildings had no reported issues beforehand, so there was no apparent critical business need seen for TV.

The overarching analysis of this section suggests that the primary determinant of collaboration activity success is the successful collaboration with technical vendors (TV). While building owners and users are crucial stakeholders for validating the proofs of concept (PoC) for prototypes, the structure for defining the collaborative organization (ID) should begin with the technical vendor (TV) and extend towards subscribers and users.

7. Usability and evaluation of DMPP in the KIEMI project

The DMPP was developed for the production of prototypes at the university. The goal has always been to produce scientific results from the prototypes. The research group is from non-commercial institutions and therefore the focus is not on achieving financial goals. This subsection clarifies the advantages of different phases of the DMPP. The KIEMI project used the DMPP model to create prototypes together with collaborative partners. This project and its approach to the subject through prototyping demonstrated the functionality of the DMPP model, especially in prototyping projects like this one. The suitability of the different phases of the DMPP model can be assessed through the KIEMI project pilot cases as follows:

Discuss requirements: Most pilot case projects involve an external partner(ID) when discussing objectives. The level of collaboration varies a lot. In low-level collaboration e.g., in pilot cases #19 and #22, the partner provided the premises to perform the measurements. The partner does not make any special requests. The output for the partner is a report which may lead to further actions. If the collaboration is closer, as when the partner takes part in further discussions, the starting point is also directed more by the partner. In these cases, the partner mostly has some issue which should be researched, e.g., they have been notified of poor indoor air quality (pilot case #10). Usually in these cases, the original task assignment expands during the pilot case and more partners join in. The DMPP is suitable for this kind of activity because the non-commercial leader – the university research team – is focused on research goals rather than financial goals. Further, the additional research/technical goals set by partners are shown to be applicable to the operation of the model within the iteration rounds. The best example of this kind of activity is pilot case #10 where the university research team led the pilot case and collected the necessary partners (e.g., ventilation technology supplier and building caretaker).

Requirements notes are an important part of documentation and their main purpose is to guide the pilot case in the selected direction. The usage of the DMPP shows the advantage of "light documentation" for getting things started; the usage of previously defined architecture models and device configurations also speeds up the operation. The term "light documentation" also means the reuse of the technological choices and definitions made in earlier pilot cases. The exception is pilot case #23, where the final report included a section on desired goals. Internal requirements are also mentioned in several cases, e.g., the research group wants to change or update some specific feature. The "light documentation" idea is based on the "Some Things Are Better Done than Described" [19]. Light documentation and process modeling is focused on the university and other research institution environments where the aim was prototyping rather than the development of commercial products. Of course, this leads to a larger amount of work if technology transfer to some partner starts from the prototype.

The **Develop software** phase uses the artifacts of previous requirements as a loose guideline. For example, UI [20] and backend [21] software developed in pilot case #09 were used in all subsequent pilot cases (excluding #11). In the DMPP, changes to the requirements are possible if it is seen to be of some benefit. Further, the requirement changes were not normally discussed with partners unless something was needed from them. The DMPP does not set requirements for the software or hardware components used, but we noticed that the usage of off-the-shelf components accelerated prototype development. The second advantage of these kinds of components is the ability to vary the prototype solutions when we have to conform to the requirements of the selected components.

Development artifacts are typically fully working prototype systems which are also the main goals of this phase for the DMPP. In the KIEMI project, this phase usually involved installing the prototype to collect data at a target provided by the partner. Most of the prototypes were working SW/HW prototypes, but there were also only SW prototypes for analyzing and visualizing the customer's collected data (#12 and #13). The main purpose of the DMPP is to produce a working prototype and therefore only the main functions of the prototype are utilized. Additionally, the documentation or testing could be done only partially. This kind of approach speeds up the development but could slow down the technological transfer later on.

The **Prepare & conduct presentation** phase is for reporting the results. In longer projects we noticed that the document reuse of skeleton reports accelerated this phase. In pilot cases #20 and #23 of the final phase of the KIEMI project we collected a skeleton report from pilot case #19. This automation sped up the reporting phase. This shows that when using the DMPP model, reporting will mostly include the same components.

Presentation and publishing of the results are the last phase in the DMPP. In successful pilot cases the partners are usually interested in further developing the prototype and the technology transfer will continue from this point. One significant advantage of the DMPP is the ultimate purpose of publishing the scientific material (pilot cases #03, #09, #10, #11, #15, and #16 have been published) and other public material from the pilot cases.

Overall analysis and DMPP's suitability for projects were shown in the KIEMI project. Two approaches were used in the project: the software development style and collaboration style. The DMPP is able to connect both styles. The project was shown to be successful for university-enterprise (AR-ID) collaboration in the context of prototype development. Further, based on the results in creating usable prototypes, the model can be seen as a success.

8. Conclusions

RQ1: Collaboration. **How was university-enterprise collaboration executed in practice using the DMPP?** The DMPP process was part of a project (Fig. 4) where the content was guided by the objectives set for the project (Management) and an individual prototype was made through collaboration (Collaboration/Piloting). The DMPP process was in the background (invisible to ID), but it was able to provide support for collaboration (AR-ID) through all of its six phases. The ability of the DMPP process to support technology transfer was highlighted in phases 1, 3, 4, and 5.

For Step 2 (Requirement Notes), the content was usually only left up to the project team (AR). Regarding companies (ID and their TV), it is unknown whether they had one of their own similar methods in place. At the very least, communication (emails) enabled ID (and their TV) to receive and store requirement-related data.

As far as Step 6 is concerned, ID received a report on the content and results of most pilot cases. For pilot cases where content was distributed through open channels (such as Project news blogs and Github in Presentation slides), ID (and TV) had the opportunity to catch up, not only with their own content, but also the content of other pilot cases.

The collaboration also demonstrated that university and corporate representatives have a very different view of technology, and therefore of pilot cases as a whole. Especially in small companies, the desire and ability to recognize the value and benefits contained in the prototype is often low, and the university needs to convince the collaborator of the benefits of a prototype that requires effort on their part.

In a longer-term project, it should be considered whether each prototype is intended for actual technology transfer or whether that stage will only come when satisfactory prototypes have been achieved. In practice, the project requires that pilot cases at the beginning of the project are conducted mainly with organizations offering test environments and only at the end does the content begin to involve technology transfer.

There was no investment in cost calculations or business models in the design of university prototypes and this may have contributed to the amount of interest shown by companies. To improve collaboration it is good to add a point where the company provides a (suitable general level) assessment of the prototype as well as the associated return on investment (ROI). With the feedback received, the research team would accumulate expertise in designing the next prototype and opportunities to produce a result that is of more interest to the company. The ability to produce prototypes valued by companies is a significant strength and advantage for a university operator that organizes projects. It is also an advantage for future project partner searches.

RQ2: Reusability. **How did the reusability of the artifacts in the DMPP steps support the workflow of the pilot case?** The use of the DMPP model led to the reuse of artifacts when the mode of operation remained the same even though the pilot cases changed. In the prototypes, we mainly used the same software and hardware components that had been used before. Further, we also always tried to introduce some new components, because this increased knowledge and expanded component-based variation. The DMPP uses light documentation to speed up prototype development, but we noticed that separate phases in different pilot cases started to contain the same type of documents. Therefore, the conclusion is that the DMPP leads to re-use of skeleton documents in different pilot cases.

RQ3: Collaboration. **How the DMPP process usage can be improved for the enterprise-university collaboration?** The approach to working with collaboration calls at the beginning of pilot cases was balancing between utilizing limited resources and the ability to identify suitable organizations. Often, actual enterprises (TVs) only emerged during requirement discussions or even later, after the prototype pilot had already commenced. To yield better results in alignment with the EU OP and its reported indicators, it is imperative that the development process includes robust involvement from technical vendors (TV) of enterprises. However, achieving enterprise participation in the project necessitates a clearer understanding of the business opportunities and the associated development costs for the enterprise.

These perspectives should be incorporated into information packages and discussions at the early stages of collaboration. Furthermore, these viewpoints should be integrated into the requirements documentation during the DMPP phase of Requirement Discussion. From the enterprise's perspective, having ample preparation time and access to relevant background information is essential to assess potential gains and the required effort, ultimately aiding in the decision-making process regarding participation. Moreover, this approach would streamline the process of suitable corporations to communicate towards to university instead of the university searching for suitable corporate partners in the area.To facilitate this, the project team (from the university side) should prepare general marketing messages and provide preliminary information packages, disseminating them to organizations in the region as early as possible, ideally during the Project Ignition phase.

The findings of the research presented above represent the context of a Finnish university and it would require more research to obtain universally applicable results. However, these observations and findings provide the basis for the possibility to extend the research to an external comparison between universities in different countries.

9. Summary

This article focused on the KIEMI research project conducted at the Pori Unit of Tampere University during 2019-2022. The project used the earlier developed Descriptive Model for Prototyping Process (DMPP) to guide university-enterprise collaboration. The project consisted of several pilot cases and prototypes, which were made in collaboration with companies, and offered real-world problems. This article reviewed and evaluated the suitability of the DMPP for this topic. The article dealt with the collaboration between university and enterprises, and reusability within the DMPP. The paper presented several pilot cases made in KIEMI, and described the usage of the DMPP. Finally, the paper evaluated the model, presented some of the challenges faced, and discussed future research topics.

Acknowledgements

This work is part of the KIEMI project and was funded by the European Regional Development Fund and the Regional Council of Satakunta.

References

[1] Saari M, Sillberg P, Grönman J, Kuusisto M, Rantanen P, Jaakkola H, et al. Reducing Energy Consumption with IoT Prototyping. Acta Polytechnica Hungarica. 2019;16(9, SI):73-91.

[2] Saari M, Rantanen P, Hyrynsalmi S, Hästbacka D. In: Sgurev V, Jotsov V, Kacprzyk J, editors. Framework and Development Process for IoT Data Gathering. Springer International Publishing; 2022. p. 41-60. Available from: https://doi.org/10.1007/978-3-030-78124-8_3.

[3] Saari M, Soini J, Grönman J, Rantanen P, Mäkinen T, Sillberg P. Modeling the software prototyping process in a research context. In: Tropmann-Frick M, Thalheim B, Jaakkola H, Kiyoki Y, Yoshida N, editors. Information Modelling and Knowledge Bases XXXII. vol. 333. IOS Press; 2020. p. 107-18.

[4] Harjamäki J, Saari M, Nurminen M, Rantanen P, Soini J, Hästbacka D. Lessons Learned from Collaborative Prototype Development Between University and Enterprises. In: 33rd International Conference on Information Modelling and Knowledge Bases EJC 2023; 2023. Available from: https://press.um.si/index.php/ump/catalog/book/785.

[5] Vorley T, Nelles J. Building Entrepreneurial Architectures: A Conceptual Interpretation of the Third Mission. Policy Futures in Education. 2009 6;7:284-96. Available from: http://journals.sagepub.com/doi/10.2304/pfie.2009.7.3.284.

[6] Zomer A, Benneworth P. The Rise of the University's Third Mission. Reform of Higher Education in Europe. 2011:81-101. Available from: http://link.springer.com/10.1007/978-94-6091-555-0_6.

[7]   Basili V, Briand L, Bianculli D, Nejati S, Pastore F, Sabetzadeh M. Software Engineering Research and Industry: A Symbiotic Relationship to Foster Impact. IEEE Software. 2018 9;35:44-9. Available from: `https://ieeexplore.ieee.org/document/8409904/`.

[8]   Salomaa M, Charles D. The university third mission and the European Structural Funds in peripheral regions: Insights from Finland. Science and Public Policy. 2021 jul;48(3):352-63. Available from: `https://academic.oup.com/spp/article/48/3/352/6126876`.

[9]   Punter T, Krikhaar RL, Bril RJ. Software engineering technology innovation–Turning research results into industrial success. Journal of Systems and Software. 2009;82(6):993-1003.

[10]   Arza V, Carattoli M. Personal ties in university-industry linkages: a case-study from Argentina. The Journal of Technology Transfer. 2017 8;42:814-40. Available from: `http://link.springer.com/10.1007/s10961-016-9544-x`.

[11]   Dusica M, Arnaud G. Industry-Academia research collaboration in software engineering: The Certus model. Information and Software Technology. 2021 4;132:106473. Available from: `https://linkinghub.elsevier.com/retrieve/pii/S0950584920302184`.

[12]   Becker-Kornstaedt U, Webby R. A comprehensive schema Integrating Software Proces Modeling and Software Measurement. IESE-Report No 04799/E. 1999.

[13]   Grönman J, Rantanen P, Saari M, Sillberg P, Vihervaara J. Low-cost ultrasound measurement system for accurate detection of container utilization rate. In: 2018 41th International Convention on Information and Communication Technology, Electronics and Microelectronics (MIPRO). IEEE; 2018. .

[14]   Soini J, Sillberg P, Rantanen P. Prototype System for Improving Manually Collected Data Quality. In: Budimac Z, Galinac Grbac T, editors. Proceedings of the 3rd Workshop on Software Quality Analysis, Monitoring, Improvement, and Applications, SQAMIA 2014, September 19-22, 2014, Lovran, Croatia. Ceur workshop proceedings. M. Jeusfeld c/o Redaktion Sun SITE; 2014. p. 99-106.

[15]   Soini J, Kuusisto M, Rantanen P, Saari M, Sillberg P. A Study on an Evolution of a Data Collection System for Knowledge Representation. In: Dahanayake A, Huiskonen J, Kiyoki Y, editors. Information Modelling and Knowledge Bases XXXI. vol. 321. IOS Press; 2019. p. 161-74.

[16]   Grönman J, Sillberg P, Rantanen P, Saari M. People Counting in a Public Event—Use Case: Free-to-Ride Bus. In: 2019 42th International Convention on Information and Communication Technology, Electronics and Microelectronics (MIPRO). IEEE; 2019. .

[17]   Object Management Group, Inc. Business Process Model and Notation; 2023. Accessed January 13, 2023. Available from: `https://www.omg.org/spec/BPMN/2.0.2/About-BPMN`.

[18]   Janne Harjamäki. Technology transfer in the Kiemi project; 2023. Accessed January 23, 2023. Available from: `https://cawemo.com/share/bb6b8086-13b7-4ab9-bb86-92cdaf9a5d18`.

[19]   Hunt A, Thomas D. The Pragmatic Programmer. Addison-Wesley; 2000.

[20]   Nurminen M, Lindstedt A, Saari M, Rantanen P. The Requirements and Challenges of Visualizing Building Data. In: 2021 44th International Convention on Information and Communication Technology, Electronics and Microelectronics (MIPRO). IEEE; 2021. .

[21]   Nurminen M, Saari M, Rantanen P. DataSites: a simple solution for providing building data to client devices. In: 2021 44th International Convention on Information and Communication Technology, Electronics and Microelectronics (MIPRO). IEEE; 2021. .

Information Modelling and Knowledge Bases XXXV
M. Tropmann-Frick et al. (Eds.)

doi:10.3233/FAIA231158

A New Global Sign Language Recognition System Utilizing the Editable Mediator: Integration with Local Hand Shape Recognition

Takafumi NAKANISHI [a,b,1], Ayako MINEMATSU [b,2], Ryotaro OKADA [a,b,3],
Osamu HASEGAWA [a,b,4] and Virach SORNLERTLAMVANICH [a,b,5]

[a] *Department of Data Science, Musashino University*
[b] *Asia AI Institute, Musashino University*
ORCiD ID: Takafumi NAKANISHI https://orcid.org/0000-0003-1029-6063

Abstract. We introduced a novel approach to global sign language recognition by leveraging the capabilities of the Editable Mediator. Traditional methods have often been limited to recognizing sign languages from specific linguistic regions, necessitating ad hoc implementation for multilingual regions. Our method aims to bridge this gap by providing a unified framework for recognizing sign languages in various linguistic areas and promoting global communication. At the core of our system is the Editable Mediator, a mechanism that determines the actual sign meaning from various local hand-shape recognitions. Instead of focusing on specific sign language notations, such as HamNoSys, our approach emphasizes the recognition of common primitive actions shared across different sign languages. These primitive actions are recognized by multiple modules, and their combinations are interpreted by the Editable Mediator to determine the intended sign-language message. This architecture not only simplifies the recognition process, but also offers flexibility. By merely editing the Editable Mediator, our system can adapt to various sign languages worldwide without the need for extensive retraining or ad hoc implementation. This innovation reduces barriers to introducing new sign language systems and promotes a more inclusive global communication platform.

Keywords. Sign language recognition, Primitive actions, Global communication platform, Global heterogeneous sign language, Action-driven recognition

1. Introduction

Communication with a diverse range of people from different linguistic backgrounds is becoming increasingly important. Sign language, especially that used by the hearing-impaired for everyday communication, has established itself as its own language system.

---

[1] Corresponding Author, Department of Data Science, Musashino University, 3-3-3 Ariake Koto-ku Tokyo 135-8181, Japan; E-mail: takafumi.nakanishi@ds.musashino-u.ac.jp.

[2] E-mail: ayako.minematsu@ds.musashino-u.ac.jp.

[3] E-mail: ryotaro.okada@ds.musashino-u.ac.jp.

[4] E-mail: osamu@ds.musashino-u.ac.jp.

[5] E-mail: virach@musashino-u.ac.jp.

For all people to communicate naturally and easily with each other, it is important not only to translate between languages but also to recognize and work seamlessly with other methods, such as sign language. It is important to develop a global communication platform to help diverse people communicate with each other.

Thus far, we have been studying sign language recognition methods [1][2][3][4]. This study focuses on methods for achieving sign-language recognition with small training data. We found it difficult to collect sufficient sign language video data. Therefore, it is generally difficult to apply machine learning methods to sign language recognition. In our research [1][2][3][4], recognition was realized by extracting time-series skeletal features from training data in advance, extracting time-series skeletal features from input videos, and computing similarity weighting. These methods [1][2][3][4] are realized in the Japanese Sign Language and can be applied to other sign languages. However, this cost is too high to be quickly applied to many sign languages.

According to [5], there are more than 400 different sign languages worldwide, depending on the country, region, and so on. For all people to communicate naturally and easily, it is necessary to recognize and compose capabilities for these 400+ sign languages that must be realized and seamlessly coordinated. We need to create a system that facilitates the application of recognition and composition to each of these sign languages. Most of the current sign language recognition methods realize specific sign language recognition for individual linguistic regions, and when sign language recognition is realized among multilingual regions, it should be implemented in an ad hoc manner. To develop multilingual sign language recognition, it is necessary to develop a new method for handling various sign systems in a unified manner.

In this paper, we introduce the concept of the "Editable Mediator," a novel mechanism that bridges the gap between local hand shape recognition and global sign language interpretation. By utilizing the Editable Mediator, we can efficiently interpret various sign languages without the need for extensive retraining or ad hoc implementation. This innovation reduces the barriers to introducing new sign language systems and promotes a more inclusive global communication platform.

Furthermore, we leverage The Hamburg Sign Language Notation System (HamNoSys) [6], a transcription system common to all signs, to realize multiple primitive action recognition modules. HamNoSys offers standardized notation for all sign languages, making it an ideal foundation for our system.

This study makes several contributions to the broader research field.

- We propose a new primitive action-driven recognition method to realize global heterogeneous sign language recognition.
- We introduce the concept of an "Editable Mediator" and its role in enhancing the flexibility and scalability of our system.
- To realize our method, we applied HamNoSys [6] to multiple primitive action recognition modules.

This paper is organized as follows. In section 2, we present some related works of our method. Section 3 provides an overview of the editable mediators and their significance in our approach. Section 4 describes the existing study, HamNoSys [6], and its integration with our method. Section 5 presents our primitive action-driven recognition method for realizing global heterogeneous sign language recognition. In Section 6, we present the results of the preliminary experiments. Finally, in section 7, we summarize the study.

2. Related Works

Our previous works [1][2][3][4] presented sign-language recognition methods. In these methods, recognition is achieved by extracting time-series skeletal features from training data in advance, extracting time-series skeletal features from input videos, and computing similarity weighting. We found it difficult to collect sufficient sign language video data. Therefore, it is generally difficult to apply machine learning methods to sign language recognition. Our previous paper [1][2][3][4] also described some related works on the realization of sign language.

Reference [7] presented a survey of machine learning methods applied to sign language recognition systems. This reference [7] states that sign language involves the use of the upper part of the body, such as hand gestures [8], facial expressions [9], lip-reading [10], head nodding, and body postures to disseminate information [11] [12] [13]. We classified hand gestures and lip reading as verbal behaviors. We classify head nodding and body postures to disseminate information as emotional behaviors. We classified facial expressions as verbal and emotional.

According to reference [3], sign language recognition methods can be divided into two categories: continuous recognition of multiple sign words and discontinuous recognition. To realize continuous recognition, there are some works such as the hidden Markov model (HMM) and dynamic time warping (DTW) [14], and methods using Random Forest, artificial neural networks (ANN), and support vector machines (SVM) [15]. To realize non-continuous recognition, there are some studies, such as the k-nearest neighbor (k-NN) method [16], SVM [17], and sparse Bayesian classification of feature vectors generated from motion gradient orientation images extracted from input videos [18]. To realize sign language recognition for non-continuous and non-time-series data, there are some works such as the method of k-NN [19], similarity calculation using Euclidean distance [20], cosine similarity [19][21], ANN [22], SVM [23], and convolutional neural network (CNN) [24]. Reference [25] provides a research survey on recognizing emotions from body gestures. Their work solved the problem of some of these sign-language recognition functions.

However, to realize these methods, it is necessary to prepare sufficient training data for sign-language recognition. It is often impossible to prepare sign-language videos and labeled training data adequately. In addition, according to [5], there are more than 400 different sign languages worldwide depending on the country, region, and so on. It is not realistic to implement a recognition system for more than 400 different sign languages in an ad-hoc manner. We must develop a recognition platform that can easily and uniformly apply each sign language.

The concept of "primitive" is proposed by Kiyoki et.al [25] in the metadatabase system architecture. The metadatable system connects several legacy databases. Each legacy database has primitive functions to connect several legacy databases through the metadatabase system.

In the realm of sign language recognition, traditional methods are often constrained by the need for extensive datasets and specific implementations for each linguistic region. Our introduction of an Editable Mediator offers a transformative approach to this challenge. At its core, the Editable Mediator utilizes a Knowledge Base that stores symbol sequences representing hand shapes, positions, and movements paired with their corresponding meanings. This design allows for seamless addition of new sign languages by simply updating the Knowledge Base with new combinations of primitive actions and their interpretations.

Drawing inspiration from [25], our method employs individual modules to recognize each basic hand movement, termed primitive action recognition modules. The integration of these modules is facilitated by the primitive action composition module, which determines the overall meaning of a sign-language sequence. This architecture negates the need for ad hoc recognition systems and offers a scalable solution capable of accommodating over 400 sign language systems globally.

Therefore, the Editable Mediator serves as a beacon for inclusive communication. It bridges the communication divide, ensuring that, irrespective of the medium or method of communication, individuals can interact freely and effectively.

3. HamNoSys (The Hamburg Sign Language Notation System)

In this study, HamNoSys (The Hamburg Sign Language Notation System) [6], a transcription system common to all signs, was used to realize multiple primitive action recognition modules. HamNoSys is a transcription system for all sign languages with a direct correspondence between symbols and gesture aspects, such as hand location, shape, and movement. We can realize each primitive action recognition function according to each handshape chart [27] in the HamNoSys.

Figure 1 shows the HamNoSys handshaped chart. The description of each hand shape in Figure 1 is composed of symbols for the basic forms and diacritics for thumb position and bending. Using this approach, the set of handshape descriptions should include all handshapes used in sign language worldwide. HamNoSys can be used internationally because they do not refer to nationally diversified finger figures.

Figure 1. HamNoSys Handshape Chart [27].

We constructed primitive action recognition modules that recognize the shape of each finger, as shown in Figure 1. All the finger-expressed signs are combinations of finger shapes, as shown in Figure 1. We can recognize all the world's sign languages by building a system that can recognize all these finger shapes. We only need to prepare a knowledge base in which combinations of finger shapes indicate what meaning. The primitive action composition module derives meaning using this knowledge base. In other words, our method can recognize various signs without training data from sign language videos by simply appending the knowledge base referenced by the primitive action composition module. This eliminates the need to collect sufficient video sign-language media content to achieve sign-language recognition. We can easily realize a unified global sign language recognition system. This method will realize a new global communication platform that avoids the communication divide and allows people to communicate freely in the current situation, where they communicate in many ways.

4. Editable Mediators

The Editable Mediator is a sophisticated system that integrates a Knowledge Base that stores special symbol sequences. These sequences represent hand shapes, positions, and movements, and are paired with the words they signify. When a new symbol sequence is introduced into the system, the mediator searches the Knowledge Base to identify and deduce the word that it represents.

The knowledge base is at the heart of an editable mediator. It not only contains pairs of symbol sequences and their associated meanings but also can incorporate types of words and specific identifiers. This includes, but is not limited to, languages such as the Japanese Sign Language or Thai Sign Language. One of the prominent features of the mediator is its ability to be enriched by contributors proficient in diverse sign languages. This collaborative approach facilitates the expansion of sign-recognition capabilities.

The process of identifying the intended word representation from a new symbol sequence is complex. The system leverages string similarity and predictive estimation techniques to search and estimate within the Knowledge Base. The symbol sequences employed within the system were consistent with those used in primitive action recognition modules, including HamNoSys. While HamNoSys is a preferred choice owing to its comprehensive coverage of all facets of sign language, the system is flexible enough to accommodate alternative symbol sequences if needed.

One of the strengths of the Editable Mediator is its adaptability and scalability. It is designed to be dynamic, particularly when introducing new sign languages or systems. The Knowledge Base, being at the core, is structured for ease of updates and edits. This ensures that the system remains versatile, catering to evolving needs and promoting a more inclusive communication platform.

5. Incorporating Editable Mediator into Primitive Action-driven Recognition Method

In this section, we delve into the integration of our Editable Mediator within the framework of the primitive action-driven recognition method. The Editable Mediator serves as a linchpin for this method, enabling a unified and scalable approach to sign language recognition across diverse linguistic landscapes. This is the cornerstone for realizing a new global communication platform that bridges the communication divide, allowing for seamless interactions in a multilingual world.

5.1. Overview

Our method is composed of three main components: preprocessing for time-series skeletal feature extraction, multiple primitive action recognition modules, and a primitive action composition module, all of which are orchestrated by an Editable Mediator, as illustrated in Figure 2.

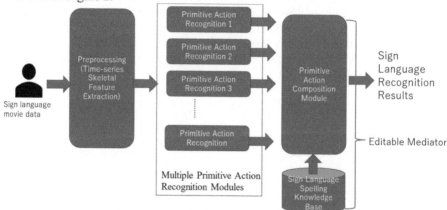

Figure 2. Overview of the primitive action-driven recognition method integrated with the Editable Mediator. This method encompasses preprocessing (time-series skeletal feature extraction), multiple primitive action recognition modules, and a primitive action composition module. Multiple primitive action recognition modules discern basic hand movements. The Editable Mediator, through its Knowledge Base, plays a pivotal role in the primitive action-composition module. It consolidates the recognition results from various primitive action recognition modules, referencing the sign language spelling knowledge base, to deduce the meaning of the input sign language.

Figure 2 provides an overview of how an Editable Mediator interacts with these components. The preprocessing stage extracts time-series skeletal features from the input sign language video data, which are then utilized by multiple primitive action-recognition modules. These modules were designed to recognize the basic hand movements and shapes of each finger based on the HamNoSys notation system.

The Editable Mediator comes into play primarily through its Knowledge Base, which is integrated into the primitive action-composition module. This module interprets the actual meaning of sign language by cross-referencing the recognition results from multiple primitive action recognition modules with a Knowledge Base. Adding new sign languages to the system is as straightforward as updating this Knowledge Base using new combinations of primitive actions and their corresponding meanings.

The Knowledge Base itself is a repository of symbol sequences, known as sign language spellings, defined by HamNoSys, and their corresponding words. This feature allows users to easily add new words to the Knowledge Base, making it the most important aspect of the proposed method. Unlike previous methods that relied heavily on labeled video content for training, our approach mitigated the need for extensive data collection. HamNoSys serves as a universal transcription system encompassing all hand shapes used in sign languages globally, thereby making our system internationally applicable.

By leveraging the Editable Mediator and its Knowledge Base, we can achieve an integrated sign language recognition system that is both flexible and globally applicable, and capable of accommodating as many as 400 different sign languages.

5.2. Preprocessing (Time-series Skeletal Feature Extraction)

Preprocessing extracts time-series skeletal features representing both hand positions each time from the sign language video data. Figure 3 shows the details of the time-series feature-extraction module.

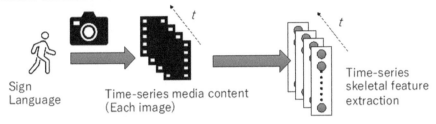

Sign Language

Time-series media content (Each image)

Time-series skeletal feature extraction

Figure 3. Preprocessing (Time-series Skeletal Feature Extraction)

First, it converts the input sign language video data into a set of images each time as a time-series media content set. Next, it extracts the features representing the positions of both hands in each image. Through this process, we can obtain multiple time series features at each time. In this study, we applied Mediapipe [28] for feature extraction. The Mediapipe can extract skeletal features of the hands, faces, arms, and body parts. This study uses the landmarks of the parts of both hands as features. The Mediapipe extracts each normalized position (x,y,z) data of 42 landmarks from each image. We obtained 126 features each time as a time-series feature. Therefore, it generates a $126 \times t$ time-series feature matrix. This matrix shows 126 motion features extracted from the sign language represented in the input video and their temporal variation.

5.3. Multiple Primitive Action Recognition Modules

The multiple primitive action recognition modules recognize the basic hand movements, as shown in Figure 4. We constructed a primitive action recognition module that recognizes the shape of each finger in HamNoSys [6][27].

From the time-series skeletal features extracted by preprocessing, all primitive action recognition modules were executed each time, and the corresponding primitive actions were derived. In other words, this module assigns a single symbol to HamNoSys, which represents hand movement each time. We can obtain a representation of the recognition results for each frame as a sequence of HamNoSys symbols. The symbol sequence extracted for each time (frame) have duplicates of the same symbol. The system deletes identical consecutive symbols.

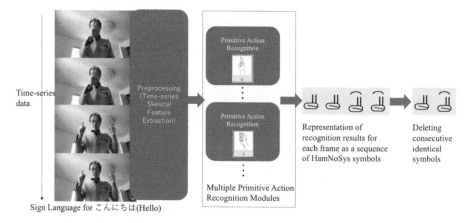

Sign Language for こんにちは(Hello)

Figure 4. An overview of multiple primitive action recognition modules

Using these modules, we can obtain symbol sequences that appear in HamNoSys from the time-series skeletal feature data.

5.4. Sign Language Spelling Knowledge Base

At the heart of our innovative approach lies the Sign Language Spelling Knowledge Base, an integral component of the Editable Mediator. This Knowledge Base is not just a static repository; it is a dynamic, user-editable platform designed to evolve and adapt to the diverse landscape of sign language. By allowing users to contribute, it harnesses the collective expertise of the global community, ensuring a comprehensive and up-to-date representation of sign languages in various regions and cultures.

The true power of the Editable Mediator is realized through this Knowledge Base. It serves as a bridge, translating intricate symbol sequences into meaningful sign-language interpretations. Each entry in the Knowledge Base consists of a symbol sequence, as defined by HamNoSys, that is paired with its corresponding word or phrase. This pairing provides direct correspondence between physical gestures and linguistic meanings.

However, the participatory nature of the Knowledge Base truly sets our method apart. By enabling users, especially those proficient in various sign languages, to contribute to and edit entries, we ensure that the system remains current and inclusive. This crowdsourced approach not only reduces the barriers to introducing new sign languages but also ensures that nuances and regional variations are captured accurately. In essence, the Sign Language Spelling Knowledge Base, through the Editable Mediator, promises a future where sign language recognition is not just a technical endeavor but a collaborative and inclusive journey.

The sign language spelling knowledge base consists of a sequence of symbols called sign language spellings, which are defined by HamNoSy,s, and a word. When users can use HamNoSys as a reference for spelling the hand shapes that make up sign language, they can easily add new words to this knowledge base. This was the most important feature of the proposed method.

Figure 5 shows how sign language spelling is composed. In general, sign language consists of multiple hand gestures. Sign language spelling describes handshapes in what order. Figure 5 shows an example of the signs of hello in Japanese. Sign language meaning hello is performed by a hand gesture with the index and middle fingers raised, followed by a hand gesture with the index and middle fingers bent. Each hand shape is assigned a symbol that is determined within the HamNoSys. Sign-language spelling is represented by one or more symbol sequences, denoted by HamNoSys.

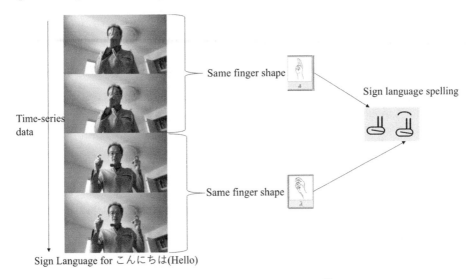

Sign Language for こんにちは(Hello)

Figure 5. How to compose sign language spelling

By introducing sign language spelling, it is possible to build a knowledge base with simple descriptions, without creating or collecting new sign language videos. The HamNoSys set of finger shapes is common to all sign languages. By applying the same methodology, it is possible to create a knowledge base for sign language recognition worldwide.

Table 1 shows an example of a sign language spelling knowledgebase. The sign language spelling knowledge base consists of a sequence of symbols called sign language spellings, which are defined by HamNoSys, and a word. This knowledge base can be created for each sign language system.

Table 1. Example of a sign language spelling knowledge base. The sign language spelling knowledge base consists of a sequence of symbols called sign language spellings, which are defined by HamNoSys, and a word.

Sign language spelling	word
	こんにちは (Hello)
	元気 (How are you?)
	久しぶり (No time long see)
	ごめんなさい (I'm sorry)
⋮	⋮

5.5. Primitive Action Composition Module

The primitive action composition module derives appropriate words by matching the symbol sequences extracted by the multiple primitive action recognition modules with each sign language spelling in the sign language spelling knowledge base.

The primitive action composition module must weigh the similarity between sign language spellings as symbol sequences. In this study, we applied the Levenshtein distance to weigh the similarity between sign language spellings. Levenshtein distance is one of the edit distances and is defined as the minimum number of times required to transform one string into the other. It is possible to derive a word that matches the sign by comparing the sequence of symbols extracted by the multiple primitive action recognition modules with sign spelling in the sign language spelling knowledge base using the Levenshtein distance.

6. Conclusion

In this study, we have presented a groundbreaking approach to global sign language recognition through the introduction of the "Editable Mediator." Traditional methods of sign language recognition are region-specific, which leads to challenges in multilingual regions. The proposed method offers a solution to this problem by providing a unified framework capable of recognizing sign languages from various linguistic backgrounds, thereby fostering global communication.

Central to our system is the Editable Mediator, a novel mechanism that bridges local hand shape recognition to derive global sign language interpretation. This mediator eliminates the need for extensive retraining or ad hoc implementation when adapting to different sign languages, making the introduction of new sign language systems more seamless and efficient.

Our approach departs from specific sign language notations, such as HamNoSys, focusing instead on recognizing common primitive actions shared across different sign languages. By leveraging the standardized notation of HamNoSys, we were able to establish multiple primitive action-recognition modules, further enhancing the efficiency of the system.

In conclusion, our research has laid the foundation for a more inclusive global communication platform, reducing barriers in sign language recognition and promoting understanding across diverse linguistic backgrounds. As communication with people from different linguistic backgrounds becomes increasingly crucial, our system offers a promising step towards a more interconnected and inclusive world.

References

[1] Nitta, T., Hagimoto, S., Yanase, A., Okada, R., Sornlertlamvanich, V., & Nakanishi, T. Realization for Finger Character Recognition Method by Similarity Measure of Finger Features, International Journal of Smart Computing and Artificial Intelligence, Vol. 6 No. 1, 2022.
[2] Hagimoto S, Nitta T, Yanase A, Nakanishi T, Okada R, Sornlertlamvanich V, Knowledge Base Creation by Reliability of Coordinates Detected from Videos for Finger Character Recognition, In proc. of the 19th International Conference e-Society 2021, FSP 5.1-F144, 2021. p.169-176.

[3] Nitta T, Hagimoto S, Yanase A, Nakanishi T, Okada R, Sornlertlamvanich V. Finger Character Recognition in Sign Language Using Finger Feature Knowledge Base for Similarity Measure, In Proceedings of the 3rd IEEE/IIAI International Congress on Applied Information Technology (IEEE/IIAI AIT 2020), 2020.

[4] Nakanishi, T., Minematsu, A., Okada, R., Hasegawa, O., & Sornlertlamvanich, V. Sign Language Recognition by Similarity Measure with Emotional Expression Specific to Signers, 32nd International Conference on Indormation Modelling and Knowledge Bases, 2022.

[5] SIL International (2018a). Sign Languages. https://www.sil.org/sign-languages

[6] Hanke, T. HamNoSys-representing sign language data in language resources and language-processing contexts. In: Streiter, Oliver, Vettori, Chiara (eds): LREC 2004, Workshop proceedings: Representation and processing of sign languages. Paris: ELRA; 2004. pp. 1-6.

[7] Adeyanju I, Bello O, Adegboye M.. Machine Learning Methods for Sign Language Recognition: A Critical Review and Analysis. Intelligent Systems with Applications 2021 12, 200056.

[8] Gupta R, Rajan S. Comparative analysis of convolution neural network models for continuous Indian sign language classification, Procedia Computer Science, 171 2020, pp. 1542-1550.

[9] Chowdhry D.A, Hussain A, Ur Rehman M.Z, Ahmad F, Ahmad A, Pervaiz M. Smart security system for sensitive area using face recognition, Proceedings of the IEEE conference on sustainable utilization and development in engineering and technology, IEEE CSUDET 2013, pp. 11-14.

[10] Cheok M.J, Omar Z, Jaward M.H. A review of hand gesture and sign language recognition techniques, International Journal of Machine Learning and Cybernetics, 10 (1), 2019, pp. 131-153.

[11] Butt U.M, Husnain B, Ahmed U, Tariq A, Tariq I, Butt M.A, Zia M.S. Feature-based algorithmic analysis on American sign language dataset, International Journal of Advanced Computer Science and Applications, 10 (5), 2019, pp. 583-589.

[12] Rastgoo R, Kiani K, Escalera S. Sign language recognition: A deep survey, Expert Systems with Applications, 164 2021, Article 113794.

[13] Lee C.K.M, Ng K.H, Chen C.H, Lau H.C.W, Chung S.Y, Tsoi T. American sign language recognition and training method with recurrent neural network, Expert Systems with Applications, 167 2021, Article 114403.

[14] Huang, Y., Monekosso, D., Wang, H., Augusto, JC. A hybrid method for hand gesture recognition, 2012 Eighth International Conference on Intelligent Environments, Guanajuato, Mexico, June 2012. pp. 297–300.

[15] Yuan,S. et al. Chinese sign language alphabet recognition is based on a random forest algorithm. 2020 IEEE International Workshop on Metrology for Industry 4.0, and IoT, June 2020. pp. 340–344.

[16] Izzah, A. and Suciati, N. Translation of sign language using generic Fourier descriptor and nearest neighbor. IJCI, vol. 3, no. 1, February 2014. pp. 31–41.

[17] Raheja JL., Mishra A, Chaudhary A. Indian sign language recognition using SVM, Pattern recognition. Image Anal., vol. 26, April 2016. pp. 434–441.

[18] Wong, S. F., Cipolla, R. Real-time adaptive hand motion recognition using a sparse Bayesian classifier. Computer Vision in Human-Computer Interaction, Berlin, Heidelberg, 2005, pp. 170–179.

[19] Mahmud, I., Tabassum, T., Uddin, Md.P., Ali, E., Nitu, AM., Afjal, MI. Efficient Noise Reduction and HOG Feature Extraction for Sign-Language Recognition. 2018 International Conference on Advancement in Electrical and Electronic Engineering (ICAEEE), 2018. pp. 1–4.

[20] Hartanto, R., Susanto, A., Santosa, P.I., Real time static hand gesture recognition system prototype for Indonesian sign language. 2014 6th International Conference on Information Technology and Electrical Engineering, Yogyakarta, Indonesia, 2014. pp. 1–6.

[21] Anand MS., Kumar NM., Kumaresan A. An efficient framework for Indian sign language recognition using wavelet transform. Circuits and Systems, Vol. 07, no. 8, June 2016. pp. 1874–1883.

[22] Hasan, M. M., Khaliluzzaman, M. D., Himel, S. A., and Chowdhury, R. T.. Hand sign language recognition for the Bangla alphabet is based on the Freeman Chain Code and ANN. 2017 4th International Conference on Advances in Electrical Engineering (ICAEE), Dhaka, September 2017. pp. 749–753.

[23] Athira, P. K., Sruthi, C. J., Lijiya, A. A signer-independent sign language recognition with co-articulation elimination from live videos: An Indian scenario. J. King Saud. Univ. - Comput. Inf. Sci., vol. 34, no. 3, March 2022. pp. 771–778.

[24] Aloysius, N., Geetha, M.: A scale space model of weighted average CNN ensemble for ASL fingerspelling recognition. Int. J. Comput. Sci. Eng., vol. 22, no. 1, May 2020. pp. 154–161.

[25] Noroozi F, Kaminska D, Corneanu C, Sapinski T, Escalera S, Anbarjafari G. Survey on emotional body gesture recognition. IEEE transactions on affective computing, 12(02), 2021. p. 505-523.

[26] Kiyoki, Y., Hosokawa, Y., Ishibashi, N. A metadatabase system architecture for integrating heterogeneous databases with temporal and spatial operations." Advanced Database Research and Development Series 10, 2000. pp. 158-165.

[27] HamNoSys Handshapes,
      https://www.sign-lang.uni-hamburg.de/dgs-korpus/files/inhalt_pdf/HamNoSys_Handshapes.pdf
[28] Mediapipe, https://google.github.io/mediapipe/

Information Modelling and Knowledge Bases XXXV
M. Tropmann-Frick et al. (Eds.)
doi:10.3233/FAIA231159

Algorithm for Generating Sketch Maps from Spatial Information Extracted from Natural Language Descriptions

Marek MENŠÍK, Petr RAPANT, Adam ALBERT

VSB - Technical University of Ostrava, 17. listopadu 15, 708 00 Ostrava,
Czech Republic

Abstract. A significant amount of real-world information is documented in simple text format, such as messages found on social networks. These messages include various types of data, including spatial details, which can be extracted through natural language processing. The extracted data can be represented as a plain topological graph, stored as tuples that describe individual edges. This paper outlines an algorithm that utilizes these tuples to generate a simplified map.

Keywords. Spatial data, Sketch map, Topology, Motion verbs, TIL

1. Introduction

A substantial part of the corpus of real-world information exists in textual records, such as messages within social networking platforms. Among their contents, these texts include spatial data, among other elements. Our research endeavors to extract spatial data from plain text, construct a topological graph representing the described area, and subsequently present it in the form of a sketch map. A sketch map is characterized as '*an outline map created based on observation rather than precise survey measurements, illustrating solely the principal features of the area.*'[1] Typically, it is a manual depiction of an area drawn without a specific scale, emphasizing the key characteristics of the region while avoiding unnecessary details. The sketch map exhibits a limited degree of positional accuracy, and as such does not accurately depict the distances, dimensions, or shapes of objects. On the contrary, it can possess a high level of logical accuracy, signifying that the spatial relationships, such as topology and spatial order, among objects are accurately portrayed.[2]

The procedure for generating a sketch map from unprocessed textual data comprises three stages, as outlined in [1]: (i) identification of spatial entities and their spatial relationships through natural language processing, (ii) development of a basic topological

---

[1] See https://www.merriam-webster.com/dictionary/sketch%20map
[2] See https://www.tariffnumber.com/info/abbreviations/12485

graph that encapsulates the identified spatial entities and their spatial connections, and (iii) transformation of this graph into a sketch map. This paper focuses on presenting initial findings related to the third stage.

The process of converting a topological graph into a sketch map entails, at its core, the dynamic arrangement of spatial entities on the medium in a manner that ensures the preservation of all established spatial relationships between them.

The conversion of a topological graph into a sketch map fundamentally entails the dynamic positioning of spatial entities on the canvas in a manner that preserves all established spatial relationships among them. Certain authors have been involved in this process. In the work of the authors [1], each entity was depicted as a rectangle and its size and position were incrementally adjusted to accommodate all spatial relationships. Their primary focus was on data that describe urbanized areas. In contrast, the authors [2] directed their efforts toward the generation of a sketch map of open landscapes, using descriptions of individual routes drawn up by orienteers. The resulting sketch map accurately portrayed the relative positioning of each spatial entity in relation to other entities.

The approach described here differs from the previous ones. In this method, we employ Transparent Intensional Logic (TIL) constructions to represent the acquired spatial data and construct a basic topological graph of the specified area. Mathematical logic tools are employed to manipulate this graph, forming individual circles within it that are subsequently concatenated to produce the final sketch map. The inception of this concept was initially introduced in [3]. The current article aims to further develop this concept by using a larger-scale example, thus improving the user's understanding.

The subsequent chapters are structured as follows: Chapter 2 provides a detailed description of the input data format employed by the algorithm, along with crucial definitions. In Chapter 3, our attention is directed towards the numbering of directions and the identification of the bounding circle within our dataset. Chapter 4 addresses the necessary data adjustments needed for the algorithm's implementation. Chapter 5 offers an extensive explanation of the algorithm itself. Chapter 6 is devoted to a case study that illustrates the practical application of the algorithm. Ultimately, Chapter 7 serves as the conclusion of this paper.

2. How We Obtain Our Data

We commence with descriptions of the journeys undertaken by the agents, which we regard as coherent both in spatial and temporal dimensions.

In the work presented in [4], we have introduced heuristic functions that operate on these journey descriptions. These functions incrementally construct a TIL representation describing spatial data.

TIL is a typed hyperintensional λ-calculus of partial functions found by Pavel Tichý in the early 1970s. TIL exploits procedural semantics, i.e., natural language expressions encode *algorithmically structured procedures* as their meaning. Tichý defined six kinds of such meaning procedures that he coined TIL *constructions* as the centerpiece of his system; see [5]. Constructions produce extensional or intensional entities, or even lower-order procedures, as their products or, in well-defined cases, fail to produce anything. TIL has been introduced and thoroughly described in numerous papers, such as [5], [6], [7], [8].

Tichý formulated six categories of these meaning procedures, which he referred to as TIL constructions, serving as the central element of his system, as detailed in [5].Constructions produce extensional or intensional entities, or even lower-order procedures, as their products or, in well-defined cases, fail to produce anything. TIL has been introduced and thoroughly described in numerous papers, such as [5], [6], [7], [8].

A journey can be informally characterized as a series of natural language sentences, with each sentence containing information pertaining to a segment of an agent's journey.To formalize these sentences, we utilize a category of *motion verbs* (such as *to go, to walk, to cross, to turn*), which bind constituents from other sentences to them through valency relationships. The valence of the verb is delineated in valency frames using *functors*. Functors establish the semantic-syntactic connection between the verb and its complement.Details are given, for example, in [9], [10], [11], [1].

As an illustration, the sentence *'Jim quickly ran from start to finish in 45 seconds.'* can be analyzed by applying the valency frame of the verb 'to ran' in the following manner:

- ACT (who): Jim

- DIR1 (from where): start

- DIR3 (to where): finish

- EXT (for how long/ how far): 45 seconds

- MANN (manner): quickly

By utilizing valency frames and the information derived from them, it becomes possible to construct a formal representation of an individual's journey by expressing it in the natural language formalized within the expressive language of TIL. [3]

$$\lambda w \lambda t \; [['ACT_{wt} \, 'Jim \, 'ran] \wedge ['DIR1_{wt} \, 'start \, 'ran] \wedge ['DIR3_{wt} \, 'finish \, 'ran]$$
$$\wedge ['EXT_{wt} \, '45 \, 'ran] \wedge ['MANN_{wt} \, 'quickly \, 'ran]] \tag{1}$$

Types:
DIR1, DIR3/$(o\pi v)_{\tau\omega}$*; ACT/* $(o\iota v)_{\tau\omega}$*; MANN/* $(o\alpha v)_{\tau\omega}$*; EXT/; Jim/* ι*; start, finish /*π*; ran/*v*, where* π *is a type of places;* v *is a type of the activity denoted by a verb.*

This approach is founded on our prior research, where we introduced an algorithm for symbolic supervised machine learning that progressively refines vague or inaccurate expressions into adequately accurate ones. For additional details, please refer to [12] and [8].

In this paper, we analyze the data extracted from the TIL constructions. This dataset encompasses information regarding the locations visited by the agents and the directions of

---

[3]For the sake of clarity, we will exclusively employ TIL language to present examples. Our calculations are conducted using TIL-Script constructions.

movement between pairs of these locations they followed. In [4], various definitions were introduced to identify spatial data within TIL constructions. Among these, the following two are instrumental in recognizing the locations visited by agents.

Definition 1 (*node, edge*). Let V be a *motion verb*, let $S = \{B|('DIR1$ or $'DIR3)$ and V are constituents of B $\}$ and let $D^V = \{C|V$ is a constituent of C $\} \setminus S$ then D^V is a set of *edges* and S is a set of *nodes*.

Definition 2 (*place, functor, value*). Let $[\alpha \, x \, v]$ be a *node* and let $[\beta \, y \, v_1]$ be the *edge* description. Then x is a *place*, α, β are *functors*, and y, v, v_1 is *values*.

A simple sentence might connect two places by verb valency with additional information. In the case of construction 1, by definition 1, $['DIR1_{wt} \, 'gym \, 'walk]$ and $['DIR3_{wt} \, 'home \, 'walk]$ are *nodes*. The rest, $['ACT_{wt} \, 'John \, 'walk], ['EXT_{wt} \, '15 \, 'walk]$, $['MANN_{wt} \, 'quickly \, 'walk]$, is an edge. By definition 2, *home*, and *gym* are *places*; they are constituents of *nodes*.

Definition 3 (*relative direction RD*). Let $['MANN \, x \, v]$ be an *edge description*, and the value x be one of the following $'straight, \, 'slightly–left, \, 'left, \, 'sharp–left, \, 'back, \, 'sharp–right, \, 'right$ and $'slightly–right$. Then x is the *relative direction*.

By employing definitions 1, 2, and 3, we extract the spatial information necessary for map sketching. Specifically, we identify a place as the point of origin for the agent's movement, identify the direction of their movement, and determine the destination place toward which the agent is traveling. As a result, we obtain input data in the form of a tuple [DIR1, direction, DIR3].

3. Numbering

Directions play a key role in map sketching. We encode the relative directions from the input data using numerical values. The mapping of relative directions to natural numbers is illustrated in Table 1.

The data presented in Table 1 correspond to the fundamental eight directions we derive, namely, straight (F), slightly left (FL), left (L), sharp left (BL), back (B), sharp right (BR), right (R), and slightly right (FR).

TIL	RD	Encoding	TIL	RD	Encoding
$'straight$	F	0	$'back$	B	4
$'slightly–left$	FL	1	$'sharp–right$	BR	5
$'left$	L	2	$'right$	R	6
$'sharp–left$	BL	3	$'slightly–right$	FR	7

Table 1. TIL representations (TIL), relative directions (RD) and their numerical representation.

Let $['MANN \, x \, v]$ be an *edge description*, and the value x be one of the following , $'slightly–left, \, , 'sharp–left, \, 'back, \, 'sharp–right, \, 'right$ and $'slightly–right$. Then x is the *relative direction*.

Drawing upon Table 1, we introduce the concept of Relative Direction Number (RDN):

Definition 4 (*relative direction number RDN*). Let *C* be a graph circle. **RDN** is the value assigned to the edge in *C* based on algorithm 1.

RDNs, along with the corresponding relative directions, are visually depicted in Figure 1.

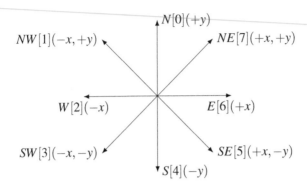

Figure 1. Relative [RDN/ASDN] and $\oplus$ function for computation of individual nodes coordinates.

In the initial phase of the map sketching algorithm, we assign Relative Direction Numbers (RDNs) to edges in accordance with Algorithm 1.

Algorithm 1. *Relative direction number (RDN) assignment*
Require: $\circ$ - numbering function (Table 2),
   G - set of tuples [α DIR1 RD DIR3] representing the graph,
   $C \subseteq G$ represents the circle,
   S - starting node, where $RD_1 = front$

$RDN_1 \leftarrow 0$
for $i := 2$ to $|C|$ **do**
   $RDN_i = RDN_{i-1} \circ RD_i$
end for

$\circ$	F	FL	L	BL	B	BR	R	FR
F	0	1	2	3	4	5	6	7
0	0	1	2	3	4	5	6	7
1	1	2	3	4	5	6	7	0
2	2	3	4	5	6	7	0	1
3	3	4	5	6	7	0	1	2
4	4	5	6	7	0	1	2	3
5	5	6	7	0	1	2	3	4
6	6	7	0	1	2	3	4	5
7	7	0	1	2	3	4	5	6

Table 2. Computation of RDN: Application of the $\circ$ function

Subsequently, we identify all bounding circles as defined by Definition 5 within our input data.

Definition 5 (*bounding circle BC*). Let G be a planar graph and C be a graph circle. If each edge of the circle C has the maximal number Cn calculated by the equation:

$$Cn = ((RDN^{out} - RDN^{in} + 8) \mod 8) \tag{2}$$

Then C is called the **bounding circle**.[4]

In situations where an edge is part of multiple circles with different Relative Direction Numbers (RDNs), it becomes necessary to execute the rotation adjustment, as detailed in Section 4.1, to derive the absolute sketch direction number (ASDN), as further defined, in order to unify all the RDNs.

For instance, let's consider a segment of a description of a bounding circle in which an agent moved "right" from point "A" to point "B," and assume that the agent arrived at node "A" from relative direction 0. In this case, our input data would be represented as [A, right, B]. Consequently, we can assign the edge from A to B with the Relative Direction Number (RDN) 6.

4. Bounding Circle Adjustment

Before we can merge two bounding circles in their overlapping portions, it is often necessary to make adjustments to them. Generally, two situations require consideration. The first situation arises when the same sections of the bounding circles are described by agents from different directions. To address this, it becomes necessary to rotate one of the bounding circles so that their common sections align in the same direction. The second situation occurs when the distances between nodes within the common sections are unequal. In this case, the nodes of one bounding circle must be repositioned to ensure that the distances between nodes in the common sections are equal, while preserving the directions of edges in the modified bounding circle.

4.1. Rotation

The shared edges of two bounding circles may be described in different directions. For example, one agent might make a left turn onto a street, while another may make a right turn onto the same street. Consequently, to merge these two bounding circles effectively, it becomes necessary to unify the RDNs associated with their common edges. This unification is accomplished through a process of rotation, whereby all RDNs are recalculated using the following equation: 3.[5]

$$RDN_{i+1} = (RDN_i + 1) \mod 8 \tag{3}$$

Definition 6 (*absolute sketch direction number ASDN*). Let e be an edge, then the *RDN* of the edge e is called **ASDN** if for every circle where the edge e is part of it, the e has the same *RDN*.

---

[4] RDN^{out} is RDN of outgoing incident edge and RDN^{in} represents RDN of the edge entering into the node.

[5] The rotation is used as many times as it is necessary to unify the RDN.

Remark: In cases where all the data are consistent, the "rotation" process yields ASDNs. However, if there is any RDN that cannot be transformed into an ASDN, it indicates data inconsistency. In such situations, the user can be informed about which specific edge is not consistent.

4.2. Node adjustment

Node adjustment involves confirming that the position of a node is consistent with its neighboring nodes, considering the RDN, and relocating it in the direction of the RDN if required. When a node is moved, the consistency of its neighboring nodes is also verified. The function ∘+ is employed to position the nodes at specific coordinates in a consistent manner.

As an illustration, if node A has coordinates [0,0] and node B is situated in direction 7, which corresponds to edge (A, B) having RDN = 7, then in accordance with the function depicted in Figure 1, node B would have coordinates [n,n], where n is greater than 0. This adjustment ensures consistent positioning based on the given direction.

5. Algorithm for Computing Coordinates of Nodes

1. Sort all *bounding circles* (BCs).

2. Pick the longest one and place any node to coordinate [0,0].

3. Go through all the nodes in the circle and according to their ASDN calculate the coordinates. Check whether there are no edges intersections. If so, make *adjust-ments*.[6]

4. Withdraw the used circle from the set.

5. From the rest of the circles find the one with the longest common part with the already processed circle. If there are known coordinates, use them. Otherwise, recalculate and *adjust* all affected BCs. [7]

6. Set one common node of the new circle to already known coordinates and continue by step [3.]

6. Case Study

In our case study, we will illustrate the functionality of the algorithm. Initially, we will showcase the input data visualized using the topological graph. We will proceed to identify bounding circles from the input data, and from this point onward, we will visualize the processed data using graph visualization for the sake of clarity. Subsequently, we will demonstrate the adjustment of bounding circles and their eventual merging to create a sketch map.

---

[6]Move nodes to other coordinates in the same direction as described in chapter 4.

[7]The longest common part means *BC* with the most common edges.

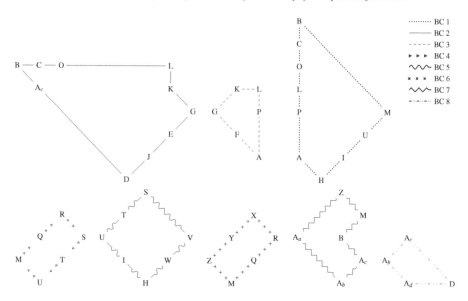

Figure 2. Eight unrotated BCs are sketched according to Table 4.

Table 3 provides a representation of our input data. The column named 'Places' contains triplets in the format (H, A, F) denoting that an agent traveled from place H through place A to place F. The 'Absolute' and 'Relative' columns present values of absolute directions and relative directions, respectively. For instance, a pair like (ne, sw) indicates that an agent arrived at place A from the northeast (place H) and proceeded to the southwest (place F). Consequently, the relative direction in this case is 0 (straight).

The absolute directions presented in Table 3 are derived from the map data and are included here solely for the purpose of validating the accuracy of our algorithm. They are not essential for the correct operation of our algorithm.

From Table 3, we identify eight bounding circles (according to definition 5), namely BC 1: L–O–C–B–M–I–H–A–P; BC 2: L–O–C–B–D–J–E–G–K and BC 3: L–K–G–F–A–P; BC 4:M–Q–R–S–T–U; BC 5: U–T–S–V–W–H–I; BC 6: Z–Y–X–R–Q–M; BC 7: M–B–A_c–A_b–A_a–Z, BC 8:A_c–D–A_d–A_b.

BCs are presented in Table 4, where the edges of bounding circles are in the form of $[[X, Y], RDN]$. By algorithm 1 we assign RDN to all edges in the bounding circles.

The visualization of bounding circles, as derived from Table 4, is depicted in Figure 2.

As there are bounding circles that share certain nodes, we have the opportunity to merge them. Initially, we merge BCs that have the most nodes in common. In this scenario, BC 1 and BC 2 (L-O-C-B are shared) will be merged first. To achieve this, we must unify the Relative Direction Numbers (RDNs) of identical edges in both BCs. For instance, the edge L-O in BC 1 has an RDN of 0, while the corresponding edge in BC 2 has an RDN of 2. Therefore, it becomes necessary to adjust (rotate) BC 2 until the RDNs match. The rotation process of all BCs is visualized in Figure 3.

Now that all bounding circles are oriented in the same direction, it becomes apparent from the visualizations of BC 1 and BC 2 in Figure 3 that the distances between the

Places	Abs	Rel	Street	Places	Abs	Rel	Street
(H,A,F)	ne,sw	F	'Bowery	(F,A,H)	sw,ne	F	'Bowery
(A,F,G)	ne,sw	F	'Bowery	(G,F,A)	sw,ne	F	'Bowery
(F,G,E)	ne,sw	F	'ChathamSQ	(E,G,F)	sw,ne	F	'Bowery
(G,E,J)	ne,sw	F	'ChathamSQ	(J,E,G)	sw,ne	F	'ChathamSQ
(E,J,D)	ne,sw	F	'ChathamSQ	(D,J,E)	sw,ne	F	'ChathamSQ
(J,D,A_c)	ne,nw	R	'MottST	(A_c,D,J)	nw,ne	L	'ChathamSQ
(D,A_c,B)	se,nw	F	'MottST	(B,A_c,D)	nw,se	F	'MottST
(A_c,B,M)	se,ne	R	'MottST	(M,B,A_c)	ne,se	L	'MottST
(B,M,U)	sw,se	R	'BayardST	(U,M,B)	se,sw	L	'MottST
(M,U,I)	nw,se	F	'BayardST	(I,U,M)	se,nw	B	'BayardST
(U,I,H)	nw,se	F	'BayardST	(H,I,U)	se,nw	F	'BayardST
(I,H,A)	nw,sw	R	'Bowery	(A,H,I)	sw,nw	L	'BayardST
(D,B,C)	se,e	BR	'PellST	(C,B,D)	e,se	BL	'MottST
(B,C,O)	w,e	F	'PellST	(O,C,B)	e,w	F	'PellST
(C,O,L)	w,e	F	'PellST	(L,O,C)	e,w	F	'PellST
(O,L,P)	w,e	F	'PellST	(P,L,O)	e,w	F	'PellST
(L,P,A)	w,e	F	'PellST	(A,P,L)	e,w	F	'PellST
(C,B,M)	e,ne	BR	'MottST	(M,B,C)	ne,e	BL	'PellST
(P,A,H)	w,ne	FL	'Bowery	(H,A,P)	ne,w	FR	'PellST
(P,A,F)	w,sw	BR	'Bowery	(F,A,P)	sw,w	BL	'PellST
(K,G,E)	nw,sw	R	'ChathamSQ	(E,G,K)	sw,nw	L	'DoyerST
(K,G,F)	nw,ne	L	'Bowery	(F,G,K)	ne,nw	R	'DoyerST
(L,K,G)	n,se	FL	'DoyerST	(G,K,L)	se,n	FR	'DoyerST
(O,L,K)	w,s	R	'DoyerST	(K,L,O)	s,w	L	'PellST
(P,L,K)	e,s	L	'DoyerST	(K,L,P)	s,e	R	'PellST
(M,Q,R)	sw,ne	F	'MottST	(R,Q,M)	ne,sw	F	'MottST
(Q,R,S)	sw,se	R	'CanalST	(S,R,Q)	se,sw	L	'MottST
(R,S,T)	nw,sw	R	'ElizabethST	(T,S,R)	sw,nw	L	'CanalST
(S,T,U)	ne,sw	F	'ElizabethST	(U,T,S)	sw,ne	F	'ElizabethST
(T,U,M)	ne,nw	R	'BayardST	(M,U,T)	nw,ne	L	'ElizabethST
(U,M,Q)	se,ne	R	'MottST	(Q,M,U)	ne,se	L	'BayardST
(U,T,S)	sw,ne	F	'ElizabethST	(S,T,U)	ne,sw	F	'ElizabethST
(T,S,V)	sw,se	R	'CanalST	(V,S,T)	se,sw	L	'ElizabethST
(S,V,W)	nw,sw	R	'Bowery	(W,V,S)	sw,nw	L	'CanalST
(V,W,H)	ne,sw	F	'Bowery	(H,W,V)	sw,ne	F	'Bowery
(W,H,I)	sw,se	R	'BayardST	(I,H,W)	se,sw	L	'Bowery
(H,I,U)	se,nw	F	'BayardST	(U,I,H)	nw,se	F	'BayardST
(I,U,T)	se,ne	R	'ElizabethST	(T,U,I)	ne,se	L	'BayardST
(Q,M,Z)	ne,nw	R	'BayardST	(Z,M,Q)	nw,ne	L	'MottST
(M,Z,Y)	se,ne	R	'MulberryST	(Y,Z,M)	ne,se	L	'BayardST
(Z,Y,X)	sw,ne	F	'MulberryST	(X,Y,Z)	ne,sw	F	'MulberryST
(Y,X,R)	sw,se	R	'CanalST	(R,X,Y)	se,sw	L	'MulberryST
(X,R,Q)	nw,sw	R	'MottST	(Q,R,X)	sw,nw	L	'CanalST
(R,Q,M)	ne,sw	F	'MottST	(M,Q,R)	sw,ne	F	'MottST
(B,A_c,A_b)	nw,sw	R	'MoscoST	(A_b,A_c,B)	sw,nw	L	'MottST
(A_c,A_b,A_d)	ne,nw	R	'MulberryST	(A_a,A_b,A_c)	nw,ne	L	'MoscoST
(A_b,A_d,Z)	se,n	FR	'MulberryST	(Z,A_d,A_b)	n,se	FL	'MulberryST
(A_d,Z,M)	s,se	BR	'BayardST	(M,Z,A_d)	se,s	BL	'MulberryST
(Z,M,B)	nw,sw	R	'MottST	(B,M,Z)	sw,nw	L	'BayardST
(M,B,A_c)	ne,se	F	'MottST	(A_c,B,M)	se,ne	F	'MottST
(A_c,D,A_d)	se,w	BR	'WorthST	(A_d,D,A_c)	w,se	BL	'MottST
(D,A_d,A_b)	se,n	FR	'MulberryST	(A_b,A_d,D)	n,se	FL	'WorthST
(A_d,A_b,A_c)	s,ne	FR	'MoscoST	(A_c,A_b,A_d)	ne,s	FL	'MulberryST
(A_b,A_c,D)	sw,se	R	'MottST	(D,A_c,A_b)	se,sw	L	'MoscoST

Table 3. Input data

BC 1	BC 2	BC 3	BC4	BC5	BC6	BC7	BC8
[[a,p],0]	[[l,o],2]	[[a,p],0]	[[m,q],7]	[[u,t],7]	[[z,y],7]	[[m,b],3]	[[ac,d],5]
[[p,l],0]	[[o,c],2]	[[p,l],0]	[[q,r],7]	[[t,s],7]	[[y,x],7]	[[b,ac],5]	[[d,ad],2]
[[l,o],0]	[[c,b],2]	[[l,k],2]	[[r,s],5]	[[s,v],5]	[[x,r],5]	[[ac,ab],3]	[[ad,ab],1]
[[o,c],0]	[[b,ac],5]	[[k,g],3]	[[s,t],3]	[[v,w],3]	[[r,q],3]	[[ab,aa],1]	[[ab,ac],7]
[[c,b],0]	[[ac,d],5]	[[g,f],5]	[[t,u],3]	[[w,h],3]	[[q,m],3]	[[aa,z],7]	
[[b,m],5]	[[d,j],7]	[[f,a],5]	[[u,m],1]	[[h,i],1]	[[m,z],1]	[[z,m],5]	
[[m,u],3]	[[j,e],7]			[[i,u],1]			
[[u,i],3]	[[e,g],7]						
[[i,h],3]	[[g,k],1]						
[[h,a],1]	[[k,l],0]						

Table 4.

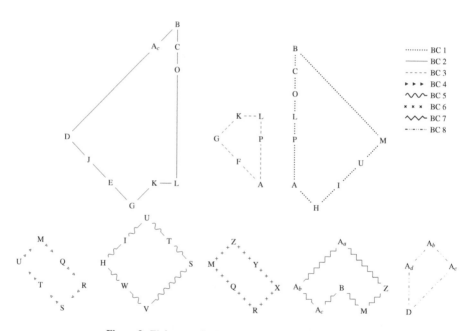

Figure 3. Eight rotated BCs are sketched according to Table 4.

shared nodes L and O are not equal. Thus, it is imperative to adjust the positions of the nodes in one of the BCs to align them with the nodes in the other BC. In Figure 4, we can observe that in BC 1, we have altered the coordinates of node L to ensure that the distance from node L to node O matches that in BC 2. This adjustment of node L's coordinates, however, affects the Relative Direction Numbers (RDNs) of the other nodes in BC 1. Consequently, we have adjusted the coordinates of nodes P, A, H, I, and M in BC 1 to preserve the original RDNs of the edges.

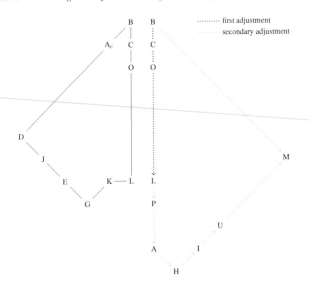

Figure 4. Node adjustment of BC 1.

As the sequence L–O–C–B maintains proportional consistency in both BC 1 and BC 2, we can now proceed with the merging process. The visualization of the merged bounding circles is depicted in Figure 5.

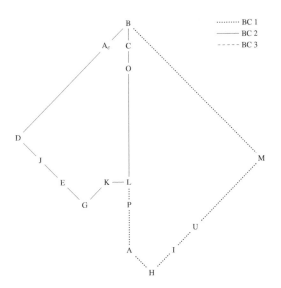

Figure 5. Marge of BC 1 and 2.

A similar process is employed for merging BC 3 with the already merged BCs 1 and 2. In this particular case, no rotation or adjustments are necessary. Figure 6 displays the merged BCs 1, 2, and 3.

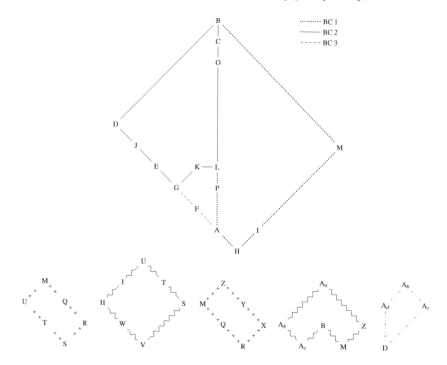

Figure 6. Merge of BC 1, BC 2 and BC 3.

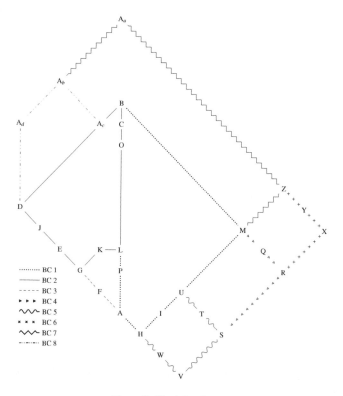

Figure 7. Final sketch map

The resulting image represents a sketch map in which the nodes are positioned relative to each other based on their direction. As noted above, the actual distances between the nodes are not pertinent; what matters is their relative placement on the sketch map.

7. Conclusion

This paper provides an overview of an algorithm designed to process tuples describing individual edges within a topological graph. These tuples are structured as [from where (place), via what (place), to where (place), change of direction (direction)]. The algorithm's output is a sketch map representing the topological graph. From the input data, the bounding circles are identified, modified, and merged to create the sketch map. It is important to note that this algorithm outline represents an initial attempt to address the challenge of generating a sketch map, and as such, it may involve computationally intensive and non-optimized procedures. The algorithm has been implemented in the PROLOG programming language.

Acknowledgements

This research has been supported by a Grant from SGS No. SP2023/065, VŠB - Technical University of Ostrava, Czech Republic, "Application of Formal Methods in Knowledge Modelling and Software Engineering VI".

References

[1] Maria Vasardani, Sabine Timpf, Stephan Winter, and Martin Tomko. From descriptions to depictions: A conceptual framework. In Thora Tenbrink, John Stell, Antony Galton, and Zena Wood, editors, *Spatial Information Theory*, pages 299–319, Cham, 2013. Springer International Publishing.

[2] Lamia Belouaer, David Brosset, and Christophe Claramunt. From verbal route descriptions to sketch maps in natural environments. SIGSPACIAL '16, New York, NY, USA, 2016. Association for Computing Machinery.

[3] Proceedings of the 33rd international conference on information modelling and knowledge bases ejc 2023. 2023.

[4] Marek Menšík, Adam Albert, Petr Rapant, and Tomáš Michalovský. Heuristics for spatial data descriptions in a multi-agent system. *Frontiers in Artificial Intelligence and Applications*, 364:68–80, 2023.

[5] Marie Duží, Bjørn Jespersen, and Pavel Materna. *Procedural semantics for hyperintensional logic*. Springer, New York, 2010.

[6] Marie Duží. *Extensional Logic of Hyperintensions*, pages 268–290. Springer Berlin Heidelberg, Berlin, Heidelberg, 2012.

[7] Marie Duzi. Communication in a multi-cultural world. *Organon F*, 21:198–218, 01 2014.

[8] Marek Menšík, Marie Duží, Adam Albert, Vojtěch Patschka, and Miroslav Pajr. Refining concepts by machine learning. *Computación y Sistemas*, 23(3):943 – 958, 2019.

[9] Jarmila Panevova. Valency frames and the meaning of the sentence. *The Prague School of Structural and Functional Linguistics*, 41:223, 1994.

[10] Bernd Heine, Heiko Narrog, Vilmos Ágel, and Klaus Fischer. Dependency grammar and valency theory. *The Oxford Handbook of Linguistic Analysis*, 2015.

[11] Thomas Herbst, David Heath, Ian F. Roe, and Dieter Götz. *A Valency Dictionary of English: A Corpus-Based Analysis of the Complementation Patterns of English Verbs, Nouns and Adjectives*. De Gruyter Mouton, 2013.

[12]   Marek Menšík, Marie Duží, Adam Albert, Vojtěch Patschka, and Miroslav Pajr. Machine learning using TIL. In *Frontiers in Artificial Intelligence and Applications*, pages 344 – 362, Amsterdam, 2019. IOS Press.

Information Modelling and Knowledge Bases XXXV
M. Tropmann-Frick et al. (Eds.)

doi:10.3233/FAIA231160

A Time-Series Multilayered Risk-Resilience Calculation Method for Disaster and Environmental Change Analysis with 5D World Map System

Shiori SASAKI [a,1] Yasushi KIYOKI [b] Amane HAMANO [c]

[a,b] *Keio University and Musashino University, Japan*
[c] *Musashino University, Japan*

Abstract. This paper presents an important application of 5D World Map System with a Risk-Resilience calculation and visualization method using time-series multilayered data for disasters and environmental change analysis to make appropriate and urgent solutions to global and local environmental phenomena in terms of short and long-term changes. This method enables the calculation of the current risk and resilience of a target region or city for disasters and rapid environmental changes, based on the analysis of past time-series changes of natural and socioeconomic factors' distribution. This method calculates the total risk and resilience to disaster as a total aggregate value that reflects the amount of change in each variable in the past, by transforming multidimensional and heterogeneous variables into a form that allows comparative and arithmetic operations through geographical normalization and projection. As an implementation and experiments, we apply our method to assessing the role of forests in urban disaster resilience as an example, by analyzing time-series changes in vegetation and forest distribution and their relationships in urban areas. Specifically, using GIS, satellite data, demographic data, urban infrastructure data, and disaster data, we analyze the relationship among urban disaster occurrence and 1) population density, 2) urban infrastructure development, and 3) forest distribution and calculate "urban-forest-disaster risk/resilience".

Keywords. CPS, Cyber-Physical-System, Sensing-Processing-Actuation, GIS, Open Data, Visualization, Knowledge Bases, SDGs, SDG9, SDG11, SDG13, SDG15, deforestation, disaster risk, disaster resilience, urban development, Global Environment

1. Introduction

Because of the impact of climate change, large-scale disasters such as forest fires, floods, inundation, landslides have been occurring frequently around the world in recent years. As the United Nations Disaster Risk Reduction (UNDRR) points out [19], it is essentially important to collect disaster information in a wide area in real time, to make it accessible and public through open data, and to detect vulnerable areas at an early stage and take countermeasures for the realization of Sustainable City (SDG9, SDG11) and Disaster Resilience (Sendai Framework [20]). In fact, many cases have been reported where it is difficult to accurately assess the current situation and identify disaster-risk hotspots due to lack of information and data.

In addition, not only detecting disaster-risk hotspots but also estimating disaster-resilience is an important and urgent task to build capacity. As Sendai Framework [20] indicates, it is important to make "action to prevent new and reduce existing disaster risks by "investing in disaster reduction for resilience" and "enhancing disaster preparedness for effective response.

One possible solution to these issues is the use of open data of socioeconomics and satellite multispectral imagery to detect the risk and vulnerability of the specific area of countries with rapid environmental changes and disasters.

The objective of our method is not only to visualize but also to calculate the risk/vulnerability and the resilience of society for disaster risks in a target area as values to make appropriate and urgent solutions to global and local environmental phenomena in terms of short and long-term changes, with a time-series and multilayered manners.

In this study, we describe a method of "Time-series Multilayered Risk-Resilience Calculation" for estimating the risk and resilience of a (possible) disaster-affected area using open satellite data and remote sensing technology. This method enables the calculation of the current risk and resilience of a target region or city for disasters and rapid environmental changes, based on the analysis of past time-series changes of natural and socioeconomic multidimensional factors. In addition, our method is applicable for open-data satellite multispectral imagery to estimate the size of disaster-affected area with relatively high accuracy. This feature makes the method widely applicable to Least Developed Countries and small local governments. In particular, the method is effective for early assessment of the situation, such as rapid confirmation of the disaster situation in wide-area disasters.

The Time-series Multilayered Risk-Resilience Calculation method is designed to be applied to the 5D World Map System [1]-[8]. "SPA-based" 5D World Map System [1]-[8] is a global and environmental knowledge-integrating and processing system for memorizing, searching, analyzing and visualizing "Global and Environmental Knowledge and Information Resources," related to natural phenomena and disasters in global and local environments.

In the implementation and experiments, we focus on deforestation and landslide phenomena as an example, which are considered to be caused by a combination of natural disasters such as heavy rainfall, floods, earthquakes, and human socio-economic activities such as land-use development, logging, farming, building etc. We conduct an implementation and experiments using open satellite data and open-source GIS software and describe the feasibility and effectiveness of our method by several experiments with the data of (a) landslide and flood risks, (b) population growth, (c) infrastructure development and (d) forest distribution in Japan (Ibaraki Prefecture in Japan, 2015 and 2020). Furthermore, the applicability of our method to a multi-dimensional world map system is also discussed.

2. Overview of SPA-based 5D World Map System

5D World Map System [1]-[8] is a knowledge representation system that enables semantic, temporal and spatial analysis of multimedia data and integrates the analyzed results as 5-dimentional dynamic historical atlas (5D World Map). The composition elements of 5D World Map are a spatial dimension (3D), a temporal dimension (4D) and a semantic dimension (5D). The "SPA-based" 5D World Map System realizes Cyber-Physical-Space integration to detect environmental phenomena with real data resources in a physical-space (real space) by various sensors as a "Sensing" process, map them to the cyber-space to make knowledge bases and analytical computing as a "Processing" process, and actuate the computed results to the real space with visualization for expressing environmental phenomena, causalities and influences as an "Actuation" process.

A semantic associative search method [9][10] is applied to this system for realizing the concept that "semantics" of words, documents, multimedia, events and phenomena vary according to the "context". 5D World Map System [1]-[8] has been providing various functionalities to calculate and express the semantics and context of various types of multimedia data [4][5][7][8]. Also, the functions for monitoring, analysing and warning with a multi-dimensional and multi-layered visualization of 5D World Map System with AI-Sensing has been utilized for monitoring SDG14, SDG9, SDG11 (Sustainable Ocean and Disaster Resilience) in United Nations ESCAP [7][31][32][33].

3. Related Studies

The multilayer visualization function of 5D World Map System and its application for ocean environmental analysis [7] and disaster-resilience monitoring [8] have been presented. Our method described in this paper is based on these research results. We extend the original multilayer visualization function not only for visualization but also for calculation of disaster risk and resilience by the normalization of geographical multiple variables.

SPA-based environmental-semantic computing for global and local environment analysis with multispectral image analysis [2] and its application for coral health monitoring [11][13] have been proposed. Also, the deforestation analyses with satellite multispectral images and SAR data analysis [12][14][17] applied to 5D World Map System, and multispectral imaging with UAV for agricultural monitoring and analysis [16][18] have been proposed. In this research, we also utilize multispectral satellite image analysis for detecting vegetation and forest areas by Normalized Differential Vegetation Index (NDVI).

There are many disaster risk visualization systems and disaster prevention maps using multispectral satellite imagery and remote sensing [21][22]. There are also open data platforms on disasters provided by national and local governments [23][24]. On the other hand, individual studies on estimating and visualizing the actual disaster area using these technologies are scattered locally in the fields of GIS, disaster prevention, and environmental engineering. A globally aggregated information platform with disaster data analysis, visualization, and sharing systems are still in the research and development stage [25]. Compared with these situations, our 5D World Map System analyzes environmental situations with multimedia and sensing data sharing as a new global knowledge sharing planform to realize a remote, interactive and real-time environmental research exchange among different areas.

Also, there are a lot of studies on disaster risk detection using satellite multispectral imagery and remote sensing. For example, a study using high-resolution satellite images to predict the risk of landslides by evaluating the predisposition to landslides from satellite images has proposed [26]. Another study proposed the extraction of reflectance characteristics that are highly relevant to landslide risk using visible and infrared images from multispectral imagery as well as our method [27]. About the cause and effect of deforestation, there is a study which discusses the causes of deforestation in the tropical areas from the aspects of slash-and-burn agriculture, population growth, poverty, and road construction [29]. Based on these references, in our experiments, we focus on population growth and road construction in the implementation, which are also cited as causes of deforestation even in the non-tropical area. We visualize their relationship with forests in the Kanto region (Ibaraki prefecture) in Japan to show the importance of forests and their effects and impacts.

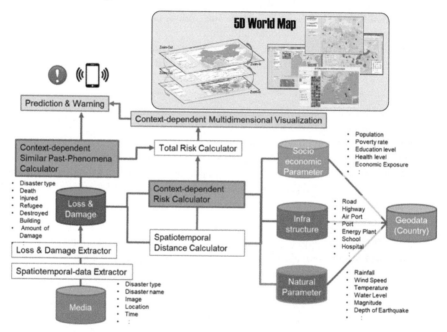

Figure 1. System structure of 5D World Map System [1]-[8] to which our Time-series Multilayered Risk-Resilience Calculation and Analytical Visualization method is applied.

4. Time-series Multilayered Risk-Resilience Calculation Method for Disasters and Environmental Changes

Our method of Time-series Multilayered Risk-Resilience Calculation is assumed to be applied to the 5D World Map System [1]-[8]. **Figure 1** shows the overall configuration of 5D World Map System for disaster data to which this method is applied.

By applying our Time-series Multilayered Risk-Resilience Calculation method to a 5D World Map System, disaster risk calculation and prediction by disaster type can be realized using the Geo Database including Socioeconomic Parameter DB, Infrastructure DB and Natural Parameter DB shown in **Figure 1** and **Figure 2**.

4.1. System Architecture

Our Time-series Multilayered Risk-Resilience Calculation method is planned to be implemented as a sub-system (Sub-system 1) of a multidimensional World Map system called "5D World Map System". **Figure 2** shows the total design of sub-systems and the connection to 5D World Map System.

This system consists of the following functions.

1) *Disaster database management function*: This function is to register and manage metadata such as images and multispectral images collected for the target area, environmental sensing data, statistical data, and infrastructure geographic data.

2) *Time-series Multilayered Risk-Resilience Calculation (Sub-system 1)*

3) *Disaster-affected area estimation & visualization function* [34] *(Sub-system 2)*

4) *Multi-layer visualization function*: Based on the results obtained by functions of 2) and 3), the other data stored in 1) such as environmental sensing data, statistical data, infrastructure geographic data, etc. are projected on the map as multiple layers.

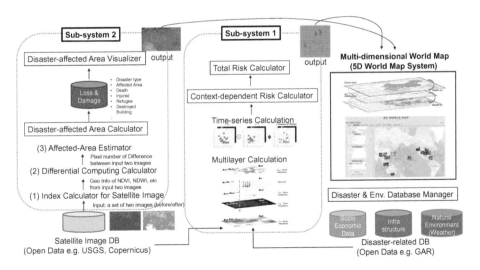

Figure 2. System structure applying our method as a Sub-system of 5D World Map System

4.2. Multilayer Risk-Resilience Calculation

The part of multilayer calculation of the Time-series Multilayered Risk-Resilience Calculation method is defined as the following 6 steps. **Figure 3** shows the visual image of the process. This process normalizes multidimensional, distributed and heterogeneous variables in a grid format and calculates the total disaster risk/resilience of a specific region as an aggregate value.

STEP 1: Set a phenomenon with spatiotemporal information as an objective variable y and set multiple phenomena with spatiotemporal information as explanatory valuables $(x_1, x_2, ..., x_n)$.

STEP 2: Collect geographical information data of y and $x_1, x_2, ..., x_n$. Commonly used geographical information data are Vector data (point/line/polygon, shape file), Raster data (image, GeoTIFF file), Mesh data (AAIGrid file), Point Cloud data, CSV text and KML/KMZ.

STEP 3: Set each geographical information data of each variable as a layer l_i for a geographical information system (GIS). The set of layers are defined as l_y and $l_{x1}, l_{x2}, ..., l_{xn}$.

STEP 4: To enable a calculation of risk or resilience among layers with various granularity, set a common grid $G := \{g_1, g_2, ..., g_m\}$. The values of each layer's grids (e.g. density of points, pixel value etc.) are expressed as a matrix or a vector such as $l_{y1} = (g_{1y1}, g_{2y1}, ..., g_{my1})$, $l_{x1} = (g_{1x1}, g_{2x1}, ..., g_{mx1})$, $l_{x2} = (g_{1x2}, g_{2x2}, ..., g_{mx2})$ and so on.

STEP 5: Normalization for each layer l_y and $l_{x1}, l_{x2}, ..., l_{xn}$

STEP 6: Create an integrated layer of explanatory variables l_X by calculating a total risk or resilience value g_{jX} with a performance of arithmetic operators (+, -, *, /) for each grid value. For example, the accumulation of values is performed, the created layer l_X and each grid's value g_{jX} of the layer are expressed as:

$$g_{jX} = \sum_{i=1}^{n} (g_{jxi})$$

$$l_X = (g_{1X}, g_{2X}, ..., g_{mX})$$

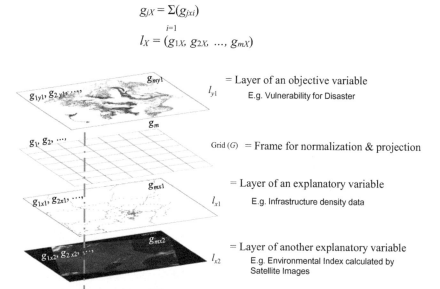

Figure 3. Multilayer Calculation of Risk-Resilience of our method

4.3. Time-series Risk-Resilience Calculation

The part of time-series calculation of the Time-series Multilayered Risk-Resilience Calculation method is defined as the following 4 steps. **Figure 4** shows the visual image of the steps. The process calculates the time-series change of each variable in a normalized grid format among a multidimensional, distributed and heterogeneous set of variables of disaster risk/resilience in the target area.

STEP 1: Set a phenomenon with spatiotemporal information as an objective variable y and set multiple phenomena with spatiotemporal information as explanatory valuables $(x_1, x_2, ..., x_n)$.

STEP 2: Collect geographical information data of y and $x_1, x_2, ..., x_n$, before $(t_i - 1)$ and after $(t_i + 1)$ the time (t_i) when disaster or environmental change occurs in the target area.

STEP 3: Set each geographical information data of each variable as a layer l_i for a geographical information system (GIS). The set of layers are defined as l_y and $l_{x1}, l_{x2}, ..., l_{xn}$.

STEP 4: Calculate the difference between the layers of before $(t_i - 1)$ and after $(t_i + 1)$.

STEP 5: If there are many times when disasters or environmental changes occur $(t_i \mid i = 1, 2, ..., q)$, the STEP 4 is repeated among $(t_1-1), (t_1+1), (t_2+1), ..., (t_q+1)$.

For the detection of disaster effect or environmental change using raster data (image, GeoTIFF file), this method uses the "Normalized Difference Environmental Index" such as Normalized Difference Vegetation Index (NDVI), Normalized Difference Water Index (NDWI), Normalized Difference Snow Index (NDSI), Normalized Burn Ratio (NBR), Normalized Difference Built-up Index (NDBI), etc., especially to estimate the size of disaster-affected area before and after the phenomenon happens. Each of these indexes is used to detect environmental changes such as landslides, floods, avalanches, wide-area forest fires and reduction of cultivated land due to buildings.

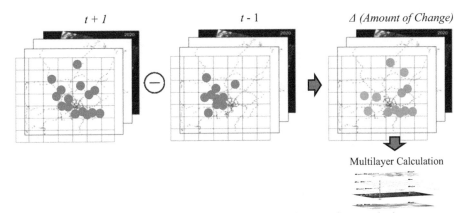

Figure 4. Time-series Calculation of Risk-Resilience of our method

5. Implementation

To realize our method of Risk-Resilience Calculation, we implement the following process with distributed time-series geographic information data, such as socioeconomic indicator data, demographic data, natural disaster data, urban infrastructure data and satellite image data. In this implementation, we apply our method to assessing the role of forests in urban disaster resilience by analyzing time-series changes in vegetation and forest distribution and their relationships in urban areas. Specifically, using GIS, satellite data, demographic, urban infrastructure, and disaster data, we analyze the relationship among disaster occurrence and 1) population density, 2) urban infrastructure development, and 3) forest distribution. From the results of this analysis, we evaluate the relationship among forest, urban development and natural disasters (hereinafter referred to as "forest-urban-disaster resilience").

In this implementation, the Time-series Multilayered Risk-Resilience Calculation is specifically realized by the following steps using GIS.

STEP 1: Visualize the base near-infrared band (NIR) using satellite multispectral imagery of the target area.

STEP 2: Calculate and visualize vegetation indices (NDVI) using satellite multispectral imagery.

STEP 3: Create virtual layers by incorporating open geographic information data such as demographics, urban infrastructure, and disaster data for the target area.

STEP 4: By switching virtual layers and overlaying them with the base map, the time-series multilayer risk-resilience is calculated to analyze "forest-urban-disaster resilience".

STEP 5: Zoom in on a part of the target area where a major change is observed to confirm the details of the relationship among forests, urban development, and natural disasters.

5.1. Data and Tools

In this implementation, the Time-series Multilayered Risk-Resilience Calculation is concretely realized for the following four types of data.
1. Using satellite multispectral images, vegetation distribution is calculated, and time-series changes (differences) are calculated.
2. Population growth rate is measured from time-series population data as demographic data.
3. As urban infrastructure data, geographic data of highway construction is used to overlay the vegetation distribution base map.
4. Data on sediment, flood, and inundation hazard zones will be used as disaster risk data to overlay the vegetation distribution base map.

QGIS [42], an open-source GIS, is used. The concrete data used for experiments are introduced in Section 6.

5.2. Data Processing

(1) Grid creation
The grid data (1km^2) is created using the investigation tool of QGIS [28][42].
. The number of grids is 13,392 in this implementation.

(2) Line and Point (Vector data)
Line and point data (e.g. transportation data) are processed to the calculable form by the following steps with shape files.

Step 1: Count the numbers of lines and points and convert them to the value of each grid

(3) Polygon (Vector data)
Polygon data (e.g. disaster occurrence) is processed to the calculable form by the following steps with shape files.

Step 1: Calculate the centroids (points) to each polygon

Step 2: Count the numbers of centroids (points) and convert them to the value of each grid

(4) Image data (Raster data)
Satellite image data (e.g. forest distribution) is processed to the calculable form by the following steps.

Step 1: Extract Band 2, 3, 4, and 5 of 10 cloud cover in the area to be analyzed from LANDSAT8 in LandBrowser [9]

Step 2: Calculate the Normalized Difference Vegetation Index (NDVI) using Band 5 (near infrared NIR) and Band 4 (visible light red R) using the following formula using Raster Calculator
$$NDVI = (NIR-R)/(NIR+R)$$

Step 3: Construct virtual raster in QGIS using Band 2, 3, 4, and 5

Step 4: Change the virtual raster to False Color using color-lamps

Step 5: Convert the raster data to polygon data (Polygonization)

Step 6: Calculate the centroids (points) to each polygon

Step 7: Count the numbers of centroids (points) and convert them to the value of each grid

(5) Total Risk-Resilience Calculation

Step 1: Time-series grid-layers of each variable are integrated by "spatial join of attributes" using data id. In this implementation, we select "equals" from geometric relations such as "intersects", "overlaps", "contains", "within", "crosses" and "touches" [35].

Step 2: For the Time-series Calculation, the difference between two input layers is calculated, and for Multilayer Calculation, the accumulation among multiple layers is performed.

6. Experiments

To examine the feasibility of the proposed method, we conducted several experiments using the time-series data of forest-related disasters in Ibaraki prefecture in the Kanto region of Japan (2015-2020) as an example (**Figure 5**). For the purpose of evaluating the role of forests in urban disaster resilience, we define the relationship between forests, urban development, and natural disasters as "forest-urban-disaster resilience," and describe a method to analyze and visualize the time-series of vegetation and forest distribution in urban areas using unevenly distributed time series geographic data, socio-economic indicator data, and natural disaster data.

First, we set a vulnerability for disaster as an explanatory variable y, and 1) disaster risk/hazard, 2) population density, 3) transportation (high-way) density, 4) forest distribution as objective variables x_1, x_2, x_3 and x_4. Second, we conduct experiments to examine the Multilayer Calculation function using the data of 2015 and the Time-series Calculation function using the data 2015 and 2020. Third, we examine the total risk values to analyze the relation among a vulnerability for disaster and 1) disaster risk/hazard, 2) population density, 3) urban infrastructure development and 4) forest distribution. Finally, we discuss the feasibility of our method to accurately assess the importance of forests and their effects and impacts.

Experiment 1: Examination on the Multilayer Calculation function
Experiment 2: Examination on the Time-series Calculation function
Experiment 3: Examination on the Total Risk-Resilience Calculation function

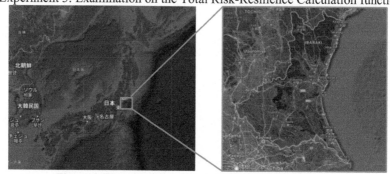

Figure 5. Target area for analysis (Ibaraki prefecture, Japan)

Data for experiments are:

- Disaster Data 1: 2015 & 2020 Landslide Disaster Precaution Area Data (Polygon, Shape file) obtained from National Land Data [13].
- Disaster data 2: 2015 & 2020 Flood Inundation Assumed Inundation Area Data (Polygon Shape file) obtained from National Land Information [14], Ministry of Land, Infrastructure, Transport and Tourism.
- Demographic data: Population distribution data of the Tokyo metropolitan area in 2015 & 2020 obtained from the Ministry of Land, Infrastructure, Transport and Tourism's National Land Survey Data [11] (Grid, Population Projection by 1km mesh of the National Land Survey Data (H30 National Bureau Estimates)).
- Urban infrastructure data: 2020 expressway time series data (Line and points, Shape file) obtained from National Land Information [12], Ministry of Land, Infrastructure, Transport and Tourism.
- Forest distribution data: satellite Landsat8 multispectral images (GeoTiff data) of Kanto region in 2015 and 2020 obtained from USGS [36] and Copernicus Open Access Hub [41].

6.1. Experiment 1: Examination on the Multilayer Calculation of the Risk-Resilience of Environmental Phenomena

Figure 6 shows the original geographical information data of Ibaraki area in 2015. (a) Disaster Risk (Polygon, Vector data), (b) Population (Grid, Vector data), (c) Highway (Line and Point, Vector data), Vegetation (NDVI, Raster data) and (d) Forest distribution (Raster data) are shown.

Figure 7 shows the same data shown in Figure 7 converted to a grid form by a data processing method described in Section 5.2. By this process, distributed and heterogeneous data are normalized and become calculable. We can grasp that the disaster risk are high in the northern part which is a mountainous area close to Tochigi prefecture, the population density is high in the middle part with relatively-big cities (Tsukuba-city, Mito-city, Hitachinama-city and Hitachi-city), the transportation density is high in the southern part close to Tokyo, and the forest density is high in the western part.

Figure 8 shows the total risk calculation result by the multilayer calculation method described in Section4.2. From this result, we can observe the total risk distribution that cannot be figured from Figure 8. From Figure 8, the independent layer's values and distribution can be observed, but total risk of each grid is difficult to estimate by human eyes. Only by this calculation, we can evaluate the total risk distribution.

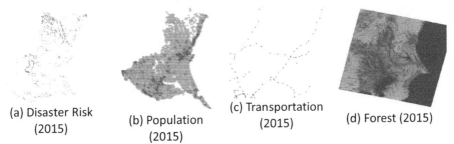

(a) Disaster Risk (2015)   (b) Population (2015)   (c) Transportation (2015)   (d) Forest (2015)

Figure 6. Original Data of Ibaraki area in 2015: **(a)** Disaster Risk (Polygon, Vector data), **(b)** Population (Grid, Vector data), **(c)** Highway (Line and Point, Vector data), Vegetation (NDVI, Raster data) and **(d)** Forest distribution (Raster data)

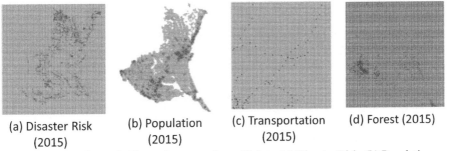

(a) Disaster Risk (2015)   (b) Population (2015)   (c) Transportation (2015)   (d) Forest (2015)

Figure 7. Data of 2015 in Figure 6 converted to grid data: **(a)** Disaster Risk, **(b)** Population, **(c)** Highway and **(d)** Forest distribution (NDVI)

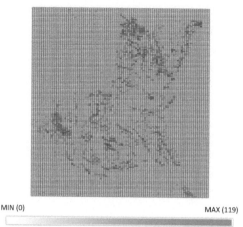

MIN (0)   MAX (119)

Figure 8. Total Risk Calculation Result (without Population) in 2015

The results of Experiment 1 in **Figure 7 – Figure 8** show that our method enables to calculate the total risk/resilience for disasters of the target area as aggregated values with multidimensional, distributed and heterogeneous variables by a normalized grid format.

6.2. Experiment 2: Examination on the Time-series Change Calculation of the Risk-Resilience of Environmental Phenomena

Figure 9, **Figure 10**, **Figure 11** and **Figure 12** show the results of time-series change calculation for geographical distribution of disaster risk, population, transportation and forest, respectively, from 2015 to 2020. From (a) 2015 and (b) 2020 of each figure, it is difficult to find the difference by human eyes. These results show that the time-series change is clearly notable with numerical values by our time-series change calculation. Also, by using a grid form, distributed and heterogeneous data are normalized and become calculable and comparative.

From **Figure 9**, we can grasp that the disaster risk increased in the northern part which is a mountainous area close to Tochigi prefecture. **Figure 10** indicates that the population density decreased in the northern coastal area around Hitachinakai-city, where a big Tsunami hit in 2011, and increased in the southern part around Tsukuba-city. **Figure 11** shows that highway junctions increased a few in the southern part close to Tokyo. **Figure 12** show that forest and vegetation are decreased seriously in the western part close to Saitama prefecture and newly developing cities (Shimotsuma-city and Yachiyo-city). These changes might be happened from land use change from agricultural area to housing area because the western part of Ibaraki is a large field of rice and vegetables.

The results of Experiment 2, shown in **Figures 9 - 12**, indicate that this method can be used to calculate the time-series change of each variable in a normalized grid format among a multidimensional, distributed and heterogeneous set of variables of disaster risk/resilience in the target area.

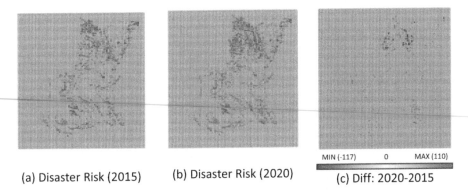

MIN (-117)   0   MAX (110)

(a) Disaster Risk (2015)   (b) Disaster Risk (2020)   (c) Diff: 2020-2015

Figure 9. Time-series Change Calculation of Disaster Risk (2020-2015): (a) disaster risk in 2015, (b) disaster risk in 2020, (c) increase or decrease in disaster risk value (grid expression, increase: red, decrease: blue)

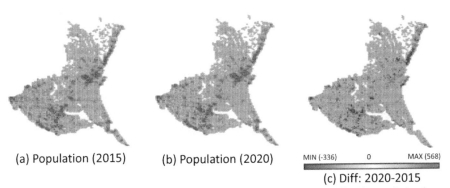

(a) Population (2015)   (b) Population (2020)   MIN (-336)   0   MAX (568)

(c) Diff: 2020-2015

Figure 10. Time-series Change Calculation of Population (2020-2015): (a) population in 2015, (b) population in 2020, (c) increase or decrease in population value (grid expression, increase: red, decrease: blue)

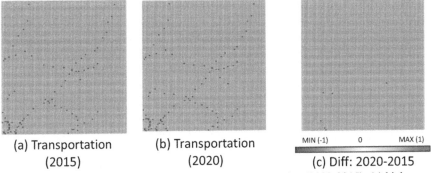

(a) Transportation (2015)   (b) Transportation (2020)   MIN (-1)   0   MAX (1)

(c) Diff: 2020-2015

Figure 11. Time-series Change Calculation of Transportation (2020-2015): (a) highway junctions in 2015, (b) highway junctions in 2020, (c) increase or decrease in the number of highway junctions (grid expression, increase: red, decrease: blue)

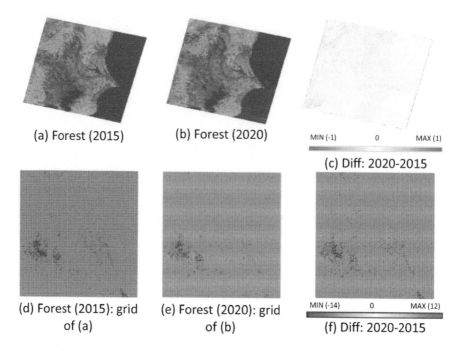

(a) Forest (2015)　　(b) Forest (2020)　　MIN (-1)　　0　　MAX (1)

(c) Diff: 2020-2015

(d) Forest (2015): grid of (a)　　(e) Forest (2020): grid of (b)　　MIN (-14)　　0　　MAX (12)

(f) Diff: 2020-2015

Figure 12. Time-series Change Calculation of Forest Distribution (2020-2015) : **(a)** forest distribution (NDVI) in 2015, **(b)** forest distribution (NDVI) in 2020, **(c)** increase or decrease of forest areas (increase: green, decrease: red), **(d)** forest distribution (grid expression) in 2015, **(e)** forest distribution (grid expression) in 2020, **(f)** increase or decrease of forest areas (grid expression, increase: red, decrease: blue)

6.3. Experiment 3: Examination on the Time-series Multilayered Calculation of the Risk-Resilience of Environmental Phenomena

Experiment 3 is a combination of the results of Experiment 1 and 2. **Figure 13 (a)** shows the result of the total risk-resilience calculation by the Time-series Multilayered Calculation method described in Section 4.2 and Section 4.3. In this calculation, we did not include population density data because we judge that it is difficult to define if a population growth contributes to disaster resilience or not. **Figure 13 (b)** shows an overlay result of Ibaraki-pref. base map [43] on the result shown in Figure 4 for a reference. **Figure 14** shows the visualization and sharing of the result of Figure 14 on 5D World Map System. From these results, we can observe that the vulnerability to disasters increased in the red part (the northern part of Ibaraki) and decreased in the blue part (the western part of Ibaraki). Conversely, the result can be interpreted that the resilience to disasters increased in the blue part (the western part of Ibaraki) and decreased in the red part (the northern part of Ibaraki).

The results of Experiment 3 in **Figures 13** and **Figure 14** show that our method enables to transform multidimensional, distributed and heterogeneous variables into a form that allows comparative and arithmetic operations through a normalization process, by reflecting the amount of change in each variable in the past to calculate a total aggregate value of risk/resilience to disaster in a specific target area.

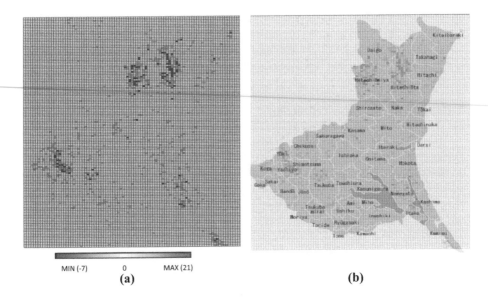

MIN (-7)   0   MAX (21)

(a)   **(b)**

Figure 13. (a) a total Risk-Resilience calculation result by the Time-series Multilayered Calculation (Ibaraki prefecture in Japan, 2015-2020), **(b)** an overlay of (a) on a Ibaraki-pref. base map [43]

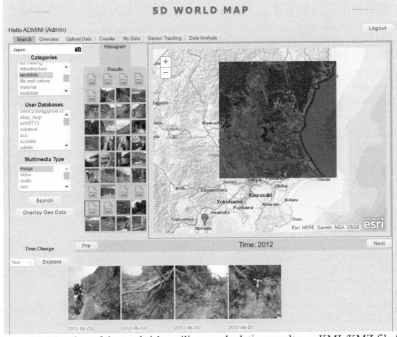

Figure 14. Mapping of the total risk-resilience calculation result as a KML/KMZ file for visualization and sharing on 5D World Map System

To increase the degree of accuracy and precision, it seems to be important to add more variables such as land use for houses, agriculture, manufacture, commercial malls, power plants and dams as infrastructure parameters and socioeconomic parameters. Also, natural parameters such as the amount of rainfall, humidity and snowfall, the frequency of serious earthquakes and forest fires should be added.

7. Conclusion and Future Direction

In this paper, "Time-series Multilayer Risk-Resilience Calculation" method for global environmental change and disaster analysis has been presented. Through the implementation and experiments, it is examined that our method enables to transform multidimensional, distributed and heterogeneous variables into a form that allows comparative and arithmetic operations through a normalization process, by reflecting the amount of change in each variable in the past to calculate a total aggregate value of risk/resilience to disaster in a specific target area.

As a future development, we will implement an automatic disaster estimation and prediction system using open data to realize a disaster resilience improvement system integrated with 5D World Map System.

Future issues include an addition of explanatory variables such as land use for houses, agriculture, manufacture, commercial malls, power plants and dams as infrastructure parameters and socioeconomic parameters, and natural parameters such as the amount of rainfall, humidity and snowfall, the frequency of serious earthquakes and forest fires etc. to increase the degree of accuracy and precision of our method.

The goal of our research is to support the realization of SDG9, SDG13, SDG11 and SDG15 in countries and regions around the world, especially in the Least Developing Countries (LDCs) that lack advanced observation equipment, technology, and financial resources. Specifically, the project will be developed with evaluation of relationships among multiple variables, and disaster prediction. We will develop our method to build a system that can predict potential disaster locations and vulnerable locations by integrating elements divided into the specific research fields.

Acknowledgement

We would like to appreciate the members of ICT & Disaster Risk Reduction Division (IDD), UN ESCAP and Asia AI Institute (AAII), Musashino University and Thammasat University for their significant discussions and experimental studies.

References

[1] Kiyoki, Yasushi, and Xing Chen. "Contextual and Differential Computing for the Multi-Dimensional World Map with Context-Specific Spatial-Temporal and Semantic Axes." Information Modelling and Knowledge Bases XXV 260 (2014): 82.
[2] Yasushi Kiyoki, Xing Chen, Shiori Sasaki, Chawan Koopipat, "A Globally-Integrated Environmental Analysis and Visualization System with Multi-Spectral & Semantic Computing in "Multi-Dimensional World Map"", Information Modelling and Knowledge Bases XXVIII, pp.106-122,2017.
[3] Sasaki, S., Takahashi, Y, Kiyoki, Y., "The 4D World Map System with Semantic and Spatiotemporal Analyzers," Information Modelling and Knowledge Bases, Vol.XXI, IOS Press, pp. 1 - 18, 2010.
[4] Sasaki, S. and Kiyoki, Y., "Real-time Sensing, Processing and Actuation Functions of 5D World Map System: A Collaborative Knowledge Sharing System for Environmental Analysis" Information Modelling and Knowledge Bases, Vol. XXVIII, IOS Press, pp. 220-239, May 2016.

[5] Shiori Sasaki, Yasushi Kiyoki, "Analytical Visualization Functions of 5D World Map System for Multi-Dimensional Sensing Data", Information Modelling and Knowledge Bases XXIX, IOS Press, pp.71 – 89, May 2017.

[6] Yasushi Kiyoki, Xing Chen, Chalisa Veesommai, Irene Erlyn Wina Rachmawan, Petchporn Chawakitchareon, "A SPA-based Semantic Computing System for Global & Environmental Analysis and Visualization with "5-Dimensional World-Map": "Towards Environmental Artificial Intelligence"" Information Modelling and Knowledge Bases XXXI, Vol. 321, pp. 285 – 305, DOI 10.3233/FAIA200021, IOS Press, 2020.

[7] Shiori Sasaki, Yasushi Kiyoki, Madhurima Sarkar-Swaisgood, Jinmika Wijitdechakul, Irene Rachmawan, Sanjay Srivastava, Rajib Shaw, Chalisa Veesommai, "5D World Map System for Disaster-Resilience Monitoring from Global to Local: Environmental AI System for Piloting SDG 9 and 11", Information Modelling and Knowledge Bases XXXI, Vol. 321, pp. 306 - 323, DOI 10.3233/FAIA200022, IOS Press, 2020.

[8] Asako Uraki, Shiori Sasaki, Yasushi Kiyoki, "A Multi-dimensional Visualization Method for Disaster Analysis on 5D World Map System", 2018 INTERNATIONAL ELECTRONICS SYMPOSIUM ON KNOWLEDGE CREATION AND INTELLIGENT COMPUTING (IES-KCIC), 139-145, 2018.

[9] Yasushi Kiyoki, Xing Chen, "A Semantic Associative Computation Method for Automatic Decorative-Multimedia Creation with "Kansei" Information" (Invited Paper), The Sixth Asia-Pacific Conferences on Conceptual Modelling (APCCM 2009), 9 pages, January 20-23, 2009.

[10] Xing Chen, Yasushi Kiyoki", A Semantic Orthogonal Mapping Method through Deep-learning for Semantic Computing", Information Modelling and Knowledge Bases XXX, Vol.312, pp.39 – 60, DOI 10.3233/978-1-61499-933-1-39, IOS Press, 2019.

[11] Yasushi Kiyoki, Petchporn Chawakitchareon, Sompop Rungsupa, Xing Chen, Kittiya Samlansin, "A Global & Environmental Coral Analysis System with SPA-Based Semantic Computing for Integrating and Visualizing Ocean-Phenomena with "5-Dimensional World-Map", INFORMATION MODELLING AND KNOWLEDGE BASES XXXII, Frontiers in Artificial Intelligence and Applications 333, IOS Press, pp. 76 – 91, Dec 2020.

[12] Irene Erlyn Wina Rachmawan, Yasushi Kiyoki, "A New Approach of Semantic Computing with Interval Matrix Decomposition for Interpreting Deforestation Phenomenon", Information Modelling and Knowledge Bases XXX, Vol.312, pp.353 – 368, DOI 10.3233/978-1-61499-933-1-353, IOS Press, 2019.

[13] Jinmika Wijitdechakul, Yasushi Kiyoki, Chawan Koopipat, "An environmental-semantic computing system of multispectral imagery for coral health monitoring and analysis", Information Modelling and Knowledge Bases XXX, Vol.312, pp.293 – 311, DOI 10.3233/978-1-61499-933-1-293, IOS Press, 2019.

[14] Irene Erlyn Wina Rachmawan. Yasushi Kiyoki, "Semantic Multi-Valued Logic for Deforestation Phenomena Interpretation", Information Modelling and Knowledge Bases XXXI, Vol. 321, pp. 401 - 418, DOI 10.3233/FAIA200027, IOS Press, 2020.

[15] Chalisa Veesommai, Yasushi Kiyoki, Shiori Sasaki, "A Multi-Dimensional River-Water Quality Analysis System for Interpreting Environmental Situations", Information Modelling and Knowledge Bases XXVIII, pp.43-62, 2017.

[16] Jinmika Wijitdechakul, Yasushi Kiyoki, Shiori Sasaki, Chawan Koopipat, "A Multispectral Imaging and Semantic Computing System for Agricultural Monitoring and Analysis", Information Modelling and Knowledge Bases XXVIII, pp.314-333,2017.

[17] Irene Erlyn Wina Rachmawan and Yasushi Kiyoki," Semantic Spatial Weighted Regression for Realizing Spatial Correlation of Deforestation Effect on Soil Degradation", International Electronics Symposium on Knowledge Creation and Intelligent Computing (IES-KCIC), September 26,2017, Surabaya Indonesia.

[18] Jinmika Wijitdechakul, Yasushi Kiyoki and Shiori Sasaki, Chawan Koopipat, "UAV-based Multispectral Aerial Image Retrieval using Spectral Feature and Semantic Computing", International Electronics Symposium on Knowledge Creation and Intelligent Computing (IES-KCIC), September 26,2017, Surabaya Indonesia.

[19] UNDRR, *"Implementing the Sendai Framework"*, SF and the SDGs, Accessed: Jan. 30, 2023. [Online]. Available: https://www.undrr.org/implementing-sendai-framework/sf-and-sdgs

[20] UNDRR, Sendai Framework, Accessed: Jan.30, 2023. [Online]. Available: https://www.undrr.org/publication/sendai-framework-disaster-risk-reduction-2015-2030

[21] NIED, J-SHIS Map, Accessed: Jan. 30, 2022. [Online]. Available: https://www.j-shis.bosai.go.jp/map/

[22] UNEP, Global Risk Data Platform, Accessed: Jan. 30, 2022. [Online]. Available: https://preview.grid.unep.ch/

[23] UNDRR, Prevention Web, Accessed: Jan. 30, 2022. [Online]. Available: https://www.preventionweb.net/

[24] UNDRR, Global Assessment Report on Disaster Risk Reduction, Accessed: Jan. 30, 2022. [Online]. Available: https://gar.undrr.org/

[25] NICT, ARIA project , Accessed: Jan. 30, 2022. [Online]. Available: https://testbed.nict.go.jp/interview/007_1.html

[26] M. Kawamura, K.Tsujino, Y. Ohtsuji, "Investigation of Sediment Disaster Mitigation GIS by Using Results of Large Area Disaster Characteristic Analysis," Journal of Disaster Science and Management, Vol.25(1), 2006, pp.35-50.

[27] H. Kasa, M. Kurodai, S. Obayashi, H. Kojima, "On the Applicability of Remote Sensing Data for Landslide Prediction Model," Journal of the Remote Sensing Society of Japan, Vol.12(1), 1992, pp.5-15.

[28] R. Furuda, GIS and satellite image analysis with QGIS (Part 3: Basic functions, Part 2), Information Geology, vol. 29, no. 4, pp. 141-149, 2018. (Japanese)

[29] M. Miyamoto, Causes of tropical deforestation: Reconsidering slash-and-burn, population growth, poverty, and road construction, Jirinshi (2010) 92: 226-234. (Japanese)

[30] Katsuhide Yokoyama, Hiroto Tauchi, Hideo Amaguchi, Akira Kawamura, Study on the relationship between urbanization on steep slopes and landslide disasters in Japan (Japanese)

[31] ESCAP SDGHELPDESK: https://sdghelpdesk.unescap.org/

[32] Closing-the-Loop - ESCAP: https://www.unescap.org/projects/ctl

[33] Yasushi KIYOKI, Shiori SASAKI, Ali Ridho BARAKBAH, "AI-Sensing Functions with SPA-based 5D World Map System for Ocean Plastic Garbage Detection and Reduction ", Information Modelling and Knowledge Bases XXXIV, Jan. 2023. DOI:10.3233/FAIA220489

[34] Yuki Nakamura, Shiori Sasaki, "Disaster-Affected Area Estimation Method with Open Multispectral-Image Data Analysis for Multidimensional World Map System ", ICBIR 2022 - 2022 7th International Conference on Business and Industrial Research, Proceedings, 616-621, Jun, 2022.

[35] Max J Egenhofer, David M. Mark, Modeling conceptual neighborhoods of topological relations, Geographical Information Systems 9(5):555-565, DBLP, September 1995.

[36] USGS: https://www.usgs.gov/

[37] Ministry of Land, Infrastructure, Transport and Tourism, National Land Numerical Data, Future Population Estimates by 1km Mesh (H30 National Bureau Estimates) (shape format version), in Japan (Japanese) https://nlftp.mlit.go.jp/ksj/gml/datalist/KsjTmplt-mesh1000h30.html

[38] Ministry of Land, Infrastructure, Transport and Tourism, National Land Numerical Data, Expressway Time Series Data, in Japan(Japanese) https://nlftp.mlit.go.jp/ksj/gml/datalist/KsjTmplt-N06-v1_2.html

[39] Ministry of Land, Infrastructure, Transport and Tourism, National Land Numerical Data, Flood Inundation Assumption Area Data, in Japan (Japanese) https://nlftp.mlit.go.jp/ksj/gml/datalist/KsjTmplt-A31-v2_1.html

[40] Ministry of Land, Infrastructure, Transport and Tourism, National Land Numerical Data, Landslide Disaster Precaution Area Data, in Japan (Japanese) https://nlftp.mlit.go.jp/ksj/gml/datalist/KsjTmplt-A33-v1_4.html

[41] Copernicus Open Access Hub, Open Hub: https://scihub.copernicus.eu/dhus/#/home

[42] QGIS: https://qgis.org/ja/site/

[43] City, town, and village offices in Ibaraki prefecture: https://www.pref.ibaraki.jp/bugai/kokusai/tabunka/en/administration/level.html

[44] Google Earth: https://earth.google.com/

Information Modelling and Knowledge Bases XXXV
M. Tropmann-Frick et al. (Eds.)

271

doi:10.3233/FAIA231161

A Knowledge Model Based on "Dark-Matter" and Parallel Spaces

Xing Chen[1] and Yasushi Kiyoki[2]

[1] *Department of Information & Computer Sciences*
Kanagawa Institute of Technology, Japan
[2] *Graduate School of Media and Governance, Keio University, Japan*

Abstract. This paper aims to analyze the phenomenon of inapplicability of experience, which means that sometimes we make mistakes when we use our past experience to solve current problems. We propose a knowledge model based on the concept of "dark-matter", which is a term used to describe the time-related data that is hidden from our observation. We use a two-dimensional matrix to represent both time-related and non-time-related data, and we call it space. We also introduce the concept of parallel spaces, which are composed of several spaces that can explain different situations and outcomes. We use case studies to illustrate how knowledge is generated and expressed using "dark-matter" and parallel spaces. We also reveal the reason for the inapplicability of experience and suggest some solutions. The contribution of this paper is that we provide a new perspective and a new model to understand and process knowledge based on "dark-matter" and parallel spaces.

Keywords. Knowledge, knowledge presentation, knowledge generation, machine learning, semantic space, spatiotemporal space

1. Introduction

People make judgments and decisions based on experience and knowledge to solve problems. However, it often happens that wrong judgments and decisions are made based on experience and knowledge. For example, in the stock trading process, people will determine the current trade based on the stock's past ups and downs and trading experience. However, decisions based on experience are not always correct. After you decide to buy, the stock may fall, or after you decide to sell, the stock may rise. This phenomenon is referred to as "the phenomenon of inapplicability of experiences" in this paper. The aim of this paper is to create a knowledge model to analyze this phenomenon. It is known that knowledge and experience build up over time. In other words, if we want to express knowledge and experience in computers, we need to create a time related knowledge model. In our previous research, we proposed a knowledge model based on a concept of "dark matter" [1].

The concept of "dark-matter" is developed based on the research works of semantic computing models [2, 3, 4, 5]. In the semantic computing models, matrixes are used to present "meaning" of data. In the models, input data are mapped through mapping matrixes into semantic spaces and presented as points in semantic spaces. Another data

---
[1] Xing Chen, 1030 Simo-Ogino, Atsugi-shi, Kanagawa 243-0292, Japan; chen@ic.kanagawa-it.ac.jp
[2] Graduate School of Media and Governance, Keio University, Japan

which present different meanings, referred to as meaning data, are also mapped to the same space. Distances of the points among input data and meaning data are performed. In this way, the semantic calculation is transmitted to calculate Euclidean distances of those points. For example, in the case for implementing semantic query, query data presenting query keywords are mapped into a semantic space and summarized as a point in the space. Retrieval candidate data are also mapped into the semantic space as other points. Euclidean distance is calculated between the query point and each retrieval candidate point. When the distance of a retrieval candidate is shorter than a given threshold, its relative retrieval candidate is extracted as the query output.

Two methods, Mathematical Model of Meaning (MMM) [4, 5] and Semantic Feature Extracting Model (SFEM) [2, 3], are developed on semantic space creation. In MMM, a common data set, for example an English-English diction is used to create the semantic space. In SFEM, the semantic space is created based on special defined data sets according to the requirement of applications.

After the semantic space is created, input data will be mapped to the space and the Euclidean distance calculation between the mapped data points in the space will be performed. Mapping matrixes are required to map input data into the semantic space. In SFEM, mapping matrixes are defined according to the applications of the models [6- 14]. Many methods are developed to create mapping matrixes for applying the model in the areas of semantic information retrieving [9, 10, 14], semantic information classifying [11], semantic information extracting [12], and semantic information analyzing on reason and results [13], etc. Furtherly a method is developed to create the mapping matrixes through deep-learning [15]. Elements of the matrixes presenting semantic spaces are previously defined, which are different from those other models, such as the artificial neural network model and deep-learning artificial neural network model [16- 19].

A mechanism is furtherly developed based on the semantic space model to implement the basic logic computation to implement true and false judgement which is the foundational mechanism required by machine learning [20]. The mechanism is applied to simulate unmanned ground vehicle control [21]. Temporal data processing is required for the ground vehicle control. In paper [1], a model is presented for the temporal data processing. In the model, the word "matter" is used to represent features of spaces which are related to the non-temporal data. The word "dark-matter" is used to represent of spaces which elements are temporally changed and "dark-matter" is also referred to as a matrix which elements are generated during training processing. In the paper [22], an exploratory research was presented on the expression of knowledge and its generation process based on the concept "dark-matter."

In this paper, a new knowledge model is created to analyze "the phenomenon of inapplicability of experiences" and a new concept of "parallel spaces" is presented based on the previous researches. Case studies are used to illustrate why "the phenomenon of inapplicability" occurred. The concept of "dark-matter" is used in this research. It is reviewed in Section 2. In Section 3, the relationship between "knowledge" and "dark-matter" is described. The phenomenon of inapplicability is also analyzed. with examples in this section. Then, the concept of "parallel spaces" is presented and illustrated with examples. Finally, the conclusions of this paper are presented.

2. The machine learning model created based on the concept "dark-matter"

In this section, the machine learning model created based on the concept "dark-matter" is briefly reviewed through an example as shown in Figure 1. This model is called "dark-matter learning model" in the following. In this model, matrix multiply is referred to as "space mapping" or simply "mapping." For example, the following equation (1) is described as to mapping a matrix **X** by a matrix **C** to a new matrix **E**.

$$\textbf{E} = \textbf{X}*\textbf{C} \qquad (1)$$

The matrix **X** is further divided into two parts as shown in Figure 1. The first part is the first column of the matrix **X**, which is referred to as "***matter***". The second part of **X** is referred to as the "***dark-matter***", which is constructed by the second to the last column of the matrix **X**. In Figure 1, "***matter***" is an index matrix correlated with sensor data. As sensor data are "visible", it is referred to as matter. Elements in the matrix of "***dark-matter***" are randomly filled. As the matrix of the dark-matter is created randomly filled, it is referred to as "chaotic space".

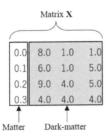

Figure 1. Creating a "chaotic space"

As pointed in the paper [22], the expression of knowledge and the knowledge generation process are correlated with "dark-matter." A machine learning model is also presented based on the concept "dark-matter" [22]. This model is referred to as the "dark-matter learning model."

The learning process is to change the "chaotic space" to "ordered space." The learning model is considered as a state machine. A state in the state machine will be changed from one to others, which is referred to as state transition. State transition diagrams are used to present the state transition. Figure 2 is an example of state transition diagram. In the figure, a circle and the number in the circle represents a state, an arrow represents a state transiting from one to another one. The numbers by the arrows represent the condition required for the state transition. For example, the state will be transited from state "0.0" to the state "0.1" if the input data is "0.0".

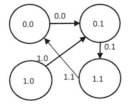

Figure 2. An example of state transition

Figure 3 presents how to create the "ordered space" from the "chaotic space" based on the state transition. The example of the state transition diagram shown in Figure 2 is used to illustrate it. In Figure 2, state "0.0" is the start state and the state transition from "0.0" to "0.1" is the first step of the state transition. Figure 3 (a) shows a chaotic space and Figure 3 (b) shows the first step state transition. In the second step, the state "0.1" transits to the state "0.3". as shown in Figure 3 (c). When all the state transition diagram shown is represented as Figure 3 (d), we say that we created an "ordered space" from the "chaotic space." In the figure, the "matter" is the first row of the matrix, and the "dark-matter" is the matrix constructed by the second, third and fourth row, painted in gray.

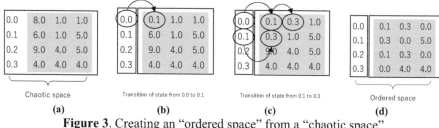

Figure 3. Creating an "ordered space" from a "chaotic space"

If X^{-1} is an inverse matrix of the matrix X, the matrix X^{-1} is referred to as an "*antimatter space*." By applying antimatter space to a matrix E, which represents actions of agents, a new matrix C is created as shown in equation (2). The calculation presented by the equation (2) is referred to as "*learning*" or "*training*" calculation.

$$C = X^{-1}*E \qquad (2)$$

In the equation "mass and energy equivalent," "**mass**" is a measure of the amount of matter that an object contains. That is, it is visible, or it can be sensed by sensors. As explained in Figure 1, "**matter**" is defined as a vector that correlates with sensor data. That is, "**matter**" can be considered the same as "**mass**." It can also be seen that the concept of energy in physics is a vector E. In equation (1), the values of the elements of the vector E and the mass in the matrix X are measurable. That is, the measurable values of E are the energy in physics and the measurable values of mass in physics is the "**matter**" that we referred to.

Next, we will take an example to analyze the relationship between equation (1) and the "energy mass equivalent" equation. Suppose that space X is a five-by-five matrix, as shown in Figure 4 (a). This assumption means that there are five different types of matter in space. The elements in the first column of the matrix are the mass of matter. In the example, the values of the "**matter**" and "**dark-matter**", which are the elements of the matrix X, are shown in Figure 4 (a). The elements of the vector E are shown in Figure 4 (b). The X^{-1}, which is the inverse matrix of X, is show in Figure 4 (c).

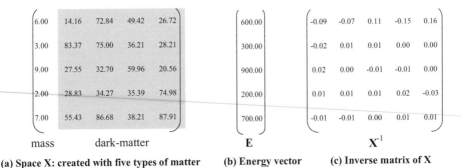

mass   dark-matter   E X^{-1}

(a) Space X: created with five types of matter   (b) Energy vector   (c) Inverse matrix of X

Figure 4. An example of a space with five different types of matter

The values of the element of the vector **C** can be calculated based on equation (2), multiplying X^{-1} by **E**, as shown in Figure 5. Therefore, we call vector **C** *"rule"* and vector **E** *"energy"*.

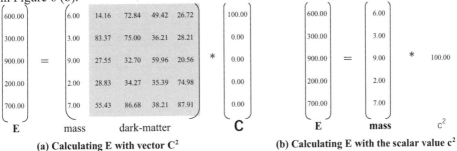

Figure 5. Multiplying X^{-1} by **E** to calculate the rule vector **C**

As shown in Figure 5, only the first element of vector **C** is a non-zero value, and all the other values of the vector are zero. When the vector **C** is given, the vector **E** can be calculated based on equation (1), as shown in Figure 6 (a). Let c^2 represent the first value of **C**, the vector **E** can be calculated by multiplying the first column of **X** by c^2, as shown in Figure 6 (b).

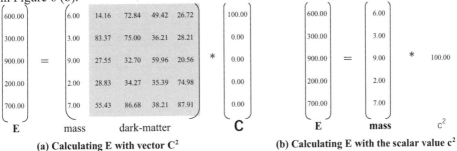

E   mass   dark-matter   C   E   mass c^2

(a) Calculating E with vector C^2 (b) Calculating E with the scalar value c^2

Figure 6. The calculated result of **E** with the vector C^2 and the scalar value c^2

In this example, if e is the i-th element of the vector **E** and m is also the i-th element of the vector **mass**, it can be found that $e = mc^2$. For example, for the first element of E and the first element of mass,

$E = 600;$
$m = 6;$
$c^2 = 100$, where, c = 10;
$600 = 6 * 10^2.$

That is,

$$e = mc^2. \tag{3}$$

In summary, if the vector **C** is defined such that the value of its first element is a non-zero value c^2 and all the other values are zero, as shown in Figure 6, the elements values of the vector **E** can be calculated by multiplying the vector **mass** by the scalar value c^2. That is, $e = mc^2$. The vector **C** is a special vector indicating that "dark-matter" is not used in the calculation. That is, the equation, $e = mc^2$, is suitable to the case that "knowledge" or "state transition" is not considered during the computation process.

3. A knowledge representation method with "dark-matter"

The relationship between "**dark-matter**" and "knowledge" is represented in the paper [22]. Let's use an example to illustrate it. Suppose that there is a maze, represented by a 4 x 4 matrix, as shown in Figure 7 (a). An agent is created in this case study which should move from a start position to a goal position. The start position of the agent is at row 2 and column 1, which is marked with the character "S". A position will be represented by row and column number as (*row number, column number*) in the following. Thus, the start position of the agent is represented as (2, 1) with the mark "S". The goal position of the agent is (2, 4) with the mark "G". The agent will go along the path shown by the arrow-mark "→". From the start position to the goal position. That is, the agent goes through the points (2,1), (2, 2), (3, 2), (4, 2), (4, 3), (4, 4) and (3, 4) and reaches to (2, 4).

By defining states of the agent as its positions on the maze matrix, a space matrix can be defined. As there are 16 possible positions for the agent on the maze matrix, 16 values from 0.0 to 1.5 are used to represent the index as shown in Figure 7 (b).

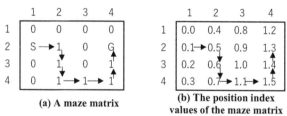

(a) A maze matrix

(b) The position index values of the maze matrix

Figure 7. A maze matrix shown for an agent moving from "S" to "G"

However, it is not always possible to calculate the action index value without the dark-matter. If the agent does not have the position sensor, but it has a laser sensor which output shows which direction that the agent can move as shown in Figure 8. The output values of the sensor are defined as follows: As shown in Figure 8 (b), the agent can move in four directions, moving to the "Down", "Left" and "Right" direction, the outputs of the sensor are defined "0100", "0010" and "0001", respectively. The direction, in which the agent can move at each position, is shown in Figure 8 (a). The sensor's output values when the agent is in different positions are shown in Figure 8 (c). For example, at the position (3, 2), the agent can move to "Up" direction, therefore, the output value of the sensor is "1000". The agent can go back from the current position to its previous position. If the agent is at the point (2, 2), the agent can move to two different positions. The agent can move back to the start position (2, 1) when it move "Left". It can also move "Down" to the next position (3, 2). The output value of the sensor at the position (2, 2) is "0110", which is the summary of the two direction "0010", "Left" and "0100", "Down".

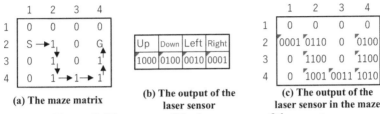

(a) The maze matrix   (b) The output of the laser sensor   (c) The output of the laser sensor in the maze

Figure 8. The output of the laser sensor of the agent

Figure 8 (c) shows a situation where the agent has the same sensor output of "1100" at two different positions: (3, 2) and (3, 4). This means that the agent can either move up or down from either position. However, if we want to define a function, f(x), that takes the sensor output as input and gives the agent's action as output, we will have a problem. The same input of "1100" will have two possible outputs: "Moving Down" or "Moving Up". This is not a valid function, because a function should have only one output for each input. Therefore, we need to use some additional information, called dark-matter, to help the agent decide which action to take.

It is not always possible to know the path at the start position as that shown in Figure 6 (b). For example, when reinforcement learning is applied to find the path from the start position to the goal position, the path is unknown at the start position. The path will be found after many trys are performed. Sometimes, many paths are found. Rewards are assigned to found paths. If the length of a path is shorter than the others, higher reward than the others is assigned to the path. During the reinforcement learning, the agent is trained to obtain the maximum reward. In this way, the optimal path from the start position to the goal position can be found. At the same time, actions of the agent at the positions on the path are determined.

When the path is unknown at the start position, it is impossible to create the space matrix as that shown in Figure 8 (a). Here, *a new method is proposed for generating the space matrix*. At the same time, *a new method for knowledge expression is also proposed*. In the methods, passed positions are recorded instead of the next positions. For example, when the agent moves from the start position (2, 1) to the position (2, 2), the passed position (2, 1) is recorded. That is, dark-matter matrix can be created based on events that have occurred instead of the events which will occurred in the future. In the following, an example is used to illustrate the method in detail. In the example, the agent has a laser sensor.

In the example, a matrix is used to show a maze as shown in Figure 9 (a). The agent can be in any positions where the "1" is marked in the matrix. The agent cannot be in the positions where "0" is marked in the matrix. Figure 9 (b) shows the output of the sensor of the agent in each position, and Figure 9 (c) shows the index values of the sensor outputs at each position. For example, when the agent is at the position (2, 2), as the agent can move to "Up", "Down" and "Left", output of the sensor is "1110", which is the summary of the value "Up", "1000", "Down", "0100" and "Left", "0010". As the agent can not be in the position (3, 1), (4, 1), (2, 3), (3, 3) and (1, 4), the output of the sensor at those positions is marked with an "X".

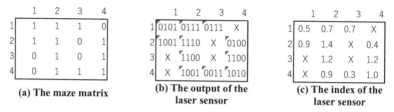

	1	2	3	4
1	1	1	1	0
2	1	1	0	1
3	0	1	0	1
4	0	1	1	1

(a) The maze matrix

	1	2	3	4
1	0101	0111	0111	X
2	1001	1110	X	0100
3	X	1100	X	1100
4	X	1001	0011	1010

(b) The output of the laser sensor

	1	2	3	4
1	0.5	0.7	0.7	X
2	0.9	1.4	X	0.4
3	X	1.2	X	1.2
4	X	0.9	0.3	1.0

(c) The index of the laser sensor

Figure 9. The output of the laser sensor of the agent

The reinforcement learning is performed as the follows. At the position (2, 1), the agent can move to two different directions "Up" and "Right". The probability value 0.5 is assigned to the two directions. That is, the agent has a 50% chance of moving "Up" and a 50% chance of moving to the "Right". When the agent moves to the position (2, 2), it has three moving directions, "Up", "Down" and "Left". Therefore, 0.33 is assigned as the probability value to the three directions. The maze is set up as follows. The target position is set at position (2, 4), and the starting position can be any position marked "1", as shown in Figure 9 (a). When the agent moves from a position to its neighbor position, it is said to have "moved a step". The number of the steps, which the agent is used to move from the start position to the goal position, is used for the reward calculation. The fewer steps the agent used, the higher the score the agent got. If the start position is at the point (2, 1), the minimum number of steps required is seven for the agent moving from the start position the goal position. When the agent moves to a direction where higher reward were obtained than the other directions, higher probability value is assigned to the direction. For example, at the position (2, 1), as moving to the "Right" can obtain higher reward than moving "Up", 0.01 is added to the probability value of moving to that "Right". Experiments were performed to find the path from the start position to the goal position. Based on the experimental results, trying about 200 times, the best path from the start position (2, 1) to the goal position (2, 4) can be found by the agent. After 2000 times trying, the probability values to the high reward directions are increased to 0.99.

To record sensor values, *a working memory mechanism is utilized*. In the mechanism, a vector is created which initial value is randomly assigned. The length of the vector is as same as the number of the steps required by the agent from the start position to the goal position. For example, when the agent started at position (2, 1) which is set as the start position, and the agent moved through positions, (2, 2), (3, 2), (4, 2), (4, 3), (4, 4), (3, 4), and reached the goal position (2, 4), there are seven steps are required. Thus, the vector is defined with seven elements with random values. Then, the value of the current sensor value is combined with the vector, thus a vector with eight elements is created, as shown in Figure 10. In Figure 10, index values of the sensor values are used. The background of the element recording the current sensor value is painted white, and the background of the elements recording the past sensor values are painted gray. For example, at the start position (2, 1), the current sensor value is 0.9, which was recorded at the first element of the vector, and the background of the first element was painted white, as shown in Figure 10 (a). The background of all the other elements were painted gray. The values of the elements from the second to the eighth were remained the random values because no sensor data were recorded. When the agent moved to position (2, 2), 1.4 which was the index value of the sensor at the position, was recorded to the first element and the previously recorded data 0.9 was moved to the second element as shown in Figure 10 (b). In the same way, when the agent moved to position (3, 2), 1.2, which was the index value of the sensor output, was recorded to the first element, and the previously recorded data were moved to the second and third elements, respectively, as shown in Figure 10 (c). After the agent moved to the goal position (2, 4), all index values of the sensor output were recorded as shown in Figure 10 (d). The index value of the sensor output at the goal position was recorded to the first element, and the index value of the sensor at the start position was recorded to the eighth element.

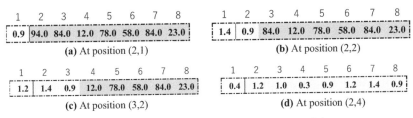

1	2	3	4	5	6	7	8
0.9	94.0	84.0	12.0	78.0	58.0	84.0	23.0

(a) At position (2,1)

1	2	3	4	5	6	7	8
1.4	0.9	84.0	12.0	78.0	58.0	84.0	23.0

(b) At position (2,2)

1	2	3	4	5	6	7	8
1.2	1.4	0.9	12.0	78.0	58.0	84.0	23.0

(c) At position (3,2)

1	2	3	4	5	6	7	8
0.4	1.2	1.0	0.3	0.9	1.2	1.4	0.9

(d) At position (2,4)

Figure 10. Working-memory and recorded index value of the sensor output

Actions of the agent are also recorded by action index value. For example, if the agent moved to the "Right" at the start position, the index value 0.1, which is the index value of moving to the "Right", was recorded. A vector $\mathbf{E}$ which records all the action index values from the start position to the end position is used, as shown in Figure 11 (c).

As shown in Figure 11 (a), the space $\mathbf{X}$ is a collection of the working-memory of the agent moved from the start position to the goal position. Its inverse matrix $\mathbf{X}^{-1}$ is shown in Figure 11 (b). By multiplying $\mathbf{X}^{-1}$ by $\mathbf{E}$, a vector $\mathbf{C}$ is generated as shown in Figure 11 (d).

$\mathbf{X} = $

0.3	0.9	1.2	1.4	0.9	58.0	84.0	23.0
0.4	1.2	1.0	0.3	0.9	1.2	1.4	0.9
0.9	94.0	84.0	12.0	78.0	58.0	84.0	23.0
0.9	1.2	1.4	0.9	78.0	58.0	84.0	23.0
1.0	0.3	0.9	1.2	1.4	0.9	84.0	23.0
1.2	1.4	0.9	12.0	78.0	58.0	84.0	23.0
1.2	1.0	0.3	0.9	1.2	1.4	0.9	23.0
1.4	0.9	84.0	12.0	78.0	58.0	84.0	23.0

(a) $\mathbf{X}$

$\mathbf{X}^{-1} = $

-0.03	2.77	-0.03	0.03	0.01	-0.03	-0.06	0.00
0.00	0.01	0.01	0.00	0.00	0.00	0.00	-0.01
0.00	-0.01	0.00	0.00	0.00	-0.01	0.00	0.01
0.00	-0.08	0.00	-0.09	0.00	0.09	0.00	0.00
-0.01	-0.02	0.00	0.01	0.00	0.00	0.00	0.00
0.02	0.03	0.00	0.00	-0.02	0.00	0.00	0.00
0.00	0.01	0.00	0.00	0.01	0.00	-0.01	0.00
0.00	-0.14	0.00	0.00	0.00	0.00	0.05	0.00

(b) $\mathbf{X}^{-1}$

$\mathbf{E} = $

0.1
0.0
0.1
0.1
0.8
0.4
0.8
0.4

(c) $\mathbf{E}$

$\mathbf{C} = $

-0.06
0.00
0.00
0.03
0.00
-0.01
0.00
0.04

(d) $\mathbf{C}$

Figure 11. Working-memory and recorded index value of the sensor output

When the vector $\mathbf{C}$ is generated, each action of the agent at each relative position can be calculated by multiply the vector of the working-memory by $\mathbf{C}$, as expressed by equation (1) introduced in Section2.

When the dark matter matrix is utilized, a unique action index value can be calculated even if the output values of the sensor are the same. For example, at the position (3, 2) and (3, 4), the index values of the sensor output value are the same 1.2, as shown in Figure 12 (a) and (b), where the index values are recorded at the first elements of the two vectors. In the working-memory, the values of the dark-matter values in the second to the eight elements of the two vectors are different, as shown in Figure 12 (a) and (b).

1	2	3	4	5	6	7	8
1.2	1.4	0.9	12.0	78.0	58.0	84.0	23.0

(a) Values of the working-memory at position (3,2)

1	2	3	4	5	6	7	8
1.2	1.0	0.3	0.9	1.2	1.4	0.9	23.0

(b) Values of the working-memory at position (3,4)

Figure 12. Working-memory and recorded index value of the sensor output

By multiplying the two vectors of the working-memory by the energy vector **E**, two different action index values 0.4 and 0.8 are obtained, as shown in equation (4) and (5). The index value 0.4 means that the agent should take the action "Moving Down" at the position (3, 2), and the index value 0.8 means that the agent should take the action "Moving Up" at the position (3, 4).

$$[1.2, 1.4, 0.9, 12.0, 78.0, 58.0, 84.0, 23.0] \times \begin{bmatrix} -0.06 \\ 0.00 \\ 0.00 \\ 0.03 \\ 0.00 \\ -0.01 \\ 0.00 \\ 0.04 \end{bmatrix} = 0.4 \qquad (4)$$

$$[1.2, 1.0, 0.3, 0.9, 1.2, 1.4, 0.9, 23.0] \times \begin{bmatrix} -0.06 \\ 0.00 \\ 0.00 \\ 0.03 \\ 0.00 \\ -0.01 \\ 0.00 \\ 0.04 \end{bmatrix} = 0.8 \qquad (5)$$

During the above process, the agent obtained skills to take appropriate actions at different positions leading it to move from the start position to the goal positions. That is, skills are acquired through experience of the agent. Considering the definition of *knowledge*, which is defined as "facts, information, and skills acquired through experience or education", it can be found that *knowledge is expressed in the dark-matter matrix* of the space matrix **X**.

4. The phenomenon of inapplicability of experience and the parallel spaces

The phenomenon of inapplicability of experience occurs when we use our experience to make judgements, but it fails to guide us correctly. Sometimes, we make wrong judgements and decisions based on experience. For example, in stock trading, we decide the current trade based on the past trends of the stock and our trading experience. However, it often happens that the stock falls when we buy, or rises when we sell.

Figure 13 shows an example of the phenomenon of inapplicability of experience. In the figure, the circles are the positions of an agent and arrows indicate position transitions.

As shown in Figure 13 (a), initially, the agent is in position 1, then it moves to the next position, position 2. When it reaches position 3, it transitions to the next position, position 4. If an agent is trained and obtains the experience as shown in Figure 13 (a), it will always move from position 3 to position 4. However, if the next position of position 3 is position 5, the phenomenon of inapplicability of experience happens as shown in Figure 13 (b).

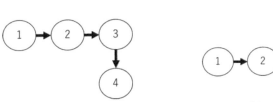

(a) The next position of position 3 should be the position based on the experience

(b) If the next position of position 3 is not position 4 but position 5, then the experience of (a) is inapplicable.

Figure 13. An example of the phenomenon of inapplicability of experience

When this phenomenon happens, it is impossible to determine which position will be the next in the current position, as shown in Figure 14. In Figure 14, both position 4 and position 5 are the next positions after position 3. In this case, we cannot empirically determine which position will be the next position of position 3.

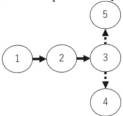

Figure 14. Both the position 4 and the position 5 will be the next position of position 3

One reason for this phenomenon is due to the lack of detection accuracy of the sensor. When the sensor's detection accuracy is insufficient, it cannot detect whether the current position should be position 3.1 or position 3.2, as shown in Figure 15 (a). Since it can only detect the current position as position 3, it cannot determine whether the next position should be position 4 or position 5. When the sensor has enough detection accuracy to detect whether the current position is position 3.1 or position 3.2, it can determine whether the next position should be position 4 or position 5, as shown in Figure 15 (b).

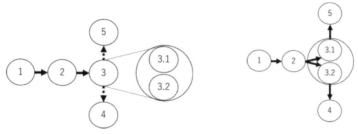

(a) Sensor's lack of detection accuracy

(b) The sensor has enough detection accuracy

Figure 15. Sensor's lack of detection accuracy causes the phenomenon of inapplicability of experiences.

The **parallel space model** proposed in this paper is a model to illustrate this phenomenon. Figure 16 is an example. In figure 16, there are an observation space and two parallel spaces, Space1 and Space2. The observation space is a projection space of the parallel spaces. That is, the observation space is a space that the sensor can detect. In Figure 16, the sensor can only detect x and y direction. It cannot detect z direction.

If two agents are trained in Space1 and Space2, respectively, they will move from position 3 to position 4 and position 5, respectively. The phenomenon of inapplicability of experience will not occur. But in the observation space, as shown in Figure 16, this phenomenon will occur. If the agent moves in Space2 based on the experience obtained from Space1, from position 3, it will move to a non-existent position in Space2, position 4. If the agent moves in Space1 based on the experience obtained from Space2, from position 3, it will move to a non-existent position in Space1, position 5. From the point of view in the observation space, from position 3, sometimes the agent moves to position 4 but sometimes it moves to position 5. In the observation space, we cannot predict what position the agent will move to from position 3 until it has moved.

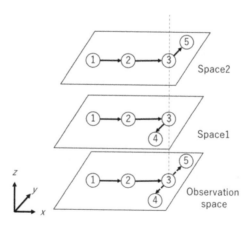

Figure 16. An example of parallel spaces

Suppose an agent is used to control an automated cleaning robot and it will clean two floors. The two floors are represented by Space1 and Space2, respectively. The robot's position on the floor plane is represented by x and y coordinates. The floor where the robot is located is represented by z-coordinates. The robot's sensors can detect positions of the robot in the x and y directions, but not the z direction. The positions of the robot are represented as 1, 2, 3 and 4 when the robot is on the Space1 floor plan. If the robot is on the Space2 floor plan, the positions of the robot are represented as 1, 2, 3 and 5. When the robot is on the floor plan Space1, as shown in Figure 17 (a), the matrix **X** is constructed with the elements of the first column are the position of the robot and the other columns are experiences and dark-matter. The inverse matrix of the matrix **X**, **X**$^{-1}$ is represented in Figure 17 (b). The elements of vector **E** are the next positions of the current positions. As shown in Figure 17 (c), the next positions are 2, 3 and 4 when the current positions are 1, 2 and 3, respectively. When the robot reached to the position 4, its next position is also 4. The rule vector **C**, shown in Figure 17 (d), is calculated multiplying **X**$^{-1}$ by **C**.

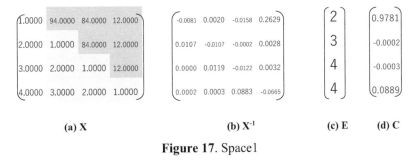

(a) **X**	(b) **X**$^{-1}$

(c) **E**   (d) **C**

Figure 17. Space1

Figure 18 shows the matrices when the robot is on the floor plan Space2. Same as those of in Figure 17, the space **X**, its inverse matrix **X**$^{-1}$, the next position vector **E** and the rule vector **C** are represented in Figure 18 (a), (b), (c) and (d), respectively.

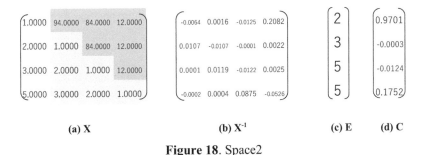

(a) **X**	(b) **X**$^{-1}$

(c) **E**   (d) **C**

Figure 18. Space2

As shown in Figure 16, on both floor plans, Space1 and Space2, the agent moves in the same way from the position 1 to the position 3. Therefore, experiences of the agent at the position 3 are the same. The experience stored in the working memory is shown in Figure 19. It is a row vector. Its first element 3.0000 represents the current robot's position, the second element 2.0000 presents its previous position and the third element 1.0000 is the start position of the robot. The last element 12.0000 is the *dark-matter*.

$$\begin{pmatrix} 3.0000 & 2.0000 & 1.0000 & 12.0000 \end{pmatrix}$$

Figure 19. Experiences stored in the working memory

Although the same experience is stored in the working memory at position 3, different next position is obtained using different rule vectors. The rule vector **C** of Space1 and the rule vector **C** of Space2 are shown in Figure 17(d) and 18(d), respectively. Multiplying the row vector stored in the working memory by the rule vector **C** respectively, the next position, 4, in the Space1, and the next position, 5, are calculated respectively, as shown in Figure 20 (a) and (b).

$$\begin{pmatrix} 3.0000 & 2.0000 & 1.0000 & 12.0000 \end{pmatrix} * \begin{pmatrix} 0.9781 \\ -0.0002 \\ -0.0003 \\ 0.0889 \end{pmatrix} = 4$$

(a) Calculating the next position at position 3 using the rule of Space1

$$\begin{pmatrix} 3.0000 & 2.0000 & 1.0000 & 12.0000 \end{pmatrix} * \begin{pmatrix} 0.9701 \\ -0.0003 \\ -0.0124 \\ 0.1752 \end{pmatrix} = 5$$

(b) Calculating the next position at position 3 using he rule of Space2
Figure 20. Calculating the next position at position 3

Space expansion is necessary when the phenomenon of inapplicability of experience happens. In the example shown in Figure 16, if only the x and y dimensions are used, experience cannot be used to decide which position, position 4 or 5 will be the next position when the current position is position 3. Adding a new sensor is one of the methods for space expansion. For example, we can add a color sensor to the cleaning robot to detect which floor it is on. Painting the floor of Space1 as yellow and the floor of Space2 as green, the output of the color sensor will be different on different floors. As a result, the space is expanded from one space to two parallel spaces, on which it can be found out which floor the robot is on and which will be the next position when the robot is at position 3.

To find out which space the agent is on, we can use sensors that can detect the next possible moving position. For example, if the cleaning robot's sensors can tell if it can move to position 4 or 5 from position 3, it can know which space it is on.

Another method is trial-and-error. Suppose the robot is on Space1. If it encounters an obstacle that prevents it from moving to position 4 from position 3, it can infer that robot is on Space2 instead of Space1.

5. Conclusion and future work

In this paper, we have reviewed the concept of *"dark-matter"* and its relation to experience and knowledge. We have also reviewed the concept of *"space"* as a matrix that is derived from experience. We have shown the characteristic of the concept of space's *"rules"* represented as vectors and how the rules can be used to generate outputs for agents based on their inputs. We have used examples to illustrate how experience and knowledge can be expressed using the concept of *"dark-matter"*. We have also reviewed the working memory mechanism that records the agent's experience and creates the space matrix. Furthermore, we have proposed a new model of *"parallel spaces"* that can explain the "phenomenon of inapplicability of experience". This model reveals why agents sometimes make wrong decisions based on their experience. The main contribution of this paper is that we have uncovered the cause of the "phenomenon of inapplicability of experience" and suggested solutions. In this paper, we have also proposed that for each space, only one rule vector is needed to calculate the output for a given input. A parallel space model can be represented by a three-dimensional matrix, where the first and the second dimensions of the matrix present *"spaces"*. However, space expansion is also needed to create a new *"space"* when the "phenomenon of inapplicability of experience" happens. We have presented two methods for space expansion: adding new sensors and trial-and-error. As our future work, we plan to develop application systems based on the proposed methods and the mechanism.

References

[1] Chen, X. and Kiyoki, Y., *"On Semantic Spatiotemporal Space and Knowledge with the Concept of "Dark-Matter","* Information Modelling and Knowledge Bases XXXIII, IOS Press, pp.110-128, 2021.

[2] Chen, X. and Kiyoki, Y., *"A query-meaning recognition method with a learning mechanism for document information retrieval,"* Information Modelling and Knowledge Bases XV, IOS Press, Vol. 105, pp.37-54, 2004.

[3] Chen, X. and Kiyoki, Y., *"A dynamic retrieval space creation method for semantic information retrieval,"* Information Modelling and Knowledge Bases XVI, IOS Press, Vol. 121, pp.46-63, 2005.

[4] Kiyoki, Y. and Kitagawa, T., "*A semantic associative search method for knowledge acquisition,*" Information Modelling and Knowledge Bases, IOS Press, Vol. VI, pp.121-130, 1995.

[5] Kitagawa, T. and Kiyoki, Y., *"A mathematical model of meaning and its application to multidatabase systems,"* Proc. 3rd IEEE International Workshop on Research Issues on Data Engineering: Interoperability in Multidatabase Systems, pp.130-135, April 1993.

[6] Chen, X., Kiyoki, Y. and Kitagawa, T., *"A multi-language oriented intelligent information retrieval system utilizing a semantic associative search method,"* Proceedings of the 17th IASTED International Conference on Applied Informatics, pp.135-140, 1999.

[7] Chen, X., Kiyoki, Y. and Kitagawa, T., *"A semantic metadata-translation method for multilingual cross-language information retrieval,"* Information Modelling and Knowledge Bases XII, IOS Press, Vol. 67, pp.299-315, 2001.

[8] Kiyoki, Y., Kitagawa, T. and Hitomi, Y., "*A fundamental framework for realizing semantic interoperability in a multidatabase environment,* " International Journal of Integrated Computer-Aided Engineering, Vol.2, No.1(Special Issue on Multidatabase and Interoperable Systems), pp.3-20, John Wiley & Sons, Jan. 1995.

[9] Kiyoki, Y., Kitagawa, T. and Hayama, T., "*A metadatabase system for semantic image search by a mathematical model of meaning,* " ACM SIGMOD Record, Vol.23, No. 4, pp.34-41, Dec. 1994.

[10] Kiyoki, Y, Chen, X. and Kitagawa, T., *"A WWW Intelligent Information Retrieval System Utilizing a Semantic Associative Search Method,"* APWeb'98, 1st Asia Pacific Web Conference on Web Technologies and Applications, pp. 93-102, 1998.

[11] Ijichi, A. and Kiyoki, Y.: "*A Kansei metadata generation method for music data dealing with dramatic interpretation*," Information Modelling and Knowledge Bases, Vol.XVI, IOS Press, pp. 170-182, May, 2005.

[12] Kiyoki, Y., Chen, X. and Ohashi, H.: "*A semantic spectrum analyzer for realizing semantic learning in a semantic associative search space*," Information Modelling and Knowledge Bases, Vol.XVII, IOS Press, pp.50-67, May 2006.

[13] Takano, K. and Kiyoki, Y.: "*A causality computation retrieval method with context dependent dynamics and causal-route search functions*," Information Modelling and Knowledge Bases, ISO Press, Vol.XVIII, pp.186-205, May 2007.

[14] Chen, X. and Kiyoki, Y.: "*A visual and semantic image retrieval method based on similarity computing with query-context recognition*," Information Modelling and Knowledge Bases, IOS Press, Vol.XVIII, pp.245-252, May 2007.

[15] Nitta T, "*Resolution of singularities introduced by hierarchical structure in deep neural networks*," IEEE Trans Neural Netw Learn Syst., Vol.28, No.10, pp.2282-2293Oct. 2017.

[16] Wiatowski, T. and Bölcskei, H., "*A Mathematical Theory of Deep Convolutional Neural Networks for Feature Extraction*," IEEE Transactions on Information Theory, PP(99) · Dec. 2015.

[17] Hochreiter, S., Bengio, Y., Frasconi, P. and Schmidhuber, J. "*Gradient flow in recurrent nets: the difficulty of learning long-term dependencies*," In Kremer, S. C. and Kolen, J. F. (eds.), *A Field Guide to Dynamical Recurrent Neural Networks*, IEEE Press, 2001.

[18] Hochreiter, S. and Schmidhuber, J., "*Long short-term memory*,". Neural computation, Vol.9, No.8, pp.1735-1780, 1997.

[19] Kalchbrenner, N., Danihelka, I. and Graves, "*A. Grid long short-term memory*," CoRR, abs/1507.01526, 2015.

[20] Chen, X. and Kiyoki, Y., "*On Logic Calculation with Semantic Space and Machine Learning*," Information Modelling and Knowledge Bases XXXI, IOS Press, Vol. 321, pp.324-343, 2019.

[21] Chen, X. Prayongrat, M. and Kiyoki, Y., "*A Concept for Control and Program Based on the Semantic Space Model*," Information Modelling and Knowledge Bases XXXII, IOS Press, Vol. 333, pp. 26-44, 2020.

[22] Chen, X., "*An Exploratory Research on the Expression of Knowledge and Its Generation Process based on the Concept of "Dark-matter"*", Information Modelling and Knowledge Bases XXXIV, IOS Press, Vol. 364, pp. 110-124, 2023.

Information Modelling and Knowledge Bases XXXV
M. Tropmann-Frick et al. (Eds.)
doi:10.3233/FAIA231162

A Spatio-Temporal and Categorical Correlation Computing Method for Inductive and Deductive Data Analysis

Yasuhiro HAYASHI [a,1], Yasushi KIYOKI [a,2],
Yoshinori HARADA [b], Kazuko MAKINO [b] and Seigo KANEOYA [b]
[a] *Musashino University*
[b] *Credit Saison Co., Ltd*
ORCiD ID: Yasuhiro HAYASHI https://orcid.org/0000-0001-9581-635X

Abstract. This paper proposes a spatio-temporal and categorical correlation computing method for induction and deduction analysis. This method is a data analytics method to reveal spatial, temporal, and categorical relationships between two heterogeneous sets in past events by correlation calculation, thereby finding insights to build new connections between the sets in the future. The most significant feature of this method is that it allows inductive and deductive data analysis by applying context vectors to compute the relationship between the sets whose elements are time, space, and category. Inductive analysis corresponds to data mining, which composes a context vector as a hypothesis to extract meaningful relationships from trends and patterns of past events. Deductive analysis searches past events similar to a context vector's temporal, spatial, and categorical conditions. Spatio-temporal information about the events and information such as frequency, scale, and category are used as parameters for correlation computing. In this method, a multi-dimensional vector space that consists of time, space, and category dimensions is dynamically created, and the data of each set expressed as vectors is mapped onto the space. The similarity degree of the computing shows the strength of relationships between the two sets. This context vector is also mapped onto the space and is calculated distances between the context vector and other vectors of the sets. This paper shows the details of this method and implementation method and assumed applications in commerce activities.

Keywords. Spatio-Temporal & Categorical Correlation Computing, Induction and Deduction Analysis, Dynamic Multi-Dimensional Vector Space Creation, Vector Composition Operator, Context-Based Data Mining

1. Introduction

In real space and online commerce, identifying factors at the connection point between customers and stores can help to increase purchasing opportunities. When analyzing the factors of connection between two sets of data, data analysts try to derive meaningful data by induction, which finds trends or patterns from events, or deduction, which finds events by making hypotheses.

---

[1] Corresponding Author: Yasuhiro Hayashi, yhayashi@musashino-u.ac.jp.

[2] Corresponding Author: Yasushi Kiyoki, y-kiyoki@musashino-u.ac.jp.

This paper proposes a spatio-temporal and categorical correlation computation method for inductive and deductive analysis. This data analysis method uses correlation calculations to reveal spatial, temporal, and categorical relationships between two heterogeneous sets of past events and thereby find insights to construct new connections between sets in the future. In general data analysis, target data is associated with extrinsic data. For example, combining commercial transaction data and weather data as external data. In this method, we analyze the relationship inherent in the two sets as the data. Concretely, the spatio-temporal and categorical relationships inherent in the sets of customers and stores in a commercial transaction are used.

The most significant feature of this method is that it allows inductive and deductive data analysis by applying context vectors to compute the relationship between the sets whose elements are time, space, and category. Inductive analysis corresponds to data mining, which composes a context vector as a hypothesis to extract meaningful relationships from trends and patterns of past events. Deductive analysis searches past events similar to a context vector's temporal, spatial, and categorical conditions. Spatio-temporal information about the events and information such as frequency, scale, and category are used as parameters for correlation computing. In this method, a multi-dimensional vector space that consists of time, space, and category dimensions is dynamically created, and the data of each set expressed as vectors is mapped onto the space. The similarity degree of the computing shows the strength of relationships between the two sets. This context vector is also mapped onto the space and is calculated distances between the context vector and other vectors of the sets.

(1) Semantic Computing by the Mathematical Model of Meaning and Meta-level System

The Mathematical Model of Meaning and Meta-level System is the core method that inspired this research. The mathematical model of meaning proposed by Kiyoki et al. [1,2] is a method for computing semantic associations between data that change dynamically according to context or situation. An orthonormal space called the metadata space is created, and media data is mapped onto the space. By calculating distances in the metadata space, this method realizes retrieval of media data that are semantically similar to the query. Suppose the context is given along with the query at the time of retrieval. In that case, the dimensionality selection control of the space is dynamically executed, and the retrieval of semantically similar media data is executed according to the context.

Furthermore, the meta-level system proposed by Kiyoki et al. [2,3] is a method that enables the integration and linkage of heterogeneous local database systems by setting up a meta-database system in the upper layer of heterogeneous local database systems. The correlation between temporal, spatial, and semantic features obtained from each local database is weighed by realizing an integrated semantic space and a mechanism for semantic distance calculation in the meta-database system. With the proposed mathematical model of meaning and the meta-level system, Kiyoki et al. aim to realize a memory processing mechanism that interprets dynamically changing meanings and sensitivities depending on context or situation [3].

Our method analyzes data in which two attributes have some relationships. The data is inputted to our method by the table join process on the meta-level of heterogeneous relational databases. Plus, our method dynamically controls dimensions to calculate correlations between two sets. Meta-level system and The Mathematical Model of Meaning are fundamental calculation models of this method.

(2) Image-Query Creation Method

The image-query creation method proposed by Hayashi, Kiyoki, and Chen [4,5] creates image queries for content-based image retrieval by combining images. In this method, an image-query creation database and image-query creation operators are set up in the query part of the content-based image database system. The combination of the image database and the operators is used to operate the color and shape features. Based on the color and shape features of the images that the searcher wants to focus on, this method dynamically controls the dimensions of the image query and the image database to be searched.

In our method, vectors of two sets are created in the integrated space of past events in various fields. Creating the vectors in the image-query creation method and calculating contextual correlation quantities in the orthogonal space of color and shape features is one of the methods that inspired this research.

(3) Emotional MaaS (Mobility as a Service)

The Emotional MaaS, proposed by Kawashima, Hayashi, and Kiyoki [6], is an application of the Mathematical Model of Meaning and Meta-Level System that calculates travel routes and facilities based on the context of tourists. MaaS provides mobility and related services to tourists across the board by highly integrating real space and information space. In this method, the context of the tourist's speed of move, distance in real space, and purpose are set in advance, and transportation and related facilities that are highly correlated with that context are weighed. The intention and situation of each traveler are described as each vector, and the context is defined by composing these vectors.

The correlation calculation and the multi-dimensional vector space creation to describe various contexts are similar to our method in this research. In addition, our approach can be applied to the commerce activity field to clarify human behaviors. The research area overlaps with that of data utilization in mobility information services.

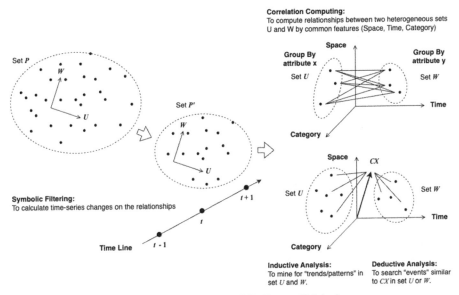

Figure 1. The Concept of The Proposed Method

2. A Spatio-Temporal & Categorical Correlation Computing Method for Induction and Deduction Analysis

2.1. Data Structure & Calculation Method

This method executes spatio-temporal and categorical correlation calculations for induction and deduction analysis. The concept of this model is shown in Figure 1. The concrete calculations are defined as follows:

The given set P is expressed as Formula 1. The elements of the set P are expressed as p_{ij}. Where $i := 1 \ldots, q$, q is the number of attributes of the set P. Furthermore, $j := 1 \ldots, r$, r is the number of elements of the set P. Also, the attributes of the set P are expressed as a_i.

$$P := \begin{matrix} a_1 & a_2 & \cdots & a_q \\ \begin{pmatrix} p_{11} & p_{21} & \cdots & p_{q1} \\ p_{12} & p_{22} & \cdots & p_{q2} \\ \vdots & \vdots & \ddots & \vdots \\ p_{1r} & p_{2r} & \cdots & p_{qr} \end{pmatrix} \end{matrix}$$

(1)

$$p_{ij} \in P \quad where \quad \{\, p_{ij} \mid i = 1 \ldots q,\, j = 1 \ldots r \,\}$$

(2)

$$a_i \quad where \quad \{\, a_i \mid i = 1 \ldots q \,\}$$

(3)

Based on the given necessary conditions about time, space, and category, selection and projection are executed on the set P. The set P reduced in number of elements and attributes by this symbolic filtering is expressed as the set P'. The set P' is assumed to have two attributes, a_x and a_y, that have significant relationships as entities. Where **1 <= x < q, 1 <= y < q, and x not equals y.**

$$a_x \quad where \quad \{\, a_x \mid 1 \leqq x < q,\, x \neq y \,\}$$

$$a_y \quad where \quad \{\, a_y \mid 1 \leqq y < q,\, x \neq y \,\}$$

(4)

Here, the set P' aggregated by the independent element $P[a_x]$ in the attribute a_x is defined as a set U.

$$U := P' \; groupby \; a_x = \begin{matrix} a_x & a_1 & a_2 & \cdots & a_q \\ \begin{pmatrix} u_{x1} & u_{11} & u_{21} & \cdots & u_{q1} \\ u_{x2} & u_{12} & u_{22} & \cdots & u_{q2} \\ \vdots & \vdots & \vdots & \ddots & \vdots \\ u_{xm} & u_{1m} & u_{2m} & \cdots & u_{qm} \end{pmatrix} \end{matrix}$$

(5)

Elements in the set U is expressed by u_{ij}. Where $i := 1 \ldots, q$, q is the number of attributes in the set U. Furthermore, $j := 1 \ldots, m$, where m is the number of elements in the set U.

$$u_{ij} \in U \quad where \quad \{\, u_{ij} \mid i = 1 \ldots q,\, j = 1 \ldots m \,\}$$

(6)

When temporal attributes in the set U are a_t, the temporal elements are expressed as $u[a_t]$. Where $\{\, a_t \mid t = 1 \ldots, tt \,\}$ and tt is an arbitrary number. When spatial attributes in the set U are a_t, the temporal elements are expressed as $u[a_t]$. Where $\{\, a_t \mid t = 1 \ldots, ss \,\}$ and ss is an arbitrary number. Furthermore, when categorical attributes in the set U are a_t, the temporal elements are expressed as $u[a_t]$. Where $\{\, a_t \mid t = 1 \ldots, cc \,\}$ and cc is an arbitrary number.

With the temporal feature extraction function tf, the spatial feature extraction function sf, and the categorical feature extraction function cf defined below, the temporal feature $u[a_{xj},\, t]$, the spatial feature $u[a_{xj},\, s]$, and the categorical feature $u[a_{xj},\, c]$ is calculated as follows:

$$u[a_{xj}, t] := tf\left(u[a_{xj}], u[a_t]\right)$$

$$u[a_{xj}, s] := sf\left(u[a_{xj}], u[a_s]\right)$$

$$u[a_{xj}, c] := cf\left(u[a_{xj}], u[a_c]\right) \tag{7}$$

Note that $u[a_x] = p[a_x], j := 1\ldots, m$, where m is the number of elements in the set U. The spatio-temporal and categorical feature vector $v[a_{xj}]$ of the set $u[a_{xj}]$ is created by this process.

$$v[a_{xj}] := \left(u[a_{xj}, t],\ u[a_{xj}, s],\ u[a_{xj}, c]\right) \tag{8}$$

Thus, the set P' aggregated by the independent element $P[a_y]$ in the attribute a_y is defined by a set W.

$$
W := P'\ groupby\ a_y =
\begin{array}{ccccc}
a_y & a_1 & a_2 & \cdots & a_q \\
\end{array}
\begin{pmatrix}
w_{y1} & w_{11} & w_{21} & \cdots & w_{q1} \\
w_{y2} & w_{12} & w_{22} & \cdots & w_{q2} \\
\vdots & \vdots & \vdots & \ddots & \vdots \\
w_{yn} & w_{1n} & w_{2n} & \cdots & w_{qn}
\end{pmatrix}
\tag{9}
$$

Elements in the set W are expressed as w_{ij}. Where $i := 1 \ldots, q$, q is the number of attributes of the set W. Plus, $j := 1 \ldots, n$, n is the number of elements in the set W.

$$w_{ij} \in W \quad where \quad \{\, w_{ij} \mid i = 1 \ldots q,\ j = 1 \ldots n \,\} \tag{10}$$

When temporal attributes in the set W is a_t, the temporal elements are expressed by $w[a_t]$. Where $\{\, a_t \mid t = 1 \ldots, tt \,\}$ and tt is an arbitrary number. When spatial attributes in the set W are a_t, the temporal elements are expressed as $w[a_t]$. Where $\{\, a_t \mid t = 1 \ldots, ss \,\}$ and ss is an arbitrary number. Furthermore, when categorical attributes in the set W are a_t, the temporal elements are expressed as $w[a_t]$. Where $\{\, a_t \mid t = 1 \ldots, cc \,\}$ and cc is an arbitrary number.

With the temporal feature extraction function tf, the spatial feature extraction function sf, and the categorical feature extraction function cf defined below, the temporal feature $w[a_{yj},\, t]$, the spatial feature $w[a_{yj},\, s]$, and the categorical feature $w[a_{yj},\, c]$ are calculated as follows:

$$w[a_{yj}, t] := tf\,(w[a_{yj}], w[a_t])$$

$$w[a_{yj}, s] := sf\,(w[a_{yj}], w[a_s])$$

$$w[a_{yj}, c] := cf\,(w[a_{yj}], w[a_c]) \tag{11}$$

Note that $w[a_y] = p[a_y], j := 1..., n$, where n is the number of elements in the set W. The spatio-temporal and categorical feature vector $v[a_{yj}]$ of the set $w[a_{yj}]$ is created by this process.

$$v[a_{yj}] := (w[a_{yj}, t],\ \ w[a_{yj}, s],\ \ w[a_{yj}, c]) \tag{12}$$

The vectors $v[a_{xj}]$ and $v[a_{yj}]$ created by Equations 8 and 12 are mapped to a multi-dimensional vector space V with time, space, and category as dimensions. The distance between vectors d_t, d_s, and d_c is calculated for each temporal, spatial, and categorical feature by the temporal feature distance function td, spatial feature distance function sd, and categorical feature distance function cd defined by Formula 13. Plus, to calculate the total correlation $score$ between mapped vectors $v[a_{xj}]$ and $v[a_{yj}]$, the similarities d_t, d_s, d_c calculated in different methods are normalized and expressed as $d_t{}'$, $d_s{}'$, $d_c{}'$ (Formula 14).

$$d_t := td\,(v[a_{xj}], v[a_{yj}])$$

$$d_s := sd\,(v[a_{xj}], v[a_{yj}])$$

$$d_c := cd\,(v[a_{xj}], v[a_{yj}]) \tag{13}$$

$$d_t' := norm(d_t)$$

$$d_s' := norm(d_s)$$

$$d_c' := norm(d_c) \tag{14}$$

The result of each normalized distance calculation is multiplied by the weights wt_t, wt_s, wt_c and calculated as a sum value $score$.

$$score := sim\,(v[a_{xj}], v[a_{yj}]) = wt_t \times d_t' + wt_s \times d_s' + wt_c \times d_c' \tag{15}$$

2.2. Context Vector for Inductive and Deductive Data Analysis

This method's originality is applying context vector CX to achieve temporal, spatial, categorical, inductive, and deductive data analysis. The context vector CX, consisting of the temporal feature cx_t, the spatial feature cx_s, and the category feature cx_c, is expressed as follows.

$$CX := (cx_t, cx_s, cx_c) \tag{16}$$

Using Formula 15, the similarity calculation between the elements $v[a_{xj}]$ of the set U and the context vector CX, or the elements $v[a_{yj}]$ of the set W and the context vector CX, enables an inductive or deductive data analysis approach.

$$score := sim\left(v[a_{xj}], CX\right)$$

$$score := sim\left(v[a_{yj}], CX\right) \tag{17}$$

Inductive analysis in this method corresponds to data mining, in which hypotheses are derived from elements of a set U or set W based on trends or patterns. Hypotheses are expressed as context vectors CX whose elements are temporal, spatial, and categorical trends or patterns. Statistics or difference calculations set the value of the context vector CX. Alternatively, when a set of context vectors CXs consisting of multiple context vectors CXs is set in advance, appropriate hypotheses are extracted by iteratively calculating the distance between the elements of the set U or W and the set of context vectors CXs.

Deductive analysis in this method corresponds to searching a set U or W for elements similar to a particular model event's temporal, spatial, and categorical features, as indicated by the context vector CX.

2.3. Spatio-Temporal and Categorical Feature Extraction Functions

2.3.1. Temporal Feature Extraction Function

This function extracts temporal average and variance. The date in the purchase history data has two facets: the usage date and the usage date interval. The extracted temporal feature vector V_T consists of the average ta of the usage dates in the n data in the purchase history, its variance tv, the average tia of the usage date interval, and its variance tiv. Note that the usage interval date is not constant.

$$V_T = (ta, tv, tia, tiv) \tag{18}$$

When each usage date data in the purchase history is expressed as p_i, the average ta of usage dates in n data is calculated as follows. Where, $i := 1, ..., n$. The $dtoi$ function converts a Gregorian date to a standard date integer. The $itod$ function converts an integer value of a date in a standard format to a date in Gregorian format. The variance tv of the date of use in n data is calculated by Formula 20. Note that absolute values are used to simplify the calculation.

$$ta := itod\left(\frac{1}{n}\sum_{i=1}^{n} dtoi(p_i)\right) \tag{19}$$

$$tv := itod\left(\frac{1}{n}\sum_{i=1}^{n}\left|dtoi(p_i) - \frac{1}{n}\sum_{i=1}^{n} dtoi(p_i)\right|\right) \tag{20}$$

When each usage date data in the purchase history is expressed as p_i, the average tia of usage date intervals for n data is calculated as follows. Where $i := 1, ..., n$. When $n>0$, the average tia and its variance tiv are obtained. When $n=0$, tia and tiv are zero. Additionally, the variance tiv of the usage date interval in n data is calculated as follows.

$$tia := itod\left(\frac{1}{n}\sum_{i=1}^{n}(dtoi(p_{i+1}) - dtoi(p_i))\right) \tag{21}$$

$$tiv := itod\left(\frac{1}{n}\sum_{i=1}^{n}\left|dtoi(p_i) - \frac{1}{n}\sum_{i=1}^{n}(dtoi(p_{i+1}) - dtoi(p_i))\right|\right)$$

(22)

2.3.2. Spatial Feature Extraction Function

This function calculates spatial features. The spatial feature vector V_S consists of the center position sa and variance sv of latitude and longitude of stores included in the n data in the purchase history.

$$V_S = (sa, sv)$$

(23)

The latitude and longitude sa corresponding to the center of gravity of the latitude and longitude in the n data is calculated by Formula 24. When the latitude and longitude of two points p, q on the earth are given as $p(latitude1, longitude1)$, $q(latitude2, longitude2)$, the great circle distance sd between p and q is calculated by Formula 25. This formula is also used for spatial similarity degree.

$$x := \frac{1}{n}\sum_{i=1}^{n}\cos\left(\frac{latitude[i]\,\pi}{180}\right) \times \cos\left(\frac{longitude[i]\,\pi}{180}\right)$$

$$y := \frac{1}{n}\sum_{i=1}^{n}\cos\left(\frac{latitude[i]\,\pi}{180}\right) \times \sin\left(\frac{longitude[i]\,\pi}{180}\right)$$

$$z := \frac{1}{n}\sum_{i=1}^{n}\sin\left(\frac{latitude[i]\,\pi}{180}\right)$$

$$sa := \left(\frac{180 \cdot atan2(z, \sqrt{x^2+y^2})}{\pi}, \frac{180 \cdot atan2(y, x)}{\pi}\right)$$

(24)

$$r := 6378.137\,[km]$$

$$x1 := r\cos\left(\frac{latitude1\,\pi}{180}\right) * \cos\left(\frac{longitude1\,\pi}{180}\right) \qquad x2 := r\cos\left(\frac{latitude2\,\pi}{180}\right) * \cos\left(\frac{longitude2\,\pi}{180}\right)$$

$$y1 := r\cos\left(\frac{latitude1\,\pi}{180}\right) * \sin\left(\frac{longitude1\,\pi}{180}\right) \qquad y2 := r\cos\left(\frac{latitude2\,\pi}{180}\right) * \sin\left(\frac{longitude2\,\pi}{180}\right)$$

$$z1 := r\sin\left(\frac{latitude1\,\pi}{180}\right) \qquad\qquad z2 := r\sin\left(\frac{latitude2\,\pi}{180}\right)$$

$$sd := 2r\,asin\left(\frac{\sqrt{(x1-x2)^2 + (y1-y2)^2 + (z1-z2)^2}}{2r}\right)$$

(25)

When each latitude and longitude data in the purchase history is expressed as p_i, the variance sv of latitude and longitude in n data is calculated as follows. Where $i := 1, ..., n$. sd is a function to calculate the great distance between p_i and the center of gravity sa of latitude and longitude in n data.

$$sv := \frac{1}{n}\sum_{i=1}^{n}|sd(p_i, sa)|$$

(26)

2.3.3. Categorical Feature Extraction Function

The Category Feature Histogram V_C is the sum of n stores' category vector data C_i in the purchase history. Where $i := 1, ..., k$. The category is expressed as tree data consisting of four levels: large, medium, small, and detailed. By converting the tree data format to vector data format, distance calculation in the vector space can be applied. When L major category, M medium category, S minor category, and D detailed category consist of l, m, *s, and d* elements, respectively, tree data T is converted to vector data C_i consisting of $k := l + m + s + d$ elements.

$$k := l + m + s + d$$

$$C_i := (c_{i1}, c_{i2}, \ldots, c_{ik})$$

$$V_C := \sum_{i=1}^{k} C_i = \sum_{i=1}^{k} (c_{i1}, c_{i2}, \ldots, c_{ik}) \tag{27}$$

2.3.4. Vector Composition Function

Given k vectors $V_i := (v_{i1}, v_{i2}, \ldots, v_{in})$ consisting of n-dimensions, this function that is named Vector Creation Operator composes a new vector by computing the sum of the same elements of those vectors. Where $2 <= i <= k$.

$$V_{composition} := composition\,(V_1, V_2, \cdots V_n) = \sum_{i=1}^{k} (v_{i1}, v_{i2}, \cdots v_{in}) \tag{28}$$

2.3.5. Distance Calculation Function

The inner product *ip* is used to calculate the semantic distance as similarity *similarity* between two context vectors V_a, V_b created by this method. Where $D := 2+4+k$. Note that if semantical distance is required between elements of two vectors, Euclidean distance calculation and geographical distance calculation are also used.

$$V_a := (v_{a1}, v_{a2}, \cdots, v_{ad})$$

$$V_b := (v_{b1}, v_{b2}, \cdots, v_{bd})$$

$$similarity := ip\,(V_a, V_b) = \sum_{i=1}^{d} (v_{ai} \times v_{bi}) \tag{29}$$

3. Assumed Implementations and Applications

This method deductively and inductively analyzes spatio-temporal and categorical associations between entities related to each other in a given set. By setting up this method as a storied function in a commercial transaction database with many commercial transactions and as a related tool for data analysts, it is possible to reveal the spatiotemporal and categorical relationships between customers and stores. The related tool should have a user interface to accept the needs of the data analyst who repeatedly tests the hypothesis, queries the database as SQL, and visualizes the results on the screen. The data to be calculated are payment systems, such as credit cards, used in real space and online. Based on information obtained from the payment system, such as the date of purchase, customer information, name of the purchasing store, and type of business, a customer and a store set are formed. The following practical applications can be assumed from these sets to be formed.

1. To clarify the purchasing habits and tendencies of all customers or specific customers in a spatio-temporal and categorical context.

2.   To clarify the spatiotemporal and categorical correlations between stores used by specific customers based on a particular purchasing context.
3.   To clarify the spatiotemporal and categorical purchasing habits and tendencies of specific customers who use specific stores.

Based on the calculation of meaningful correlations between customers and stores obtained through a series of analytical processes, new business marketing is expected to enhance the Well-Being and happiness of each customer and each store.

4. Conclusion

This paper described a spatio-temporal and categorical correlation computing method for induction and deduction analysis. This method's originality applies context vector CX to achieve temporal, spatial, and categorical correlation calculation between two heterogeneous sets as inductive, and deductive data analysis. Inductive analysis corresponds to data mining, which composes a context vector as a hypothesis to extract meaningful relationships from trends and patterns of past events. Deductive analysis searches past events similar to a context vector's temporal, spatial, and categorical conditions. By repeating the analysis, insights will be found to build new connections between sets in the future. This paper also described the proposed method's assumed implementation and applications in commercial activities.

As the next step, we will develop a proto-type system that applies the proposed method and experiments to evaluate effectiveness and feasibility, and business deployment.

References

[1] Yasushi Kiyoki, Xing Chen, "A Semantic Associative Computation Method for Automatic Decorative-Multimedia Creation with "Kansei" Information" (Invited Paper), The Sixth Asia-Pacific Conferences on Conceptual Modelling (APCCM 2009), 9 pages, January 20-23, 2009.
[2] Yasushi Kiyoki and Saeko Ishihara: "A Semantic Search Space Integration Method for Meta-level Knowledge Acquisition from Heterogeneous Databases," Information Modeling and Knowledge Bases (IOS Press), Vol. 14, pp.86-103, May 2002.
[3] Kiyoki, Y., Chen, X., Veesommai, C., Wijitdechakul, J., Sasaki, S., Koopipat, C., & Chawakitchareon, P.: "A semantic-associative computing system with multi-dimensional world map for ocean-environment analysis", Information Modelling and Knowledge Bases XXX, pp. 147-168.
[4] Hayashi, Y., Kiyoki, Y., and Chen, X.: "An Image-Query Creation Method for Expressing User's Intentions by Combining Multiple Images", Information Modelling and Knowledge Bases, Vol.XXI, IOS Press, pp. 188-207, 2010.
[5] Hayashi, Y., Kiyoki, Y., and Chen, X.: "A Combined Image-Query Creation Method for Expressing User's Intentions with Shape and Color Features in Multiple Digital Images", Information Modelling and Knowledge Bases, Vol. XXII, IOS Press, pp. 258-277, 2011.
[6] Kawashima, K., Hayashi, Y., Kiyoki, Y., Mita., T.: "A Mobility and Activity Integration System Supporting Sensitivity to Contexts in Dynamic Routing - Emotional MaaS -", Information Modelling and Knowledge Bases, Vol. XXXIII, IOS Press, pp. 297-308, 2021.
[7] UN SDGs-3, Ensure healthy lives and promote well-being for all at all ages, https://sdgs.un.org/goals/goal3, 2023/01/28.
[8] Tal Ben-Shahar, "Even Happier: A Gratitude Journal for Daily Joy and Lasting Fulfillment," McGraw Hill, 2009.
[9] Kahneman, D, and A Deaton. 2010. "High income improves evaluation of life but not emotional well-being." Proceedings of the National Academy of Sciences 107 (38): 16489-16493.

Information Modelling and Knowledge Bases XXXV
M. Tropmann-Frick et al. (Eds.)
© 2024 The Authors.
doi:10.3233/FAIA231163

Browser Fingerprinting: Overview and Open Challenges

Marko HÖLBL[a,1], Vladimir ZADOROZHNY[b], Tatjana WELZER DRUŽOVEC[a],
Marko KOMAPARA[a] and Lili NEMEC ZLATOLAS[a]

[a] *University of Maribor, Faculty of Electrical Engineering and Computer Science,
Maribor, Slovenia*
[b] *University of Pittsburgh, School of Computing and Information, Pittsburgh, USA*

ORCiD ID: Marko Hölbl https://orcid.org/0000-0002-9414-3189

Abstract. The central concept of browser fingerprinting is the collection of device-specific information for identification or security purposes. This chapter provides an overview of the research conducted in the field of browser fingerprinting and presents an entry point for newcomers. Relevant literature is examined to understand the current research in the field of browser fingerprinting. Both research in the field of crafting browser fingerprints and protection against it is included. Finally, current research challenges and future research directions are presented and discussed.

Keywords. Browser fingerprinting, profiling, user privacy, web tracking

1. Introduction

The web is a platform that we access using browsers. In recent years, with the introduction of technologies such as HTML5 and CSS3, the web has become more dynamic and utilized than ever before. Since the beginning of the web, we strive to improve the user experience by sharing device-specific information. However, this fact and the diversity of the devices connecting to the web have paved the way for device fingerprinting. A device fingerprint collects information about the software and hardware of a device for identification purposes. Typically, a fingerprinting algorithm consolidates the data into an identifier. A browser fingerprint is data collected specifically through interaction with a device's web browser [1]. This data is often needed for browsing to function adequately. Therefore, it cannot be remedied easily.

The concept of browser fingerprinting is simple – collect device-specific data for identification and security purposes through a browser. Websites are often required to track users to maintain a session for various reasons, such as maintaining logged-in status, language preferences, or shopping cart status. The most widely used technology for this purpose are cookies, and in recent years, they have grown increasingly problematic due to their misuse, such as for advertising [2]. Since cookies are stored locally (on the user's computer), user information leakage or tampering can be accomplished easily [3]. This

---

[1] Corresponding Author: Marko Hölbl, Faculty of Electrical Engineering and Computer Science, University of Maribor, Koroška cesta 46, 2000 Maribor, Slovenia; E-mail: marko.holbl@um.si

resulted in a growing mistrust of cookies. Many browser add-ons were developed to address the issue by disabling or deleting cookies. Additionally, private or incognito browsing modes gained popularity. Given the negative connotation of cookies and techniques for their prevention [4], browser fingerprinting has emerged as a new standard in user tracking. Additionally, in the EU, websites need to issue so-called cookie notifications [5], which can impact the user experience of websites when using cookies [6].

A browser fingerprint is a compilation of information about a user device's hardware, operating system, browser, and configuration. It is the process of collecting data using a web browser to generate a device's (potentially unique) identifier (i.e., fingerprint). A server can collect various data from different available APIs (Application Programming Interfaces) and HTTP metadata interfaces using a simple browser-based script. An API, the interface that provides access to specific objects and methods, even enables access to hardware, such as the microphone and camera. However, it requires authorization to do so. Each browser features many such APIs, which are easily accessible via JavaScript, making information collection effortless. Unlike other identification methods, such as cookies, which rely on a unique identifier (ID) explicitly recorded in the browser, browser fingerprinting is less explicit and more concealed.

More information about the client's software and hardware are required to adapt to a wider variety of devices. These unique details, such as the browser's User-Agent, can be gathered from several sources, such as the HTTP message header, the user's IP address, and the screen resolution. Some examples of data that a website can acquire are shown in Table 1.

Table 1. Sample of Data Acquired by a Web Browser [7,8].

Characteristic	Value
User agent	Mozilla/5.0 (Macintosh; Intel Mac OS X 10_15_7) AppleWebKit/537.36 (KHTML, like Gecko) Chrome/114.0.0.0 Safari/537.36
Accept	text/html,application/xhtml+xml,application/xml;q=0.9,image/avif,image/webp,image/apng,*/*;q=0.8,application/signed-exchange;v=b3;q=0.7
Content encoding	gzip, deflate, br
Content language	en-US,en,sl
List of plugins	Plugin 0: PDF Viewer; Portable Document Format; internal-pdf-viewer. Plugin 1: Chrome PDF Viewer; Portable Document Format; internal-pdf-viewer. Plugin 2: Chromium PDF Viewer; Portable Document Format; internal-pdf-viewer. Plugin 3: Microsoft Edge PDF Viewer; Portable Document Format; internal-pdf-viewer. Plugin 4: WebKit built-in PDF; Portable Document Format; internal-pdf-viewer.
Cookies enabled	yes
Use of local storage	yes
Use of session storage	yes
Timezone	UTC+02:00 Europe/Paris
Screen resolution and color depth	1512x982x30
Platform	MacIntel
Do Not Track	yes
Canvas	Chi fordhank glyphs vext quiz Cwm fjordbank glyphs vext quiz
WebGL Vendor	Google Inc. (Apple)
WebGL Renderer	ANGLE (Apple, Apple M1 Pro, OpenGL 4.1)

This chapter aims to give an overview of existing work and, in this way, provide an entry point into the field and, secondly, lay the groundwork for future research in the field by identifying current challenges.

This chapter's structure is as follows. This section introduced browser fingerprinting, and related definitions and contributions were described. A discussion of existing research in the field of browser fingerprinting is given in Section 2. Section 3 provides a summary of defense mechanisms to tackle browser fingerprinting. Later, a discussion and open research challenges are discussed in Section 4. Section 5 gives the conclusions.

2. Overview of Browser Fingerprint Research

Before 2010, cookie technology was associated with browser uniqueness. Cookies maintain the user status (the so-called session) and can return this data if needed. Cookies store client data, so it is a challenge to assure privacy. Many browser users disable cookies with plug-ins, and current browsers include privacy options that disable cookies.

Mayer [9] studied Internet anonymity in 2009. He showed in a tiny experiment that browser fingerprints may identify users, although Eckersley [10] of the Electronic Frontier Foundation first demonstrated a practical implementation of the idea in 2010. When visiting a web page, the web server can embed JavaScript code or gather information about the user's browsing device. As opposed to cookies, browser fingerprints cannot be disabled. A cookie a user can delete or deactivate using adequate privacy options. Browser fingerprints may be used for cross-domain identification.

Due to the great attractiveness of user tracking with the help of browser fingerprinting, the field is very active, with much research in the field. Mowery and Shacham [11] investigated HTML Canvas fingerprint characteristics. Faiz Khademi et al. [12] examined browser fingerprint detection and protection. Vastel et al. [13] examined browser fingerprints across time.

Browser fingerprint-related research can be categorized according to several study directions, including feature acquisition or defense mechanisms, both of which are addressed in this chapter.

Since browser fingerprinting seeks to identify the user, researchers focus on high-entropy, long-lasting, and preferably cross-browser fingerprint approaches. Modern browsers have strong functionality and extensive interfaces, giving many possible ways in which to create browser fingerprints.

One of the more widely used techniques for acquiring browser fingerprints is using JavaScript code. In this way, browser information such as operating system or browser version can be gained. Much research has utilized this approach, e.g., [3,4,9,10]. For example, Mowery et al. used a plug-in known as NoScript and its whitelist for the characteristics of a fingerprint [14]. Mulazzani et al. [15] have optimized the techniques to enable JavaScript engine detection to leverage the JavaScript parsing engine's properties and, in this way, fingerprint a browser.

Many browser plug-ins block JavaScript scripts because it is too powerful and thus can be abused. In 2013, Unger et al. used CSS (Cascading Style sheet) for fingerprints [16], while in 2015, Takei et al. used browser CSS features for fingerprint collection [17]. Different browser rendering engines read CSS differently; hence, attribute implementation states vary. Browser fingerprints are created by exploiting Web browser request differences. In 2021, Laperdrix et al. [18] suggested infusing style sheets for fingerprint traits. It uniquely identifies browser extensions from the visited website.

As modern browsers with HTML5 support have many capabilities, they pose a risk, as shown in [11]. In this work, text and WebGL scenes were used to create fingerprints. Compared to others, the homogeneity and high entropy make it very utilizable. Later, Acar et al. [19] advanced this approach.

As discussed in [10], WebGL properties can be used to demonstrate how different hardware renders WebGL. However, in 2015, Nakibly et al. [20] suggested fingerprinting the device by detecting the CUP and GPU clock variations during a difficult rendering workload. The WEBGL_debug_renderer_info interface provides the precise device model, according to Laperdrix et al. [21]. Google's Bursztein et al. [22] created a browser fingerprint mechanism utilizing JavaScript and Canvas in 2016. Cao et al. enhanced WebGL hardware fingerprint detection in 2017 [23]. They uniquely identified over 99% of test devices via 31 rendering jobs. Schwarz et al. [24] used numerous JavaScript functionalities not described in MDN docs in 2019.

In 2016, Englehardt et al. developed a Web Audio API-based fingerprint [25] similar to WebGL. Oscillator Node, an audio script, generates the unique audio fingerprint in this study [26]. Many browsers were tested, as well as many hardware and software combinations to get fingerprint data. However, it turned out that Web Audio API alone is unreliable.

Browser plugins add convenience and additional functionality to browsing. Sjosten et al. [27] suggested using Web Accessible Resources to identify browser plug-in installations in 2017. Chrome and Firefox need web page extension resources, and the URL "extension:///" lets you check if the plug-in exists. In this way, most plug-ins can be detected. However, specific extensions do not have this property available. Starov et al. [28] used several approaches to identify browser plug-ins. Namely, many plug-ins alter web page DOMs, and detecting relevant modifications reveals relevant users' plug-in installations and consequentially exposes a user. Sanchez-Rola et al. [29] presented an attack for access control to identify browser plug-ins using time side channels. In 2019, Starov et al. [30] upgraded past browser plug-ins' side effects studies, including injecting script or style tags, empty placeholders, or page messages.

Fuhl et al. [31] correlated the mouse movement trajectory to the human eye, which could be used as a fingerprint. However, these techniques need further validation and research. Abgral et al. utilized cross-site scripting attacks [32] to fingerprint HTML parsers in different browsers. This method yields fingerprints that are hard to mislead and difficult to reproduce since they presume a running HTML parser. Fifield and Egelman [33] suggested measuring font glyph screen sizes to recognize web browser fingerprints in 2015. The authors mainly utilize the rendering of browsers for identification. In a test of over 1,000 browsers, 34% could be identified in this way. Authors in [34] examined HTML5's misuse of the battery API to utilize the properties of short-term batteries to identify users. Sanchez-Rola et al. [29] introduced time-based device fingerprint recognition in 2018, which measures execution clock difference using JavaScript codes to identify users. Wu et al. [35] suggested a website user delay fingerprint in 2021. After IP address translation, users may switch browsers and use virtual machines with 80% recognition.

Based on the overview of current research, the following challenges in browser fingerprint can be highlighted: (1) Most techniques depend on JavaScript, which is an omnipresent and vital part of most of today's web pages. Nevertheless, research in the field of browser fingerprinting should try to develop non-JavaScript-dependent techniques. Some examples include research by Takei et al. [17] and Wu et al. [35]. (2) Research in the field of cross-browser fingerprinting should address aspects like matching recognition featuring weighting and techniques for obtaining more reliable and high-entropy fingerprint characteristics. There is already some research conducted in this direction [4,16]. (3) From the research overview, we can see that most of the fingerprinting properties depend on a device's software (e.g., plug-ins) or hardware properties that can be gathered through the web browser. The challenge here is to fingerprint co-used devices (e.g., in public places, using the same networks). Research is already ongoing in this direction. Fuhl et al. showed how to exploit user activity to create fingerprints and proved its practicality [31].

A brief overview of different approaches to browser fingerprinting is presented in Table 2.

Table 2. Categorization of Research on Brower Fingerprinting Techniques.

Technique is based on	Example Reference
JavaScript	[3,4,9,10,14,15]
CSS	[16–18]
Hardware	[20,21,23,29,34]
HTML5 features	[11,19–26]
Plug-ins / Extensions	[27,28,30,36]

3. Overview of Browser Fingerprint Defense Research

Browser fingerprints, especially those acquired without the user's knowledge, pose a major threat to privacy. Browser fingerprints are best used to precisely monitor and secure users when they don't wish to be tracked. Scholars explore browser fingerprint defense to provide a secure and effective way for users who want to remain concealed.

Browser fingerprint protection research increased after Eckersley et al.'s [10] study highlighted the browser tracking potential. However, there are examples of browser plug-ins or add-ons that further facilitate fingerprinting, like Firegloves [37]. This plug-in returns random results when data on browser properties is gathered, which makes identifying such users simpler. On the other hand, tools like FP-Block [38] generate site-specific fingerprints without affecting continuous or cross-domain tracking. Additionally, authors in [12] proposed to monitor web objects running on the user's browser to check for the intention of fingerprinting. Additionally, they employ protection techniques using randomization, filtering, and even blacklists of relevant websites.

In 2014, Besson et al. noted that randomization is not difficult, but how to randomize is. This work models trackers and fingerprint recognition tools using information theory channels and presents a randomization approach to assure program privacy without fingerprints. Nikiforakis et al. [39] proposed a randomization approach where developers can balance effectiveness and usability using different randomization algorithms. Laperdrix et al. [40] use software variety and dynamic reconfiguration to automatically construct varied browsers for the randomized return of phony fingerprints. Since a virtual machine environment is needed for the implementation, this can significantly impact efficiency. Another study by Trickel et al. [41] created CloakX to hide browser plug-in fingerprints by randomizing the accessible resource path. The technique uses JavaScript code rewriting and the DOM proxy Droxy to intercept and rewrite extension requests, thus assuring protection during browser plug-in installation.

Another direction of browser fingerprinting defense was proposed by Wu et al. [42], namely unification. In their work, the authors suggested unifying WebGL and proposed an approach called UNIGL. Additionally, Fiore et al.'s [43] proposed a concept in which fake data (used for fingerprinting) are generated to cope with browser fingerprinting. However, it needs to be changed continuously to protect regardless of whether genuine and false fingerprint tracking would be possible.

An interesting technique was proposed by Yokoyama and Uda [44]. The authors employ local agents to modify the browser fingerprint value and, in this way, prevent fingerprinting. Another approach was proposed in [45], where Chromium was changed to protect against Flash and Canvas browser fingerprinting, but without influencing the two technologies. Laperdrix et al. [46] also offered a Firefox-based upgrade with fingerprint protection against AudioContext, and Mitropoulos et al. presented a training technique [47] for known cross-site scripting attacks to gather browser fingerprints [32]. ElBanna and Abdelbaki later created a method to reduce browser fingerprinting [48] for WebGL and Canvas fingerprint monitoring.

Based on the overview of current research on browser fingerprint protection, it is evident that this can be done using additional plug-ins or modified versions of browsers. Still, the main remaining challenges include: (1) It is difficult for a user (browser) to determine whether the website's intention is legitimate or malicious. For instance, it is unclear to the user whether or not their screen resolution is being considered when designing the site's layout. For example, it is difficult to determine if retrieving the screen resolution information is to adapt the web page layout or for browser fingerprinting purposes. (2) The use of unification with a small number of users is questionable. It requires the support of vendors, international standards organizations, and technical committees to, for example, unify WebGL and Canvas rendering.

4. Discussion and Open Challenges

The development of browser fingerprinting technology is consistent with the growing concern for privacy among individuals. Traditional tracking using cookies has shown shortcomings, as cookies can be stolen [49], modified or forged, and even injected [50]. Google recently announced that they plan to ban third-party cookies as more and more users block cookies or install protection plug-ins. If this happens, browser fingerprinting will become more important to assure statefulness and legitimate user tracking.

Based on the review of existing research, we anticipate the following directions for future research:

(1) **Machine learning and AI** will play an important role. One of the directions will be algorithms automatically matching fingerprints, as presented in [16,51]. Considering the evolution of fingerprinting techniques and approaches [10,13], a matching algorithm is required. Efficient rule-based matching algorithms were already developed [10,13,52,53]. With further progress in machine and deep learning, this technology is becoming preferable when developing browser fingerprinting techniques. For instance, [9,12] present a clustering algorithm to extract fingerprint signs autonomously. Additionally, machine learning algorithms, such as neural networks, are becoming increasingly popular [11,13] for fingerprinting. It is anticipated that in future research, combining browser fingerprinting and machine learning will increase.

(2) **Browser fingerprinting applications** [54–57] exploit two aspects: the immutability of browser fingerprints and the use of browser fingerprints – gathering them through browser feature collection. However, with research in the field of browser fingerprinting, hardware fingerprinting, and the evolution of browser fingerprinting

[58–61], additional potential applications are emerging (e.g. cross-browser fingerprinting or cross-domain tracking).

(3) As browsers and network technologies continuously develop, many technologies will disappear or be discontinued. For example, Microsoft, Google, and Adobe have discontinued technical support for Flash. Therefore, new approaches that are **less dependent on specific technology** need to be developed.

Despite the fact that browser fingerprinting has been around for a significant amount of time and its maturity, legislation, regulation, and technical specifications have fallen behind practice [62]. Regarding information leakage, previous studies [63] have focused more on the technical aspect of securing device information. Research in [36] demonstrates that browser fingerprinting technology can impact personal privacy. Vendors are continuously monitoring the progress in the field and upgrading their products to prevent the acquisition of specific features that could help with browser fingerprinting. However, in the long term, the fundamental remedy still lies in regulation, legislation, and governance to guide technology development.

5. Conclusions

Current research on browser fingerprinting has yielded significant results that can be used for tracking users. There are two sides to the coin – on the one hand, browser fingerprinting can be used instead of cookies for maintaining the state of a user and, on the other, misused for tracking. The combination of browser fingerprinting and traditional user identity tracking can be applied positively, like identity tracking, user authentication, and for security. In this chapter, we have given an overview of browser fingerprinting from two aspects – acquiring and protecting against it. Further, we have discussed various challenges and future directions of the research field, which is intended to help facilitate further research in this interesting and, for online privacy, very important field.

Acknowledgement

The authors acknowledge the financial support from the Slovenian Research and Innovation Agency (Research Core funding No. P2-0057, the bilateral project BI-US/22-24-147) and the financial support of the ATHENA (Advanced Technology Higher Education Network Alliance) European University project, funded by the European Union, Erasmus+, European universities initiative, grant agreement number 101004096.

References

1.   Wikipedia. Device fingerprint [Internet]. 2023 [cited 2023 Jul 6]. Available from: https://en.wikipedia.org/wiki/Device_fingerprint
2.   Mathews-Hunt K. CookieConsumer: Tracking online behavioural advertising in Australia. Comput Law Secur Rep. 2016;32(1):55–90.

3. Kwon H, Nam H, Lee S, Hahn C, Hur J. (In-)security of cookies in HTTPS: cookie theft by removing cookie flags. IEEE Transactions on Information Forensics and Security. 2020;15.
4. Cranor LF. Cookie monster. Commun ACM. 2022;65(7):30–2.
5. GDPR.eu. Cookies, the GDPR, and the ePrivacy Directive [Internet]. 2023 [cited 2023 Jul 7]. Available from: https://gdpr.eu/cookies/
6. Kulyk O, Hilt A, Gerber N, Volkamer M. this website uses cookies": Users' perceptions and reactions to the cookie disclaimer. In: European Workshop on Usable Security (EuroUSEC). 2018.
7. Electronic Frontier Foundation (EFF). Cover Your Tracks [Internet]. 2023 [cited 2023 Jul 6]. Available from: https://coveryourtracks.eff.org/
8. AmIUnique.org. Am I Unique? [Internet]. 2023 [cited 2023 Jul 6]. Available from: https://amiunique.org/
9. Mayer JR. Any person… a pamphleteer: Internet Anonymity in the Age of Web 2.0. 2009.
10. Eckersley P. How unique is your web browser? In: Privacy Enhancing Technologies. Berlin, Heidelberg: Springer Berlin Heidelberg; 2010. p. 1–18.
11. Mowery K, Shacham H. Pixel Perfect: Fingerprinting canvas in HTML5. In: Proceedings of W2SP. San Francisco, CA, USA; 2012. p. 1–12.
12. Khademi A, Zulkernine M, Weldemariam K. FPGuard: detection and prevention of browser fingerprint- ing. In: DBSec 2015: Data and Applications Security and Privacy XXIX. Cham: Springer; 2015. p. 293–308.
13. Vastel A, Laperdrix P, Rudametkin W, Rouvoy R. FP-STALKER: Tracking Browser Fingerprint Evolutions. In: 2018 IEEE Symposium on Security and Privacy (SP). IEEE; 2018.
14. Mowery K, Bogenreif D, Yilek S, Shacham H. Fingerprinting information in JavaScript implementations. In: Proceedings of W2SP. Krakow, Poland; 2011.
15. Mulazzani M, Reschl P, Huber M. Fast and reliable browser identification with javascript engine fingerprinting. In: Workshop on Security and Privacy (W2SP). Citeseer; 2013.
16. Unger T, Mulazzani M, Fruhwirt D, Huber M, Schrittwieser S, Weippl E. SHPF: Enhancing HTTP(S) session security with browser fingerprinting. In: 2013 International Conference on Availability, Reliability and Security. IEEE; 2013.
17. Takei N, Saito T, Takasu K, Yamada T. Web browser fingerprinting using only cascading style sheets. In: 2015 10th International Conference on Broadband and Wireless Computing, Communication and Applications (BWCCA). IEEE; 2015.
18. Laperdrix P, Starov O, Chen Q, Kapravelos A, Nikiforakis N. Fingerprinting in Style: Detecting Browser Extensions via Injected Style Sheets. In: 30th USENIX Security Symposium (USENIX Security 21) [Internet]. USENIX Association; 2021. p. 2507–24. Available from: https://www.usenix.org/conference/usenixsecurity21/presentation/laperdrix
19. Acar G, Eubank C, Englehardt S, Juarez M, Narayanan A, Diaz C. The web never forgets: Persistent tracking mechanisms in the wild. In: Proceedings of the 2014 ACM SIGSAC Conference on Computer and Communications Security. Vienna, Austria; 2014. p. 674–89.
20. Nakibly G, Shelef G, Yudilevich S. Hardware Fingerprinting Using HTML5. CoRR [Internet]. 2015;abs/1503.01408. Available from: http://arxiv.org/abs/1503.01408

21. Laperdrix P, Rudametkin W, Baudry B. Beauty and the beast: Diverting modern web browsers to build unique browser fingerprints. In: 2016 IEEE Symposium on Security and Privacy (SP). IEEE; 2016.

22. Bursztein E, Malyshev A, Pietraszek T, Thomas K. Picasso: lightweight device class fingerprinting for web clients. In: Proceedings of the 6th Workshop on Security and Privacy in Smartphones and Mobile Devices. Vienna, Austria; 2016.

23. Cao Y, Li S, Wijmans E. (Cross-) browser fingerprinting via os and hardware level features. In: 24th Annual Network and Distributed System Security Symposium. Scottsdale, Arizona, USA; 2017.

24. Schwarz M, Lackner F, Gruss D. JavaScript template attacks: Automatically inferring host information for targeted exploits. In: Proceedings 2019 Network and Distributed System Security Symposium. Reston, VA: Internet Society; 2019.

25. Englehardt S, Narayanan A. Online tracking: a 1- million-site measurement and analysis. In: Proceedings of the 2016 ACM SIGSAC Conference on Computer and Communications Security. Vienna, Austria; 2016.

26. Queiroz JS, Feitosa EL. A Web Browser Fingerprinting method based on the Web Audio API. Comput J. 2019;62(8):1106–20.

27. Sjösten A, Van Acker S, Sabelfeld A. Discovering browser extensions via web accessible resources. In: Proceedings of the Seventh ACM on Conference on Data and Application Security and Privacy. New York, NY, USA: ACM; 2017.

28. Starov O, Nikiforakis N. XHOUND: Quantifying the fingerprintability of browser extensions. In: 2017 IEEE Symposium on Security and Privacy (SP). IEEE; 2017.

29. Sanchez-Rola I, Santos I, Balzarotti D. Clock around the clock: time-based device fingerprinting. In: Proceedings of the 2018 ACM SIGSAC Conference on Computer and Communications Security. Toronto, Canada; 2018.

30. Starov O, Laperdrix P, Kapravelos A, Nikiforakis N. Unnecessarily Identifiable: Quantifying the fingerprintability of browser extensions due to bloat. In: The World Wide Web Conference. New York, NY, USA: ACM; 2019.

31. Fuhl W, Sanamrad N, Kasneci E. The Gaze and Mouse Signal as additional Source for User Fingerprints in Browser Applications. CoRR [Internet]. 2021;abs/2101.03793. Available from: https://arxiv.org/abs/2101.03793

32. Abgrall E, Traon Y Le, Monperrus M, Gombault S, Heiderich M, Ribault A. XSS-FP: Browser Fingerprinting using HTML Parser Quirks. CoRR [Internet]. 2012;abs/1211.4812. Available from: http://arxiv.org/abs/1211.4812

33. Fifield D, Egelman S. Fingerprinting web users through font metrics. In: Financial Cryptography and Data Security. Berlin, Heidelberg: Springer Berlin Heidelberg; 2015. p. 107–24.

34. Olejnik Ł, Acar G, Castelluccia C, Diaz C. The leaking battery - a privacy analysis of the HTML5 Battery Status API. In: Data Privacy Management, and Security Assurance. Cham: Springer International Publishing; 2016. p. 254–63.

35. Wu T, Song Y, Zhang F, Gao S, Chen B. My Site Knows Where You Are: A Novel Browser Fingerprint to Track User Position. In: ICC 2021 - IEEE International Conference on Communications. 2021. p. 1–6.

36. Karami S, Ilia P, Solomos K, Polakis J. Carnus: Exploring the privacy threats of browser extension fingerprinting. In: Proceedings 2020 Network and Distributed System Security Symposium. Reston, VA: Internet Society; 2020.

37.   Boda K, Földes ÁM, Gy. Gulyás–portal. eu G. Cross-browser fingerprinting test 2.0.

38.   Ferreira Torres C, Jonker HL, Mauw S (Sjouke). FP-Block: Usable Web Privacy by Controlling Browser Fingerprinting. In: Pernul G, Ryan PYA, Weippl E, editors. Computer Security – ESORICS 2015. Switzerland: Springer Nature Switzerland AG; 2015. p. 3–19. (Lecture Notes in Computer Science (LNCS) series; vol. 2).

39.   Nikiforakis N, Joosen W, Livshits B. PriVaricator: deceiving fingerprinters with little white lies. In: Proceedings of the 24th International Conference on World Wide Web. Florence, Italy; 2015.

40.   Laperdrix P, Rudametkin W, Baudry B. Mitigating Browser Fingerprint Tracking: Multi-level Reconfiguration and Diversification. In: 2015 IEEE/ACM 10th International Symposium on Software Engineering for Adaptive and Self-Managing Systems. 2015. p. 98–108.

41.   Trickel E, Starov O, Kapravelos A, Nikiforakis N, Doupé A. Everyone is Different: Client-side Diversification for Defending Against Extension Fingerprinting. In: 28th USENIX Security Symposium (USENIX Security 19) [Internet]. Santa Clara, CA: USENIX Association; 2019. p. 1679–96. Available from: https://www.usenix.org/conference/usenixsecurity19/presentation/trickel

42.   Wu S, Li S, Cao Y, Wang N. Rendered Private: Making GLSL Execution Uniform to Prevent WebGL-based Browser Fingerprinting. In: 28th USENIX Security Symposium (USENIX Security 19) [Internet]. Santa Clara, CA: USENIX Association; 2019. p. 1645–60. Available from: https://www.usenix.org/conference/usenixsecurity19/presentation/wu

43.   Fiore U, Castiglione A, Santis Alfredo D, Palmieri F. Countering browser fingerprinting techniques: Constructing a fake profile with Google chrome. In: 2014 17th International Conference on Network-Based Information Systems. IEEE; 2014.

44.   Yokoyama S, Uda R. A proposal of preventive measure of pursuit using a browser fingerprint. In: Proceedings of the 9th International Conference on Ubiquitous Information Management and Communication. New York, NY, USA: ACM; 2015.

45.   Baumann P, Katzenbeisser S, Stopczynski M, Tews E. Disguised Chromium browser: Robust browser, Flash and Canvas fingerprinting protection. In: Proceedings of the 2016 ACM on Workshop on Privacy in the Electronic Society. Sofia, Bulgaria; 2016.

46.   Laperdrix P, Baudry B, Mishra V. FPRandom: Randomizing core browser objects to break advanced device fingerprinting techniques. In: Lecture Notes in Computer Science. Cham: Springer International Publishing; 2017. p. 97–114.

47.   Mitropoulos D, Stroggylos K, Spinellis D, Keromytis AD. How to train your browser: preventing XSS attacks using contextual script fingerprints. ACM Transactions on Privacy and Security. 2016;19(1):1–31.

48.   ElBanna A, Abdelbaki N. NONYM!ZER: Mitigation framework for browser fingerprinting. In: 2019 IEEE 19th International Conference on Software Quality, Reliability and Security Companion (QRS-C). IEEE; 2019.

49.   Sivakorn S, Polakis I, Keromytis AD. The cracked cookie jar: HTTP cookie hijacking and the exposure of private information. In: 2016 IEEE Symposium on Security and Privacy (SP). IEEE; 2016.

50. Calibri F, Chen H, Duan X, Zheng J, Jiang J. Path leaks of HTTPS Side-Channel by cookie injection. In: International Workshop on Constructive Side-Channel Analysis and Secure Design. Springer; 2018. p. 189–203.

51. Laperdrix P, Avoine G, Baudry B, Nikiforakis N. Morellian analysis for browsers: Making web authentication stronger with canvas fingerprinting. In: Detection of Intrusions and Malware, and Vulnerability Assessment. Cham: Springer International Publishing; 2019. p. 43–66.

52. Liu X, Liu Q, Wang X, Jia Z. Fingerprinting web browser for tracing anonymous web attackers. In: 2016 IEEE First International Conference on Data Science in Cyberspace (DSC). IEEE; 2016.

53. Liangfeng Z, Yi W, Yuanyi W, Rui K. Statistics-based browser fingerprinting technology. Information Network Security. 2019;11:49–55.

54. Nikiforakis N, Kapravelos A, Joosen W, Kruegel C, Piessens F, Vigna G. Cookieless monster: Exploring the ecosystem of web-based device fingerprinting. In: 2013 IEEE Symposium on Security and Privacy. IEEE; 2013.

55. Rochet F, Efthymiadis K, Koeune F, Pereira O. SWAT: Seamless web authentication technology. In: The World Wide Web Conference. New York, NY, USA: ACM; 2019.

56. Jia Z, Cui X, Liu Q, Wang X, Liu C. Micro-honeypot: Using browser fingerprinting to track attackers. In: 2018 IEEE Third International Conference on Data Science in Cyberspace (DSC). IEEE; 2018.

57. Qingxuan X. Fake order recognition system based on browser fingerprint. Electronic Production. 2019;2.

58. Li X, Cui X, Shi L, Liu C, Wang X. Constructing browser fingerprint tracking chain based on LSTM model. In: 2018 IEEE Third International Conference on Data Science in Cyberspace (DSC). IEEE; 2018.

59. Bird S, Mishra V, Englehardt S, Willoughby R, Zeber D, Rudametkin W, et al. Actions speak louder than words: Semi-supervised learning for browser fingerprinting detection. CoRR [Internet]. 2020;abs/2003.04463. Available from: https://arxiv.org/abs/2003.04463

60. Qixu L, Xinyu L, Cheng L, Junnan W, Langping C, Jiaxi L. An android browser fingerprint recognition method based on bidirectional recurrent neural network. Computer Research and Development. 2020;57(11):2294–311.

61. Muñoz-Garcia Ó, Monterrubio-Martin J, Garcia-Aubert D. Detecting browser fingerprint evolution for identifying unique users. International Journal of Electronic Business. 2012;10(2):120–41.

62. Laperdrix P, Bielova N, Baudry B, Avoine G. Browser Fingerprinting: A Survey. ACM Trans Web [Internet]. 2020 Apr;14(2). Available from: https://doi.org/10.1145/3386040

63. Jérôme Segura. Operation Fingerprint: A Look Into Several Angler Exploit Kit Malvertising Campaigns [Internet]. MalwareBytes. 2016 [cited 2023 Jul 2]. Available from: https://www.malwarebytes.com/blog/news/2016/03/ofp

Information Modelling and Knowledge Bases XXXV
M. Tropmann-Frick et al. (Eds.)
© 2024 The Authors.
This article is published online with Open Access by IOS Press and distributed under the terms
of the Creative Commons Attribution Non-Commercial License 4.0 (CC BY-NC 4.0).
doi:10.3233/FAIA231164

Identification and Analysis of Factors Impacting e-Inclusion in Higher Education

Maja PUŠNIK [a,1], Katja KOUS [a], Tatjana WELZER DRUŽOVEC [a],
and Boštjan ŠUMAK [a]

[a] *University of Maribor, Faculty of Electrical Engineering and Computer Science,*
Maribor, Slovenia

ORCiD ID: Maja Pušnik https://orcid.org/0000-0003-0087-1044

Abstract. In this chapter, we investigate the complex process of analyzing and understanding the factors that influence individuals' access to and participation in digital education within the Higher Education context. While the digital transformation in Higher Education Institutions (HEI) has produced numerous benefits for both students and educators, it has also brought forth challenges, particularly for students with special educational needs and disabilities (SEND). A literature review was conducted, to gain insight into the specific requirements of this student demographic. This review aimed to identify the multifaceted factors that impact e-inclusion within Higher Education. Our research resulted in the identification of 24 different factors that should be considered when evaluating e-inclusion within HEI. These factors serve as essential indicators in the assessment of the accessibility and inclusivity of digital education, allowing for a more multifaceted understanding of the dynamics in the Higher Education landscape.

Keywords. Inclusion, Higher Education, accessibility, SEND students

1. Introduction

E-inclusion, or digital inclusion, addresses the challenge of ensuring all individuals have equal opportunities to access and benefit from digital technologies and online resources. When studying the factors impacting e-inclusion in Higher Education Institutions (HEI), researchers and practitioners analyze a range of elements that can either enable or hinder the participation of diverse individuals in digital learning environments. With the introduction of changes in HEI new challenges emerged, especially in the COVID time when the teaching environment moved online. The transformation included adapting both learning materials and teaching methods to the demands of online teaching and learning. During this time, it was crucial to emphasize the importance of including all students, regardless of their obstacles, and creating an environment where all participants had an equal opportunity for success and development in HEI. In many cases this involved adaptations and innovations in the educational process, to enable individuals with different needs to reach their full potential. Although the included changes improved the students' experience and enriched the educational community, and

---

[1] Corresponding Author: Maja Pušnik, Faculty of Electrical Engineering and Computer Science, University of Maribor, Koroška cesta 46, 2000 Maribor, Slovenia; E-mail: maja.pusnik@um.si.

contributed to better preparedness for the contemporary world, several issues were raised regarding the inclusion of different students.

One of the goals of this research is to understand and contribute to creating an inclusive digital learning environment that provides equal opportunities for all students to succeed in their educational pursuits, focusing on equality versus equity. Although digitalization in HEI has many positive effects, such as saving time, money, energy, increasing safety and a flexible environment, there are several negative impacts of digitalization, which present obstacles for some students, especially students with different disabilities or special needs. In this research, we have focused mainly on digital accessibility and researched factors, classified in one of the following categories, influencing e-inclusion: Infrastructure and Access, Digital Skills and Literacy, Socioeconomic Factors, Inclusive Pedagogical Approaches, Institutional Policies and Support, Cultural and Social Factors, Student Engagement and Motivation. The infrastructure and access present the availability and quality of technological infrastructure, such as internet connectivity and computing devices, and played a significant role in e-inclusion. Factors like broadband availability, affordability, and reliable access to devices can influence a student's ability to engage in online learning. Digital skills, literacy and proficiency in using digital technologies are also crucial for effective participation in e-learning. Assessing the digital skills and literacy levels of students and understanding gaps or barriers they face can help identify strategies to enhance their competence and confidence in using digital tools. Socioeconomic factors are also important in impacting e-inclusion. Students from low-income backgrounds face financial constraints in accessing the necessary technology and Internet services, and understanding those factors can guide the development of targeted support programs. Inclusive pedagogical approaches influence the design and delivery of online courses, which play a role in promoting e-inclusion. Pedagogical strategies that consider diverse learning styles, accessibility requirements, and multiple modes of engagement, can contribute to a more inclusive online learning environment. Institutional policies, practices, and support mechanisms also influence e-inclusion significantly. This includes policies related to digital accessibility, student support services, training programs for HEI, and the delivery of assistive technologies for students with disabilities. Cultural and social factors, such as cultural norms, social expectations, and individual attitudes toward technology, also impact e-inclusion. It is essential to consider cultural diversity and social dynamics within HEI to ensure access and participation in digital learning. Student engagement and motivation affects student success crucially in online learning. Identifying strategies to enhance students' interest, interaction, and sense of belonging in digital learning environments can contribute to their e-inclusion. By analyzing these factors and their interactions, policymakers, educators, and institutions can develop strategies and interventions to promote e-inclusion in Higher Education.

The main aim of the research is to understand which factors influence inclusive digital capabilities in HEI, to enable equal educational opportunities for all students, especially students with special needs (SEND). The foundation of this study is built upon the Technological Pedagogical Content Knowledge (TPACK) framework, a framework for teachers to effectively integrate technology into their teaching, combining knowledge of technology, pedagogy (teaching methods), and subject matter expertise (content knowledge). Therefore our research is based on three essential domains [11]: Technological Knowledge (TK), Pedagogical Knowledge (PK), and Content Knowledge (CK). TK refers to an understanding of the various digital tools, technologies, and resources available for educational purposes. PK includes the understanding of effective teaching methods, strategies, and approaches. It encompasses the knowledge of instructional techniques, classroom management, assessment practices, and student engagement strategies. CK relates to a deep understanding of the subject matter being taught. It involves expertise in the specific content area, including key concepts, theories, principles, and methodologies [11]. By integrating the domains TK, PK, and CK, educators can design and deliver instruction effectively that optimizes the use of technology to support learning objectives. Through the TPACK framework, this study explores and identifies factors, good practices, and challenges that contribute to successful digital inclusion in Higher Education, ultimately promoting effective and inclusive integration of technology in teaching and learning processes.

2. Method

This research employed a systematic approach to identify relevant factors for digital inclusion in HEI, focusing on accessible education for students, including SEND students. The identification of factors was conducted through a literature search using specific keywords, including "Factors", "Digital Inclusion", "E-inclusion", "Higher Education", "Accessible Education", "Students" and "Pedagogy" or "Teaching." The search was performed across scientific databases including WoS, ScienceDirect, IEEExplore, ACM and Google Scholar. To ensure the relevance of the findings, only literature in the English language was considered, published from 2017 onwards.

A total of 133 papers were identified through this process. From the identified papers, 206 factors were recognized as contributing to digital inclusion in Higher Education, although 24 distinct factors were extracted after analysis and classification. The screening of the literature, which involved the efforts of all the authors, led to the identification of 87 good practices that have shown positive outcomes in promoting digital inclusion. Additionally, 63 challenges were extracted from the literature, representing the obstacles and barriers that need to be addressed to enhance digital inclusion. By employing this methodology and considering a wide range of sources, this research provides a foundation for understanding the factors, good practices, and challenges related to digital inclusion in Higher Education.

3. Identification of good practices and challenges

A total of 87 good practices were identified throughout the research process. In the first cycle 30 best practices were extracted, based on their recurring mentions in the literature. Each of these practices was highlighted at least once in the reviewed sources, indicating their presence in the context of digital inclusion. Subsequently, in the second cycle, a more rigorous criterion, excluding papers, which did not address e-inclusion within their contents, was applied, to narrow down the selection further. Out of the 30 identified best practices, 16 practices stood out as particularly impactful, as they were identified consistently at least three times in the literature. These practices not only addressed digital inclusion, but also emphasized a broader sense of inclusion across diverse educational settings. The research resulted in the following good practices, providing a basis for the identified factors: Variety in Content Presentation, Modern Teaching Methods, Structured Lectures, Practical Examples, Extended Time, Assistive Technologies, Small Groups, Self-Monitoring, Low Physical Effort, Positive Personal

Relationships, Positive Group Relationships, Peer Integration, Structured Feedback, University Regulations, Shared Responsibility and Adapted Learning. However, from the same identified body of research, we also identified 63 challenges for SEND students, from which 6 groups of challenges were extracted, as presented in **Table 1**.

Table 1. Challenges

Challenge	Description
One solution does not fit all	An individual problem needs an individual solution, and there is no one general solution (Blind learners, Deaf learners, Autism, Dyslexia, Muscular dystrophy, Chronic fatigue all have different needs).
Some solutions just do not work	Researchers advise to repeat the content, however, sometimes the content is being repeated too often and it causes dullness. It is also advised to provide everything online (in advance even). However, that can cause dependence on the online platform, and have a negative influence.
Professors mean well but overdo it	Combining several sensory inputs to make the class more diverse and interesting can be discomforting. PowerPoint is often used inefficiently, accessible word processing and presentation styles are not always included, in addition to unreadable graphs, drawings and non-structured Word documents. Also, if HEI provides too much help it has a negative impact, as students may feel their disability was more prominent, and they perceived a strong emphasis on their weaknesses rather than on their strengths.
Social environment	An unfriendly atmosphere, compulsory class attendance, crowded classrooms, and large lecture halls can have a negative effect. In many cases, peers don't know how to communicate with SEND students, increasing the negative environment.
Physical environment	Not adapted infrastructure and existing facilities which have difficulties in accommodating SEND students using a wheelchair, in addition to impracticalities such as cables on the floor and ergonomic barriers (acoustics, furniture, etc.).
Personal issues of students	Loneliness and fear of not knowing how to act in classrooms, hesitation when asking questions in class or conversing with other students. Poor concentration and organizational skills, and becoming overwhelmed by the volume of work also contributes to barriers in HEI, causing SEND students to be segregated from "regular school classes" and "mainstream school programs".

4. Identification of factors

The primary outcome of this study is the development of a list of the factors influencing inclusive digital education. This list incorporates extended essential elements from the TPACK framework [11]. As part of the research process, analysis resulted in the identification of 24 factors that influence digital inclusion in education. To enhance the clarity and positive direction of these factors, negative aspects were transformed into positive counterparts. For instance, factors such as "Insufficient or limited teacher training" were reframed as "Informed, trained, aware, and educated staff/university." This reframing aims to emphasize the importance of equipping educators and institutions with the necessary skills and knowledge to foster digital inclusion.

To facilitate a more organized understanding, similar factors were categorized together, based on their common characteristics: student's perspective, teacher's perspective, school's perspective, pedagogic approach, external environment and tools and technology. By integrating these components a general perspective on the effective integration of technology in educational settings is provided, while promoting inclusivity. This categorization also allows a clearer overview of the factors influencing digital inclusion. Additionally, the identified best practices and barriers were integrated into the definition and description of the identified factors, presented in the following sections. This integration ensures that the list of factors not only acknowledges the existing barriers, but also offers practical guidance and strategies to overcome them.

4.1. Student's perspective

In the student's perspective category, two main factors were identified, F1 and F2, presented in the **Table 2**.

Table 2. Factors in a student's perspective

Factor	Points in this category
F1 Digital literacy	Student learning in digital education, including digital skills and literacy training, access to devices and software, students' tech proficiency, and device reliability. Infrastructure challenges like limited network access and assistive technology also play a role. Students with disabilities face specific challenges, such as the absence of sign language interpreters and difficulties with screen readers. These limitations can hinder student participation in the curriculum and limit access to the necessary support [1][2][12].
F2 Student's motivation	Emphasizes educational strategies to boost learner motivation and engagement. It also highlights the significance of communication skills, organization, and self-awareness, particularly in terms of seeking support from Disability Team staff. The participants' mind-set is identified as a crucial factor [3][4][5][9].

4.2. Teacher's perspective

In the teacher's perspective category, three main factors were identified, F3, F4 and F5, presented in **Table 3**.

Table 3. Factors in a teacher's perspective

Factor	Points in this category
F3 Teacher's ethics	Addresses critical aspects of teachers' attitudes in education, including their ethical compass concerning a rigid curriculum and the impact of teacher attitudes on teaching, the importance of positive attitudes towards inclusive education and high expectations for SEND students, which correlate with teachers' readiness to provide appropriate support [2][4][13].
F4 Teacher's motivation	Explores teacher development, focusing on their motivation and self-regulation in teaching, highlighting the positive impact of the participants' awareness of SEND students, which increased their motivation for teaching and emphasized the need for training in disability and inclusive education [5][6].
F5 Teacher's knowledge	Provides key insights into effective teaching practices and teacher attitudes. Teachers with high self-efficacy employ student-centered strategies that prioritize flexibility, responsiveness, and student success, fostering self-regulation. It also highlights a lack of awareness and skills in assistive technology (AT) among educators. Additionally, it underscores the role of continuous learning in teaching [2][7][8][14].

4.3. School's perspective

In the teacher's perspective category, five main factors were identified, F6, F7, F8, F9 and F10, as presented in **Table 4**.

Table 4. Factors in a school's perspective

Factor	Points in this category
F6 Collaboration and communication encouragement	Emphasizes the importance of collaboration between teachers and schools, highlighting its essential role in education. It also stresses the need for increased collaboration between schools, parents, and vulnerable learners to protect SEND students from violence. These points revolve around schools' efforts to promote collaboration, engage parents and caregivers, and ensure all voices, including students, teachers, parents, and school administration [15][16].
F7 Curriculum flexibility	Discusses essential supports and instructional strategies for SEND students. These include curriculum modifications, structural adjustments, assessment accommodations, and instructional methods like cooperative learning and universal design for learning. The school plays a vital role in providing these supports, such as offering flexible curriculum options, adapting settings, and granting extra time for students with extensive needs [2].
F8 Training and education on inclusiveness	Highlights the impact of training on instructors' willingness to support SEND students. Teaching methodology and awareness-raising training are linked to higher willingness. Specialized courses boost instructors' willingness to provide accommodations. It stresses the importance of school-based personnel having the skills to offer individualized support, and emphasizes the need for ongoing skill development. Additionally, it highlights desirable instructor attitudes, such as receptiveness to feedback, being firm, fair, and motivating [2][8].
F9 Leadership and support	Emphasizes the critical role of school leadership in shaping the perception of digital accessibility within an organization. It highlights the leadership's attitude toward interactions with students, the institution's desired image, and the importance of school support in staff education [16].
F10 Clear policy	Addresses the necessity of a well-defined university-level policy to accommodate students with disabilities effectively by addressing digital technologies, support services, and resource allocation. It also emphasizes the importance of a school's inclusion policy focused on accommodating students with special needs and the commitment to creating an unbiased, diverse, and inclusive environment, along with the corresponding actions to achieve this goal [12].

4.4. Pedagogic approach

In the pedagogic approach perspective category, six main factors were identified, F11, F12, F13, F14, F15 and F16, as presented in **Table 5**.

Table 5. Factors in a pedagogic approach perspective

Factor	Points in this category
F11 Flexibility	Addresses the value of flexible strategies for SEND students, and highlights the benefits of flexible grouping and cooperative peer learning to provide necessary support and foster collaboration among students. Furthermore, implementing diverse instructional and assessment options through Universal Design for Learning (UDL) ensures curriculum access for all students, accommodating various learning styles [9][10][5].

F12 Personalization	Highlights the use of individual educational plans for students with special needs, addressing various learning backgrounds, prerequisites, and adaptive instructions. It also emphasizes the importance of understanding students' diverse needs, the flexibility of creating individual plans at the beginning of the academic year, and the possibility of making accommodations as the year progresses. Additionally, the factor underscores the significance of involving students in the planning process, considering their feedback for a tailored approach [17][18].
F13 Modern pedagogical approaches	Discusses various pedagogical approaches and practices for delivering study content, including peer tutoring, cooperative teaching, video instruction, lecture methods, online and hybrid instruction. It also mentions strategies like providing lecture outlines and notes, engaging students visually, using teaching aids and technology, and enhancing lectures with appealing study extensions. Additionally, it acknowledges the effectiveness of Social Stories as a learning tool [19].
F14 Feedback	Addresses various aspects of feedback in education, including self-testing, progress checkers, and the importance of the student voice. It also highlights different feedback channels, such as professor-to-student feedback, student-to-student feedback, and feedback from students to professors. Additionally, it emphasizes the mechanisms that enable anonymous feedback from students [20][21].
F15 Consistency	Emphasizes the significance of consistency in various aspects of education, including lecture structure, school organization and feedback provision, access to student work, and clear, written expectations from students [22].
F16 Motivation	Emphasizes the importance of consistency and coherence in education, while advocating for clear accessibility processes to enhance product development efficiency. It also recognizes that inconsistent support can limit curriculum access. Furthermore, it discusses the value of motivational techniques, such as gamification in engaging students based on their interests and needs [3][16][22][23].

4.5. External environment

In the external environment category, three main factors were identified, F17, F18 and F19, as presented in **Table 6**.

Table 6. Factors in an external environment

Factor	Points in this category
F17 Government	Highlights the absence of governmental support, effective legislation, and educational policies, as well as the lack of interventions to promote inclusive practices in education [27].
F18 Peers	Discusses the importance of fostering welcoming environments through strategies like peer support. It also highlights the significance of student-student interactions for socialization and learning purposes, emphasizing the integration of students with special needs into working groups without making it mandatory [23][21].
F19 Caregivers and parents support	Recognizes caregivers as crucial in planning for the successful inclusion of students with extensive support needs, as per IDEIA. It emphasizes the importance of providing a platform to encourage family and caregiver support in students' educational activities [2].

4.6. Tools and technology

In the tools and technology category, five main factors were identified, F20, F21, F22, F23 and F24, as presented in **Table 7**.

Table 7. Tools and technology domain

Factor	Points in this category
F20 Assistive Technology access	Identifies access to assistive technology (AT) as crucial for the full participation of individuals with disabilities in various educational and community settings. This category addresses the importance of adapted and accessible equipment, the lack of such equipment, and the various types of AT that can enhance the learning experience for individuals with disabilities [2][23].
F21 Infrastructure and physical environment	Identifies the need for various accessibility tools, such as sign language interpreters and hearing aid-compatible systems. It also highlights issues related to improper facilities, classroom size, and unwelcoming environments, emphasizing the importance of appropriate classroom conditions for inclusive education [19][23][25][26].
F22 Developing new ICT tools and new ways of using them	Addresses the importance of research and development in the field of ICT, emphasizing the need for exploring new ways of using ICT and developing new tools. It highlights the involvement of various stakeholders, including people with disabilities, and the significance of partnerships and collaboration to support innovative practices in education and technology [27].
F23 Inclusion assessment	Addresses the lack of agreed-upon criteria and tools to measure the efficiency of inclusion in education. It emphasizes the need for criteria and tools for evaluating inclusion at both the teacher and school levels [24].
F24 Periodical assessment	Highlights the importance of establishing a schedule for inclusion assessment, defining key performance indicators, and creating an inclusion index to monitor progress and effectiveness in inclusion efforts [23].

5. Conclusion

The research focuses on identifying factors, good practices, and challenges related to digital inclusion in HEI. The main research method was a literature review, where the key emphasis was to identify factors influencing the creation of an inclusive digital education environment, including accessible digital content and the availability of inclusive technologies. The literature review was performed by several researchers on different digital libraries. The research activities resulted in 16 good practices, 6 main barriers and 24 factors, which were categorized based on their characteristics: Student's perspective, Teacher's perspective, School's perspective, Pedagogic approach, External environment and Tools and technology.

To provide a more complete framework for advancing digital inclusion in educational settings, it is crucial to refine and expand the identified factors further. The future research will focus on selecting and validating the most impactful factors using methods such as surveys and workshops. This selection process will involve a thorough analysis of factors and a comprehensive exploration of their impact on e-inclusion in HEI. In addition to incorporating insights from TPACK [11], which is a framework used in the field of education to describe the knowledge and skills that teachers need to effectively integrate technology into their teaching practices, other existing frameworks will also be used, such as SELFIE (Self-reflection on Effective Learning by Fostering the use of Innovative Educational technologies) [28][29] and the Index for inclusion [30][31]. The final objective is establishing a set of comprehensive factors that can be utilized to evaluate inclusion in different Higher Education Institutions.

Acknowledgments

This research was conducted within the activities of the SET4Includion (Self-Evaluation Tools for e-Inclusion in HEI) project, co-funded by the Erasmus+ Programme of the European Union. The authors acknowledge the financial support from the Slovenian Research Agency (Research Core Funding No. P2-0057).

References

[1]   Starks, A.C., Reich, S.M. "What about special ed? ": Barriers and enablers for teaching with technology in special education. Comput. Educ. 2022, 193, 104665.

[2]   Orlando, A.M. Klinepeter, E.; Foster, M. Retrospectives on factors influencing inclusive opportunities for college students with extensive support needs. Int. J. Incl. Educ. 2016, 20, 1239–1251.

[3]   Frank, H., McLinden, M., Douglas, G. Accessing the curriculum; university based learning experiences of visually impaired physiotherapy students. Nurse Educ. Pract. 2020, 42, 102620.

[4]   Coubergs, C., Struyven, K., Vanthournout, G., Engels, N. Measuring teachers' perceptions about differentiated instruction: The DI-Quest instrument and model. Stud. Educ. Eval. 2017, 53, 41–54.

[5]   Griful-Freixenet, J., Struyven, K., Vantieghem, W. Exploring pre-service teachers' beliefs and practices about two inclusive frameworks: Universal Design for Learning and differentiated instruction. Teach. Teach. Educ. 2021, 107.

[6]   Moriña, A., Carballo, R. The impact of a faculty training program on inclusive education and disability. Eval. Program Plann. 2017, 65, 77–83.

[7]   Woodcock, S., Sharma, U., Subban, P., Hitches, E. Teacher self-efficacy and inclusive education practices: Rethinking teachers' engagement with inclusive practices. Teach. Teach. Educ. 2022, 117, 103802.

[8]   Abdella, A.S. Instructors' willingness to provide instructional accommodations for students with disabilities in selected universities of Ethiopia. Int. J. Incl. Educ. 2018, 22, 671–682.

[9]   Carrington, S., Saggers, B., Webster, A., Harper-Hill, K., Nickerson, J. What Universal Design for Learning principles, guidelines, and checkpoints are evident in educators' descriptions of their practice when supporting students on the autism spectrum? Int. J. Educ. Res. 2020, 102, 101583.

[10] Courey, S.J., Tappe, P., Siker, J., LePage, P. Improved Lesson Planning With Universal Design for Learning (UDL). Teach. Educ. Spec. Educ. J. Teach. Educ. Div. Counc. Except. Child. 2013, 36, 7–27.

[11] Kurt, S. TPACK: Technological Pedagogical Content Knowledge Framework; Frameworks & Theories; 2019.

[12] Chen, W. Students with Disabilities and Digital Accessibility in Higher Education under COVID-19. 29th International Conference on Computers in Education Conference, ICCE 2021 - Proceedings, 1, 656–662.

[13] Mouchritsa, M., Romero, A., Garay, U., & Kazanopoulos, S. Teachers' Attitudes towards Inclusive Education at Greek Secondary Education Schools. Education Sciences 2022: 12(6), 404, doi: https://doi.org/10.3390/educsci12060404

[14] Väyrynen, S., Paksuniemi, M. Translating inclusive values into pedagogical actions. International Journal of Inclusive Education 2020, 24(2), 147–161, doi: https://doi.org/10.1080/13603116.2018.1452989

[15] European Agency for Special Needs and Inclusive Education. Inclusive Digital Education. Association for Educational Communications and Technology (AECT) 2022. Retrieved from https://link.springer.com/10.1007/978-3-031-14775-3

[16] AbilityNet. Attitudes to Digital Accessibility 2022.

[17] Weiss, S., Muckenthaler, M., Heimlich, U., Kuechler, A., Kiel, E. Teaching in inclusive schools. Do the demands of inclusive schools cause stress? International Journal of Inclusive Education 2021, 25(5), 588–604, doi:https://doi.org/10.1080/13603116.2018.1563834

[18] Tops, W., Van Den Bergh, A., Noens, I., Baeyens, D. A multi-method assessment of study strategies in higher education students with an autism spectrum disorder. Learning and Individual Differences 2017, 59(June), 141–148, doi: https://doi.org/10.1016/j.lindif.2017.09.003

[19] Onuigbo, L., Osadebe, N. E., Achebe, N. E. Classroom environment required for meeting the information needs of students with hearing impairment in Nigerian universities. International Journal of Inclusive Education 2020, 24(3), 266–287, doi: https://doi.org/10.1080/13603116.2018.1459887

[20] Edwards, M. Inclusive learning and teaching for Australian online university students with disability: a literature review. International Journal of Inclusive Education 2022, 26(5), 510–525, doi: https://doi.org/10.1080/13603116.2019.1698066

[21] MRSEC Education Group. Inclusive Teaching Practices 2023.

[22] Deng, M., Wang, S., Guan, W., Wang, Y. The development and initial validation of a questionnaire of inclusive teachers' competency for meeting special educational needs in regular classrooms in China. International Journal of Inclusive Education 2017, 21(4), 416–427, doi: https://doi.org/10.1080/13603116.2016.1197326

[23] Haegele, J., Zhu, X., Davis, S. Barriers and facilitators of physical education participation for students with disabilities: an exploratory study. International Journal of Inclusive Education 2018, 22(2), 130–141. doi: https://doi.org/10.1080/13603116.2017.1362046

[24] Dimitrellou, E., Hurry, J., Male, D. Assessing the inclusivity of three mainstream secondary schools in England: challenges and dilemmas. International Journal of Inclusive Education 2020, 24(10), 1097–1113. doi:https://doi.org/10.1080/13603116.2018.1511757

[25] Lopez-Gavira, R., Moriña, A., Melero-Aguilar, N., & Perera-Rodríguez, V. H. Proposals for the Improvement of University Classrooms: The Perspective of Students with Disabilities. Procedia - Social and Behavioral Sciences 2016, 228(June), 175–18, doi: https://doi.org/10.1016/j.sbspro.2016.07.026

[26] Gale, L., Bhushan, P., Eidnani, S., Graham, L., Harrison, M., McKay-Brown, L., Sivashunmugam, C. Overcoming barriers to inclusion in education in India: A scoping review. Social Sciences & Humanities Open 2022, 5(1), 100237, doi: https://doi.org/10.1016/j.ssaho.2021.100237

[27] Watkins, A., Tokareva, N., Turner, M. ICTs in Education for People with Disabilities – Review of Innovative Practice.

[28] Bocconi, S., Panesi, S. and Kampylis, P. Fostering the Digital Competence of Schools: Piloting SELFIE in the Italian Education Context. IEEE Rev. Iberoam. Tecnol. del Aprendiz (2020)., vol. 15, no. 4, pp. 417–425.

[29] E. C. European Union, "SELFIE A tool to support learning in the digital age." 2023.

[30] Centre for Studies on Inclusive Education, "Index for Inclusion: developing learning and participation in schools," 2020.

[31] T. Booth and M. Ainscow, Index for Inclusion: developing learning and participation in schools. 2011.

Information Modelling and Knowledge Bases XXXV
M. Tropmann-Frick et al. (Eds.)
© 2024 The Authors.

doi:10.3233/FAIA231165

Opportunities and Pitfalls of IT Architectures for Edge Computing

Luka ČETINA[a,1] and Luka PAVLIČ[a]

[a] *University of Maribor, Faculty of Electrical Engineering and Computer Science,*
Maribor, Slovenia
ORCiD ID: Luka Četina https://orcid.org/0009-0000-0267-1092,
Luka Pavlič https://orcid.org/0000-0001-5477-4747

Abstract. Networks and data centres are under a lot of stress due to the rapid growth of connected devices and the significant amount of data that they produce. While data centres are struggling with heavy workloads, the cloud-native IT solutions underutilise the increasingly powerful clients. By bringing computational capabilities closer to the edge, the Edge Computing direction offers a way to alleviate the pressure on data centres, reduce network traffic, and opens the way for novel applications that would take full advantage of the benefits it brings. Edge Computing can also supplement existing applications by giving them the resources to run new, more complex operations, or improve existing ones partially. Edge applications are less reliant on the cloud, and provide more stability and customisation to globally distributed systems.

Keywords. Edge Computing, Cloud Computing, IT architectures

1. Introduction

The number of devices with Internet connectivity is growing rapidly, as well as the volume of data these devices produce, causing increasing strain for the network [1]. Currently, the prevalent paradigm is Cloud Computing, wherein all the data from devices are sent to the cloud for storage and processing [2]. With applications being deployed worldwide and users creating large quantities of data, sending and processing everything in a central location is becoming unsustainable. Networks are struggling to handle the data being sent, and energy usage of data centres is expected to triple in the next decade [3]. Reducing the load for data centres is not only beneficial for the environment, but also for businesses, as less energy means more savings, especially at times when energy costs are high. Edge Computing is sometimes heralded as the solution for these problems, and, while it is no silver bullet, it presents an opportunity to rethink the classic cloud paradigm in domains where the centralisation of storage and processing power is becoming a burden and hindering innovation.

Edge Computing is not a new technology, but rather a topology that brings processing power closer to the places where data are produced and consumed, also called the edge [4]. The edge is where people and things interact with the digital world, and devices such as mobile phones, smart devices, cars and game consoles, which facilitate

---

[1] Corresponding Author: Luka Četina, Faculty of Electrical Engineering and Computer Science, University of Maribor, Koroška cesta 46, 2000 Maribor, Slovenia; E-mail: luka.cetina@um.si

this interaction are called edge devices. In Edge Computing, data produced on the edge are not sent to the cloud, but are processed on nearby edge nodes, which are devices deployed close to the edge, capable of running computations [3]. The nodes process the data and produce an answer in real time, which is then sent to edge devices. Due to the many different types of devices, the line between an edge device and an edge node is not always clear. A mobile phone, for example, is an edge device, as it enables the interaction between people and the digital world, yet it also has computing power which can be used to process the produced data [5]. In this paradigm, edge nodes can process some of the data edge devices produce, thereby reducing the amount of data that must be transported to the cloud and processed there. This alleviates the pressure on data centres, and enables edge devices to shift the load onto edge nodes in real time [1].

However, the potential benefits of this are irrelevant if they are not exploited through innovative IT solutions taking advantage of them. As pointed out by [6], while the infrastructure enables edge computing, IT solutions help us realise the benefits. This raises the question of how to design IT solutions not only to work in an edge environment, but also to take full advantage of the benefits it offers. It is also important to be aware of the pitfalls of Edge Computing, as it may not be beneficial in every domain.

The objectives of this chapter are presenting the benefits of utilising Edge Computing on the one hand, and avoiding possible obstacles when designing suitable IT architectures. This is why we present several aspects of Edge Computing specifics related to IT architectures:

- The nature of Edge Computing (advantages, differences between Cloud and Edge Computing),
- The current state and trends while developing edge computing-enabled systems,
- The advantages and limitations of IT architectures for Edge Computing,
- The characteristics of edge computing-enabled system development (typical architecture, different system types, best development practices).

The rest of the chapter is organised as follows. In the next Section, Edge Computing concepts are presented in detail. The current state-of-the-art and future trends are presented in Section three. Possible edge computing opportunities and pitfalls from the IT architecture point of view are presented in Sections four and five. The Chapter is concluded with Section six.

2. Edge computing IT architectures

Edge-computing-based IT solutions can be classified as solutions, designed specifically to take advantage of unique features of edge systems, such as: bandwidth scalability, low-latency offload, privacy-preserving denaturing and WAN-failure resiliency [7].

A typical edge IT solution architecture is three-tier, and is composed of:

- **Edge devices,** which typically run the part of the solution that produces and consumes data. These devices typically do not have enough resources for virtualization, which makes development more challenging, as multiple versions of the software have to be produced to work on different devices. The software is typically installed using application stores, which is a common practice in smartphones, and increasingly in desktop operating systems.

- **Edge nodes** typically run microservices that handle requests from edge devices and communicate with the cloud. Since these devices have more resources available compared to the edge devices, virtualization such as containers is used typically.
- **Cloud** typically contains the services that handle more complex operations, data storage and provide an overview of the entire system.

The described architecture is a basic blueprint, where additional tiers can be added or existing ones removed, such as the cloud. Depending on how well the IT solutions take advantage of the edge architecture, we can classify them into three types, as shown in Figure 1.

Edge-enhanced, device-native IT solutions typically run on devices, and do not require the cloud or edge nodes to function satisfactorily. They can, however, take advantage of edge nodes if they are available, and use their resources to offer new functionalities or improve existing ones.

Edge-enhanced, cloud-native IT solutions are currently the most common type of edge-based IT solutions. Cloud and edge solution development share some similarities, which means that adapting a cloud-native solution to work on the edge is easier than developing a new one, designed specifically for the edge .

Edge-native IT solutions are designed to work in an edge system and utilise its resources fully. They require edge nodes to be available at all times, and lose functionality when otherwise. Despite edge-enhanced, cloud-native solutions being the most common, edge-native solutions are expected to be the most revolutionary and popularise Edge Computing further. While they are in a large part reliant on the underlying infrastructure, history shows that novel applications drive hardware acceptance. A nice example are spreadsheets, which popularised personal computers in the 80's [7].

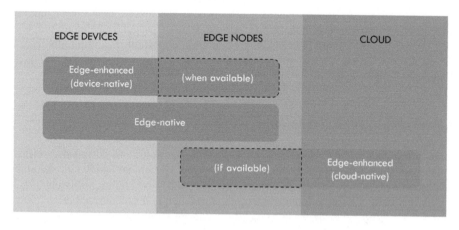

Figure 1: Types of edge-computing-based IT solutions

3. Current trends

The area of Edge Computing-based IT solutions is still developing, therefore the cloud-native solutions being extended to the edge are currently the most common. Even the platforms and tools used most were often intended for cloud-native development [7]. Even so, tends show that edge-native solutions are becoming more common, and the framework and tool ecosystem is evolving as well [8] with tools like OpenYurt [9], KubeEdge [10] and EdgeX [11]. Because the area of Edge Computing is still evolving standardisation is becoming an issue, and should be addressed as noted by [12], while [13] found service migration, security and privacy preservation and deployment as the most pressing issues.

Currently the most researched topic in Edge Computing is Machine and Deep Learning on the edge, followed closely by computational offloading. Less commonly researched topics are security and privacy in Edge Computing, its use in smart cities and homes and the industrial Internet. In 2021 COVID-19 was a hot topic, as a number of articles were published on how Edge Computing could be used to help during the pandemic [8]. Edge-based IT solutions are currently used typically for video surveillance and video processing [1], [7], [8], while another common use is running Deep Learning on the edge [1]. In recent years a number of authors have addressed the topic of combining edge-based IT solutions with technologies like Blockchain and 5G networks [8]. There has also been an increase in the number of articles dealing with the application of Edge Computing in Smart Healthcare and intelligent analysis in recent years [14], as well as combining Edge Computing and technologies such as digital twins, that can be used to provide support for remote working, retail industries and digital advertising [13].

Future research directions of Edge Computing research involve accelerating AI services and improving the efficiency of edge AI, integration with the upcoming 6G and using low-delay edge networks to create digital twins. While Edge Computing is currently focused on supplementing the cloud, it is expected to decouple from the cloud in the future, and instead become edgeless computing, where devices communicate with each other instead of via the cloud. There might be no need for performing computations on the cloud, as devices will be able to share processing power as needed. The cloud could still function as a data repository, but the processing would happen on devices closer to the data source [13].

4. Opportunities

In an edge-based IT architecture the resources for performing basic computations are deployed much closer to end devices than in a cloud-based architecture, therefore edge devices can perform complex operations that would not be feasible without the help of edge nodes. Using those resources, edge devices can offer advanced functionalities that would otherwise be too demanding. That is crucial, as many edge devices are portable (eg. mobile phones, smartwatches, wearables), meaning they have very limited resources compared to the cloud. Due to being highly portable the chances of such devices being in an area where Internet connectivity may be limited or non-existent is high, which presents a challenge for IT solutions that are not designed to work offline. With strategically placed edge nodes, portable edge devices could offer functionalities with high added value in real time, without being dependent on the cloud [1].

Edge-based IT solutions that complement human cognition are often touted as a killer, or revolutionary application of Edge Computing, and the authors in [7] are convinced that they will drive wider adoption of Edge Computing. Such solutions help improve tasks such as face-recognition, long-term memory or navigation, making them of immense value to people with cognitive impairment. The aforementioned use cases can be quite demanding computationally, which means that most devices portable enough to be carried around easily, will struggle to perform them in real time. Current solutions designed to help people with cognitive impairment often rely on humans to perform desired tasks, as is the case for the app "Be My Eyes", where volunteers help people with impaired vision read labels or navigate their environment via video call [15]. A similar solution based on Edge Computing could make use of nearby computational resources, and perform at least some operations without involving volunteers, thereby empowering people who would otherwise be reliant on others.

Due to the large amount of data gathered by web giants like Facebook and Google and many instances of questionable uses of those data, many countries are passing a stricter regulative, detailing which data can be stored and how they can be processed, to respect users' privacy. This can mean, for example, that data gathered from EU citizens can only be kept in data centres located in the EU, or additional safety measures must be taken [16]. If a solution uses a single data centre located in the US and all data are sent there, violations of the data regulative can occur quickly. In an edge-based IT architecture data are kept and processed as close to the source as possible, and only necessary data are sent to the cloud. Since less data are transferred over the network, they are less likely to be intercepted by a malicious third party, which is beneficial to users and companies alike. A key enabler of cloud-based solutions is the assumption that all data will eventually be uploaded to the cloud, where they will be processed and stored. The authors in [5] pointed out that companies often shy away from sharing data due to safety concerns and data transfer costs, which limits possible collaboration and innovation. An edge-network connecting all parties could be established, where edge-nodes would intercept the produced data and send them to all relevant systems, ensuring that data are shared as they are created, reducing the need for intensive batch transfers of data between different systems. The authors saw the most potential in Healthcare, where sensitive data are handled and are rarely shared, due to security risks and outdated systems. Edge-based IT solutions could enable wider collaboration and data sharing, bringing value for organisations and better services for individuals.

Because edge-based IT solutions are deployed close to the edge they can adapt better to the needs of an environment than traditional cloud-based ones. Different edge-nodes can run different versions of the solutions, making sure that, while on the move, users always have access to the solution that is most relevant to their current environment. Companies with many geographically distributed stores or warehouses can also benefit from using Edge Computing-based IT solutions, as it allows them to adapt their system easily to the needs and specifics of each location. A great example of this is the American fast food franchise Chick-fil-A, which abandoned its cloud-based IT solution in favour of an edge-based one [17]. The cloud-based solutions were used to help them coordinate work in the restaurant and provide better service to the customers, but was entirely reliant on the cloud, meaning that it ceased to function in cases of Internet outage. The company also discovered that a uniform solution might not be the best option, as different restaurants were struggling with very different issues and needed a system more adapted to their needs. They decided to develop an edge-based solution and deploy it on an edge node installed in each restaurant. Along with the edge node they installed hundreds of sensors, tracking everything from the queue length to the temperature of the oil in the fryer, and used all those data and the edge node to predict which items would be in demand and must be prepared in advance. Kubernetes [18] was used, to make redeployment and updates as simple as possible, as one of their goals was to create a system that could be customised easily for each individual restaurant. The edge-based solution depends only on the sensors and edge nodes, which means that Internet outages are no longer a major concern.

Edge Computing-based IT solutions can take advantage of edge nodes to take the pressure off the cloud in times of increased traffic. This can be beneficial to web stores that see a high increase in traffic a couple times a year when their servers struggle to process all requests. The most common requests, like adding or removing an article from the basket, are trivial, but can cause problems due to how often they are performed. Such operations could be performed by edge nodes, to give users a responsive experience and synchronised with the cloud in the background, thereby improving the user experience and reducing the number of requests the cloud has to handle [5].

5. Pitfalls

Edge-based IT architectures have great potential, but are in large part dependent on the underlying infrastructure [7], which can be expensive to set up and maintain. Before we decide to develop an edge-based IT solution we must know exactly what we want to achieve and if an edge-based architecture will help or hinder us. Not only is setting up the infrastructure demanding, but deploying our solution to all edge devices and nodes can also be a challenge, due to the large number of devices that can vary greatly in resources and availability [19]. If a device is unavailable during redeployment, the older and the newer versions of the solution must be able to coexist until all devices are updated. Shipping even a small fix can require a redeploy, which takes quite a bit of time and resources. If we are not aware of the unique properties of Edge Computing-based IT solutions, we might find that the cost of maintaining and managing the infrastructure nullifies the benefits of using Edge Computing. Most edge devices are not capable of virtualization, which means that many different versions of the solution must be developed, one for each type of device [5]. Many edge nodes also means that there are more potential points of attack, making it harder to prevent data breaches and maintain data security.

Despite offering more independence from the cloud, most edge-based IT solutions are still dependent on the cloud in some way. When the calculations the solutions need to run are too complex for edge nodes, the solution loses some functionality if the cloud is not available to handle the excess load. The IT solution that offers cognitive assistance mentioned above, would only be capable of running basic operations without edge nodes, making it useless for users who need a response in real-time. Scalability is another issue, as the underlying edge infrastructure is difficult to upgrade due to devices being numerous and distributed geographically. If the number of requests increases suddenly our solution might run out of resources quickly, and be unable to provide responses to all requests. Cloud-native solutions, on the other hand, can scale up quickly to receive more resources when needed. When developing Edge Computing-based IT solutions we must anticipate that the load might have to be reduced, shifted or stopped entirely at any moment. Therefore, one of the main benefits of edge-based IT architectures – independence from the cloud, can turn quickly into a weakness if used improperly [20].

6. Conclusion

Edge-based IT solutions are gaining traction, and many organisations are wondering whether they are the right fit for their use case. Edge based IT solutions have many advantages, such as offering complex functionalities on devices with very limited resources, adapting to the environment and transferring less data through the network. However, they are limited by their dependency on the underlying infrastructure, which can be expensive and hard to manage due to the large number of geographically distributed edge nodes. The most common type of edge-based IT solution is currently the edge-enhanced, cloud-native IT solution, but edge-native IT solutions are evolving quickly, and are expected to become the most common and provide the killer application of Edge Computing. Because the area of Edge Computing is still evolving, it lacks tools, frameworks and standardisation. Current trends for Edge Computing research include improving edge AI and integration with promising technologies such as digital twins, 6G and finding further use cases with Blockchain.

This chapter introduces the concept of Edge Computing and IT architectures that are used commonly. We present current trends, different types of edge-based IT solutions and the opportunities as well as pitfalls they bring.

Acknowledgements

The authors acknowledge financial support from the Slovenian Research Agency (Research Core Funding No. P2-0057)

References

[1]   K. Cao, Y. Liu, G. Meng, and Q. Sun, "An Overview on Edge Computing Research," *IEEE Access*, vol. 8, pp. 85714–85728, 2020, doi: 10.1109/ACCESS.2020.2991734.

[2]   L. Mei, W. K. Chan, and T. H. Tse, "A Tale of Clouds: Paradigm Comparisons and Some Thoughts on Research Issues," in *2008 IEEE Asia-Pacific Services Computing Conference*, Dec. 2008, pp. 464–469. doi: 10.1109/APSCC.2008.168.

[3]   B. Varghese, N. Wang, S. Barbhuiya, P. Kilpatrick, and D. S. Nikolopoulos, "Challenges and Opportunities in Edge Computing," in *2016 IEEE International Conference on Smart Cloud (SmartCloud)*, Nov. 2016, pp. 20–26. doi: 10.1109/SmartCloud.2016.18.

[4]   B. Gill and D. Smith, "The Edge Completes the Cloud: A Gartner Trend Insight Report".

[5]   W. Shi, J. Cao, Q. Zhang, Y. Li, and L. Xu, "Edge Computing: Vision and Challenges," *IEEE Internet Things J.*, vol. 3, no. 5, pp. 637–646, Oct. 2016, doi: 10.1109/JIOT.2016.2579198.

[6]   I. Verma, "Developing at the edge: Best practices for edge computing," Red Hat Developer. Accessed: Feb. 13, 2023. [Online]. Available: https://developers.redhat.com/blog/2020/07/16/developing-at-the-edge-best-practices-for-edge-computing

[7]   M. Satyanarayanan, G. Klas, M. Silva, and S. Mangiante, "The Seminal Role of Edge-Native Applications," in *2019 IEEE International Conference on Edge Computing (EDGE)*, Jul. 2019, pp. 33–40. doi: 10.1109/EDGE.2019.00022.

[8]   B. Liu, Z. Luo, H. Chen, and C. Li, "A Survey of State-of-the-art on Edge Computing: Theoretical Models, Technologies, Directions, and Development Paths," *IEEE Access*, vol. 10, pp. 54038–54063, 2022, doi: 10.1109/ACCESS.2022.3176106.

[9]   "An open platform that extends upstream Kubernetes to Edge | OpenYurt." Accessed: Oct. 03, 2023. [Online]. Available: https://openyurt.io/

[10]   "KubeEdge." Accessed: Oct. 03, 2023. [Online]. Available: https://kubeedge.io/

[11]   T. L. Foundation, "EdgeX Foundry | The Open Source Edge Platform," https://www.edgexfoundry.org. Accessed: Oct. 03, 2023. [Online]. Available: https://www.edgexfoundry.org

[12]   M. Mahbub and R. M. Shubair, "Contemporary advances in multi-access edge computing: A survey of fundamentals, architecture, technologies, deployment cases, security, challenges, and directions," *J. Netw. Comput. Appl.*, vol. 219, p. 103726, Oct. 2023, doi: 10.1016/j.jnca.2023.103726.

[13]   X. Kong, Y. Wu, H. Wang, and F. Xia, "Edge Computing for Internet of Everything: A Survey," *IEEE Internet Things J.*, vol. 9, no. 23, pp. 23472–23485, Dec. 2022, doi: 10.1109/JIOT.2022.3200431.

[14]   J.-H. Syu, J. C.-W. Lin, G. Srivastava, and K. Yu, "A Comprehensive Survey on Artificial Intelligence Empowered Edge Computing on Consumer Electronics," *IEEE Trans. Consum. Electron.*, pp. 1–1, 2023, doi: 10.1109/TCE.2023.3318150.

[15]   "Be My Eyes - See the world together." Accessed: Mar. 13, 2023. [Online]. Available: https://www.bemyeyes.com/

[16]   "Data protection under GDPR," Your Europe. Accessed: Apr. 14, 2023. [Online]. Available: https://europa.eu/youreurope/business/dealing-with-customers/data-protection/data-protection-gdpr/index_en.htm

[17]   B. Chambers, "Enterprise Restaurant Compute," chick-fil-atech. Accessed: Mar. 14, 2023. [Online]. Available: https://medium.com/chick-fil-atech/enterprise-restaurant-compute-f5e2fd63d20f

[18]   "Production-Grade Container Orchestration," Kubernetes. Accessed: Apr. 17, 2023. [Online]. Available: https://kubernetes.io/

[19]   "IBM Edge Computing Field Guide".

[20]   J. Wang, Z. Feng, S. George, R. Iyengar, P. Pillai, and M. Satyanarayanan, "Towards scalable edge-native applications," in *Proceedings of the 4th ACM/IEEE Symposium on Edge Computing*, in SEC '19. New York, NY, USA: Association for Computing Machinery, Nov. 2019, pp. 152–165. doi: 10.1145/3318216.3363308.

Information Modelling and Knowledge Bases XXXV
M. Tropmann-Frick et al. (Eds.)
© *2024 The Authors.*
This article is published online with Open Access by IOS Press and distributed under the terms
of the Creative Commons Attribution Non-Commercial License 4.0 (CC BY-NC 4.0).

327

Subject Index

Author Index